FROM THE REALITY
of God
TO VICTORY
in Christ

SCIENTIFIC AND BIBLICAL EVIDENCES SO CONVINCING
AN IGNORAMUS COULD TEACH YOU

John M. Carney

From The Reality of God to The Victory In Christ
Copyright © 2013 John M. Carney

All Rights Reserved.

Published 2013.

No part of this publication may be reproduced, distributed, or transmitted in any form or by any means, including photocopying, recording, or other electronic or mechanical methods, without the prior written permission of the publisher, except in the case of brief quotations embodied in critical reviews and certain other noncommercial uses permitted by copyright law. For permission requests, write to the publisher, addressed "Attention: Permissions Coordinator," at the address below.

First published by Faith Books & MORE

ISBN 978-1-939761-15-6

Printed in the United States of America
This book is printed on acid-free paper.

3255 Lawrenceville-Suwanee Rd.
Suite P250
Suwanee, GA 30024
publishing@faithbooksandmore.com
faithbooksandmore.com

Ordering Information:
Quantity sales. Special discounts are available on quantity purchases by corporations, associations, and others. For details, contact the publisher at the address above.

Orders by U.S. trade bookstores and wholesalers. Please contact Ingram Book Company: Tel: (800) 937-8000; Email: orders@ingrambook.com or visit ipage.ingrambook.com.

Disclaimer
The purpose of this book is to empower, educate, and offer hope. The authors of the book achieved that through their own experiences, expertise, and research. Consequently, this book should only be used as a road map. This book is not intended to be nor is it represented as legal advice. The authors are not liable or responsible, to any person, or entity, for any and all claims, demands, damages, causes of action, suits in equity of whatever kind or nature, caused or alleged to have been caused, directly or indirectly, by the information contained in this book or the authors' past or future negligence or wrongful acts.

CONTENTS

Preface 1
Chapter 1
Introduction 5
Chapter 2
"What Is Truth?" 13
Chapter 3
Thermodynamics: Truth in Science Points to GOD 41
Chapter 4
Cause & Effect: Truth in Science Points to GOD 63
Chapter 5
Symbols of Evolution Lack Substance
Law of Biogenesis: Truth in Science Points to GOD 87
Chapter 6
Laws of Probability: Truth in Science Points to GOD 131
Chapter 7
The Holy Inspired Bible and the Canon 145
Chapter 8
Truth in Biblical Prophecy: Promise of a Messiah King 171
Chapter 9
Messiah Arrives: Prophesies Fulfilled Christ Is King 189
Chapter 10
The Subtle Resistance of the Skeptics 209
Chapter 11
Messiah Has Arrived: Christ's Promises and Death 243
Chapter 12
The Death, Burial & Resurrection of Christ: Historical Fact 289
Final Remarks
Why Was This Book Written? 335
Notes 341

PREFACE

The year was 1925. A momentous event was about to take place. Things of enormous impact in history often occur in obscure places. Such was the case in a small American town in the state of Tennessee where a battle was to begin that would shape the educational culture for generations to come. In the long run, it influenced more than American education. It has been referred to as "The Monkey Trial."

F. LaGARD SMITH, a former district attorney, Professor of Law at Pepperdine University, and author of *ACLU: The Devil's Advocate*, gives his insight as to what was taking place:

"It began as a test case for the ACLU. Then as a clever Chamber of Commerce ploy. Then as a battle of egos. Then as a media circus. In the end, it heralded the most crucial, though perhaps least understood, battle for the control of America's spiritual mind. More than any other single case, the sensational 1925 Scopes 'monkey trial' in Tennessee changed the philosophical landscape in America, paving the way not only for significant change in public education, but, more importantly, for unprecedented implementation of the liberal-left agenda." (F. LaGard Smith, ACLU: The Devil's Advocate, p.197, (1996), Marcon Publishers, 770-101 Wooten Rd., Colorado Springs CO 80915).

Dr. BERT THOMPSON, in his book, *The History of Evolutionary Thought*, provides more historic details of the Scopes trial on how it was used to promote evolution in the public schools:

"*The history of evolutionary thought* is marked with important events—the publication of Darwin's *Origin of Species*, Huxley's debate with Wilberforce, and many others. But few of these events are comparable (in many ways) to the milestone which the Scopes trial represents. The year was 1925. The place was Dayton, Tennessee. The man was John Thomas Scopes, a young science teacher and football coach" (Bert Thompson, Ph.D., *The History of Evolutionary Thought*, p.157, (1981), Apologetics Press, Inc.).

John Thomas Scopes was not the instigator of the event. He was, in a political sense, the pawn that was used to begin the conflict of what would be taught in our nation's public schools. Dr. Thompson continues to explain what took place:

"The occasion was in essence, instigated by the American Civil Liberties Union. The A.C.L.U. advertised in Tennessee newspapers that it would finance a court trial for any teacher who would be willing to test the constitutionality of the Tennessee law (the Butler Act) which forbade the teaching of evolution in public schools. A New Yorker working in Tennessee, George Rappelyea, saw the advertisement in a Chattanooga paper, and persuaded the county superintendent of schools and the head of the county board of education that a trial would be beneficial. …Rappelyea met with John Thomas Scopes in a drugstore" (ibid.).

The meeting between Rappelyea and Scopes resulted in Scopes agreeing to openly state that he had taught evolution in the classrooms against Tennessee law forbidding such to take place. When Scopes was brought to trial in July, 1925, in Dayton, Tennessee, so much national attention had been generated for the event that it had attracted two major figures who engaged in the prosecution and defense of John Thomas Scopes. The prosecution was led by the famous William Jennings Bryan, and for the defense, the successful criminal lawyer, Clarence Darrow. This local trial became a monumental event in history. Thompson provides some background of the leading prosecutor and that of the attorney for the defense:

"….The leader of the prosecution team was William Jennings Bryan (the 'great commoner'), three-time nominee for the Presidency by the Democrats, and formerly Woodrow Wilson's Secretary of State. …The defense was led by the renowned criminal lawyer and agnostic, Clarence Darrow. He was a favorite defense attorney for known criminals and had worked with the A.C.L.U. before" (ibid., p.159).

Clarence Darrow's strategy for defense was an all-out attack on the character and credibility of those who believed in the Biblical creation of Genesis. According to NORMAN L. GEISLER, a Christian apologist, Darrow repeatedly accused his opponents of "bigotry, ignorance, and hatred," calling them "**bigots and ignoramuses**":

"….He did believe that passing and defending the Tennessee creation law was 'bigotry' and used the word bigotry or bigot six times on only two pages of trial transcript (Hilleary, 75, 87). Bryan said on the witness stand, 'I am perfectly willing that the world shall know that these gentlemen have no other purpose than ridiculing every Christian who believes in the Bible.' Darrow snapped back, 'We have the purpose of preventing bigots and ignoramuses from controlling the education of the United States and you know it, and that is all' (ibid., 299, emphasis added). (Norman L. Geisler, *Baker Encyclopedia of Christian Apologetics*, p.180, (1999), Baker Books, Grand Rapids, MI, 49516-6287. Geisler's source: W. Hilleary and W. Metzger, *The World's Most Famous Court Trial*.)

Geisler also quotes Darrow with: "You know that there is no suspicion which possesses the minds of men like bigotry and ignorance and hatred" (ibid., 181; from Hilleary, ibid., p.87).

And thus, the accusations and attacks continued successfully. The actual results of the trial turned out to be anti-climatic, with a legal verdict in favor of Tennessee law:

"For his part, William Jennings Bryan successfully convinced Judge John Raulston that the sole question was whether the legislature had the right to determine public school curricula. ...It was left to Darrow's streetfighter instincts to save the day. Through a bit of crafty maneuvering...Darrow played on Bryan's ego and coaxed Bryan into taking the witness stand himself in defense of Fundamentalism. Under Darrow's fierce examination, Bryan quickly became muddled, and to the gasps of his literalist supporters, even stated that the six days of the creation in Genesis were not literal twenty-four hour days. ...Not at all enticed by Darrow's appeal to a broader concern regarding human freedom, the jury deliberated for only nine minutes and returned the obvious verdict: 'Guilty'" (F. LaGard Smith, *ACLU: The Devil's Advocate*, p.199, (1996), Marcon Publishers, Colorado Springs, CO 80915).

The impact of the Scopes Trial and its national attention brought some drastic changes in how legislators perceived the legality of evolution and natural selection being taught in the public schools. Smith explains what took place shortly after the trial ended:
"Although the prosecution emerged victorious, if greatly embarrassed, the long-range victory went to the ACLU and the broader liberal cause. Over the next two years, anti-evolution legislation was defeated in twenty-two states" (ibid.).

It is sad to note that William Jennings Bryan died just a few days after the trial. The stigma of Darrow's accusations continues to this day toward anyone whose faith and scientific examination compels them to defend the inspiration and reality of an intelligent Creator God who created humankind and sent forth His Son Christ Jesus to bring salvation to everyone who believes. The condescending, materialistic, natural selection believing, scientific elite continue to look down their noses at such as "**bigots and ignoramuses**." It is the purpose of this author, who, in their judgment, would be considered just another "ignoramus," to expose the shallowness of materialistic natural selection as a façade and an empty hypothesis in comparison to the reality of our God and Father and His Son, the resurrected Jesus Christ, and His master-plan for all of humanity.

Chapter 1
INTRODUCTION

CHAPTER 1

FIRST, this book was written to clear up some of the myths of evolution being taught in schools. Public educational systems and most media networks have maintained a steady barrage of devious propaganda about unproved naturalistic philosophy, commonly referred to as "Evolution" or "Natural Selection." If you have been educated through the public school system you have most likely been through program after program of naturalistic philosophy. Since its beginning, this teaching has changed world views of moral principles and human worth.

SECOND, the most enjoyable reason this book was written is to let the reader know there is abundant evidence available so that anyone capable of reading at a standard high school level today (or at 8th grade level for those over 65) can find overwhelming scientific data that points to the reality of God. For those who have reading difficulties, there are several DVD'S available that provide more than sufficient evidence for most people to realize that God is real.

But we're not going to stop there. This book brings readers an advanced study of Biblical evidence beginning with a foundation of historical and inspirational (God-breathed) facts. These facts provide an understanding of why the Holy Bible was written and how the reader will know this unique collection of literature could never have originated simply by man's imagination. It had to be motivated by an eternal, intelligent Designer to bring His highest level of creation—humanity—into a loving relationship with their Creator, showering grace, truth, and love upon any person willing to learn.

What are my qualifications to write this book, you may ask? Do I have a Ph.D. in science or theology? No. Do I have a Bachelor's degree? No. Do I have a formal degree in anything? Not really. I am an eleventh-grade high school drop-out. My grades were so bad I flunked most of my classes except gym with maybe two D's in the others. If you were able to talk to any of my former teachers they would probably tell you my D's were the result of over-achievement!

Sometime after I turned thirty I went down to Emily Griffith Opportunity School and took a G.E.D. high school equivalency test and passed it. Later I took a history class in *Western Civilizations* at Colorado University extension in downtown Denver, which I passed with a satisfactory grade. That's about it for my formal education. My training is the result of years of Bible study under a variety of

INTRODUCTION

teachers and mentors plus intense study in my after-work hours, and the prayers, love, and encouragement of my wife Inez, with whom I have been married for fifty-nine years.

It began in earnest, with my search to find God after I returned from active duty in the army as a Korean War Veteran. That was in 1953. I went to work in a factory, stacking 8x8x16 and 12x12x16 concrete blocks on pallets. After work I'd hit the bars and party with my drinking buddies until 2:00 a.m. when the bars closed.

It was during that time that I met Inez, the woman who would end up becoming my wife. We dated for about three months, then one night after we had been at a party I asked her to marry me. She said, "Ask me again when you're sober." I did, and in 1954 we were married by a Justice of the Peace.

The first years were a tough adjustment for both of us. I still wanted to party and drink with my friends. Inez had become a Christian about a year before she moved from Alabama to Denver, Colorado. She was trying to live as Jesus taught. Thus, being married to a man who was living in a world of darkness was no help. Over the next year and a half we had our share of arguments. I began searching for answers as to how to rid myself of the life I was living, knowing there is a God up there somewhere who judges people like me, a man with no clue of what to do to find this man, Christ, to rid myself of condemnation.

Inez began to attend a church in Englewood. A few weeks later, she placed her membership with that church, and she continued to ask me to join her on Sundays at that little congregation worshipping in a converted garage on South Broadway. We were renting a place in Littleton at that time, waiting for the first house we bought to be finished. Two young men stopped by the house. They introduced themselves as "elders." Elders? They were both younger than I was, and I was only twenty-four years old. They wanted to study the Bible with us. I invited them in. They had been coming once a week for about three weeks when I challenged them on something they were teaching. It did not check out with my limited knowledge of the Bible. They became angry and left.

It was at this point that Inez asked me if I would like to study with the minister at the church where she'd placed her membership. By then I had been going with her most of the time. I agreed, and began to study with him on what the Bible taught

CHAPTER 1

concerning salvation. As I read from the Scriptures it became so simple and clear what I should do. So after three study periods the preacher asked me if I believed that Jesus was the Son of God and that He is the way to eternal life. I said yes. Then he said something like this: "Well, then there is nothing stopping you from being baptized tonight."

I was silent. I had a serious decision to make! I wanted to do this, but my nature as a procrastinator said not right now. Wait. Yet I knew I needed to do it. So I picked a time the following week, after work, at night, when only the minister, my wife, and the minister's wife would be present. Right after I made that decision to wait a few days I had serious second thoughts. What if I died before I was baptized? What would my condition be before God and my new Lord, Jesus Christ? Needless to say, I was certainly anxious for that day to arrive. I was baptized into Christ. That was in December of 1955. I was saved! All of my former sins and character flaws were forgiven. After that, things would never be the same.

For the first two years after I became a Christian the life changes were frustrating. It wasn't easy to change from stopping at the bar after work and going fishing on Sunday to attending morning and evening worship services with people whose lifestyles were completely different from what I was used to. It was a tough learning experience to understand why it was so important to share communion with other Christians and to fully comprehend why it was necessary for Jesus to die and be raised on the third day from the dead. It took a while to realize that I was no longer serving just myself, but I was now serving Christ. At first, I was reluctant to allow the Holy Spirit to reshape my image to be like that of my Lord, Jesus Christ. Yet change I did.

One of the hardest challenges was the fact that a lot of my friends whom I had hung around with since junior high (middle school) no longer called to let me know when they were having a party or going out to the midget auto races. But I soon made new friends with other Christians with whom I shared common interests. I began to study the Bible seriously.

By the time I was twenty-eight, Inez and I had begun to study the Bible with some of our former friends and with our neighbors. Then one day one of our elders at the church asked me to help teach a class on Sunday mornings. I agreed. After about

INTRODUCTION

three or four weeks the elder informed me he couldn't be in class any longer and asked if I would take over. Hesitantly, I said yes, and I ended up teaching that class for the rest of the year.

Several years went by. I enjoyed teaching, learning more, and going into deeper spiritual topics. Then sometime in the mid-1960s I began to get some extremely provocative questions from the class. Is God real? Can I prove it? About the same time I was receiving questions about whether or not one could prove Christ was actually raised from the dead, because there were a lot of alleged contradictions in the New Testament.

I had always assumed that most people accepted the Bible as authentic, especially those attending my classes at church. But at that point, with my limited education, I found I could not give them satisfactory answers. I had no educational background in science with the exception of limited 8th and 9th grade science classes and I had no formal education in the New Testament outside my personal Bible studies. Never before had I been challenged on whether the Bible was inspired, whether history and science would offer convincing evidence on the reality of God and the resurrection of Christ.

Right away I knew I was lacking in two critical subjects. I realized I desperately needed to learn more. My faith in Christ and the Holy Scriptures compelled me to reason that God would not have inspired some forty authors from different periods of history and different backgrounds to write these Scriptures without some way to verify their authenticity. My ignorance in science was clearly evident. I needed to vastly improve my education, and I knew there had to be evidence out there that I wasn't aware of. I began to search in all of the Christian bookstores in the area for anything on science and creation.

The first book I bought was titled, *The Genesis Flood* by Henry M. Morris and John C. Whitcomb, (1967), 10th printing. This book provided scientific evidence that was current with excellent documentation. I knew I was on the right track. The next book I purchased was an excellent source on evidence for the New Testament and the resurrection of Christ, *Evidence That Demands a Verdict*, Vol.1, by Josh McDowell, (1972). That was the beginning.
From then until now, about forty years later, I have accumulated some 67 books on

CHAPTER 1

the refutation of Darwin's "Natural Selection by Spontaneous Generation," how the four basic laws of science point to the reality of an Eternal, Intelligent Creator (God), how truth in prophecy points to Jesus Christ as the promised Messiah, how internal and external evidence substantiates this fact, and how the resurrection of Jesus Christ from the dead is an established, historical fact. In summary, these sources explain how all the accumulated evidence clearly validates the authenticity of the God-breathed inspiration of the selected men who wrote the books of the Old and New Testaments (The Holy Bible). From the book of Genesis onward, the scriptures lay out how our God, through an ingenious strategy, defeated both His and humanity's greatest adversary, the one called Satan, and how God's immeasurable grace and love provide for us the means to be free from the bondage to Satan and to have the promised everlasting life in Christ Jesus.

After years of teaching Bible classes on Sunday mornings and small groups in homes, including classes on the historical facts concerning the resurrection of Christ with scientific evidences about creation and the impossibility of accidental natural selection, I was approached by our minister about the possibility of a Sunday morning class on the evidences for the creation by an Intelligent Creator (God), the credibility of the Holy Bible, and the historical fact of the resurrection of Christ. We discussed this for a period of time and he asked if I would teach that class. I said I would.

The class was an immediate success. What was surprising to me was the number of students from the younger generations—the 20-, 30-, and 40-year-olds—that turned up. We were having classes of 45 to 50 students, nearly all who remained all the way through the thirteen-week study. It was so successful I was asked to teach the same subject again the following year.

From this beginning, I decided to write a fictional book titled, *Welcome to Tranquility* about a retired couple and their friendship with a small-town minister living in the mountains of Colorado. It would tell about how land developers changed the culture of the town. When confronted by the local minister, they revealed their true hostility to Christianity. I included one chapter to debate the subject of creation versus evolution. Then I decided to write this book, *From the Reality of God to the Victory in Christ*, using the material from my classes to reach anyone interested in finding the truth.

INTRODUCTION

Believe me, I am certainly not the first person to write on this most critical subject. Otherwise, I would not have all the material for my studies. But the difference is that the authors who produced the excellent books I used as sources were Ph.D.s and other well-educated people. Many Bible-believers who are not college or high school graduates have expressed to me that books on the science of creation are just too deep for them to understand. The same problem applies to those without a Christian background who know very little about the Bible and Christianity. They think apologetics it just too difficult. And after all, they say, wasn't the issue about life happening accidentally settled with the discovery of evolution and natural selection? And doesn't that cast serious doubts about God's existence? This book was written to demonstrate that even a high school drop-out with only a G.E.D. can use the accumulated evidence in a way that is easy to understand and can be taught by someone who is not a Ph.D.!

I believe that by the time you finish this book you will have two very clear choices. Either you will deliberately turn your back on the evidence presented and willfully decide not to believe, or you will come to understand that Almighty God is real, that He has prepared a way for you to put your complete trust in His Son, Jesus Christ, and that through Christ you will have a new life and confidence of your Victory in Him.

Chapter 2
WHAT IS TRUTH?

"See to it that no one takes you captive through hollow and deceptive philosophy, which depends on human tradition and the basic principles of this world rather than on Christ" (Colossians 2:8 NIV).

CHAPTER 2

A DIALOGUE BETWEEN TWO MEN
"You are a king, then!" said Pilate.
"Jesus answered, "You are right in saying I am a king. In fact, for this reason I was born, and for this I came into the world, to testify to the truth. Everyone on the side of Truth listens to me."
"What is truth?" Pilate asked. With this he went out again to the Jews and said, "I find no basis for a charge against him" (John 18:37-38).

This is an incident that had a monumental impact on the Roman government. A secular Roman judge, Pontius Pilate, governor of a Roman-occupied area called Judea, in a secular court hearing, was interrogating a Jew named Jesus who had just admitted that he was a king. But not a kingdom that Pilate was familiar with. Then Jesus made this statement: "I came into the world to testify to the truth."

Testify to the truth? To a secular politician like Pontius Pilate "truth" could be a subjective thing without boundaries, without certainties. So he asked, "What is truth?"

In this book, truth is what we are looking for, not another lie. No one I know of deliberately looks for a confirmed, deliberate lie in which to believe, although some may prefer to believe in an unproven delusion because they may have convinced themselves that is preferable to the alternative. So, let's begin with the definition of "truth" as it is used in John 18:37-38.

According to W.E. Vine's *Expository Dictionary of Biblical Words*, "The word 'truth' in John 18:37, 38 in the Greek text is 'aletheia.' The word has an absolute force in John 14:6; 17:17; 18:37, 38; in Eph. 4:21, where the R.V., 'even as truth is in Jesus,' gives the correct rendering, the meaning is not merely ethical truth, but truth in all its fullness and scope, as embodied in Him" (p. 1171) {1}.

This Is The "Truth" Everyone Should Be Looking For!

But in order to reach the secular world we first have to know something of tangible, secular truths because we are living in a world of materialists. If their only background and education has been in tangible things then we must begin with the

WHAT IS TRUTH?

established truths in the world of science. Demonstrated, established truths in the world of science are called LAWS, such as "The Law of Gravity." There are two major philosophies that influence how people think and that shape their worldviews in our present day culture. Both point to evidence in science to give validation for their belief-systems. Christians, however, place their trust in the intangible, eternal truths found in the Holy Bible, above all other truths, and the laws of science only help to establish the reality of the eternal truth of God as our Creator and our Savior. Both philosophies play an important part in determining the lifestyles of individuals.

One philosophy is secular and materialistic. In this worldview all known processes are the result of accidental, natural selection, including the universe and the origin of life itself. This philosophy is being taught in our public school systems and universities as science. We know it as "Evolution by Means of Natural Selection." To simplify its meaning as it applies to the field of science let's use the definition given in the *Baker Encyclopedia of Christian Apologetics* by Norman L. Geisler:

"**Evolution**...covers three basic areas: the origin of the universe, the origin of first life, and the origin of new life forms. Respectively, these are called cosmic evolution, chemical evolution, and biological evolution. ...In the broad sense, evolution means development, but more specifically it has come to mean the theory of common ancestry. It is the belief that all living things evolved by natural processes from earlier and more simple forms of life. ...Naturalistic evolution believes the entire process is natural including the origin of the universe and first life by spontaneous generation" (p.224) {2}.

Brief History Of Evolutionary Origins

Materialists in general wrap themselves around the philosophy made famous by Charles Darwin. However, Darwin was not the originator of evolutionary philosophy. We need to go back over 2,500 years to a Greek named Thales (pronounced Thay-leez) of Miletus (640-546 B.C.). Bert Thompson, Ph.D., in his book, *The History of Evolutionary Thought*, comments on the work of Thales as being: "The oldest name mentioned in Greek science." He was born in Miletus in Ionia, but traveled much into Greece proper, Crete, and Egypt. One of the seven "wise men" of ancient Greece...he founded the earliest school of Greek philosophers. ...His greatest

CHAPTER 2

claim to fame was through his astronomy, and as the father of geometry. ...Thales began with the single natural cause—water, which in turn developed into the other elements. He held that these first developed into the bodies of plants, then into simpler animals, and finally into more complex forms such as man. Thales felt that all unsuccessful forms supposedly reverted back to those elements from which they sprang" (pp. 28, 29) {3}.

There were others in history that held similar beliefs of some form of life coming from non-life, but for brevity's sake we're going to jump ahead to the 19th century to the four most prominent advocates of natural selection.

Charles Lyell (1797-1875) — Uniformitarianism

Charles Lyell, according to John C. Whitcomb, Jr., Th.D., and Henry M. Morris, Ph.D., in their book, *The Genesis Flood*, was known as:

"...the high priest of uniformitarianism," and author of the famous textbook, *Principles of Geology*, was a young English attorney who had enthusiastically accepted the doctrine of gradual geological changes. ...James Hutton (1726-1797)...a Scottish geologist, had taught that many of the geological processes now operating in the earth had been active for extremely long periods in the past, and that such gradual processes could account for the world as we see it today. Lyell also adopted the theories of William ('Strata') Smith (1769-1839), 'the father of stratigraphic geology,' who believed that rock layers always occur in the same sequence, depending on the type of fossils they contain. ...But Lyell went even farther than his predecessors, in his insistence that all geologic processes had been very gradual in the past and in utter abhorrence for anything suggestive of sudden catastrophes" (p. 95) {4}.

Here we see prominent, well-known scientists beginning to question the Genesis account of God's six-day creation and a global flood. As Whitcomb and Morris have emphasized, "...Charles Lyell's uniformitarianism has been accepted as the true philosophy of geology in all major centers of scientific learning in the world today" (p. 96) {5}.
It is interesting to note that Charles Darwin was a disciple of Lyell's. In fact, he used uniformitarianism as a foundation for much of his theory of organic evolution.

WHAT IS TRUTH?

Whitcomb and Morris went on to say, "Charles Darwin, a disciple of Lyell, built his theory of organic evolution upon the uniformitarian foundation which Lyell had laid. Nor was Darwin reluctant to acknowledge his debt of gratitude to Lyell...in his book, *The Origin of Species*" (p. 96) {6}.

Later, in his *Life and Letters of Charles Darwin*, Darwin gives credit to Charles Lyell for Darwin's own personal beliefs. "...I am proud to remember that the first place, namely, St Jage, in the Cape De Verde archipelago, in which I geologized, convinced me of the infinite superiority of Lyell's views over those advocated in any other work known to me" (p. 60) {7}.

Charles Lyell and Charles Darwin were not alone. They were part of a small group of historical figures to appear on the scene in the 1800's that made a rather stunning impact on philosophy and science. Another prominent Englishman involved was Herbert Spencer. According to Thompson, in his book, *The History of Evolutionary Thought*, Spencer had a profound influence on Darwin:

Herbert Spencer (1820-1903)

Thompson explains: "Such a man was Herbert Spencer (1820-1903). The Englishman Spencer, and geologist Charles Lyell, probably influenced Charles Darwin more than any other two men of the Darwinian era...and may ultimately be responsible for more of the acceptance of the theory of evolution than they are given credit for. ...Herbert Spencer...was not a scientist as such, but a philosopher" (p. 65) {8}.

As Thompson continues to point out, Spencer, like Darwin, were far more interested in avoiding any supernatural explanation. Materialistic naturalism dominated their research:

"Herbert Spencer was a confirmed naturalist—and that may be stating the matter too simply. Even from his younger years he leaned heavily toward totally naturalistic explanations he saw. ...Spencer's bias against the supernatural was so compelling that he could not even think about supernatural manifestations being possible" (p. 66) {9}.

Herbert Spencer, in his mind, subjectively eliminated any form of a Creator God. He chose to concentrate his thinking toward only a tangible, materialistic answer to

CHAPTER 2

how things came to be. Therefore, as Thompson indicates, his mind centered on naturalism:

"Because of his naturalistic attitude, he was led (as Darwin and Huxley were) to accept evolution. He (and they) had rejected special creation and was (were) looking for something to take its place" (p. 67) {10}.

I can't help thinking of what the New Testament writer, Paul, wrote to the Thessalonians, who were Christians living in Macedonia:

"…and in every sort of evil that deceives those who are perishing. They perish because they refused to love the truth and so be saved. For this reason God sends them a powerful delusion so that they will believe the lie" (2 Thessalonians 2:10-11).

I will return to this scripture later, but I want to make note of the fact that there is such a thing as "powerful delusion." But for now, we need to move on to the most famous of the 19th century natural selection advocates.

Charles Darwin (1809-1882)

To begin with, the *Baker Encyclopedia of Christian Apologetics*, by Norman L. Geisler, provides a brief biographical and historical background on Charles Darwin:

"Charles Robert Darwin, (1809-1882) was born in Shrewsbury, England, the son of a physician. As a naturalist, he won sponsors and government backing for an expedition on the military sailing ship HMS Beagle, where he made his famous observations on the differences in finches. Later he used what he had learned on this ship as evidence for his theory of Evolution" (p. 181) {11}.

Darwin's work caused a significant scientific controversy, as Bert Thompson notes in his book, *The History of Evolutionary Thought*:

"In 1842 Darwin wrote out a brief statement of the theory he had formed to account for the origin of species, with a more complete draft being drawn up in 1844" (p. 107) {12}.

WHAT IS TRUTH?

"On November 24, 1859, *The Origin of Species by Natural Selection* first appeared. All 1,025 copies of the first edition were sold the first day. Its publication insured that Darwin would receive major credit for the hypothesis of organic evolution by natural selection. And so he has!" (p. 108) {13}.

Charles Darwin was a contemporary of Alfred Russell Wallace. Wallace, like Darwin, was a naturalist working from Malaya. The problem was, as Thompson states, that "Wallace had summarized what Darwin had been working on for over 20 years. ...He wrote the paper in a matter of days and sent it to Darwin with the request that Darwin take it to Lyell for his opinion. ...Both Darwin's and Wallace's work were read before the Linnaean Society in 1858, with little attention given to both" (pp. 107-108) {14}.

Alfred Russell Wallace's essay did not get the recognition it deserved, while Charles Darwin's book received outstanding notoriety. According to Thompson:

"The success of Darwin's book was phenomenal. In 17 years it had sold 16,000 copies—a remarkable achievement in that day and time" (p. 108) {15}.

Lyell, Spencer, Darwin, and Wallace were not without contemporary adherents. Other notable characters came forth and joined forces with them. One significant adherent of natural selection was a man by the name of Thomas Henry Huxley.

Thomas Henry Huxley (1825-1894)—"Darwin's Bulldog"

Thomas Huxley became an aggressive combative defender of evolution. Huxley constantly promoted natural selection science most eloquently through debate, lectures, and writing. By 1860, Huxley had already become famous as the champion of Darwinism. Henry M. Morris wrote in *The Troubled Waters of Evolution*:

"Thomas Huxley...was probably more responsible than any other single individual for the rapid and widespread acceptance of Darwinian evolution, through his constant and effective speaking and writing. Huxley was an evolutionist before Darwin, but the latter's book gave him the needed scientific support for it, or so he thought. He became known as 'Darwin's Bulldog'" (p. 58) {16}.

CHAPTER 2

History is full of examples of scientists and — surprising as it may seem — theologians who succumbed to the notion that perhaps God used natural selection as the means to bring everything into being. Many were simply not aware that even during those rude awakening years of scientific upheaval and theories that had tremendous impact on 19th century philosophy, there were, during that same period of history, contemporary scientists who made a serious discovery so factual that it is known as a natural "law" of science, that completely demolishes the hypothesis of life coming into being by accidental spontaneous generation. Spontaneous generation, by the way, is the starter mechanism of life for Darwinian evolution. Later, in another chapter, it will become evident why this scientific law cannot be overlooked as solid evidence for an intelligent Creator (God).

Could religion and Darwinism become united in principle on creation through evolutionary methods? Not according to Thomas Huxley. Thompson points out that: "Huxley considered men fools for believing in...'the myths of Genesis.' ...'But my sole point is to get the people who persist in regarding them as statements of fact to understand that they are fools'" {17}.

You see, it was already in the minds of serious skeptics who made it their predominant goal to publicly reject the God-breathed Holy Scriptures to reject anything that had to do with a supreme being, such as God, who held humanity responsible to acknowledge, believe, and trust in Him as their creator whom they should glorify and serve. Was Huxley open-minded enough to consider the God of the Bible as Creator? According to Huxley's own admission, he was not. In Huxley's own words:

"I really believe that the alternative is either Darwinism or nothing, for I do not know of any rational conception or theory of the organic universe which has any scientific position at all beside Mr. Darwin's" {18}.

Dr. Asa Gray — American Botanist

In the United States, the influence of Charles Darwin spread among Americans, such as Dr. Asa Gray (1810-1888), a professor of botany at Harvard. Before the publication of *The Origin of Species*, Gray and Darwin had exchanged letters on the subject of species. In 1859, therefore, when Darwin published *The Origin of Species*, Gray was already familiar with Darwin's work. However, Gray's views departed from Darwin and Huxley on the issue of a Divine Creator. As Thompson describes:

"Asa Gray was a peculiar case. He was considered by many to be a Christian because of his strong stand that a Creator was necessary to make Evolution work. ...Anyone even vaguely familiar with his speeches and writings knows that Christianity took a back-seat to science as far as he was concerned. ...If ever there was a theistic evolutionist, it was Asa Gray. He tried desperately throughout his entire adult life to 'merge' evolution with the Bible. He never succeeded" {19}.

There is another historical figure one cannot ignore whose philosophy still maintains a huge dominance in our educational system.

John Dewey (1859-1952)

Norman Geisler, in his book, *Baker Encyclopedia of Christian Apologetics*, gives a historical background of the man who has impacted our educational system probably more than most people would imagine:

"John Dewey (1859-1952) has been called the father of modern American education, on which he had immense influence. As a philosopher and writer he is closely identified with the philosophy of instrumentalism, also known as progressivism or pragmatic humanism. Through the American educational system, his views have influenced virtually every American of the twentieth century. Dewey signed the *Humanist Manifesto* and was a leader in the movement to turn education toward secular humanism. ...Born and educated in Vermont, Dewey took his doctorate at Johns Hopkins University. There he studied the pragmatism of C.S. Pierce...and the philosophies of G.S. Morris (a neo-Hegelian), and T.H. Huxley. Dewey taught at the universities of Michigan and Chicago and was at Columbia University from 1904 to 1930. ...As a secular humanist, Dewey rejected belief in a theistic God. ... Dewey concluded that modern science made belief in a supernatural origin of the universe untenable" {20}.

CHAPTER 2

In Dewey's book, *A Common Faith*, he wrote: "The impact of astronomy eliminated the older religious creation stories...geological discoveries have displaced creation myths which once bulked large...biology has revolutionized conceptions of soul and mind...and this science has made a profound impression upon ideas of sin, redemption and immortality" {21}.

Geisler summarizes John Dewey's philosophy with these remarks: "Since there is no creator, human beings were not created. For Dewey modern men and women think in scientific and secular terms, thus, they must now take a naturalistic view of origins. ...Humanity is a result of naturalistic evolutionary processes, not the special creation by any kind of God" {22}.

Two of John Dewey's most notable doctrines were Pragmatism (whatever works is true) and Relativism (denial of the possibility of an absolute truth; truth itself is subjective). It is through Dewey that "progressivism or human pragmatism" has stamped a huge impact on our public schools and our universities. Geisler put it these words:

"Through the American educational system, his views have influenced virtually every American of the twentieth century. Dewey signed the *Humanist Manifesto* and was a leader in the movement to turn education toward secular humanism" {23}.

In Europe, there was one more critically influential person in the field of science that so impressed Charles Darwin that he included about twelve pages on the subject of embryology as evidence for natural selection in his book, *The Origin of Species*.

NOTE: According to *the Columbia Encyclopedia*, (1993), 5th Ed., p.755, Dewey also taught at the University of Minnesota, (1888-1889).

John Dewey's philosophy was taught at four different universities (in Minnesota, Michigan, Chicago, and at Columbia). He taught for a period of 42 years (from 1888 to 1930). Think of how many young, impressionable minds he must have changed and how his teachings affected their worldviews! Think of the impact upon our society! These young minds then went out into the workplace. Many earned doctorates and began teaching the next generation. And the next generation did the same and went out to teach the next generation! And the beat goes on.

WHAT IS TRUTH?

Ernst Haeckel

The Columbia Encyclopedia gives a brief description of Haeckel's life:

"Haeckel, Ernst Heinrich…1834-1919, German biologist and philosopher…taught (1862-1909) at the University of Jena. An early exponent of Darwinism in Germany, he evolved a mechanistic form of MONISM based on his interpretation of Darwin's theories and set forth in his speculative works on science. …Although many of his works have proved erroneous, they attracted a large following and stimulated research" {24}.

In a later chapter there will be more information on Haeckel's embryology theories and why they have been proven to be false.

Thus we have what I believe to be the six most influential figures in the emergence of evolution by natural selection of the 19th century. Think of how many people Charles Lyell, Charles Darwin, Thomas Huxley, Ernst Haeckel, Asa Gray, and John Dewey have influenced over the past 150 years.

Darwinian Evolution Defined (Subtle-Miniscule-Increments)

The Darwinian hypothesis depends upon huge expanses of time, and subtle, miniscule increments of change in determining the outcome of the necessary acquired characteristics. The problem comes when it is put to the test by known, tested, and established laws of science. It comes up highly lacking in substance. Nevertheless, it has had horribly tragic effects upon humanity.

The Impact Of Materialistic Natural Selection

Materialistic natural selection has produced such philosophies as Marxism, Nazism, and Secular Humanism. Common tenets include "Survival of the fittest," no moral absolutes, and whatever works—moral or immoral. The by-products are hostility to Judaism/Christianity and Racism, which leads to the idea of "weeding out the unfit."

CHAPTER 2

Why would such philosophies as these produce racism? In these worldviews human beings are "biological organisms" no different from ordinary house flies. Henry M. Morris explains the natural result of their reasoning:

"In dealing with man strictly as a biological organism in a 'great chain of being' with all other organisms, the human 'species' (Homo sapiens) has been divided by evolutionary biologists into various 'subspecies' or races, in the same way that other species are subdivided. In evolutionary terminology, a race is an incipient species; if racial development is progressive and beneficial in the 'struggle for existence,' then that race will be preserved and others may die out, so it eventually becomes a new and better species. Homo erectus may have evolved into Homo sapiens, and, someday, it is theorized, a particularly virile race among the latter may evolve into, say, Homo supremus (superman)! …This concept was particularly dominant among the 19th century evolutionists, and it produced a number of aberrant philosophies" {25}.

Although organizations such as Hitler's Nazi party and the Ku Klux Klan have been publicized as the dominant adherents of **racism**, it did not begin with them. Take a look at the writings of Charles Darwin and Thomas Huxley:

CHARLES DARWIN: "The more civilized so-called Caucasian races have beaten the Turkish hollow in the struggle for existence. Looking to the world at no very distant date, what an endless number of the lower **races** will have been eliminated by the higher civilized races of the world" (emphasis added) {26}.

THOMAS HUXLEY: "No rational man, cognizant of the facts, believes that the **average Negro** is the equal, much less the superior, of the white man" (emphasis added) {27}.

On the subject of evolutionists and racism, Morris, made this comment:
"Modern day evolutionists, for the most part, do not regard any one race of men as intrinsically superior or inferior to any other. **Nevertheless, the very concept of 'race' is fundamentally a category of evolutionary biology, and leading evolutionary biologists recognize this.** George Gaylord Simpson says: '**Races of man have, or perhaps one should say "had," exactly the same biological significance as the subspecies of other species of mammals**'" (emphasis added) {28}.

WHAT IS TRUTH?

To the evolutionist, man is not made in the image of God as stated in the Bible (Genesis 1:27). Humans are simply another species of animal. Seemingly, a more advanced species, but nevertheless, a mammal. The Human (Homo sapiens) is just matter, and matter is all there is. Seems harmless on the face of it, doesn't it? But is it really? To answer that question one only need look at how materialistic evolution has impacted our culture. First, let's look at the philosophy of Friedrich Nietzsche.

FRIEDRICH NIETZSCHE (1844-1900)

For historical background, Edward McNall Burns, in his book, *Western Civilizations*, describes the life of Friedrich Nietzsche:

"Friedrich Nietzsche also revealed a decided influence of the idea of evolution. But Nietzsche was not a scientist, nor was he interested in the nature of matter or in the problem of truth. ...Born in 1844, the son of a Lutheran minister, he was educated in the classics at Leipzig and Bonn and at the age of twenty-five was made a professor of philology at the University of Basel. Ten years later he was forced to retire on account of ill health. He spent the next decade of his life in agony, wandering from one resort to another in a fruitless quest for relief. ...In 1888 he lapsed into hopeless insanity, which continued until his death in 1900" {28}.

Nietzsche's philosophy and influence has had a horribly detrimental impact on western culture. It is delusional, bitter, and extremely hostile to both Christianity and Judaism. Follow the word-picture that Burns provides in his description:
"His cardinal idea is the notion that natural selection should be permitted to operate unhindered in the case of human beings as it does with plants and animals. He believed that such a constant weeding out of the unfit would eventually produce a race of supermen—not merely a race of physical giants but men distinguished above all for their moral courage, for their strength of character. Those who should be allowed to perish in the struggle are the moral weaklings, the ineffective and craven ones, who have neither the strength nor the courage to battle nobly for a place in the sun. But before any such process of NATURAL SELECTION could operate, religious obstacles would have to be removed. Nietzsche therefore demanded that the moral supremacy of CHRISTIANITY and JUDAISM should be overthrown. ...They exalt into virtues qualities which ought to be considered vices—humility, non-resistance, mortification of the flesh, and pity for the weak

CHAPTER 2

and incompetent. The enthronement of these qualities prevents the elimination of the unfit and preserves them to pour their degenerate blood into the veins of the race" (emphasis added) {29}.

Does this bring to mind someone who brought this sort of evil upon humanity?

Adolph Hitler (1889-1945)

Adolf Hitler was one of a group of seven men who formed the "National Socialist German Workers Party" in 1919. Shortly thereafter, he became their leader. Interestingly, at their beginning, Hitler and the party were strongly influenced by Nietzsche's philosophy. Jacques Barzun, in his book, *From Dawn to Decadence*, states:

"It was the mistake of Hitler and his intellectual aides to include Nietzsche among the early prophets of their social and racial dogmas. They soon found he did not suit the role—quite the opposite—and within a short time he was quietly cast aside" {30}.

Although Nietzsche may not have fit the ideal of perfection for the Nazi party, according to Barzun, because he held no enthusiasm for "populism," it seems rather clear that Hitler and the party did share Nietzsche's disdain for what both he and Hitler considered inferior races, Judaism and Christianity. Burns records some of Hitler's early history:

"He became an ardent admirer of certain Jew-baiting politicians in Vienna; and he associated Judaism with Marxism, he hated that philosophy also. He likewise became a convert to extreme Nordicism, doting the qualities of the proud German nation" {31}.

Who can forget the horrific conspiracy of this man in his leadership of Nazi Germany to exterminate all living Jews and the religion of Judaism? It has a name that will probably never be forgotten, the Holocaust. This is the name that commemorates the attempted extermination of a whole race of innocent people who were methodically and forcibly imprisoned in concentration camps to work as slaves and ultimately sent to their deaths in gas chambers. According to *the Columbia Encyclopedia*, "By the end of the war [World War II] six million Jews had been systematically murdered" {32}.

He deceitfully manipulated the Protestant and Catholic churches in Germany to continue his Fascist-Socialist agenda to gain total power, pretending to be the protector of Christianity against the Russian Bolshevik persecution of Russian Orthodox churches and religion. But this was never his real intention. Neither Judaism nor Christianity would be safe from Adolf Hitler's ultimate objectives. In their book, *Totalitarian Dictatorship and Autocracy*, Friedrich and Brzezinski make this extremely clear:

"The Russian Orthodoxy was intimidated and subdued, and the church no longer represented an effective impediment to totalitarian rule. ...The Fascists and Nazis claimed to fight this policy, which had aroused the indignation of the Western world by erecting a totalitarian dictatorship strong enough to withstand the Bolshevik onslaught. But in conjunction with this claim they propounded views which made religion purely a function of political needs. They insisted upon a 'political faith' which must be the cardinal point of reference. Adolf Hitler put this quite clearly and unequivocally in *Mein Kampf*: 'For myself and all true National Socialists there exists only one doctrine: nation and fatherland. What we have to fight for is to make secure the existence and expansion of our race and our nation, to rear its children and to keep pure the blood, the freedom and independence of the fatherland...'" {33}.

What Hitler's ultimate intentions were for Christians there is no doubt: Total elimination! Friedrich and Brzezinski quote from an author by the name of Hermann Rauschning:

"What is to be thought of this concern of Hitler's for truly inner religiosity can be seen from one of the conversations Rauschning has reported to us: 'What do you think, will the masses ever become Christian again? Never! ...But the priests...will betray their God to us...and replace the cross by the swastika. They will celebrate the pure blood of our nation instead of the blood of their previous redeemer...' Hitler planned to tackle the problem of the churches after the war as 'the last great problem' and to transform them into organizations for celebrating the racial 'faith' in which he believed" {34}.

CHAPTER 2

The more I read from the promoters of the evolutionist worldview the more I see this consistent pattern of hostility toward Christians and Jews. It may be more subtle in our Western Culture than in Nazi Germany, but it is still present today. In fact, some atheistic evolutionists are becoming more and more open in their hostility. But before we examine today's conflict we must not forget that the 19th century produced a small but determined group of individuals who were rebellious to the thought of obedience to their Creator, even denying His reality. There is one more person neither we nor history can ignore.

Karl Marx (1818-1883)

While it is true that Marx's main thrust in his writings was the advancement of political-social economic systems through what he considered an inevitable evolution of change, Marx was the prominent instigator of evolution in social/political economics. J.D. Bales, in his book, *Two Worlds: Christianity and Communism*, reminds us that Marx was an atheist:

"Communists deny that communism is a religion or a religion substitute. They view all religion as evil. Lenin affirmed that 'every religious idea, every idea of God, is utter able vileness. ...Although some individuals may have reacted against corruption, and turned to communism as a substitute faith, yet it must be remembered that Marx was an atheist before he became a communist" {35}.

Solid evidence of the malice that was deliberately directed toward Christian people by the atheistic communists is beyond question. Friedrich and Brzezinski remind us that this is critical to the Totalitarian philosophy:

"'Religion is the opium of the people!' This famous slogan of the Communist-Marxist movement conveys a good part of the totalitarian approach—its hostility to all organized religion" {36}.

Atheists, agnostics, and other historical critics have openly condemned the Spanish Inquisition and some of the atrocities that occurred during the Crusades, and rightly so. Wrong is wrong no matter who does it, whether they bear the name of Christian or not. However, the same critics rarely mention, and many times ignore, the millions who suffered and died under the totalitarian socialist dictatorships of the

WHAT IS TRUTH?

Marxists and the Fascists. According to *The New Foxe's Book of Martyrs*, (Rewritten and Updated by Harold J. Chadwick), the persecution and death toll continues to this day:

"During the first quarter of the twentieth century, there was no systematic persecution of Christians. Then in 1924, Joseph Stalin gained control of the USSR and the communist form of government was fully established. Over the years, atheistic Communism spread throughout the world, especially after World War II, during the period of 1945 to 1975. From the beginning, the Communists persecuted Christians, destroyed their churches, imprisoned them, tortured them, and killed them. During the height of Communism worldwide, an average of **330,000 Christians were killed every year.** ...According to the 1997 *World Christian Encyclopedia*, **between 155,000 and 159,000 Christians are killed for their faith throughout the world every year.** [In] Communist nations, such as Cuba and China...Christians are still being persecuted. ...In China today, it is said that there is no official government policy of persecution, and that it is not illegal to be a Christian. Yet Christians continue to be harassed and arrested by the police, and underground churches are sought out and their meeting places destroyed" (emphasis added) {37}.

Richard Dawkins—Evolutionist/Athiest

Richard Dawkins made this statement in regard to religion and faith: "I think a case can be made that faith is one of the world's great evils, comparable to the smallpox virus but harder to eradicate" {38}.

This statement was made in The Humanist 57 (January/February 1997: 26). It seems evident that Darwinian atheists are not interested in peaceful co-existence. As of yet, in the USA, persecution remains subtle, preferring to gain victories through the courts.

NOTE: It should be mentioned that after the 1991 dissolution of the USSR, the majority of the persecution of Christians is being carried out by those of the Muslim faith (pp. 326, 327).

CHAPTER 2

William Provine

Dr. William Provine is a distinguished professor of Ecology and Evolutionary Biology. What he had to say in a "keynote address" at a university in Tennessee should be critical in understanding the evolutionist worldview. In an article, in *Reason & Revelation*, July, 2008, titled "The Bitter Fruits of Atheism," Kyle Butt quotes the words of Mr. Provine:

"On February 12, 1998, William Provine, a professor in the Department of Ecology and Evolutionary Biology at the distinguished Cornell University, took the podium on the campus of the University of Tennessee in Knoxville. He was invited to give the keynote address at the second annual Darwin day. ...Dr. Provine's introductory comments are recorded in the following words: 'Naturalistic evolution has clear consequences that Charles Darwin understood perfectly. 1) No gods worth having exist; 2) No life after death exists; 3) No ultimate foundation for ethics exists; 4) No ultimate meaning in life exists; and 5) Human free will is nonexistent... The first four implications are so obvious to modern evolutionists that I will spend little time defending them'" {39}.

It should be mentioned that several Theistic evolutionists have defended Charles Darwin, insisting that Darwin's theory of natural selection did not necessarily mean that Darwin was an atheist. However, when one reads from what he has written it appears that Provine is right about Darwin. Dr. James D. Bales, in his book, *How Can Ye Believe?* agrees with Provine on Darwin's views of God and Creation:

"For some reason or another, Darwin was determined not to believe in God, although he admitted more than once that it is reasonable to believe in God, and unreasonable to reject God. Thus he wrote: 'This follows from the extreme difficulty of conceiving this immense and wonderful universe, including man with his capacity for looking far backwards and far into futurity, as the result of blind chance or necessity. When thus reflecting I feel compelled to look at a First Cause having an intelligent mind in some degree analogous to that of man; and I deserve to be called a Theist. This conclusion was strong in my mind about the time, as far as I can remember, when I wrote the "Origin of Species;" and it is since that time that it has very gradually, with many fluctuations, become weaker. But then arises the doubt, can the mind of

WHAT IS TRUTH?

man, which has, as I fully believe, been developed from a mind as low as that possessed by the lowest animals, be trusted when it draws such grand conclusions? …Nevertheless you have expressed my inward conviction, though far more vividly and clearly than I could have done, that the universe is not the result of chance. But then with me the horrid doubt always arises whether the convictions of man's mind, which has been developed from the mind of the lower animals, are of any value or at all trustworthy. Would anyone trust in the conviction of a monkey's mind, if there are any convictions in such a mind?' {40}.

The Grand Delusion

Charles Darwin gives substantial evidence of allowing his passions to interfere with reason. When this happens, the result is the development of a delusion. *Webster's Collegiate Dictionary, Tenth Edition*, defines a "delusion" as it applies in this case: "2 a: something that is falsely or delusively believed or propagated" {41}.

What Darwin conceived in his mind is a delusion of immense proportions. It became a fixation in his thinking to avoid what reason had suggested—that the universe is the result of "a First Cause having an Intelligent mind" —and to continue in his pursuit of his grand delusion. Charles Darwin, of course, was not alone. It became the fixation of his associates of like mind, such as Thomas Huxley, John Dewey, Ernst Haeckel, Friedrich Nietzsche, Karl Marx, and the generations that followed, who were willing to forsake truth and reason to follow the **Grand Delusion**. This is not a sudden whim of the 19th century. It is almost as old as humanity.

2 Thessalonians 2:10-12 warns about "…every sort of evil that deceives those who are perishing. They perish because they refused to love the truth and so be saved. For this reason God sends them a **powerful delusion** so that they will believe the lie and so that all will be condemned who have not believed **the truth** but have delighted in wickedness" (emphasis added).

DAN BARKER, a professed atheist and staunch defender of Darwin's natural selection, made this statement in his book, *Godless*: "Darwinism shows us that all living organisms are the result of a natural evolutionary process." Okay, Mr. Barker, tell us, how does the "natural evolutionary process" work? Read carefully, Dan Barker's explanation:

CHAPTER 2

"But evolution is not blind chance. It is design that incorporates randomness—not intelligent design, but design by laws of nature, by the limited number of ways atoms interact mathematically and molecules combine geometrically" {41}.

Did you catch that? **"It is design that incorporates randomness—not intelligent design, but design by the laws of nature..."** (emphasis added). Design without a designer? Perhaps Mr. Barker needs to look again at Webster's definition of design. Here is how *Merriam Webster's Collegiate Dictionary, 10th edition*, defines the word "DESIGN": 1 a. a particular purpose held in view by an individual or group; b. deliberate purposive planning; 2 a. mental project or scheme in which means to an end are laid down..." {42}.

A design automatically includes a deliberate planned design by an intelligent designer! "Randomness," from the word "random" is: "n. a haphazard course—at random: without definite aim, direction, rule, or method;" adj. 1 a. lacking a definite plan, purpose or pattern" {43}.

If I understand him correctly, what Dan Barker is telling us is that evolution (natural selection) is an unintelligent, incoherent effect lacking any sort of definite plan or purpose that is an efficiently operating scheme which reason would indicate is a deliberate, intelligent design, but it isn't. Because as Dan Barker insists, "evolution is not blind chance." It is "randomness" that produces "design." Sorry, Mr. Barker, but that sounds like an irrational delusion to me. Later in another chapter of this book that statement will be compared to what the laws of science actually tell us.

Where is this delusional type of thinking leading our culture? It leads to the devaluation of human beings to the level of a dog or a pig, and in some cases, of even lesser value. In an article, "The Bitter Fruits of Atheism" (Part 1), Kyle Butt, M.A., comments on an article in 1983, by Peter Singer:

"It is an easily ascertainable fact that belief in atheistic evolution devalues human life, demoting it to the base level of animal status. Such thinking logically leads to the adoption of measures that destroy innocent human life, but are still viewed by atheistic thinkers as 'moral.' For instance in 1983, Peter Singer published an article in...Pediatrics titled 'Sanctuary of Life or Quality of Life?' In the article, he contended that there is no moral burden to keep alive human infants who are born with mental retardation or other developmental problems such as Downs syndrome."

WHAT IS TRUTH?

Here is a quotation from Peter Singer's article, as listed in Kyle Butt's article:

"We can no longer base our ethics on the idea that human beings are a special form of creation…so why should we believe that the mere fact that a being is a member of the species Homo sapiens endows its life with some unique, almost infinite value? …If we compare a severely defective human infant with a nonhuman animal, **a dog or a pig, for example, we will often find the nonhuman to have superior capacity, both actual and potential, for rationality, self-consciousness, communication, and anything else that can plausibly be considered morally significant. …Species membership alone, however, is not morally relevant.** … If we can put aside the obsolete and erroneous notion of the sanctity of all **human life,** we may start to look at human life as it really is: at the quality of life that each human being has or can achieve" (emphasis added) {44}.

When we look at this statement by Peter Singer it is easy to see the delusional thinking that led to the 1973 legalization of abortion. In the eyes of advocates for atheistic evolution and humanism, an unborn child is simply another mammal, no different from a cow, dog, or pig. After all, if it's okay to kill cattle for food we should be able to snuff out a human unborn child (a "fetus"—NOTE: Humanists/Atheists do not like to use the word "child" to refer to the unborn). Humanist and evolutionist Julian Huxley, grandson of Sir Thomas Huxley, chose these words to describe why humanists/evolutionists perceive that man is just another "natural phenomenon":

"I use the word 'humanist' to mean someone who believes that man is just as much a natural phenomenon as an animal or plant; that his body, mind and soul were not supernaturally created but are products of evolution, and that he is not under the control or guidance of any supernatural being or beings, but has to rely on himself and his own powers" {45}.

Do we wonder why abortions are so numerous when those whom we have trusted to save lives now find it profitable to terminate—to slaughter—innocent human lives? To the humanist way of thinking, an unborn human child is no different than an unborn chicken inside the egg. Kyle Butt, in the July 2008, *Reason & Revelation* article mentioned previously, estimates:

CHAPTER 2

"In the United States, this murderous practice has been legal since January 22, 1973, and has resulted in the deaths of more than **48 million innocent human lives in this country alone**" (emphasis added) {46}.

It is not just technical and scientific differences that divide atheistic Darwinist philosophy from Christian creationist philosophy, that inevitably divide Darwinists and Christians morally. Within the atheist community there is a more subtle agenda behind the division. An Atheist by the name of Aldous Huxley wrote:

"I had motives for not wanting the world to have meaning; consequently, assumed it had none, and was able without any difficulty to find reasons for this assumption. …For myself, as no doubt for most of my contemporaries, the philosophy of meaninglessness was essentially an instrument of liberation. The liberation we desired was simultaneously liberation from a certain political and economic system and liberation from a certain system of morality. **We objected to the morality because it interfered with our sexual freedom**" (emphasis added) {47}.

Kyle Butt M.A., is the Associate Editor of *Reason & Revelation* (R&R), a monthly publication of Apologetics Press, which provides Biblical and Scientific evidence for the reality of God and His message. Kyle wrote two articles in R&R in 2008, one in July and one in August, titled: "THE BITTER FRUITS OF ATHEISM," (Parts I & II). In these articles he comments on the impact of atheism on society. He makes some clear observations on the atheist agenda:

"Following Huxley's argument, if we assume that the world was not created by God, and that there is ultimately no real meaning to human existence, then we can have sex with whomever, whenever, and in whatever way we choose. Evolutionary atheism offers sexual deviance a blank check to be filled out in whatever way each 'naked ape' chooses. Numerous examples can be shown in which atheistic evolution is used to explain and defend sordid sexual perversions" {48}.

In these articles, "The Bitter Fruits of Atheism," Parts I & II, Kyle Butt has included some of the thoughts of the author James Rachels, a strong Darwinian Natural Selection advocate, from his book, *Created from Animals: The Moral Implications of Darwinism*:

NOTE: Included in Part II, are quotations from several atheists/evolutionists on their liberal worldview, on rape, homosexuality, and pedophilia.

WHAT IS TRUTH?

"Some unfortunate humans—perhaps because they have suffered brain damage—are not rational agents. What are we to say about them? The natural conclusion, according to the doctrine we are considering, would be that their status is that of mere animals. And perhaps we should go on to conclude that they may be used as non-human animals are used—perhaps as laboratory subjects, **or as food**" (1990, p.186 emphasis added) {49}.

Does anyone not see that the thoughts for the future agenda of humanity by Darwinists such as Rachels and Singer are hardly different than that of Nietzsche and Hitler? Are not the deaths of 6,000,000 Jews by Hitler, the deaths of over 9,000,000 Christians by Stalin, and the 48,000,000 legalized abortions that have taken place in this nation by abortion advocates evidence enough that something is wrong with Atheistic Humanist Darwinism? Have our eyes been blinded by the constant indoctrination through our schools, secular universities, newspapers, and television programming?

This is not intended to make a blanket statement that all atheistic Darwinists are planning some violent form of vicious, cold-blooded, brutal murder of all Christians. Most of them would probably not advocate such evil intentions, although there is a growing number who would like to eliminate all Christian influence in our educational systems and in public forums. They certainly wouldn't mind if churches and Christianity would simply disappear. In fact, they would be delighted.

Think about young, pregnant girls facing the serious dilemma of raising a child when they are, in many cases, teen and pre-teen children themselves, who are being encouraged and often coerced and pressured into aborting their unborn babies. How little many of them know about how our Lord Jesus loves and forgives them because they, so often, simply do not know what they are doing!

As a Christian, a less than-perfect, flawed human being saved by the grace of God, washed by the blood of Jesus Christ, and pardoned from every sin I have ever committed, I am compelled to write this book because the facts concerning the reality of God are overwhelming. The promise of eternal salvation foretold by the prophets and fulfilled in Christ's death, burial, and resurrection are real. They are offered to everyone who is willing to accept Christ Jesus as their Lord and Savior.

CHAPTER 2

Yes, I realize there have been people in the past and a few in the present who profess Christianity, but their actions demonstrate they have another agenda. Our Lord Jesus Christ never advocated such evil behavior as the Spanish Inquisition, the intolerant and murderous escapades by several of the Crusaders, and the terror spread by the Ku Klux Klan in the 19th, 20th, and 21st centuries. Jesus said, "By this all men will know that you are my disciples, if you love one another" (John 13:35).

THIS BRINGS US BACK TO THE QUESTION: "WHAT IS TRUTH?" CHRISTIANITY AND ATHEISTIC EVOLUTION ARE TWO DIAMETRICALLY OPPOSED BELIEF SYSTEMS.

Atheistic Natural Selection Humanists believe everything that exists is matter.

Bible-believing Christians believe in both matter and spirit. Matter is everything that is tangible. Spirit is that which is intangible.

In his speech previously referenced, Dr. William Provine gave five clear examples of the difference between Atheistic Materialism and Biblical Matter and Spirit.

Dr. Provine—
1) NO GODS WORTH HAVING EXIST.

The Bible—
Romans 1:20: "For since the creation of the world God's invisible qualities—his eternal power and divine nature—have been clearly seen, being understood from what has been made, so that men are without excuse."
Acts 17:24; "The God who made the world and everything in it is the Lord of heaven and earth and does not live in temples built by hands."

Dr. Provine—
2) NO LIFE AFTER DEATH EXISTS.

The Bible—
John 3:16: "For God so loved the world that he gave his one and only Son, that whoever believes in him shall not perish but have eternal life."

WHAT IS TRUTH?

Luke 16:22-25: (The rich man and the beggar, Lazarus) "The time came when the beggar died and the angels carried him to Abraham's side. The rich man also died and was buried. In hell, where he was in torment, he looked up and saw Abraham far away, with Lazarus by his side. So he called to him, 'Father Abraham, have pity on me and send Lazarus to dip the tip of his finger in water and cool my tongue, because I am in agony in this fire.' But Abraham replied, 'Son, remember that in your lifetime you received your good things, while Lazarus received bad things, but now he is comforted here and you are in agony."

In the Atheist worldview MATTER (i.e., the Universe, the Earth, humans, mammals) is all that exists. Therefore, the inner-man, (the intangible spirit within man), does not exist! To admit that an inner spiritual man does exist, would render void everything in the atheist's belief system.

Dr. Provine—
3) NO ULTIMATE FOUNDATION FOR ETHICS EXISTS.

The Bible—
Matthew 22:36-40: "'Teacher, which is the greatest commandment in the Law?' Jesus replied: 'Love the Lord your God with all your heart and with all your soul and with all your mind. This is the first and greatest commandment. And the second is like it: Love your neighbor as yourself. All the Law and the prophets hang on these two commandments.'"
Matthew 6:14-15: "For if you forgive men when they sin against you, your heavenly Father will also forgive you. But if you do not forgive men their sins, your Father will not forgive your sins."

Dr. Provine—
4) NO ULTIMATE MEANING IN LIFE EXISTS.

The Bible—
Matthew 5:16: In the same way, let your light shine before men, that they may see your good deeds and praise your Father in heaven."

CHAPTER 2

Galatians 6:10: "Therefore, as we have opportunity, let us do good to all people, especially to those who belong to the family of believers."

Ephesians 2:8-10: "For it is by grace you have been saved, through faith—and this not from yourselves, it is the gift of God—not by works, so that no one can boast. For we are God's workmanship created in Christ Jesus to do good works, which God prepared in advance for us to do."

ALEXANDER CAMPBELL, in his debate with Robert Owen, in April, 1829, asked these questions: **"What is man? Whence came he? Whither does he go?"** {50}. **If there is no meaning to life for humanity then we are nothing more than a cow only with a larger brain capacity and having the use of two five-fingered (in most cases) hands with the ability to build things; no more. If we die we cease to exist. This very dreary and depressing suggestion flies in the face of everything the Bible tells us! No wonder the humanists do not want the responsibility of being subjected to standing before the God of heaven and earth, because they are in rebellion! Herein lies the difference. Christians are here for a purpose: "as we have opportunity" to "do good to all people" and to give glory and honor to our "Father in heaven."**

Dr. Provine—
5) HUMAN FREE WILL IS NONEXISTENT.

The Bible—
Joshua 24:15: "But if serving the LORD seems undesirable to you, then choose for yourselves this day whom you will serve, whether the gods your forefathers served beyond the river, or the gods of the Amorites, in whose land you are living. But as for me and my household, we will serve the LORD."

THE FINAL AND MOST IMPORTANT POINT THAT PLACES CHRIST AND CHRISTIANITY IN DIAMETRICAL OPPOSITION TO ACCIDENTAL NATURAL SELECTION ATHEISIM

IF there is no life after death, then Christ has not been raised from the dead. IF Christ was not raised, then neither will those who put their trust in Christ be raised from the dead. "IF only for this life we have hope in Christ, we are to be pitied more

WHAT IS TRUTH?

than all men" (1 Corinthians 15:19 emphasis added).

IF these fleeting moments we have on this planet is all there is and no more, then the statement made by an atheist named Quentin Smith sums up the futility of our lives and all we have done: "THE MOST REASONABLE BELIEF IS THAT WE CAME FROM NOTHING, BY NOTHING AND FOR NOTHING" (emphasis added) {51}.

Wow, isn't that something to look forward to?

But not according to the Bible. 1 Corinthians 15:20 promises: "BUT CHRIST HAS INDEED BEEN RAISED FROM THE DEAD!" (emphasis added).

After over fifty years of Bible study and over forty years of study in the scientific evidence that not only refutes the natural selection, evolutionist philosophy, but vividly points out the reality of God, our Creator, I will point out in this book the four scientific laws that demonstrate God is real. I will then take the reader on a journey through the Old and New Testaments to point out how Biblical prophecy, revealed by God to the prophets, began in the very first book of the Bible and continued throughout until the arrival of the promised Messiah, Jesus Christ. Then through a detailed study of the historical events that point out the historically recorded resurrection of Jesus Christ, I will show that we can know with assurance that our faith will lead us to victory In Christ!

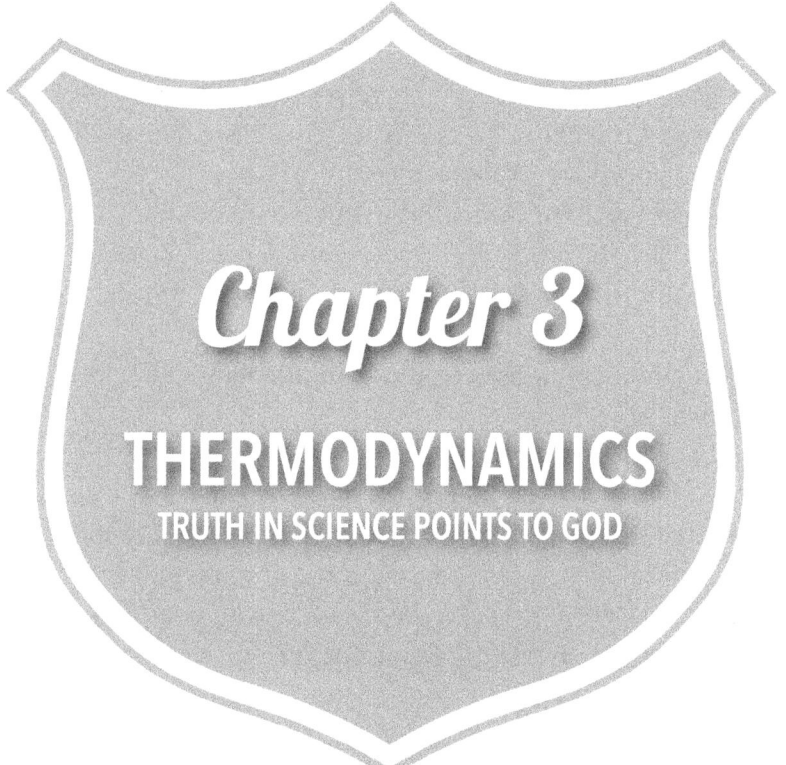

Chapter 3
THERMODYNAMICS
TRUTH IN SCIENCE POINTS TO GOD

"Manned space flight is an amazing achievement, but it has opened for mankind thus far only a tiny door for viewing the awesome reaches of space. An outlook through this peephole at the vast mysteries of the universe should only confirm our belief in the certainty of its Creator. I find it as difficult to understand a scientist who does not acknowledge the presence of a superior rationality behind the existence of the universe as it is to comprehend a theologian who would deny the advance of science" (WERNHER VON BRAUN, Ph.D., 1912-1977, Director of NASA) {1}.

CHAPTER 3

Dr. Von Braun could not have stated it in a more common sense way: The "tiny door for viewing" enriched everyone who was aware of it—that looking "through this peephole at the vast mysteries of the universe should only confirm our belief in the **certainty of its Creator**" (emphasis added).

In the previous chapter I stated that there are two primary philosophies in our culture that compete for our minds. There are other significant religious philosophies to be sure, such as Judaism and the recent emergence of Islam, but in our culture here in the United States at this point in history the two that have the most influence are the secular humanist philosophy of Darwinism, or natural selection, and Christianity. **Since they both compete for our minds, they are in competition for our souls!** If the universe and life began as the result of an unintended accident then there is no intelligent Creator. If there is no intelligent Creator there is no God.

Take note of the comments of three reputed evolutionists who reject the presence of an Intelligent Creator:

VICTOR L. STENGER: "Only fundamentalist Christians who insist on a literal interpretation of the Bible refuse to accept the biological evidence for evolution. ... But it is fair to say that *there is not a single shred of evidence that demands that we hypothesize that the universe was created*, and we can now at least provisionally understand how all we are and all we know could have come about by chance" {2}.

ERNST MAYR (an evolutionary biologist): "No educated person any longer questions the validity of the so-called theory of evolution, which we now know to be a simple fact" {3}.

RICHARD LEWONTIN (a Harvard geneticist): "The problem is to get [people] to reject irrational and supernatural explanations of the world, the demons that exist only in their imaginations, and to accept a social and intellectual apparatus, Science, as the only begetter of truth" {4}.

ARE THE EVOLUTIONISTS RIGHT? DO THE BASIC FUNDAMENTAL LAWS OF SCIENCE POINT TOWARD DARWINISM OR IS IT POSSIBLE THAT SCIENCE ACTUALLY POINTS TOWARD AN INTELLIGENT CREATOR?

What Do We Know About the Universe?

Is the Universe eternal? In other words, has it always been here? What do the Laws of science tell us about the Universe?

A British astronomer by the name of SIR FRED HOYLE came up with what is known as the "Steady State Theory." Hoyle described it this way:

"This idea requires atoms to appear in the Universe continually instead of being created explosively at some definite time in the past" (*Frontiers of Astronomy*, pp. 317-318, New York, Harpers, 1955).

Hoyle clarified his statement further when he asserted, "The old queries about the beginning and the end of the universe are dealt with in a surprising manner—by saying that they are meaningless, for the reason that the Universe did not have a beginning and it will not have an end" (ibid., p. 321) {5}.

Another prominent theory was proposed the same year known as "The Eternal Oscillation" cosmology that proposes: "a continually oscillating universe eternally fluctuating between periods of expansion, as at present, and collapse into the super-dense condition." The most prominent advocate of this theory is the physicist-astronomer GEORGE GAMOW. "Gamow insists, "Thus there is no more room in this theory for a genuine divine Creation than there is in the steady-state theory" {6}.

In later years, Sir Fred Hoyle changed his views. We will come back to Hoyle later. Let's take a look at what the laws of science actually tell us. The sources of information I will be using are from reputable authorities and not from me: scientists such as Henry M. Morris, Ph.D. and Bert Thompson, Ph.D. plus Norman L. Geisler, professor of apologetics and philosophy, and Lee Strobel, an investigative journalist. That means what you will be reading comes from Ph.D. scientists, a professor of apologetics, and an investigative journalist and not from a retired paint salesman. To begin with, we need to understand that science is not the enemy of the Christian. Notice what JOHN POLKINGHORNE, a physicist and theologian had to say about science, as quoted in LEE STROBEL'S book, *The Case for a Creator*, p. 69:

CHAPTER 3

"Science and religion...are friends, not foes, in the common quest for knowledge. Some people may find this surprising, for there's a feeling throughout our society that religious belief is outmoded, or downright impossible, in a scientific age. I don't agree. In fact, I'd go as far as to say that if people in this so-called 'scientific age' knew a bit more about science than many of them actually do, they'd find it easier to share my view" {7}.

Is John Polkinghorne right? He claims that: "SCIENCE AND RELIGION...ARE FRIENDS NOT FOES, IN THE COMMON QUEST FOR KNOWLEDGE."

REMEMBER, we are searching for the truth! Is it possible that the field of science actually supports what is written in the Bible? The answer is a definite yes! To demonstrate this fact we will begin with the Laws of Thermodynamics.

Thermodynamics

What are we talking about when we refer to the Laws of Thermodynamics? First, let's define the word. *WEBSTER'S NEW WORLD DICTIONARY of the American Language* provides the simplest explanation: "**thermo-**, [< Gr. therme, heat], a combining form meaning: heat, as in thermodynamics: "**dynamic**, ...[<Fr. < Gr. dynamikos <dynamis, power] 1. relating to energy or physical force in motion: opposed to static. **thermodynamics**- the science that deals with the relationship of heat and mechanical energy and the conversion of one into the other" {8}.

One of the most trustworthy laws of science that we have today was discovered because of the experiments made by these three men:

NICOLUS LEONARD SADI CARNOT (1796-1832)
RUDOLPH JULIUS EMANUEL CLAUSIUS (1822-1888)
WILLIAM THOMPSON KELVIN (1824-1907)

HENRY M. MORRIS, Ph.D. and founder of the Institute for Creation Research (ICR), has written several books on the subject of Creation and Science. His research has opened the doors for creating awareness among Christians and scientists alike on the vast amount of scientific evidence available which confirms

THERMODYNAMICS: TRUTH IN SCIENCE POINTS TO GOD

the testimony of those ancient writers who received the God-breathed inspiration to write the 66 books of the Holy Bible. Dr. Morris, in his book, *The Twilight of Evolution*, made these comments regarding the works of Carnot, Clausius, and Kelvin who developed the Second Law of Thermodynamics:

"The second law of thermodynamics was originally developed by Carnot, Clausius, and Kelvin, starting from work on the engineering problems of steam engines. In its early forms, it was developed at about the same time as Darwin's publication of *The Origin of Species*. However, its broader implications were only gradually becoming understood by the end of the 19th century. Even today, it is obvious that most people, especially most evolutionists, have very little understanding of the tremendous implications of the second law" {9}.

The Laws of Thermodynamics

Dr. Morris lists several of the laws of conservation: "Conservation of mass, conservation of linear momentum, conservation of electric charge, conservation of angular momentum, and conservation of energy are the most important. And without a doubt, the one truly universal conservation law is that of energy conservation. Energy, defined as 'capacity for doing work,' actually includes everything in the physical universe. Because of mass-energy equivalence, all forms of matter are, in a very real sense, merely forms of energy. Energy may also appear as mechanical, electrical, electro-magnetic, chemical, light, heat, sound, and other types of energy" {10}.

The First Law of Thermodynamics

Morris furnishes a statement of explanation by Dr. A.R. Ubbelohde, a Professor of Thermodynamics: "The First Law of Thermodynamics is merely another name for the Law of Conservation of Energy.... This Law states that energy can be transformed in various ways, but can neither be created nor destroyed" {11}.

It is interesting to note that certain evolutionists have suggested that this Universe we live in simply evolved from "literally nothing," to which Dr. Ubbelohde states: "The First Law of Thermodynamics states that energy...can neither be created nor destroyed."

CHAPTER 3

The Second Law of Thermodynamics

As stated by Dr. Morris, "the tremendous implications of the second law" have only recently been understood, especially due to the fact that the Second Law of Thermodynamics points directly to an Intelligent Creator and nullifies the Darwinian hypothesis of an eternal universe. Remember the statement that George Gamow made that the universe is: **"a continually oscillating universe eternally fluctuating between periods of expansion, as at present, and collapse into the super-dense condition."**

Dr. Morris, in his book *Scientific Creationism*, gives a well-defined explanation of why the Second Law of Thermodynamics ("Law of Energy Decay") makes null and void the evolutionist claims of an eternal universe, because the universe is not eternal:

"The Second Law (Law of Energy Decay) states that every system, left to its own devices, always tends to move from order to disorder, its energy tending to be transformed into lower levels of availability, finally reaching the state of complete randomness and unavailability for further work. When all energy of the cosmos has been degraded to random heat energy, with random motion of molecules and uniform low-level temperature, the universe will have died a 'heat death'" {12}.

The Third Law of Thermodynamics

The *Baker Encyclopedia of Christian Apologetics*, by Norman L. Geisler, describes the third Law: "There is an absolute temperature scale, with an absolute zero temperature. The Third Law of Thermodynamics states that absolute zero can be approached very closely, but it can never be reached" {13}.

How the Laws of Thermodynamics Control the Universe

The Second Law of Thermodynamics (or Entropy) points to the fact that everything in the Universe, including all matter and energy, is wearing out. This in turn answers

---

NOTE: There is also the "Zeroth Law," basically meaning that any object will eventually reach the temperature of its surroundings" (see end note) {36}.

THERMODYNAMICS: TRUTH IN SCIENCE POINTS TO GOD

the question, "Is the Universe is eternal?" Many scientists have now reached the same conclusion as that of a well-recognized astronomer by the name of ROBERT JASTROW.

BERT THOMPSON holds an M.S. and Ph.D., in microbiology. He has written several books on Christian evidences and apologetics. In his book, *The Scientific Case for Creation*, he quotes Dr. Jastrow's conclusion:

"And concurrently there was a great deal of discussion about the fact that the second law of thermodynamics, applied to the Cosmos, indicates the Universe is running down like a clock. If it is running down, there must have been a time when it was fully wound up" {14}.

"THE SECOND LAW OF THERMODYNAMICS, APPLIED TO THE COSMOS, INDICATES THE UNIVERSE IS RUNNING DOWN LIKE A CLOCK"

JESSE L. GREENSTEIN, in 1959, who at that time was Head of the Department of Astronomy at California Institute of Technology, agrees with Dr. Thompson and Dr. Jastrow concerning "Dying Stars":

"An irreverent physicist once rephrased the laws of thermodynamics to read: (1) you can't win, (2) you can't even break even, (3) things are going to get worse before they get better and (4) who says things are going to get better? When applied to stellar processes, the first law reminds us that stars do not create energy, but only convert energy from one form to an equivalent quantity of another form; that is, they convert to radiant energy the energy contained in their gravitational potential and in that fraction of their mass which is consumed in thermonuclear reactions. They can never produce more energy than they start out with… But the second law reminds us that this cannot go on forever. A star can never recapture the energy it wastes into the sink of space; its life history is irreversible" {15}.

In science, the Second Law of Thermodynamics is also referred to as "entropy." According to its universal usage, entropy means: "2 a: the degradation of the matter

CHAPTER 3

and energy in the universe to an ultimate state of inert uniformity" {16}. Therefore, whether a scientist refers to the running down of heat-energy in stars as "Entropy" or as the "Second Law of Thermodynamics" they are one and the same.

What has astounded most scientists over the years is the fact that this particular law has been mentioned in the Bible more than once! According to Dr. Jastrow, after he mentions that "the Universe is running down like a clock," he admitted: "When that occurred, and Who or what wound up the Universe were questions that bemused theologians, physicists, and astronomers, particularly in the 1920's and 1930's" {17}.

Frankly, it should cause any physicist or astronomer to wonder how this information could have been known to ancient peoples thousands of years before Clausius, Kelvin, and Carnot made their discoveries in thermodynamics!

The 102nd Psalm is the prayer "of an afflicted man" who pours out his lament before the LORD. In this prayer he acknowledges the power and majesty of the LORD:

"But you, O LORD, sit enthroned forever, your renown endures for all generations" (Psalm 102:12).

READ WHAT THE PSALMIST WRITES IN VERSES 25-26:

"In the beginning you laid the foundations of the earth, And the heavens are the work of your hands. They will perish, but you remain; They will all wear out like a garment. Like clothing you will change them, And they will be discarded" (Psalm 102:25-26).
THE FOUNDATIONS OF THE EARTH AND THE HEAVENS WHICH GOD CREATED "WILL PERISH." "THEY WILL ALL WEAR OUT LIKE A GARMENT." *That raises the question, "How did this person know that the earth and heavens were wearing out and would "perish"?*
This is an inspired-by-God version of the Second Law of Thermodynamics in action! It describes Entropy in motion. Josephus, the Jewish historian, claims with good authority that all the Old Testament Scriptures were written and completed from the time of "Artaxerxes" (a Persian King) about 400 years before the birth of Christ. The only logical conclusion is that this fact was known over 2,000 years before it was discovered in the 19th century.

THERMODYNAMICS: TRUTH IN SCIENCE POINTS TO GOD

The words of Psalm 102:25-26 were quoted in the New Testament book of Hebrews (1:10-11). This knowledge was given to writers who were without scientific backgrounds by direct inspiration from God. How could this not but point to the reality of God?

Fact #1: The Bible Revealed That Everything In the Universe Is Wearing Out

Another observation which is obvious from the first fact is that if everything in the Universe is wearing out then would it not seem logical that there must have been a beginning? This is exactly the conclusion scientists such as Dr. Jastrow had been driven to:

Dr. ROBERT JASTROW: "Most remarkable of all is the fact that in science, as in the Bible, the World begins with an act of creation. That view has not always been held by scientists. Only as a result of the most recent discoveries can we say with a fair degree of confidence that the world has not existed forever; that it began abruptly, without apparent cause, in a blinding event that defies scientific explanation" (written in 1977, recorded in Bert Thompson's book, *The Scientific Case for Creation*, pp, 20-21) {17}.

Then in 1978, Thompson records Jastrow's conclusion:

"Now both theory and observation pointed to an expanding Universe and a beginning in time. ...About thirty years ago science solved the mystery of the birth and death of stars, and acquired new evidence that the Universe had a beginning" (1978, pp. 47, 105).

Who is this Dr. Robert Jastrow that Thompson is quoting and why would his testimony have authority on the subject of thermodynamics, especially the Law of Entropy (the wearing out of our Universe)? Dr. BERT THOMPSON explains in his book, *The Scientific Case for Creation*, pp. 20-21:

"In his book, *God and the Astronomers*, Dr. Jastrow explained why attempts to prove an eternal Universe failed. 'Now three lines of evidence—the motions of the

CHAPTER 3

galaxies, the laws of thermodynamics, and the life story of the stars—pointed to one conclusion; all indicated that the Universe had a beginning' (1978, p. 111). JASTROW—WHO IS CONSIDERED BY MANY TO BE ONE OF THE GREATEST SCIENCE WRITERS OF OUR TIME—CERTAINLY IS NO CREATIONIST. But as a scientist/astronomer, he has written often the inescapable conclusion that the Universe had a BEGINNING" (emphasis added). Thompson continues with his personal conclusion: 'The evidence states that the Universe had a beginning. The Second Law of Thermodynamics, as Dr. Jastrow has indicated, has demonstrated this to be true" {18}.

This is the place where I believe it is necessary to explain the differences in terminology when one is referring to [1] a scientific Law; [2] a scientific Theory; and [3] a scientific Hypothesis. Here is the simplest way I know to explain the differences.

[1] SCIENTIFIC LAW (also referred to as natural law): A Law in science, or a natural Law, is a scientific fact that has been established by continuous observation and repeated demonstrations which have been tested and retested over and over again, such as the Law of Gravity, where everyday occurrences and experiences demonstrate its truth. A rock in my hand will automatically fall to the ground if I let it go. The same is true with the Second Law of Thermodynamics (Entropy): everything wears out!

[2] THEORY: A Theory has a much looser definition. According to Webster's Dictionary, a theory in science would involve: "3. A formulation of apparent relationships or underlying principles of certain observed phenomena which has been verified to some degree; 4. That branch of art or science consisting in a knowledge of its principles and methods rather than its practice" {19}. (Such as the Theory of Evolution.)

[3] HYPOTHESIS: The simplest explanation is the one given by Webster's Dictionary: "…an unproven theory, proposition, etc., tentatively accepted to explain certain facts or (working hypothesis) to provide a basis for further investigation, argument, study, etc. {20}.

These three are the most commonly used terms when one reads from the books and articles of scientists when referring to the data or proposals they make. Which of

THERMODYNAMICS: TRUTH IN SCIENCE POINTS TO GOD

the three carries the greatest authority? It is always the LAWS of science that have the greatest authority, such as, in this case, the Second Law of Thermodynamics.

Dr. HENRY MORRIS explains why:

"It is well to note at this point the implications of the First and Second Laws of Thermodynamics with respect to the origin of the universe. It should be stressed that these two Laws are proven scientific laws, if there is such a thing. They have been experimentally tested, measured and confirmed, thousands of times, on systems both extremely large and extremely small, and no scientist today doubts their full applicability in the space-time coordinates accessible to us. Therefore the cosmic implications of the two Laws are profound" {21}.

Do you see the difference between a scientific Law and a scientific Theory? THE SECOND LAW OF THERMODYNAMICS HAS BEEN TESTED AND CONFIRMED, whereas the Theory of Natural Selection (Evolution) records only some limited examples that evolutionists suggest are evidence of accidental natural selection, most of which have been proven to be false. These will be covered in another chapter.

There are still a few holdouts that balk at the idea of a Universe that is wearing out. The most widely used argument is that the Law of Entropy applies only to a closed system. The example they like to use is the earth and the sun in our solar system. They claim the sun produces enough energy to override the earth's energy loss. They are, to say the least, completely incorrect. As Dr. MORRIS continues to explain:

"….By far the most common response by evolutionists to the problem posed by the Second Law is to deny its applicability to open systems such as the earth. Since there is enough energy reaching the earth from the sun to more than offset the loss of energy in its processes due to entropy, they say, the problem is irrelevant. However this response is itself irrelevant. …In all systems, the Second Law describes a tendency to go from order to disorder. …Now if one examines closely all such systems to see what it is that enables them to supersede the Second Law locally and temporarily (in each case, of course, the phenomenon is only ephemeral, since the organism eventually dies and the building eventually collapses)" {22}.

CHAPTER 3

To simplify why the evolutionists' argument that the sun continues to supply energy to the earth, therefore, the process could continue forever, let's use the example given—the sun. Have evolutionists already forgotten that this SUN that supplies energy to the earth is a STAR? Science tells us, without exception, that all stars wear out. They use up their energy. The Sun that we draw our energy from is no exception! It is wearing out! Remember that JESSE L. GREENSTEIN, an astronomer, had reached this conclusion about stars that are dying, referring to the Second Law of Thermodynamics:

"But the Second Law reminds us that this cannot go on forever. A star can never recapture the energy it wastes into the sink of space; its life history is irreversible" {23}.

Are we beginning to see the direct implication of Entropy on the question, "Is the Universe eternal?" According to leading scientists, the Second Law of Thermodynamics points to the facts that:
(1) The Universe and everything in it is wearing out. It is not eternal.
(2) The Universe and everything in it must have had a beginning.

There is no way to escape these facts logically or scientifically. Most of the respected scientists have come to this conclusion. Here is a list of well-qualified scientists who have commented on the Law of Entropy:
ROBERT JASTROW: "Now three lines of evidence—the motions of the galaxies, the laws of thermodynamics, and the life story of the stars—pointed to one conclusion; all indicated that the Universe had a beginning" {24}.

ARTHUR EDDINGTON (renowned British astronomer) as quoted by Dr. Jastrow, in his book, *God and the Astronomers*: "Arthur Eddington, the most distinguished British astronomer of his day wrote, 'If our views are right, somewhere between the beginning of time and the present day we must place the winding up of the universe' {25}.

JEREMY RIFKIN in his book, *Entropy: A New World View*: "Now, however, a new world view is about to emerge. ...The Entropy Law will preside as the ruling paradigm over the next period of history. ALBERT EINSTEIN said that it is the premier law of all of science. SIR ARTHUR EDDINGTON referred to it as the

THERMODYNAMICS: TRUTH IN SCIENCE POINTS TO GOD

supreme metaphysical law of the entire universe. The Entropy Law is the second law of thermodynamics. ...There will be those who will stubbornly refuse to accept the fact that the Entropy Law reigns supreme over all physical reality in the world. They will insist that the entropy process only applies in selective instances and that any attempt to apply it more broadly to society is to engage in the use of metaphor. Quite simply, they are wrong" (pp. 6, 8 emphasis added) {26}.

JOHN ROSS on "The Second Law of Thermodynamics," Letter-to-the-Editor, *Chemical and Engineering News, vol. 58*: "There are no known violations of the second law of thermodynamics. Ordinarily the second law is stated for isolated systems, but the second law applies equally well to open systems" {27}.

BERT THOMPSON, Ph.D., and BRAD HARRUB, Ph.D., in their book, *Investigating Christian Evidences*, referring to a June 25, 2001, Time magazine article: "The cover of the June 25, 2001 issue of Time magazine announced: 'How the Universe Will End: Peering Deep Into Space and Time,' scientists have just solved the biggest mystery in the cosmos" {28}.

Five pages later, on page 12, Thompson and Harrub sum up the evidence after they list the conclusions of scientists, such as Robert Jastrow, Sir James Jeans, Henry Morris, and Michael D. Lemonick's article in the 2001 Time magazine article on: "Matter hardly can be eternal because everyone knows (and as every knowledgeable scientist readily admits), eternal things do not run down. Furthermore there is going to be an end at some point in the future. And eternal entities have neither beginnings nor endings" {29}.

HENRY M. MORRIS: "The Second Law requires the universe to have had a beginning; the First Law precludes its having begun itself. The only possible reconciliation of this problem is that the universe was created by a Cause transcendent to itself" {30}.

One physicist in May of 1980 was brought to acknowledge the reality of the impact that understanding Thermodynamics has brought into the world of science. Here is what he was forced to admit:

CHAPTER 3

H.S. LIPSON: "Therefore if we wish to regard the birth of an animal as regulated by the principles of thermodynamics, we must believe that the developing arrangement of atoms is that of the lowest internal energy. My mind boggles! If living matter is not, then, caused by the interplay of atoms, natural forces and radiation, how has it come into being? ...I think, however, that we must...admit that the only acceptable explanation is creation. I know that this is anathema to physicists, as indeed it is to me, but we must not reject a theory that we do not like if the experimental evidence supports it" {31}.

The overwhelming evidence that has been demonstrated time and time again has caused astronomers, physicists, and engineers to come to this reality as stated by H.S. Lipson: "The only acceptable explanation is CREATION" (emphasis added). Are we beginning to see how truth in science points to the reality of God? The book of Genesis chapter one, verse one states:

"In the beginning God created the heavens and the earth."

"IN THE BEGINNING" GOD created the Universe and everything in it, including all species of life. Where did the writer of Genesis get this information?

Where did the psalmist get the scientific data that "In the beginning" God created the heavens and the earth? (Psalm 102:25).
Where did the psalmist get the scientific data that "They will perish," and "they will all wear out like a garment"? (Psalm 102:26).

Were these statements just a couple of "shoot from the hip" conjectures by the writers of Genesis and this Psalm? If so, then one has to explain a lot of other "guesswork" such as the following:
"He sits enthroned above the circle of the earth..." (Isaiah 40a:22).

According to Thompson and Harrub: "The Hebrew word Isaiah used for 'circle' is the word khug, which means literally something with 'roundness,' a 'SPHERE.' ... How did Isaiah know the Earth to be a sphere? Just a lucky guess?" (emphasis added) {32}.

And how about this?

THERMODYNAMICS: TRUTH IN SCIENCE POINTS TO GOD

"All streams flow into the sea, yet the sea is never full. To the place the streams come from, there they return again" (Ecclesiastes 1:7).

"If clouds are full of water, they pour rain upon the earth." (Ecclesiastes 11:3a). Today we realize what the writer of Ecclesiastes is describing is the "HYDROLOGIC CYCLE" Thompson and Harrub comment on when scientists first became aware of it, giving the example of the Mississippi River. "The Mississippi River, when moving at normal speed, dumps 6,052,500 gallons of water per second into the Gulf of Mexico. …Where, pray tell, does all that water go? The answer, of course, lies in the hydrologic cycle so well illustrated in the Bible. …The idea of a complete water cycle was not fully understood or accepted until the sixteenth and seventeenth centuries…from experiments of Pierre Perrault and Edme Mariotte. …Astronomer Edmund Halley also contributed valuable data to the concept of a complete water cycle. More than 2,000 years prior to their work, however, the Scriptures had indicated a water cycle. How?" {33}.

In JOB 38:16, Job was questioned by God about the "springs of the sea" and "the recesses of the deep," places Job had never been. Job is one of the oldest books in the Bible. You can read about the fresh water springs in the ocean and the "recesses"—"deep trenches"—in the oceans and several other recently discovered facts that were mentioned in the Scriptures long before science discovered them in Thompson's and Harrub's *Investigating Christian Evidences*, pages 145 to 160. However, there is one more fact of science I would like to mention, which Bert Thompson, who has an earned Ph.D. in Microbiology, and Brad Harrub, who also has an earned Ph.D. in Neurobiology and Anatomy, concerning the blood we humans have in our bodies:

"FOR THE LIFE OF A CREATURE IS IN THE BLOOD" (Leviticus 17:11a).

There is a book among those of the Old Testament named "Leviticus." It was written by Moses, the leader of the Israelites selected by God to lead the nation of Israel from the bondage of slavery to freedom in a land that what was promised beforehand.

LEVITICUS is the section of the Old Testament where the laws of worship in the tabernacle, moral laws, and holy days were given. In the seventeenth chapter special attention is given to the serious priority of "blood" and the significant role it plays.

CHAPTER 3

It cannot be overlooked. Therefore, time will be spent in this chapter looking at the physical importance attached to blood. Later special attention will be given to the spiritual impact of blood in the New Testament:

"For the life of a creature is in the blood, and I have given it to you to make atonement for yourselves on the altar; it is the blood that makes atonement for one's life" (Leviticus 17:11).

To clarify the physical priority that "blood" has to the life of every human being, read these comments presented by two doctors of medicine, Dr. Brad Harrub and Dr. Bert Thompson:

"Moses told the Israelites (Leviticus 17:11-14) that 'The life of the flesh is in the blood.' [Note: This expression can be found in the 1611 King James; the New King James; the 1901 American Standard; and the New American Standard Version] He was correct. Because the red blood cells can carry oxygen (due to hemoglobin in the cells) life is made possible. In fact, the human red blood cells carry, for example, approximately 270,000,000 molecules of hemoglobin per cell (see Perutz, 1964, pp.64-65). If there were any less, there would not be enough residual oxygen to sustain life after, say, a hard sneeze or a hefty pat on the back. We know today that the 'life of the flesh is in the blood.' But we didn't know that in George Washington's day. How did the 'father of our country' die? We bled him to death (see Havron, 1981, p.62). People felt that the blood was where evil 'vapors' were found, and that getting rid of the blood would make a person well again. Today, of course, we know that is not true. Think of how often blood transfusions have made life possible for those who otherwise would have died. Today we know the truth of the matter. How did the Biblical writer know it?" {34}.

Moses wrote about the life in the blood some 1,500 years before the birth of Christ. Yet science still didn't know this until some years after President George Washington's time (1732-1799). I have to agree with Thompson and Harrub. How did Moses know unless God inspired him?

"The Entropy Law reigns supreme over all physical reality in the World" (Jeremy Rifkin).

The Truth is that the Second Law of Thermodynamics (Entropy) demonstrates that the Universe had a beginning. Not only that, it is wearing out—running down! Isn't

THERMODYNAMICS: TRUTH IN SCIENCE POINTS TO GOD

this what the Bible has told us way before scientists were able to discover these facts in the 19th century?

"In the beginning God created the heavens and the earth." (Genesis 1:1).
The creation text in Genesis was written over 3,000 years ago.

The Second Law of Thermodynamics demonstrates that the Universe did have a beginning. It certainly points to the truth written in Genesis, which states that the Universe had a beginning.

The Second Law also points out something else. It demonstrates that the Universe and everything in it is wearing out:

"In the beginning you laid the foundations of the earth, And the heavens are the work of your hands. They will perish, but you remain; they will all wear out like a garment. Like clothing you will change them and they will be discarded" (Psalm 102:25-26).

The question remains—where did these biblical writers get their information? The writers did not get it from clausius or kelvin. It had to be from someone intelligent enough to have understood how a complex law of science works, and be capable of putting it into motion! That someone was present beforethe existence of the earth and any human being that has ever lived!

Evolutionists have tried to avoid the fact that the Universe had a beginning and will have an ending. The Second Law of Thermodynamics has brought out feelings of insecurity among some atheistic evolutionists. Even Dan Barker, probably one of the most talented and formidable debaters among them, could only offer two basic arguments:

DAN BARKER: "I guess by telling this tactic, I'll never use it again. Here's what you do: If the theist brings up the second law of thermodynamics, ask if he or she knows how many laws of thermodynamics there are. If the answer is "no," this is a

---

NOTE: The New Testament writer of the letter to the Hebrews, quoted from this text (Hebrews 1:10-12). The author of Hebrews wrote the letter over 1,900 years ago. He was quoting from Psalm 102:25-26 written hundreds of years before that.

CHAPTER 3

good indicator that the person you are debating is superficially informed about the topic, probably recycling an argument from a creationist book, and has no real understanding of the science. ...But the argument still needs to be rebutted on its merits. ...It is easy to point out that the earth, bombarded by energy from the sun, is not a closed system, and...our observed universe is probably indeed a 'CLOSED SYSTEM' (if that means anything)" (emphasis added) {35}.

As for the number of Laws of Thermodynamics, there are four listed in Norman L. Geisler's *Baker Encyclopedia of Christian Apologetics*: pp.723-725: [1] The "Zeroth Law," [2] the "First Law," [3] the "Second Law," [4] the "Third Law." Another fact, which JOHN D. MORRIS, Ph.D., brings up, is that the theory of evolution points to an opposite direction contrary to the Second Law:

"Creationists have long cited the Second Law of Thermodynamics as an anti-evolution argument. The Second Law, or the Law of increasing Entropy, operates throughout the universe, as far as we can tell, and has never been seen to be violated in time or space. ...But what does it mean? Entropy is a measure of the state of randomness or disorder in a system. While the total amount of energy remains the same [according to the First Law of Thermodynamics] the usefulness of that energy spontaneously degrades as the process proceeds—i.e., its entropy increases. ... Things are becoming less ordered and less energetic all the time. On the surface, this is the opposite of evolution, which states that things have become more complex through time as molecules evolved into people" {36}.

Evolutionists, however, such as Dan Barker and others, contend that the Earth is an "open system" drawing energy from the sun, which provides energy for seeds to grow, plants to mature, life to continue to grow more complex, and onward and upward.

NOTE: Dan Barker, like others who use this argument, ignores the fact that the "Sun" is a "Star"! And like other stars, the sun is slowly using up its energy and will eventually burn out. At that point, the earth, which is dependent upon the sun for its continued supply of heat energy, will also suffer an eventual heat death, as will all life (unless Christ should return before that happens).

THERMODYNAMICS: TRUTH IN SCIENCE POINTS TO GOD

Notice the explanation offered by Denis Alexander, a theistic evolutionist:

DENIS ALEXANDER (ON THE LAW OF ENTROPY): "The concern behind the question is therefore that evolution appears to be a story about going 'uphill' in terms of the increased complexity and organization of systems, which is contrary to the second law. But of course one has to consider the system taken as a whole, which includes the energy derived from both the sun and the earth, without which life would be impossible. Photosynthesis provides a classic example, in which energy from the sun is translated into cellular energy using the chemical chlorophyll inside plant cells. In a further example, the molten interior of our planet is constantly releasing heat through the earth's crust, but also from vents at the bottom of oceans where complete ecosystems thrive on the energy so provided. So the important point to grasp here is that indeed the entropy of the system taken as a whole is increasing, including the sun in this equation, but as one system (the sun) 'runs down' so another system (life) 'runs up.' There is therefore no violation of the second law of thermodynamics" {37}.

There Are Serious Flaws With Alexander's Explanation.

(1) He states that: "Photosynthesis provides" an "example, in which energy derived from the sun is translated into cellular energy using the chemical chlorophyll inside plant cells." But, he doesn't explain where the "photosynthesis" process or the "chlorophyll" came from. Did they just pop into existence from nothing or were they brought into existence from the energy from the sun? DR. JOHN MORRIS explains why just energy from the sun alone would be harmful to plant life:

"First, there must be an energy conversion mechanism already present to convert the raw energy into useful forms. In the plant, the marvelous mechanism of photosynthesis must pre-exist the plant or the abundant energy cannot be utilized. In fact, unbridled solar energy will kill a plant; it must be converted into useful forms before the plant can use it. It fuels the plant's activities and growth. Photosynthesis is as yet incompletely understood by today's scientists, and it certainly did not create itself. But the plant already possesses this ability and passes it on to each generation. Second, there must be a plan in place to direct this now-useful energy into useful work. In living things, the marvelously complicated DNA

CHAPTER 3

code contains that plan. Nothing random here. This code is copied and maintained using just the right form of energy. But the machines that manufacture those energy molecules are specified by the code. Which came first, the fuel to copy the code or the code for the fuel's manufacture? ...Evolutionary innovation is thought to occur through unguided mutation and natural selection. How many random tries would it take to either devise a complicated process (like photosynthesis) or write a complex code (like DNA)? Both must be present for life to function and continue. ...An open system and raw energy are insufficient. Thus, evolution violates a basic law of science...the requirements for overcoming its implications are not met by nature" {38}.

Dr. Morris is right when he questions how random mutations or acquired characteristics could produce a remarkably complex code like DNA. Later, in another chapter, it will be explained why life could not have happened by accidental mutations or acquired characteristics, no matter how much time is allotted for them.

NORMAN GEISLER, in his book, *Baker Encyclopedia of Christian Apologetics*, agrees with Dr. Morris that the Second Law of Thermodynamics applies not only to the Universe, but to all living things as well:

"Calories of sun energy do not help a creature grow new eyes with which to see the sun's light. It does not even charge a creature's batteries so that it can live indefinitely. Entropy happens in both the individual organism's life cycle and in species' life" {39}.

DR. JOHN D. MORRIS, Ph. D., sums it up with what is needed:
"A universal tendency toward randomness dominates, and the requirements for overcoming its implications are not met by nature. They are met by intelligence of a surpassing level far exceeding ours" {40}.

As we bring this chapter to a close, I want to remind you, the reader, these are not the words of the author (a retired paint salesman) who presented these facts. These are the words of educated and respected scientists who are telling us the Universe and all matter had a beginning and will have an end, and that this is what was written in the Bible in the book of Genesis, chapter one, verse one: "In the beginning..." and in the 102nd Psalm, verses, twenty-five and twenty-six: "they will all wear out like a garment."

THERMODYNAMICS: TRUTH IN SCIENCE POINTS TO GOD

After all, what we are looking for is truth, isn't it?

"They are met by intelligence of a surpassing level far exceeding ours" (John D. Morris, Ph.D.).

CHAPTER 4

The previous chapter exposed two important facts.
FIRST: The Universe is wearing out.
SECOND: Therefore the Universe had a beginning.

Which raises the question, if the Universe had a beginning, what then, would have caused it? This question is answered by another scientific law:

The Law of Cause and Effect
(Also known as the Law of Causality)

NORMAN L. GEISLER explains what this law means:

"The principle of causality may be stated in various ways, some more easily accepted than others. For example, it may be stated:
1. Every effect has a cause. This form is clearly self-evident, and it is analytic, in that the predicate is reducible to its subject. Other ways to state the principle are not analytic, nor so self evident:
2. Every contingent being is caused by another.
3. Every limited being is caused by another.
4. Everything that comes to be is caused by another.
5. Nonbeing cannot cause being."

Geisler explains further: "For example, 'Every thing that begins has a cause' is the same as 'Everything that comes to be is caused by another.' Also, 'Every dependent being is caused by another' is the same as 'Every contingent being is caused by another'" {1}.

"Every thing that comes to be is caused by another. The Universe came to be [had a beginning]. Therefore the Universe was caused by another" {2}.

The Law of Cause and Effect has strong philosophical implications.

This form of reasoning is not new according to WILLIAM LANE CRAIG, Ph.D., Research Professor of Philosophy at Talbot School of Theology, author of several articles in theological and philosophical journals plus over a dozen books such as

CAUSE & EFFECT: TRUTH IN SCIENCE POINTS TO GOD

Atheism and Theism. In an interview with LEE STROBEL, an investigative journalist; in Strobel's book, *The Case for a Creator*, Craig gives the historical background for Cause and Effect:

"Aristotle...In his view, both God and the universe are eternal. Of course, that contradicted the Hebrew notion that God created the world out of nothing. ...One prominent Christian philosopher on the topic was John Philoponus of Alexandria, Egypt, who lived in the fourth century. He argued that the universe had a beginning. When Islam took over North Africa, Muslim theologians picked up on these arguments, because they also believed in creation. So while this tradition was lost to the Christian West, it began to be highly developed within Islamic medieval theology. One of the most famous Muslim proponents was al-Ghazali, who lived from 1058 to 1111. ...As formulated by al-Ghazali, the argument had three simple steps: Whatever begins to exist has a cause. The universe began to exist. Therefore the universe has a cause" {3}.

As it is applied in the field of science, the Law of Cause and Effect states that every material effect must have a preceding, sufficient cause. For example, a fly landing on the back of a large male African elephant would not cause the elephant to collapse. In contrast, the Mesa Verde Cliff Dwellings are an effect that had a sufficient cause—intelligent human design. We will come back to the Cliff Dwellings later, but before that, it needs to be established why the Law of Causality is a critical dividing point between those who believe in creation by God and those who deny the need for, or the existence of, a supernatural, intelligent Creator.

The "Something From Nothing" Hypothesis

In 1997, HENRY M. MORRIS, compiled a list of quotations from hundreds of scientists, called, *That Their Words May Be Used Against Them*. In this book I discovered how far atheistic evolutionists are prepared to go in their insistence that the universe was not the result of a special creation by an intelligent, creative God. Read what these scientists are now presenting in the way of an explanation for the existence of the universe:

CHAPTER 4

"From a historical point of view probably the most revolutionary aspect of the inflationary model is the notion that all the matter and energy in the observable universe may have emerged from almost nothing" (ALAN H. GUTH and PAUL J. STEINHARDT: from "The Inflationary Universe," *Scientific American*, vol. 250 (May 1984), p.116-128).

"EMERGED FROM ALMOST NOTHING"? They are not through yet. There is more.

"The inflationary model of the universe provides a possible mechanism by which the observed universe could have evolved from an infinitesimal region. It is then tempting to go one step further and speculate that the entire universe evolved from literally nothing" (ALAN H. GUTH and PAUL J. STEINHARDT: from "The Inflationary Universe," *Scientific American*, vol. 250 (May 1984), p.116-128).

Is this "inflationary model" an empirical, demonstrable fact that Guth and Steinhardt are presenting? NO, it is not! Notice the words: "…MAY HAVE EMERGED FROM ALMOST NOTHING"—"A POSSIBLE MECHANISM"—"AND SPECULATE…"

And speculate what? "…THAT THE ENTIRE UNIVERSE EVOLVED FROM LITERALLY NOTHING!"

Later, in 1997, Guth, still a believer in the speculation that everything in the Universe evolved from "nothing," wrote this:

"So in the inflationary theory the universe evolves from essentially nothing at all, which is why I frequently refer to it as the ultimate free lunch" (GUTH, ALAN H., "Cooking Up a Cosmos," Astronomy, vol. 25 (September 1997), pp. 54-57) {4}.

So where did the Universe come from, Mr. Guth? His answer—"The universe evolves from essentially nothing at all." As Alan Guth stated, it's what he calls "THE ULTIMATE FREE LUNCH" (emphasis added).

EDWARD P. TYRON, Professor of physics, Hunter College and CUNY, said:
"In 1973, I proposed that our Universe had been created spontaneously from nothing

(ex nihilo), as a result of established principles of physics. This proposal variously struck people as preposterous, enchanting, or both" (TYRON, EDWARD P., "What Made the World?" *New Scientist*, vol. 101, (March 8, 1984) p.14).

"So my proposal of creation ex nihilo was accompanied by a prediction that our Universe is finite and hence 'closed'" (TYRON, EDWARD P., "What Made the World?" *New Scientist*, vol. 101, (March 8, 1984) p.15).

"So I conjectured that our Universe had its physical origin as a quantum fluctuation of some pre-existing true vacuum, or state of nothingness" (TYRON, EDWARD P., "What Made the World?" *New Scientist*, vol. 101, (March 8, 1984) p.15) {5}.

Uh, let's see if we can understand what Professor Tyron is telling us. The "Universe had been created SPONTANEOUSLY from NOTHING!" And, he "CONJECTURED" that the "Universe had its physical origin as [a] STATE OF NOTHINGNESS." Do you suppose this is why some people thought Professor Tyron's conjecture (in other words, a guess), was "PREPOSTEROUS"? (emphasis added).

Not to be outdone by the other evolutionists, here is Victor L. Stenger:

"Only fundamentalist Christians who insist on a literal interpretation of the Bible refuse to accept the biological evidence for evolution. But what will these churchmen and their flock say about the latest conclusion of physical cosmology, that the universe is probably the result of a random quantum fluctuation in a spaceless, timeless void? In other words, physicists are now claiming that the hundreds of billions of stars and galaxies, including the earth and humanity, are not conscious creations but an accident. There is no Creator, because there was no creation" (STENGER, VICTOR L., "Was the Universe Created?" *Free Inquiry* (Summer 1987), p. 28).

"So what had to happen to start the universe was the formation of an empty bubble of highly curved space-time. How did this bubble form? What caused it? Not everything requires a cause" (STENGER, VICTOR L., "Was the Universe Created?" *Free Inquiry* (Summer 1987), p. 29).

CHAPTER 4

"Much is still in the speculative stage, and I must admit that there are yet no known empirical or observational tests that can be used to test the idea of an accidental origin" (STENGER, VICTOR L., "Was the Universe Created?" *Free Inquiry* (Summer 1987), p. 30) {6}.

Alright, let's see if we can understand what Mr. Stenger is trying to tell us. First, he makes it emphatically clear that "THERE IS NO CREATOR, BECAUSE THERE WAS NO CREATION." Well, that seems clear enough. Stenger does not believe in a "Creator." Why does Mr. Stenger deny the existence of a Creator? "Because there was no creation." What, then, caused the Universe to come into being? Stenger's answer: "NOT EVERYTHING REQUIRES A CAUSE."

What scientific proof does Stenger have to persuade someone that the Universe had no cause? Here is his answer: "MUCH IS STILL IN THE SPECULATIVE STAGE, AND I MUST ADMIT THERE ARE YET NO KNOWN EMPERICAL OR OBSERVATIONAL TESTS THAT CAN BE USED TO TEST…AN ACCIDENTAL ORIGIN" (emphasis added). Another way of stating what Victor Stenger is saying is that there is no way he can prove this by any sort of scientific test or observation because it's all just a hypothesis, but this is what he believes regardless of the lack of proof.

Dr. BERT THOMPSON compares what Steinhardt, Guth, Tyron, and Stenger have speculated with what the Law of Cause and Effect actually requires:

"Indisputably, the most universal and most certain, of all scientific laws is the Law of Cause and Effect, or as it is commonly known, the Law of Causality. …Simply put, the Law of Causality states that **every material effect must have an adequate antecedent cause.** …There is no question of its acceptance in the world of experimental science or in the ordinary world of personal experience" {7}.

"This is an interesting turn of events. Evolutionists such as Stenger, Tyron, Guth and Steinhardt insist that this marvelously intricate Universe is "'simply one of those things which happen from time to time' as the result of a 'random quantum fluctuation in a spaceless, timeless void' that caused matter to evolve from 'literally

---

NOTE: "Antecedent" means "a preceding event, condition, or cause" {8}.

CAUSE & EFFECT: TRUTH IN SCIENCE POINTS TO GOD

nothing.' This suggestion, of course, is in clear violation of the First Law of Thermodynamics...which states that neither matter nor energy may be created or destroyed in nature. Furthermore, science is based on the time-honored principles of observation, reproducibility, and empirical data" {9}.

BERT THOMPSON, in his book, *The Scientific Case for Creation*, points to a quote from Dr. ROBERT JASTROW'S book, *Until the Sun Dies*, p.21, (1977) on what is the common sense approach to the subject of a Universe evolving "without any adequate cause":

"Jastrow had discussed this very problem—a Universe without any adequate explanation for its own existence and, worse still, without any adequate cause for whatever theory scientists might set forth in an attempt to elucidate how it did originate. As Jastrow noted: 'This great saga of cosmic evolution, to whose truth the majority of scientists subscribe, is the product of an act of creation that took place twenty billion years ago [according to evolutionary estimates–BT]. Science, unlike the Bible, has no explanation for the occurrence of that extraordinary event. The Universe, and everything that has happened in it since the beginning of time, are a grand effect without a known cause. An effect without a cause? That is not the world of science; it is a world of witchcraft, of wild events and the whims of demons, a medieval world that science has tried to banish. As scientists, what are we to make of this picture? I do not know'" {10}.

"An effect without a cause? That is not the world of science; it is a world of witchcraft, of wild events and the whims of demons, a medieval world that science has tried to banish" (Robert Jastrow)

Dr. WILLIAM LANE CRAIG, Research Professor of Philosophy at Talbot School of Theology, author of numerous articles and books, was interviewed by Lee Strobel in his book, *The Case for a Creator*, on the subject of Causality (the Kalam argument), and the unreasonable assertions of evolutionists, such as Stenger's assumption: "Not everything requires a cause." Although Stenger is not mentioned in this text, it has become a common argument among atheists and skeptics. Here is

CHAPTER 4

Dr. Craig's reply:

"To me, this is absolutely bewildering! …Things don't just pop into existence, uncaused, out of nothing."

Dr. Craig continues to explain why.

"In the first place," he replied, "this first premise (whatever begins to exist has a cause) is intuitively obvious once you clearly grasp the concept of absolute nothingness. …But in atheism, the universe just pops into being out of nothing, with absolutely no explanation at all. I think once people understand the concept of absolute nothingness, it's simply obvious to them that if something has a beginning, that it could not have popped into being out of nothing but must have a cause that brings it into existence."

At this point in the interview, LEE STROBEL pressed Dr. Craig for "something more substantial." He asked, "Can you offer anything harder than just intuition? What scientific evidence is there?"

CRAIG'S REPLY:

"Well, we certainly have empirical evidence for the truth of this premise. This is a principle that is constantly confirmed and never falsified. We never see things coming into being uncaused out of nothing. Nobody worries that while he is away at work, say, a horse might pop into being, uncaused, out of nothing, in his living room, and be there defiling the carpet. We don't worry about those kinds of things, because they never happen" {11}.

"This is a principle that is constantly confirmed and never falsified. We never see things coming into being uncaused out of nothing" (William Lane Craig, Ph.D.).

Notice that Guth, Steinhardt, Tyron, and Stenger propose the Universe "may have emerged from almost nothing," that "the entire universe evolved from literally nothing," and that it sprung "spontaneously from nothing." After all, "not everything requires a cause," "it was just another accidental happening." Oh really? Common sense alone would cause one to question this type of reasoning. Proposals such as these by Guth, Steinhardt, Tyron, and Stenger come from no empirical, demonstrated observations, but from hypothetical speculations.

However, other scientists were beginning to realize that if the Universe did have a beginning, this raised the question: What caused it in the first place?

BERT THOMPSON, points out that even the reputed skeptic DAVID HUME admitted: "…in a letter to John Stewart: 'I never asserted so absurd a Proposition as that **anything might arise without a cause**" (see Greig, 1932, p.187, emphasis in original.; Craig, 1984, p.75) {12}.

Although Hume was not an advocate for the Law of Cause and Effect, he did not want to be classified as publicly asserting that things (like the Universe) might just come into being without any type of cause. To do that would openly imply that he would have left common sense behind for his own personal delusion. Earlier in this chapter I used the Mesa Verde Cliff Dwellings as an example of intelligent human design. Let's examine that in more detail.

The Mesa Verde Cliff Dwellings

If you were to be the first person to discover the famous Cliff Palace located near the four-corners area of the United States in the southwestern part of Colorado and after walking through it and examining all the intricate detailed structures built up out of natural rock placed in minute detail with both circular and rectangular structures and multi-storied towers, would you believe that all that as caused by natural erosion of the rocks and soil over millions of years or would you believe the site was the result of detailed intelligent planning and design by intelligent minds? I doubt seriously that any physicist, astronomer, biologist, or anthropologist would think otherwise.

You see, there is far too much evidence that the Mesa Verde Cliff Palace buildings could not have just happened by accidental natural causes or that they just happened to pop into existence without any cause at all. No one in their right minds would think that!

CHAPTER 4

Before any type of construction began in the concave part of this cliff, human minds were laying out the details of what they were going to do. It had to be structurally sound; it had to have purpose; it had to accommodate the needs of a large group of people. This required a lot of detailed intelligent planning! Why then would anyone reasonably think otherwise?

DR FRED HOYLE came to the same conclusion about the necessity of some kind of "purposeful intelligence" to produce life here on earth:

"The likelihood of the spontaneous formation of life from inanimate matter is one to a number with 40,000 noughts after it. ...It is big enough to bury Darwin and the whole theory of evolution. There is no primeval soup, neither on this planet nor on any other, and if the beginnings of life were not random they must therefore have been the product of purposeful intelligence" {13}.

Everything one finds in the complex structure of the Mesa Verde Cliff Palace consists of natural material, including the cliff, the rocks, and the logs used in the structures. The people who built and lived there were flesh and blood, living matter. There was just one particular additive in the human being that is not matter, and that is the human mind. This is where the difference lies. It is the difference between matter and mind.

Is there any difference between matter and mind or is matter all there is?

Bert Thompson, Ph.D., lists a quote from, as he describes him, "the eminent evolutionary astronomer, Robert Jastrow, who currently is serving as the director of the Mount Wilson Observatory," on the subject of matter:

ROBERT JASTROW: "The Universe is the totality of all matter, animate and inanimate, throughout space and time. If there was a beginning, what came before? If there is an end, what will come after?" {14}.
In 1983, VICTOR F. WEISSKOPF, Professor Emeritus & Former Head, Physics, MIT, made these rather significant comments in the American Scientist, vol. 71 (September/October), on "The Origin of the Universe":
"No existing view of the development of the cosmos is completely satisfactory, and this includes the standard model, which leads to certain fundamental questions and problems." (p. 474).

CAUSE & EFFECT: TRUTH IN SCIENCE POINTS TO GOD

"The theory of the inflationary universe is still beset with a number of difficulties" (p. 480).

"The hypothesis of the periodic universe is not without its own problems. It could well be that the entropy of the universe increases each time, in which case one again arrives at the problem of a real beginning: the first Primal Bang" (p. 480).

"Indeed, the Judeo-Christian tradition describes the beginning of the world in a way that is surprisingly similar to the scientific model. Previously it seemed scientifically unsound to have light created before the sun. The present scientific view does indeed assume the early universe to be filled with various kinds of radiation long before the sun was created. The Bible says about the beginning: 'And God said, Let there be light, and there was light. And God saw the light, that it was good'" (p.480) {15}.

Professor Emeritus Weisskopf was quoting from Genesis, chapter one:

"And God said, Let there be light: and there was light. And God saw the light, that it was good:" (Genesis 1:3-4a King James Version, 1611).

Since there are scientists who have included God into the possibilities for the beginning of the Universe, this should be a good place to include God as a probable cause for the effect we call the Universe. This is in keeping with our subject, The Law of Cause and Effect.

The major point of evidence in determining what would be a preceding, sufficient cause for the existence of the Universe might be, at first, the most difficult to grasp. But once the reader fully understands it you will have achieved the same realization that several respected scientists did when they discovered the truth.

To begin with, BERT THOMPSON, Ph.D., in his book, *The Scientific Case for Creation*, has logically laid out a method of approaching the subject:

"Since it is apparent that the Universe is not eternal, and since it likewise is apparent that the Universe could not have created itself, the only remaining alternative is that the Universe **was created** by something (or Someone): (a) that existed before it, i.e., some eternal uncaused First Cause; (b) superior to it — the created cannot be

CHAPTER 4

superior to the creator; and (c) of a different nature since the finite, dependent Universe of matter is unable to explain itself. As Hoyle and Wickramasinghe observed: 'To be consistent logically, we have to say that the intelligence which assembled the enzymes did not itself contain them'" (1981, p. 139).

"Everything that exists can be classified as either MATTER or MIND. There is no third alternative. The argument, then, is this:
1. Everything that exists is either matter or mind.
2. Something exists now, so something eternal exists.
3. Therefore either matter or mind is eternal.
    A. Either matter or mind is eternal.
    B. Matter is not eternal, as per evidence cited above.
    C. Thus, it is MIND that is eternal" (emphasis added) {16}.

When we think or talk about the mind in our normal human capacity most people, generally speaking, are thinking of or referring to our human brain. If one were to read dated scientific and medical literature, the capacity to think and feel and move—even our consciousness— is attributed to the human brain. Therefore, it shouldn't surprise us when Darwinists suggest that the mind is nothing more than a function of the brain, which, of course, is matter.

LEE STROBEL, in his book, *The Case for a Creator*, describes why Darwinists have difficulty perceiving anything beyond the human brain:

"According to Darwinists, the physical world is all that there is. At some point, the human brain evolved, with its raw processing power increasing over the eons. When the brain reached a certain level of structure and complexity, people became 'conscious'—that is, they suddenly developed subjectivity, feelings, hopes, a point of view, self awareness, introspection, that 'hidden voice of our private selves.' As far back as 1871, Darwin advocate THOMAS HUXLEY said: 'Mind [or consciousness] is a function of matter, when that matter has attained a certain degree of organization.' Darwinists today agree that 'conscious experience is a physical and not a supernatural phenomenon,' as sociobiologist EDWARD O. WILSON said" {17}.

Perhaps this would be a good place to look into the Biblical definition of the "mind" as it is used in the Scriptures and compare them with Huxley's definition.

CAUSE & EFFECT: TRUTH IN SCIENCE POINTS TO GOD

"...to be made new in the attitude of your MINDS; and to put on the new self, created to be like God in true righteousness and holiness" (Ephesians 4:23-24 emphasis added).

"'For who has known the MIND of the Lord that he may instruct him?' But we have the MIND of Christ" (1 Corinthians 2:16 emphasis added).

"Oh, the depth of the riches of the wisdom and knowledge of GOD! How unsearchable his judgments, and his paths beyond tracing out! Who has known the MIND of the Lord? Or who has been his counselor?" (Romans 11:33-34 emphasis added).

For secular materialists, such as with the evolutionist Thomas Huxley, the mind consists of the brain only, which is matter. Now compare this with the text in 1 Corinthians 2:16 and substitute "BRAIN" (matter) for "MIND":

"Who has known the BRAIN (matter) of the Lord? ...But we have the BRAIN (matter) of Christ."

Again, in Romans 11:34, substitute "BRAIN" (matter) for "MIND":

"Who has known the BRAIN (matter) of the Lord [GOD]?" (Romans 11:34a).

Common sense tells us something is missing in defining the MIND as matter. It just doesn't make sense!

The Christian is not using the same brain (matter) of Christ. It is obvious that the meaning of the "mind" used in the Bible in these three scriptures has to be different from the atheist/materialist description. Now let's take a look at W.E. VINE'S, *An Expository Dictionary of Biblical Words*, as the word "mind" is used in the same three Scriptures in the Bible:

"NOUS: mind denotes, speaking generally, the seat of reflective consciousness, comprising the faculties of perception and understanding, and those of feeling, judging and determining. Its use in the N.T. may be analyzed as follows: ...(b) counsels, purpose, Rom. 11:34 (of the mind of God)...1 Cor. 1:10; 2:16, twice (1)

NOTE: The Greek word for "mind" as a noun is "NOUS."
NOTE: The Greek word for "mind" as a verb is "PHRONEO."

of the thoughts and counsels of God, (2) of Christ, a testimony to His Godhood; Eph.4:23; (c) the new nature, which belongs to the believer by reason of the new birth..." {18}.

"I. PHRONEO...signifies (a) to think, to be minded in a certain way; (b) TO THINK OF, BE MINDFUL OF. It implies moral interest or reflection, not mere unreasoning opinion."

Vine provides a good example in COLOSSIANS 3:2: "Set your mind," lit., 'mind (the things above)'" {19}.

In the New International Version, it reads:

"Set your MINDS on things above, not on earthly things" (Colossians 3:2 emphasis added).

The "THINGS ABOVE" are listed in verses 12a-14:

"Clothe yourselves with compassion, kindness, humility, gentleness and patience" (v. 12a).

"Bear with each other and forgive whatever grievances you may have against one another. Forgive as the Lord forgave you" (v. 13).
"And over all these virtues put on love, which binds them all together in perfect unity" (v. 15).

The "EARTHLY THINGS" are as follows:

"Put to death, therefore, whatever belongs to your earthly nature: sexual immorality, impurity, lust, evil desires and greed, which is idolatry" (v. 5).

Atheistic evolutionists strongly maintain that the mind is a function of brain matter, and through the millions of years of hypothetical evolution, it has acquired complex abilities such as self-awareness, feelings, reasoning power, etc. This is where the difference is so critical between how Christians and creationists in general understand true reality. In truth, the mind is far more than a blob of cerebral matter. The mind is intangible. It is a critical part of what is known as that inward part of the human species that lives on after the body has passed into death.

CAUSE & EFFECT: TRUTH IN SCIENCE POINTS TO GOD

"Therefore we do not lose heart. Though outwardly we are wasting away, yet inwardly we are being renewed day by day. For our light and momentary troubles are achieving for us an eternal victory that far outweighs them all. So we fix our eyes not on what is seen, but on what is unseen. For what is seen is temporary, but what is unseen is eternal" (2 Corinthians 4:16-18).

In the sixteenth verse, the New American Standard reads: "But though our outer man is decaying, yet our inner man is being renewed day by day."

The "inner man" is that "unseen," that intangible part of man which is "eternal" while the "outer man" (the body) is "wasting away."

Isn't this, in truth, what the Second Law of Thermodynamics constantly points out? Our human body is wearing out, "wasting away," "decaying!" Scientifically and Biblically we know this to be true. It is a fact of life. But what about this claim of that inward man? Atheists such as Dan Barker refuse to accept the possibility of an intangible spirit.

DAN BARKER, a former ordained minister, who has converted to atheism, made this statement in his book, *Godless*: "The word 'spirit' has never been defined, except in terms that tell us what it is not: immaterial, intangible, no corporeal, supernatural. No one has ever described what a spirit is." Barker then is left with his only other conclusion, which is materialistic evolution: "'Nature,' on the other hand, means something. Darwinism shows us that all living organisms are the result of a natural evolutionary process. We have been fashioned by the laws of nature." {20}.

Later, in another chapter, which will be devoted to the highly touted evidence for evolution, I will point out the delusional nature of the belief in natural selection. But, for now, time will be spent on the scientific evidence for the reality of that inner person, the mind, which is separate and apart from the material brain.

WITH THE NEW SCIENTIFIC DATA BEING RELEASED, THINGS ARE BEGINNING TO CHANGE. SCIENTISTS, SUCH AS, WILDER PENFIELD, SIR CHARLES SHERRINGTON, AND JOHN ECCLES, IN THEIR RESEARCH AND REPEATED DEMONSTRATIONS HAVE REACHED THE CONCLUSION THAT THE INNER PERSON, "THE HUMAN SOUL," IS A REALITY.

CHAPTER 4

LEE STROBEL, in his book, *The Case for a Creator*, devoted several pages to the subject of "The Evidence of Consciousness: The Enigma of the Mind":

"Amazingly, many scientists and philosophers are now concluding that the laws of physics and chemistry cannot explain the experience of consciousness in human beings. They are convinced that there is more than just the physical brain at work, but there also is a nonmaterial reality called the 'soul,' 'mind,' or 'self' that accounts for our sentience.

Did you catch that? Scientists are now coming to the realization that those words written down in a collection of books called the Bible that had its beginning more than 3,000 years ago exposed us to the human complex nature in first chapter in Genesis:
"So God created man in his own image, in the image of God he created him; male and female he created them" (Genesis 1:27).

If we knew nothing else at this point, we would know that humankind has been created "in the IMAGE of GOD," No other creature mentioned in the Bible has ever been described as being created in the image of God.

Strobel continues to describe how scientists had to cope with their struggle to explain why they were beginning to do an about-face in their understanding of how the brain and the mind "are actually distinct from each other":

"One scientist whose opinions were reversed on the issue is WILDER PENFIELD, the renowned father of modern neurosurgery. He started out suspecting that consciousness somehow emanated from the neural activities in the brain, where synapses can fire an astounding ten million billion times a second. 'Through my own scientific career, I, like other scientists, have struggled to prove that the brain accounts for the mind,' he said. But through performing surgery on more than a thousand epileptic patients, he encountered concrete evidence that the brain and mind are actually distinct from each other, although they clearly interact. ...In other words, Penfield ended up agreeing with the Bible's assertion that human beings are both BODY and SPIRIT. 'To expect the highest brain mechanism or any set of

---

NOTE: "Sentience" means feeling or sensation. In fact, they cite its very existence as strong evidence against the purely naturalistic theory of Darwinian evolution in favor of a Creator who imbued humankind with his image.

reflexes, however complicated, to carry out what the mind does, and thus perform all the functions of the mind, is quite absurd'" {22}.

Strobel records how Penfield's evidence from surgery and electrical stimulation brought him to realize what the Bible has consistently recorded to the point where he made this statement: "What a thrill it is, then, to discover that the scientist, too, can legitimately believe in the EXISTENCE of the SPIRIT" (emphasis added) {23}.

Penfield was not alone in his findings. Other scientists have reached almost parallel conclusions. Penfield applied electrical stimulation of "'the proper motor cortex of conscious patients and challenge [them] to keep one hand from moving when the current was applied. The patient would seize this hand with the other hand and struggle to hold it still.' Thus one hand under the control of the electrical current and the other hand under the control of the patient's MIND fought against each other. Penfield risked the explanation that the patient had not only a physical brain that was stimulated to action but also a NONPHYSICAL REALITY that interacted with the brain'" (emphasis added) {24}.

"SIR CHARLES SHERRINGTON, a Nobel Prize winner described as a 'genius who laid the foundations of our knowledge of the functioning of the brain and spinal cord,'' declared five days before his death: "For me now, the only reality is the human SOUL" (emphasis added) {25}.

"What a thrill it is, then, to discover that the scientist, too, can legitimately believe in the existence of the spirit"(Wilder Penfield).

In 2003, Bert Thompson, Ph.D., and Brad Harrub, Ph.D., teamed up to write a book, "*Investigating Christian Evidences*," (377 pages). BRAD HARRUB earned his Ph.D. in neurobiology and anatomy from the University of Tennessee. Dr. Harrub studied the works of Dr. John Eccles, an Australian physiologist "…who won the Nobel Prize in Physiology or medicine in 1963 for his discoveries relating to the neural synapses within the brain… [Dr. Eccles] documented that the MIND is more than merely physical." Here is what Thompson and Harrub had to say about Dr. Eccles:

CHAPTER 4

"Anyone familiar with neurophysiology or neurobiology know the name of SIR JOHN ECCLES. ...But for those who might not be familiar with this amazing gentleman, we would like to introduce Dr. Eccles via the following quotation, which comes from a chapter ('The Collapse of Modern Atheism') that philosopher NORMAN GEISLER authored for the book, The Intellectuals Speak Out About God...Geisler wrote: 'The extreme form of materialism believes that MIND (or soul) is matter. ...**However, from a scientific perspective much has happened in our generation to lay bare the clay feet of materialism. Most noteworthy among this is the Nobel Prize winning work of Sir John Eccles. His work on the brain demonstrated that the mind or intention is more than physical. He has shown that the supplementary motor area of the brain is fired by mere intention to do something, without the motor cortex of the brain (which controls muscle movements) operating.** So, in effect, the mind is to the brain what an archivist is to a library. The former is not reducible to the latter'" (1984, pp. 140-141 emphasis added) {26}.

Why, you might ask, is this particular evidence so critical? Because, you see, most (not all) Darwinian evolutionists and atheists believe that the MIND is simply MATTER, that is part of the complex nature of the brain, which, of course, is also matter. To their way of thinking, MATERIALISM is all there is! But notable, renowned scientists, such as, Wilder Penfield, Sir Charles Sherrington, Dr. John Eccles, and his co-author, Sir Karl Popper, a notable philosopher of science, in their book, The Self and Its Brain (1977), have produced "scientifically demonstrated" evidence that the MIND is "NON-MATERIAL" and can operate independently from the material brain.

There is more to come. Continuing on, Thompson and Harrub have an interesting quote from Norman Cousins book, *Nobel Conversations*:

"NORMAN COUSINS, who moderated a series of conversations among four Nobel Laureates, including Dr. Eccles, made the following statement: '...Nor was Sir John Eccles claiming too much when **he insisted that the action of non-material mind on material brain has been not merely postulated but scientifically demonstrated**" (1985, p.68 emphasis added) {27}.

NOTE: An "archivist" is a person who is in charge of an "archive," which is a place where historical or public documents are preserved.

CAUSE & EFFECT: TRUTH IN SCIENCE POINTS TO GOD

DR. JOHN ECCLES, as the result of his "SCIENTIFICALLY DEMONSTRATED" work which pointed out that our actions of the intangible inner self—that inward, conscious, personality with free will emotions to be angry and hateful or loving and caring—is not dictated by some uncontrollable, naturalistically-acquired characteristics. The Bible describes it as that part of every human being that is created in the image of God. Here is the word picture Eccles used to describe his conclusions, which Thompson and Harrub recorded in their book on page 29:

"In an article titled 'Modern Biology and the Turn to Belief in God' that he [Eccles] wrote for the book, The Intellectuals Speak Out About God, Eccles Concluded: 'Science and religion are very much alike. Both are imaginative and creative aspects of the human mind. The appearance of a conflict is a result of ignorance. **We come to exist through a divine act.** That divine guidance is a theme throughout our life; at our death the brain goes, but that divine guidance and love continues. Each of us is a unique, conscious being, a divine creation. It is the religious view. **It is the only view consistent with all the evidence.** And, one more time we agree.'" (1984, p. 50 emphasis added) {28}.

ALEXANDER CAMPBELL, President of Bethany College, was a well-known leader in the Restoration movement and a famous debater of the 1800's. Robert Owen, a famous atheist of his time and also an excellent debater, had charged that Christianity was detrimental to humanity as a narcotic and on every occasion challenged clergymen to debate the grounds for belief in a living God. Campbell accepted Owens' challenge and was involved in a debate with him in April, 1829. In his first response to Robert Owens, Alexander Campbell raised the following questions:

"…It is not the momentary affair of empire, or the evanescent charms of dominion—nay, indeed, all these things are but the toys of childhood, the sportive excursions of youthful fancy, contrasted with the question, What is man? Whence came he? Whither does he go? Is he a mortal or an immortal being? Is he doomed to spring up like grass, bloom like a flower, drop his seed into the earth, and die forever? Is there no object of future hope? No God—no heaven—no exalted society to be known or enjoyed? …These are the awful and sublime merits of the question at issue. It is not what we shall eat, nor what we shall drink, unless we shall be proved to be mere animals; but it is shall we live or die forever?" {29}.

CHAPTER 4

"What is man? Whence came he? Whither does he go?"
(Alexander Campbell)

Today the issue remains the same. It has not changed. What is it that makes the human creature different from an ape? Secular humanists/atheists would argue that humans are only an advanced species of animal and no more. The debate continues and will continue until the eternal divine Creator decides to end it once and for all. The answer to the question, WHAT IS MAN? takes us back to Genesis, the first chapter: "So God created man in his own image, In the image of God he created him; male and female he created them" (Genesis 1:27).

WHAT IS IT THAT DEFINES HOW MANKIND (MALE & FEMALE) WERE CREATED IN GOD'S IMAGE? WHAT IS GOD?

In the fourth chapter of the Gospel of John in the New Testament Jesus was talking with a Samaritan woman by a well called "Jacob's well" by a town named Sychar. During the conversation the woman said: "Our fathers worshipped on this mountain, but you Jews claim that the place where we must worship is in Jerusalem" (v. 20); to which Jesus replied that there will be a time that neither Samaritan nor Jew will be required to worship God at a specific geographical site, that: "...true worshippers will worship the Father in spirit and truth, for they are the kind of worshippers the Father seeks" (v. 21-23). Then He makes it clear who and what God is:
"GOD IS SPIRIT, and his worshippers must worship in spirit and in truth" (John 4:24 emphasis added).

The Bible speaks about two separate parts of man: The "inner man"—the "unseen," "eternal" part of man and the "outer man"—the body and brain—which is wearing out (2 Corinthians 4:16-18). God created man and woman in His own image (Genesis 1:27). "God is Spirit." In Luke chapter 24 Jesus describes the spirit. Jesus makes an appearance to His disciples after His resurrection from the dead. The disciples were shaken up because they "...thought they were seeing a spirit" (v. 37). Jesus reassures them they were not:

CAUSE & EFFECT: TRUTH IN SCIENCE POINTS TO GOD

"See My Hands and My feet, that it is I Myself; touch Me and see, for a SPIRIT does not have flesh and bones as you see that I have" (Luke 24:39 New American Standard Bible—NASB emphasis added).

The point is that a spirit does not consist of matter (such as "flesh and bones"). A SPIRIT is an intangible (non-material), conscious, thinking, feeling, being.

Therefore, the connection is that man's inner being, his mind, is a conscious, thinking and feeling immaterial SPIRIT! This part of man is real, and eternal! This answers the question, "What is man?"

The answer to the question, "WHENCE CAME HE?"—in other words, where did he come from?—is described in the following Scriptures:

"Furthermore, we had earthly fathers to discipline us, and we respected them; shall we not much rather be subject to the FATHER of SPIRITS, and live? (Hebrews 12:9 NASB emphasis added).

This seems reasonably clear. When the Hebrew writer refers to "earthly fathers" he speaks of fathers of the "outer man" (flesh and bones). The "Father of spirits" refers to the "inner man" (the SPIRIT of man, which includes his mind).

"Then the dust will return to the earth as it was" (Ecclesiastes 12:7).

Let's summarize what we know about God. God is an eternal, super-intelligent MIND, a conscious, thinking, feeling, loving, intangible SPIRIT. He is not clothed in a material, flesh-and-blood body (except when He chose to appear in a human body). Man has been created in the IMAGE of God; therefore it is not his material body that is in God's image. It is the fact that man possesses an intangible, intelligent MIND; a thinking, feeling, conscious SPIRIT.

THIS IS HOW MAN WAS MADE IN THE IMAGE OF GOD—THE MIND (OR SPIRIT)! ACCORDING TO PENFIELD, SHERRINGTON, ECCLES, AND POPPER, IT IS A DEMONSTRATED, SCIENTIFIC FACT!

NOTE: Genesis 2:7 tells us that: "...the LORD God formed man of dust from the ground" (the outward flesh and blood part of man). Ecclesiastes 12:7 says "the SPIRIT will return to GOD who gave it" (NASB).

CHAPTER 4

"WE COME TO EXIST THROUGH A DIVINE ACT. ...IT IS THE ONLY VIEW CONSISTENT WITH ALL THE EVIDENCE" (Dr. John Eccles, emphasis added).

LET'S SUMMARIZE THE EVIDENCE ON THE LAW OF CAUSE & EFFECT and how it applies to the Creation of the Universe.

FIRST, everything that exists can be classified as either Matter or Mind.
SECOND, the Universe consists of all the Matter there is.
THIRD, the Law of Entropy confirms the fact that the Universe is not eternal. It had a beginning.
FOURTH, Matter is incapable of creating itself. The Universe and life itself is far too complex for anything like that to be possible. Therefore, all Matter (such as the Universe) is an Effect.
FIFTH, the Law of Cause and Effect points to a Preceding and Capable, Uncaused First Cause. The only other thing that exists outside of Matter is Mind. Therefore, it would have to be a preceding, uncaused, intangible, Super Intelligent, Eternal Mind. The only Mind that is qualified to create such a complex Universe and humanity is God who is Spirit. Nothing else within reason would qualify.

"NOR WAS SIR JOHN ECCLES CLAIMING TOO MUCH WHEN HE INSISTED THAT THE ACTION OF NON-MATERIAL MIND ON MATERIAL BRAIN HAS NOT BEEN MERELY POSTULATED BUT SCIENTIFICALLY DEMONSTRATED" (NORMAN COUSINS emphasis added).

"Oh, the depth of the riches both of the wisdom and knowledge of God! How unsearchable are His judgments and unfathomable His ways! For WHO HAS KNOWN THE MIND OF THE LORD, OR WHO BECAME HIS COUNSELOR?" (Romans 11:33-34 NASB).

It appears the Writer of Hebrews in the New Testament had it right what he wrote in the third chapter:

"For every house is built by someone, but the builder of all things is God" (Hebrews 3:4 NASB).

CAUSE & EFFECT: TRUTH IN SCIENCE POINTS TO GOD

"MESA VERDE NATIONAL PARK is truly America's premier archaeological wonder. ...The Park tells the story of a civilization's dynamic growth over 700 years. The beauty and complexity of the homes and villages here speak eloquently of the ancient peoples who built them" (emphasis added) {30}.

"Step into a room and smell centuries' old soot. Look out the window, and appreciate the same views the original architects enjoyed" {31}.

We know the "ARCHITECTS" of Mesa Verde were intelligent Human MINDS who designed and built these dwellings. Doesn't it seem reasonable that it would take a preexisting, Intelligent ARCHITECT, with a MIND capable of creating this incredibly complex Universe?

"For since the creation of the world His invisible attributes, His eternal power and divine nature, have been clearly seen, being understood through what has been made, so that they are without excuse" (Romans 1:20 NASB).

Chapter 5

SYMBOLS OF EVOLUTION LACK SUBSTANCE
THE LAW OF BIOGENESIS
TRUTH IN SCIENCE POINTS TO GOD

CHAPTER 5

We began this book with the interrogation of a prisoner by the Roman Governor Pontius Pilate. The incident is found in the Gospel of John, chapter 18, verses 37-38: "Pilate said to the prisoner named, Jesus: 'You are a king, then!' said Pilate. Jesus answered, 'You are right in saying I am a king. In fact, for this reason I was born, and for this I came into the world, to testify to the truth. Everyone on the side of truth listens to me.' To which, Pilate asked the question: 'WHAT IS TRUTH?'" (emphasis added).

IN SCIENCE—
Truth is: the Universe had a Beginning and is Wearing Out.
Truth is: every effect (such as the Universe) must have a Preceding, Sufficient Cause.
Truth is: the most Sufficient Cause would be an Existing, Intelligent, Designing, Mind who existed before the Universe Began.

ALL THESE FACTS POINT TOWARD AN INTELLIGENT, PRE-EXISTING BEING WHOM THE BIBLE REFERS TO AS "GOD" (Genesis 1:1).

Why is it then that famous, outspoken scientists and philosophers insist there is no need for a belief in God because Charles Darwin's theory of natural selection (evolution) has been proven to be a fact? They claim the evidence is such that to disbelieve in evolution is to identify one's self as ignorant and anti-science. Following are some quotes from evolutionists.

First, so we don't have misunderstandings of what evolution is and how it is being taught, here is an explanation from, THEODOSIUS DOBZHANSKY provided by HENRY M. MORRIS in *That Their Words May Be Used Against Them*, on page, 109:

"Evolution is a process which has produced life from non-life, which has brought forth man from an animal, and which may conceivably continue doing remarkable things in the future. In giving rise to man, the evolutionary process has, apparently for the first and only time in the history of the Cosmos, become conscious of itself" (Dobzhansky, Theodosius, 'Changing Man,' p. 409, Science, vol. 155, no.3761, January 27, 1967) {1}.

SYMBOLS OF EVOLUTION LACK SUBSTANCE

Really? "EVOLUTION IS A PROCESS WHICH HAS PRODUCED LIFE FROM NON-LIFE"? I want the reader to understand that evolutionary "process" is not valid scientific truth. There is one Law of science alone that refutes and nullifies any such process from taking place, which I will bring up later in this chapter, but I want to make the reader aware of what is being taught at almost every level of education in the public schools, from elementary school on through high school and universities. It is becoming extremely difficult for anyone with a background of Christian education or simply the belief in Creation by God to get a position as a public school science teacher or as a science professor in most state colleges or universities. That is why it is critical to expose the highly-touted symbols of evidence for evolution which are instances of hoax, or in some extreme cases, complete fraud. Certainly, most are instances where evolutionists have simply made some mistakes in their data. Some of these mistakes have been conceded by scientists who wanted to set the records straight.

Those in science and philosophy who are atheistic evolutionists and purely materialists openly claim there is no supernatural Creator God. Everything, including earth and humanity, simply "evolved" as did religion (when man developed the capacity to think more complexly about why things happen). Read the following quotations from some leading Darwinian evolutionists:

JULIAN HUXLEY, in an "Associated Press Dispatch, November, 27, 1959, address at the Darwinian Centennial Convocation, Chicago University, [see *Issues in Evolution*, edited by Sol Tax (University of Chicago Press, 1960)] made this statement:

"In the evolutionary system of thought there is no longer need or room for the supernatural. The earth was not created, it evolved. So did all the animals and plants that inhabit it, including our human selves, mind and soul, as well as brain and body. So did religion. Evolutionary man can no longer take refuge from his loneliness by creeping for shelter into the arms of a divinized father figure whom he himself created" (p. 252) {2}.

WAYNE JACKSON, ERIC LYONS, and KYLE BUTT, in their book, *Surveying the Evidence*, comment on the remarks made by: "Evolutionist Neil deGrasse Tyson of the Hayden Planetarium in New York...He referred to a recent poll taken of

CHAPTER 5

members of the U.S. National Academy of Sciences which revealed that 15 per cent did not indicate they were atheists, and asked: "How come the number isn't zero? ...That should be the subject of everybody's investigation. That's something that we can't just sweep under the rug" (p. 10) {3}.

To which, the authors (Jackson, Lyons, and Butt) made these comments:

"One wonders what Tyson would suggest if Louis Pasteur, Isaac Newton, Carolus Linnaeus, and other brilliant **theistic** scientists from the past were members of this group? Kick them out for not being atheists, even though their contributions to science likely far exceed...most current members of the U.S. National Academy of Sciences?" (p. 10) {4}.

EUGENIE SCOTT is Director of the National Center for Science Education and one of the most influential members of the aggressively hostile group of Darwinian scientists who have been blocking any attempt to include intelligent design (creation science) factual information into public school classrooms. Scott prepared a list of steps that could be taken to prevent intelligent creation from being taught in classrooms. The list includes: "25 things 'parents and teachers, and even scientists' can do to help evolution win its battle over creation" {5}.

"For instance," Eugenie Scott wrote: "...'scientists using God to explain natural phenomena of **any kind** violates the practice of methodological naturalism, in which scientific explanations are limited only to natural causes" (2004, p.119 emphasis added).

In other words, any idea that contains a hint of a supernatural, non-material Creator is, according to their definition, "unscientific" {6}.

Is Eugenie Scott alone in her materialistic worldview assessment by refusing to acknowledge God's creative design of "ANY KIND" in the scientific process of information? Absolutely not! In fact, Jackson, Lyons, and Butt state that in the National Academy of Science's book, *Science and Creationism*, the "steering committee" members, including Stephen J. Gould, Eugenie Scott, Francisco Ayala, and others: "...put it like this: '[T]he teaching of evolution should be an integral part of science instruction, and creation science is in fact not science and should not be presented as such in science classes'" (1999, p. 2) {7}.

SYMBOLS OF EVOLUTION LACK SUBSTANCE

This appears to be standard procedure in nearly all departments of the sciences. It provides the domination method in the assessment of evidences. HENRY M. MORRIS, in his book, *That Their Words May Be Used Against Them*, lists a quotation from the National Association of Biology Teachers' "Statement on Teaching Evolution":

"Whether called 'creation science,' 'scientific creationism,' 'intelligent-design theory,' 'young-earth theory' or some other synonym, creation beliefs have no place in the science classroom" (p. 1).

"Courts have thus restricted school districts from requiring creation science in the science curriculum and have restricted individual instructors from teaching it. All teachers and administrators should be mindful of these court cases, remembering the law, science and NABT support them as they appropriately include the teaching of evolution in the science curriculum" (p. 3) {8}.

"THE TEACHING OF EVOLUTION SHOULD BE AN INTEGRAL PART OF SCIENCE INSTRUCTION AND CREATION SCIENCE IS IN FACT NOT SCIENCE AND SHOULD NOT BE PRESENTED AS SUCH IN SCIENCES CLASSES" (National Academy of Science).

Should students have a choice in the evidence they would have available in order to make a decision? Not according to the National Academy of Science "steering committee!" If the evidence for evolution is factual and unreasonable to challenge, why do they run away and hide in their Darwinian castle when Christian scientists challenge them to a debate? This is getting to be the standard operating procedure after they clearly lost the majority of debates in the 1980's and continued to lose in the 1990's. In fact, this is the advice of EUGENIE SCOTT, the Executive Director of the National Center for Science Education, in 1996: **"Avoid Debates"** (Emphasis in quoted text) {9}.

This is not the only occasion where this has happened. In the *Skeptical Inquirer*, in the May/June 2007, magazine, there is an article on "Debating Creationists" by Charles L. Rulon, professor emeritus at Long Beach City College. In his opening

CHAPTER 5

remarks in a debate with a scientist on intelligent design, here is what he had to say about debating creationists:

"So why am I here? Have I actually deluded myself into thinking that I have some silver bullet arguments to convert the creationists in today's audience? Hardly, as I discovered from decades of frustrating personal experiences. The only way creationists have been defeated, so far, from introducing their anti-evolution beliefs into public school science classes has been in court cases where their phony science has been exposed. So, again, why am I here today? Because I believe that science educators have a duty to defend the scientific method from irrational attacks. ... That's why I agreed to debate today. Even so, there are excellent reasons for science educators not to debate the anti-evolutionists."

Rulon gives five reasons why evolutionists should not debate "creationists":

"First, in science's search for truth, it's the rigorous application of the scientific method that counts, not oratory skills. Yet, repeatedly, the overwhelming majority of debates before public audiences are won not by the actual scientific content but by the emotional rapport, public speaking skills, likeability, and believed authority of the debaters. How could it be otherwise, given the audiences' lack of expertise in being able to recognize fake science? The creationists know this and most are excellent debaters, now with impressive and entertaining Power Point presentations. A second reason for not debating…if a scientist debates, it's 'proof' that a scientific controversy actually exists. If he declines, it's 'proof' that evolutionists are running scared" ("Debating Creationists," pp. 63, 64).

It isn't hard to understand why those who teach evolution via natural selection by spontaneous generation are reluctant to debate their position, but there is more.

The "fourth reason" is the one that is most glaring, exposing a lack of objective intent. Rulon doesn't believe it is fair to give creationists equal time:

"A fourth reason for not debating creationists is that in debates equal time is given to both sides" {10}.

SYMBOLS OF EVOLUTION LACK SUBSTANCE

Can you imagine that? It's just not fair to be giving those "creationists" EQUAL TIME! In fact, Mr. Rulon believes it is better to let the "courts" silence those troublesome creation scientists who believe in intelligent design.

Is "the established fact" of "biological evolution" really an established fact? Not by a long shot! This chapter is going to establish how the alleged facts and proofs for biological natural selection have fallen by the wayside. Many of them are still being taught and are in public school textbooks. Here are the most popular symbols of evidence for evolution.

SYMBOL #1: "THE GREAT BIOGENIC LAW" by ERNST HAECKEL (Also known as "Embryonic Recapitulation")

One of the earliest evidences used to validate Charles Darwin's theory in his book, *The Origin of Species*, was Ernst Haeckel's highly touted "Great Biogenic Law." When you read the research evidence that has been accumulated you find out that it turned out to be strong evidence of fraud. BERT THOMPSON, Ph.D., in his book, *The History of Evolutionary Thought*, describes what took place after its introduction in 1859 and onward:

"In Europe, the leading proponent of Darwinian evolution besides Huxley was Ernst Haeckel. In fact, he was so anti-Christian and pro-evolution that Darwinians thought it might even hurt their cause. As it turned out, Haeckel's activities apparently diverted attacks from Darwin to Haeckel himself, thereby indirectly aiding Darwin's cause. Haeckel was a German anatomist. ...Haeckel is responsible for formulating the "great biogenic law," which states that the ontogeny (development of the individual) recapitulates (repeats) the phylogeny (development of the race). The general idea is that embryos, in their development, repeat the evolutionary history of their ancestors. Darwin had regarded embryonic recapitulation as a very strong evidence of evolution (he devoted 12 pages to embryology as a proof of this theory in *The Origin of Species*."

What was touted to be the "great biogenic law" in truth turned out to be THE GREAT BIOGENIC FRAUD! Thompson comments on what Haeckel did to deceive the public with the use of embryos:

CHAPTER 5

"Haeckel is now looked upon with disrepute, as is his "biogenic law." ...The illustrations and drawings that Haeckel used...(he was an accomplished artist) were nothing but lies and forgeries. As Davidheiser points out: 'He even faked his drawings, which created a scandal in his day.'"

As Thompson continues to point out, it was known among Haeckel's peers:

"Even scientists of Haeckel's day recognized the falsehoods. Professor L. Rutimeyer of the University of Basel and Professor Wilhem His, Sr. of the University of Leipzig openly accused Haeckel of falsifying his drawings, and backed up their accusations with facts!" {12}.

But this doesn't tell the whole story, nor should Thompson's book be expected to do so, because it deals with the history of how evolutionary thought developed. The lengths Haeckel employed to convince the unsuspecting public is nothing short of deception. LEE STROBEL, an investigative journalist and atheist at the time of his research, began to see what others had found. After studying the evidence, he became a believer and now confidently declares he is a Christian. Let's follow where his research has taken him in his book, *The Case for a Creator*, where he interviews several scientists about the scientific evidence for the reality of God:

Strobel's first interview began with JONATHAN WELLS, Ph.D. in religious studies and Ph.D. in molecular and cell biology. In the year 2000, Dr. Wells wrote the book, *Icons of Evolution*, with the sub-title, *Why Much of What We Teach about Evolution Is Wrong*. Wells' book exposes such things as what Strobel refers to as "THE SINS OF HAECKEL." Strobel is meticulous in investigating the details in his interview with Dr. Wells:

"THREE PROBLEMS' WITH HAECKEL'S DRAWINGS"
"I was hungry for details. 'What was it specifically that bothered you?' I asked.
"'There are three problems with these drawings,' he said. 'The first is that the similarities in the early stages were faked.'
"He leveled the accusation without emotion in his voice, but nevertheless it was a stunning charge. 'Faked?' I repeated. 'Are you sure?' It seemed inconceivable that the books I had relied upon as a student could have so blatantly misled me.
"'You can call them fudged, distorted, misleading, but the bottom line is that they

SYMBOLS OF EVOLUTION LACK SUBSTANCE

were faked,' he replied. 'Apparently in some cases Haeckel actually used the same woodcut to print embryos from different classes because he was so confident of his theory that he figured he didn't have to draw them separately. In other cases he doctored the drawings to make them look more similar than they really are. At any rate, his drawings misrepresent the embryos.'
"'That's amazing!' I said. 'How long has this been known?'
"'They were first exposed in the late 1860's, when his colleagues accused him of fraud.'" {13}.

At this point, I would think one would reasonably conclude that since HAECKEL'S FRAUD has been exposed since the 1860s, surely by now this has been discredited by present day science writers and is no longer in the biology textbooks in our public schools, right?

THINK AGAIN! Strobel questioned Dr. Wells about this very thing, mentioning the fact that "the drawings" were in his books when he was in school:

"'Wait a minute—I saw these drawings in books that I studied when I was a student in the 1960's and 70's—more than a hundred years later. How is that possible?'"

To that Dr. Wells replied:

"'It's worse than that!' he declared. 'They're still being used, even in upper-division textbooks on evolutionary biology'" {14}.

In Lee Strobel's interview, Dr. Wells addresses the other problems:

"'The minor problem is that Haeckel cherry picked his examples. ...He only shows a few of the seven vertebrate classes. For example, his most famous rendition has eight columns. Four are mammals, but they're all placental mammals. [NOTE: placental mammals are dogs, cats, and humans. They are not marsupials, such as the kangaroo.] There are two other kinds of mammals that he didn't show, which are different. The remaining four classes he showed—reptiles, birds, amphibians, and fish—happen to be more similar than the ones he omitted. He used a salamander to represent amphibians instead of a frog, which looks very different. So he stacked the deck by picking representatives that came closest to fitting his idea—and then he went further by faking the similarities.'"

CHAPTER 5

As Strobel continued his interview, he questioned Wells about the "MAJOR" problem:

"If that's the minor problem," I said sarcastically, "then what's the major one?'

"Wells explained: 'To me, as an embryologist, the most dramatic problem is that what Haeckel claimed is the early stage of development is nothing of the sort. It's actually the midpoint of the development. ...If you go to the earlier stages, the embryos look far more different from each other. But he deliberately omits the earlier stages altogether.'"

Strobel asked: "Why is that important?"

"Dr. Wells explained: 'Remember Darwin claimed that because the embryos are most similar in their earlier stages, this is evidence of common ancestry. He thought that the early stage showed what the common ancestor looked like—sort of like a fish. But embryologists talk about the "developmental hourglass." ...You see, vertebrate embryos start out looking very different in the early cell division stages. The cell divisions in a mammal, for example, are radically different from those in any of the other classes. There's no possible way you could mix them up. In fact, it's extremely different within classes. The patterns are all over the place'" {15}.

Dr. Wells explained that "the midpoint" was what "Haeckel claimed in his drawings was the early stage—the embryos become more similar, though nowhere near as much as Haeckel claimed."

Strobel asked the obvious question: "'If they're so misleading, then why did scientists continue to publish them for generation after generation of students?'"

I want the reader to catch the reason this form of deceit has been taught to biology students for so many years after the evolutionists knew that Haeckel's drawings were "faked!"

DR. WELLS EXPLAINS: "'One explanation that's often given...is that although the drawings are false, they teach a concept that's basically true. Well, this is not true. Biologists know that embryos are not most similar in their earliest stages'" {16}.

SYMBOLS OF EVOLUTION LACK SUBSTANCE

"ALTHOUGH THE DRAWINGS ARE BASICALLY FALSE, THEY TEACH A CONCEPT THAT'S BASICALLY TRUE. WELL, THIS IS NOT TRUE" (JONATHAN WELLS)

A good example of what Wells stated in Strobel's book is found in 2009, in the book, *Why Evolution Is True*, by Jerry A. Coyne, an evolutionist:

"Noting this principle, Ernst Haeckel, a German evolutionist and Darwin's contemporary, formulated a 'biogenetic law' in 1866, famously summarized as 'Ontogeny recapitulates phylogeny.' This means that the development of an organism simply replays its evolutionary history. But this notion is true only in a limited sense. ...Haeckel's law has fallen into disrepute not only because it wasn't strictly true, but also because Haeckel was accused, largely unjustly, of fudging some drawings of early embryos to make them look more similar than they are. Yet we shouldn't throw out the baby with the bathwater. Embryos still show a form of recapitulation" {17}.

"Haeckel's law has fallen into disrepute not only because it wasn't strictly true, but also because Haeckel was accused, largely unjustly, of fudging some drawings of early embryos. ...Embryos still show a form of recapitulation" (Jerry A. Coyne).

This book was written in 2009! Just one year or less before I started to write this book! Coyne, a professor of ecology and evolution, may not believe that Haeckel's drawings, according to Dr. Jonathan Wells, "ARE FALSE," but, in fact, Haeckel manipulated the embryos with the intention to deceive!
BERT THOMPSON AND WAYNE JACKSON, in their book, *Christian Evidences*, record "SIR ARTHUR KEITH bluntly stating:

"It was expected that the embryo would recapitulate the features of its ancestors from the lowest to the highest forms in the animal kingdom. Now that the appearances

CHAPTER 5

of the embryo at all stages are known, the general feeling is one of disappointment; the human embryo at no stage is anthropoid in appearance. The embryo of the mammal never resembles the worm, the fish, or the reptile. **Embryology provides no support whatsoever for the evolutionary hypothesis**" {18}.

Christian Evidences also quotes DR. GEORGE G. SIMPSON: "To use the words of Dr. George G. Simpson, the famous evolutionist: "It is now firmly established that ontogeny does not repeat phylogeny" {19}.

The conclusion is that one of the key evidences for evolution mentioned in Charles Darwin's book, *The Origin of Species*, has been proven to be false and dishonest. Let us now give closer investigation to the rest of the symbolic evidence for natural selection.

SYMBOL #2: THE ARCHAEOPTERYX

For Charles Darwin and his colleagues it was critical to locate some form of transitional fossil to support their theory (which is actually a hypothesis). Lo and behold, what should appear shortly after the publication of *The Origin of Species* right out of Germany, but the highly-prized transitional fossil known as the "Archaeopteryx," the ideal missing link between the reptile and bird. It is still used as evidence today. In his book, *Why Evolution Is True*, Jerry A. Coyne has it presented as evidence:

"If evolution is true, then we should expect to see the reptile-bird transition in rocks between 70 and 200 million years old. And there they are. The first link between birds and reptiles was actually known to Darwin, who curiously, mentioned it only briefly in later editions of The Origin, and then only as an oddity. It is perhaps the most famous of all transitional forms: the crow-sized Archaeopteryx lithographica, discovered in a limestone quarry in Germany in 1860" {20}.

Richard Dawkins, on the other hand, believes it is wise to use some caution when jumping upon such seemingly transitional forms of one species moving up "a ladder" to another. In his book, *The Greatest Show On Earth*, he explains why:

SYMBOLS OF EVOLUTION LACK SUBSTANCE

"But the pernicious legacy of the Great Chain of Being also feeds the challenge 'Where are the intermediates between major animal groups?' And, nearly as discreditably, underlies the tendency of evolutionists to answer such a challenge by trotting out particular fossils, such as Archaeopteryx, the celebrated 'intermediate between reptiles and birds. Nevertheless, there is something else going on underneath the Archaeopteryx fallacy, and it is of general importance; ...Zoologists have traditionally divided the vertebrates into classes: ...like mammals, birds, reptiles and amphibians." {21}.

Dawkins continues by explaining how scientists differ in their method of species classification, such as birds: "...All birds are descended from a single ancestor that would also have been called a bird and would have shared with modern birds the key diagnostic characters—feathers, wings, a beak, etc. ...Reptiles are not a good class in this sense. This is because, at least in conventional taxonomies, the category explicitly excludes birds. ...Some reptiles...are closer cousins to birds than they are to other reptiles" {22}.

KYLE BUTT and ERIC LYONS, in their book, *Truth Be Told: Exposing the Myth of Evolution*, explain why the Archaeopteryx is not really a transitional reptile to bird, as presented by many Dawinians:

"One of the most unusual birds of the past is known as Archaeopteryx (AR-kee-OP-ter-iks). Even though Archaeopteryx [meaning 'ancient' (Greek archae) 'wing' (pteryx)] had feathers, and was about the size of a pigeon, controversy has surrounded this creature for a long time, because it also had some features that are similar to a small dinosaur—it had teeth in its beak and claws on its wings. Actually, however, such characteristics...do not prove that it was a missing link between reptiles and birds. ...Some modern birds have claws on their wings, but no one thinks of them as being missing links. The HOATZIN of South America has claws when it is young, which it uses to climb trees. The TOURACO of Africa also has claws. And if you have ever seen an OSTRICH up close, you might have noticed that it has three claws on each wing that it can use if it is attacked. ...Fossil studies have shown that other true birds, which are now extinct, also had teeth. The presence of teeth, then, does not mean that Archaeopteryx was a dinosaur-to-bird link. This strange bird also had feathers, just like birds today, and the feathers were fully formed. Archaeopteryx did not have half scales/half feathers, but fully formed feathers" (emphasis added) {23}.

CHAPTER 5

Has the Archaeopteryx escaped the attention of LEE STROBEL'S investigative research in his book, *The Case for a Creator*? No, it has not. In fact, it was one of the "images" he remembered from high school. When offered an opportunity to interview Dr. JONATHAN WELLS about the highly-touted missing link between reptile and bird, he asked Wells this question:

"'Doesn't archaeopteryx fill the gap between reptiles and modern birds?' I asked Wells.

"'There are several problems with that,' came his reply. 'Does it show Darwinian Evolution? Well, no, for the same reason that Corvettes don't illustrate Darwinian evolution. We need more than an immediate form to show that; we would need to know how you get from one to the other. The question is, do you get from a reptile to a bird—which is an astonishingly huge step—by some totally natural process or does this require the intervention of a designer? An archaeopteryx, as beautiful as it is, doesn't show us one way or the other. Besides, we see strange animals around today, like the duck-billed platypus, which nobody considers transitional but which has characteristics of different classes'"

"The question is, do you get from a reptile to a bird—which is an astonishingly huge step—by some totally natural process or does this require the intervention of a designer?" (Jonathan Wells, Ph.D.).

This prompted Strobel to ask the question:

"'But the archaeopteryx is a half-bird, half-reptile, right?'

Wells reply:
"'No, not even close,' he insisted. 'It's a bird with modern feathers, and birds are very different from reptiles in many important way—their breeding system, their bone structure, their lungs, their distribution of weight and muscles. It's a bird, that's clear—not part bird and part reptile'" {24}.

NOTE: Dr Wells is right—it is an "astonishingly huge step." Later in this chapter a scientist will show us why.
NOTE: The "*Truth Be Told: Exposing the Myth of Evolution* book has further information on this subject and has some detailed illustrations of these birds which are beautifully done.

SYMBOLS OF EVOLUTION LACK SUBSTANCE

ALAN FEDUCCIA, an ornithologist with many years' experience as a biologist, has made several comments regarding the Archaeopteryx. One such comment was recorded in HENRY M. MORRIS'S book, *That Their Words May Be Used Against Them*, p.191:

"Other evidence suggests that Archaeopteryx had an advanced aerodynamic morphology. (i) It had the feathers of modern birds, unchanged in structural detail over 150 million years of evolution, including microstructure, like regular spacing of barbs throughout the feather's length and clear impressions of barbules. I conclude that Archaeopteryx was arboreal and volant, considerably advanced aerodynamically, and probably capable of flapping, powered flight to at least some degree. Archaeopteryx probably cannot tell us much about the early origins of feathers and flight in true protobirds because Archaeopteryx was, in the modern sense, a bird" (Feduccia, Alan, 'Evidence from Claw Geometry Indicating Arboreal Habits of Archaeopteryx," Science, vol. 259 (February 5, 1993), pp.792) {25}.

This highly inflated example of reptile-to-bird evidence for Darwinian evolution has been around for nearly 150 years. More and more of those who believe in evolution have backed away from the Archaeopteryx because the more the evidence is scrutinized, the more doubtful evolutionists and creation scientists have become, until now some scientists are saying, NO! It is not what it has been claimed to be. As Jonathan Wells and Alan Feduccia have both clearly stated, ARCHAEOPTERYX IS...A BIRD! The complexity that natural selection advocates propose in trying to support such a hypothetical concept is explained by an aerospace engineer. Notice the immense problems acquired characteristics face with birds.
In the January, 2010, issue of the *Reason & Revelation* monthly journal, a scientist by the name of JERRY FAUSZ, with a Ph.D. in Aerospace Engineering, wrote a fascinating article on the complexity of flight by "flying creatures," such as eagles and hawks, and the characteristics necessary to perform these tasks:

"MORPHING FLIGHT: BEYOND IRREDUCIBLE COMPLEXITY:
Researchers and observers have long recognized that birds and various other flying creatures change the positioning of their body structures in flight in order to perform specific maneuvers or adjust their aerodynamic profile to accommodate changing flight conditions. This adaptive orientation of body shape has been dubbed 'morphing' in the popular literature...the ability that birds possess to change the form or geometry of their bodies for increased maneuverability, as well as for stable flight in a wide variety of ambient conditions" 30 (1):1.

CHAPTER 5

Dr. Fausz continues: "Clearly, research in aircraft technology and design continues to draw ideas and inspiration from **nature's** flyers. It is also clear that **our** technical capabilities seriously lag behind **their natural** abilities" 30 (1):2.

"Indeed, morphing flight is a highly multi-disciplinary skill. The different disciplinary facets of morphing may be broken down as follows:

"SENSING…Flying creatures and machines must be able to detect or sense the condition of the atmosphere around them, as well as their own position and structural configuration, in order to be able to carry out the activity of flying in a given environment.

"COMPUTATION…The sensor inputs from eyes, ears, etc., as well as specialized sensor systems, must be integrated and processed in the brain for biological flyers, or alternatively, the flight computer if one is considering the sensor systems of flying machines. The processing that must be carried out includes specialized algorithms for flight stability, guidance, navigation, and control. …In biological flyers, these commands are electrical impulses from the brain that stimulate specific muscles and organs. …Given the computational requirements of flight locomotion, it may not be surprising that the size of a bird's brain with respect to its body size is, on average 10 times that of the reptiles with whom they are assumed to share common ancestry (Jerison 2004)" 30 (1):3.

"…the size of a bird's brain…is on average, 10 times that of the reptiles with whom they are assumed to share common ancestry (Jerison 2004)" (Jerry Fausz).
"ACTUATION…Morphing flight requires highly specialized structures, but it also requires equally specialized actuators to move and position those structures. … Natural flyers…require a specialized skeletal structure and attached musculature to perform their amazing feats of aerial acrobatics. …Multiple components of bird anatomy have been studied in the literature with respect to the irreducible complexity they possess regarding the bird's ability to fly.

NOTE: Because of the length of the article and the detailed technical language it has been condensed to include a simplified explanation of what is involved with how birds change their wing shape and body movements to reduce "aerodynamic drag," etc.

NOTE: Think about the increase in complexity that would be required just for the brain alone, in accidental, acquired characteristics to INCREASE "10 TIMES" THE "SIZE" OF THE BRAIN in the process of becoming a BIRD from that of a REPTILE.

SYMBOLS OF EVOLUTION LACK SUBSTANCE

For example, MATTHEW VANHORN discussed the amazing complexity of bird feathers (2004), CALEB COLLEY pointed out how bats use their ears (hearing) for echolocation (2204), and irreducible complexity has been examined in general terms with regard to various components of bird physiology (Fausz, 2008). ...The IRREDUCIBLE COMPLEXITY associated with bird feathers and other components of bird physiology are enough of a challenge to the Darwinian notion of natural selection to render it **impractical**. However, when one considers the system level implications of morphing flight, and the necessity of simultaneous development of multiple combinations of these physical components, NATURAL SELECTION as an explanation for morphing flight capability is seen to be **absolutely irrational**" 30 (1):3 & 30 (1):4 (emphasis added) {26}.

I believe Dr. Fausz described it most adequately—the obvious amount of intricate intelligent design involved in the creation of a bird is definitely BEYOND IRREDUCIBLE COMPLEXITY." The chance for accidental natural selection of a bird from a reptile is beyond any sort of mathematical probability, a subject to which I intend to devote one whole chapter later in the book.

SYMBOL #3: ARCHAEORAPTOR—ANOTHER "FAKE" IN THE FOSSIL MARKET

LEE STROBEL, in his book, *The Case for a Creator*, mentions another case study. This has to do with the production of what turns out to be the "fake-fossil" industry that now exists:

"Paleontologists, however, have been on a frenzy to try to locate an actual reptilian ancestor for birds. ...their zeal has resulted in some recent embarrassments for science. Wells was more than willing to regale me with some examples."

Dr. JONATHAN WELLS will provide the details:

"'A few years ago the *National Geographic* Society announced that a fossil had been purchased at an Arizona mineral show that turned out to be "the missing link between terrestrial dinosaurs and birds that could actually fly." ...They called it the archaeoraptor, and it had the tail of a dinosaur and the forelimbs of a bird. *National*

CHAPTER 5

Geographic magazine published an article in 1999 that said there's now evidence that feathered dinosaurs were ancestors of the first bird. ...Well, the problem was that it was a fake! ...A Chinese paleontologist proved that someone had glued a dinosaur tail to a primitive bird. He created it to resemble just what the scientists had been looking for. ...Fakes are coming out of these fossil beds all the time... because the fossil dealers know there's big money in it.'"
After Dr. Wells made this statement Strobel made this comment in his book:

"I remained skeptical about that charge until I subsequently read an interview with ornithologist Alan Feduccia, an evolutionary biologist at the University of North Carolina at Chapel Hill. When a reporter for Discover magazine raised the archaeoraptor fraud, Feduccia said:

"'Archaeoraptor is just the tip of the iceberg. There are scores of fake fossils out there, and they have cast a dark shadow over the whole field. When you go to these fossil shows, it's difficult to tell which ones are faked and which ones are not. I have heard there is a fake-fossil factory in northeast China, in Liaoning Province, near the deposits where many of these recent alleged feathered dinosaurs were found.'

"Asked what would motivate such fraud, Feduccia replied: 'Money. The Chinese fossil trade has become a big business. These fossil forgeries have been sold on the black market for years now, for huge sums of money. Anyone who can produce a good fake stands to profit'" {27}.

Let the buyer beware! It may not be what you think it is!

This is not the only time wishful-thinking scientists looking for that ultimate "missing-link," have been hoodwinked. Missing-link fossils have become the cherished **"sacred relics"** of the evolutionists. Preceding the arrival of Martin Luther, the selling of "sacred relics" had become an extremely profitable business for the Catholic church. In his book, *Western Civilizations, Their History and Their Culture*, historian EDWARD McNALL BURNS, commented on the sacred relics market: "According to Erasmus, the churches of Europe contained enough wood of the true cross to build a ship" {28}.

NOTE: I thought the "archaeoraptor" should be included because of the previous reptile-to-bird fossil that was highly-touted, but failed.

SYMBOLS OF EVOLUTION LACK SUBSTANCE

As we continue, more will surface on the authenticity of the symbols ("sacred relics") of Darwinian evolution. There are probably a lot more than we will be able to cover because they keep coming out even as I have been writing this book. Just beware of that "new missing-link fossil."

Human fossils and the antiquity of man

It was necessary in the Darwinian scheme of things that the human species descended from the next most similar species, the primates. Thus it should come as no surprise that in the recovery of human fossil remains anthropologists would be looking for the primate (ape/chimpanzee) link to the most primitive human species. The ideal geographic location for such to arrive would be, of course, Africa. Why Africa? Because in the minds of Darwin and Huxley, the indigenous races of Africa and Asia were thought to be the "lower races" and to be the more primitive of the human species. HENRY M. MORRIS, Ph.D., in his book, *Scientific Creationism*, explains why:

"Evolutionists apply evolutionary theory not only to man's origin but also to his later history, interpreting his societies and cultures, and even his economic and political systems, in terms of naturalistic development from one form into another" {29}.

"In dealing with man strictly as a biological organism in a 'great chain of being' with all other organisms, the human 'species' (Homo sapiens) has been divided by evolutionary biologists into various 'subspecies' or races, in the same way that other species are subdivided. ...This concept was particularly dominant among the 19th century evolutionists. ...It is significant that Charles Darwin gave his book, *The Origin of Species by Natural Selection*, the provocative subtitle 'The Preservation of Favored Races in the Struggle for Life.' Though in his book the discussion centered on races of plants and animals, it was clear that he also included the various races of men in the same concept. As a matter of fact, he made his convictions on the subject quite clear...from one of his published letters, in which he wrote: 'The more civilized so-called Caucasian races have beaten the Turkish hollow in the struggle for existence. Looking to the world at no very distant date, what and endless number of the lower races will have been eliminated by the higher civilized races throughout the world.'"

SYMBOLS OF EVOLUTION LACK SUBSTANCE

Similarly, THOMAS HUXLEY, the leading evolutionary protagonist of the last century, said:

"No rational man, cognizant of the facts, believes that the average negro is the equal, still less the superior, of the white man' (1).

"Modern-day evolutionists, for the most part, do not regard any one race of men as intrinsically superior or inferior to any other. Nevertheless, the very concept of 'race' is fundamentally a category of evolutionary biology, and leading modern evolutionists recognize this" {30}.

In his book, *That Their Words May Be Used Against Them*, Morris has recorded the words of the evolutionist GEORGE GAYLORD SIMPSON, who wrote in 1966:

"Moreover, races are evanescent in the course of evolution. A given race may change, disappear by fusion with others, or die out altogether while the species as a whole simply continues its evolutionary course. Races of man have or perhaps one should say 'had' exactly the same biological significance as the subspecies of other species of mammals" (p. 474) {31}.

Morris also records in the same book a quotation from the writings of HENRY FAIRFIELD OSBORN made in 1926:

"...This is the recognition that the genus homo is subdivided into three absolutely distinct stocks, which in zoology would be given the rank of species, if not of genera...the Caucasian, the Mongolian, and the Negroid. ...The Negroid stock is even more ancient than the Caucasian and Mongolian, as may be proved by an examination not only of the brain, of the hair, of the bodily characters, such as the teeth, the genitalia, the sense organs, but of the instincts, the intelligence. The standard of intelligence of the average adult Negro is similar to that of the eleven-year-old youth of the species Homo sapiens" {32}.

HENRY M. MORRIS has devoted several pages in this same book to the predominant thinking of the Darwinists' philosophical view of the human origin. It seems to explain why so much of their research is being done in Africa. That is where there appears to be the largest population of primates, from which, they perceive, the human "species" of today have descended.

CHAPTER 5

SYMBOL #4: JAVA MAN (Pithecanthropus erectus): IS HE, OR ISN'T HE?

"Pithecanthropus erectus" (Java Man) has been one of the most popular symbols of the alleged evolution of man. As far back as 1958, one of my favorite history books has him up front, in a photograph, with replicas of "Four Types of Stone Age Men" with "Java Man" on the left of the other three. So you see, "Java Man" has been given his own place in history. The man responsible for his fame is Eugene Dubois. MARVIN L. LUBENOW, in his book, *Bones of Contention*, an in-depth study of human fossils, exclaims: "Java Man! Breathes there a man or woman with soul so dead who has not heard of Java Man? Java Man is like an old friend. We learned about him in grade school. They called him the ape-man and told us that he was our evolutionary ancestor. The artist's drawings of that beetle-browed, jaw-jutting fellow were quite convincing" {33}.

In EDWARD McNALL BURNS book, *Western Civilizations*, he acknowledges the "famous" "Java Man" among his "Four Types of Stone Age Men": "During this time at least four species of men inhabited the earth. One was the famous Pithecanthropus erectus, or 'erect ape man,' whose skeletal remains were found on the island of Java in 1891" {34}.

LEE STROBEL, the author of several apologetic books, was convinced as a youth, like so many other young people, growing up with textbooks that describe "Java Man" as an authentic evolutionary discovery:

"That kind of certainty about human evolution was engendered in me as a youngster, when I would devour my *World Book Encyclopedia*. One of my favorite entries was 'Prehistoric Man,' where I would linger for hours, fascinated by the part-ape, part-human nicknamed 'Java Man'" {35}.

MARVIN L. LUBENOW has spent more than 20 years involved in some serious inquiry into human fossils. In fact, he has written a book on human fossils, titled, *Bones of Contention*. He is a creationist. In his book he devotes about six pages to the history and research on "Java Man":

CHAPTER 5

"The story has been told many times. Before the turn of the century, a Dutch anatomist, Eugene Dubois, went to the Dutch East Indies (now Indonesia) in search of the 'missing link' between apes and humans. In 1891, along the bank of the Solo River in Java, he found a skullcap that seemed to him to have a combination of human and ape features. A year later, about fifty feet away, he found a thigh bone (femur), very human in appearance, that he assumed belonged with the skullcap. Dubois named his 'transitional form,' which is now dated by evolutionists at about half a million years, Pithecanthropus erectus. However, to the general public he will always be known affectionately as Java Man" {36}.

Lubenow continues on to reveal detailed information as to the questionable research and excavation process that Dubois used in his discovery and assessment of these fossils, and his conclusions:

"My conclusions on Dubois and Java Man are as follows: (1) Java Man is not our evolutionary ancestor but is a true member of the human family, a post-Flood descendant of Adam, and a smaller version of Neandertal; (2) Dubois seriously misinterpreted the Java Man fossils, and there was abundant evidence available to him at that time that he had misinterpreted them; (3) the evolutionists' dating of Java Man at half a million years is highly suspect; (4) more modern-looking humans—possibly including Wadjak Man—were living as contemporaries of Java Man; and (5) Java Man was eventually accepted as our evolutionary ancestor in spite of the evidence because he could be interpreted to promote evolution. The historical and scientific questions regarding Java Man are as legitimate today as they were when the fossils were first discovered" {37}.

Human nature, in the case of that missing piece of information for which one has been diligently searching, is tempted to leap across objective reasoning and pounce on something that could possibly be that highly coveted object, regardless of the serious lack of evidence. Darwinian evolutionists are no exception. "Java Man" spurred Dubois onward, past some basic necessary evidence needed to confirm his discovery. In Dubois' mind, this was it! This was all the evidence he needed to believe that here was the final missing link; part ape—part man. Dubois was not alone in his rush to judgment. Later in this chapter we will see it happen again with another more recent discovery in Africa. But first, notice what Lee Strobel and Dr. Jonathan Wells have to say about the problem with "Java Man" and why imagination plays a heavy roll in making their pronouncements.

SYMBOLS OF EVOLUTION LACK SUBSTANCE

LEE STROBEL confides how he was completely taken in by Dubois and the "Java Man" story: "As a youngster beginning to form my opinions about human evolution, I wasn't aware of what I have more recently discovered: that Dubois' shoddy excavation would have disqualified the fossil from consideration by today's standards" {38}.

JONATHAN WELLS EXPLAINS TO STROBEL HOW IMAGINATION TAKES OVER WHEN CONFRONTED WITH SCANTY, UNPROVEN EVIDENCE:

"One of the major problems with paleoanthropology is that compared to all the fossils we have, only a miniscule number are believed to be creature ancestral to humans. ...Often, it just skull fragments or teeth. So this gives a lot of elasticity in reconstructing the specimens to fit evolutionary theory. For example, when *National Geographic* hired four artists to reconstruct a female figure from seven fossil bones found in Kenya, they came up with quite different interpretations. One looked like a modern African-American woman; another like a werewolf; another had a gorilla-like brow; and another had a missing forehead and jaws that looked a bit like a beaked dinosaur" {39}.

Before this chapter is brought to a conclusion, I will list more examples of from-ape-to-man discoveries regarding age dating and anthropological postulations.

In other words, from the perspective of an evolutionist who happens to be an anthropologist, since he or she assumes that living creatures began from non-life to life then advanced through natural selection to more complex life to primate then primate to man in small minute steps, his/her imagination views fossil discoveries as evidence in natural selection's advancement.

SYMBOL #5: PILTDOWN MAN

OH, GIVE ME SOME BONES TO BUILD AN APE-MAN AND MY IMAGINATION WILL MAKE MY DREAMS COME TRUE!

NOTE: According to Merriam-Webster's Collegiate Dictionary, 10th Edition: "**postulate**...a hypothesis advanced as an essential presupposition, condition or premise of a train of reasoning" {40}.

CHAPTER 5

In their book, *The Truth About Human Origins*, Brad Harrub Ph.D. and Bert Thompson Ph.D., explain the history of Piltdown Man and the final results of their research:

"Piltdown was an archaeological site in England where in 1908 and 1912 fossil remains of humans, apes, and other mammals were found. In 1913, at a nearby site, researchers found an ape's jaw with a canine tooth worn down like a human's. And thus another missing link was put forth—one that possessed the skull of a human and the jawbone of an ape. Piltdown was proclaimed genuine by several of the most brilliant British evolutionists of the day—Sir Arthur Smith-Woodward, Sir Arthur Keith, and Grafton Elliot Smith. How did these fake fragments of bone fool the best scientific minds of the time? Perhaps the desire to be part of a great discovery blinded those charged with authenticating it. Of course, the deception did far more than dupe a few evolutionists. ...Museums worldwide proudly displayed copies and photographs of the Piltdown remains. Books and periodicals also spread the news across the globe. ...In 1953, Piltdown Man was exposed as a forgery. The skull was modern and the teeth on the ape's jaw had been filed down and treated bio-chemically to make them appear 'old.' No missing link here" (pp. 89-90) {41}.

SYMBOL #6: NEBRASKA MAN

GIVE ME A TOOTH TO BUILD AN APE-MAN AND MY IMAGINATION!

The evolutionists were still searching. After all, the missing links must be out there somewhere! Darwinists know this just has to be true! Then just a few years after their discovery of Piltdown Man, which as yet, was not known to be a fraud, there was another find. Harrub and Thompson describe what happened:

"The June 24, 1922 *Illustrated London News* presented on its front cover a man and a woman who had been reconstructed from a single tooth found in the state of Nebraska. The artist even incorporated clothing and imaginary surroundings into the drawings of this alleged 'missing link.' When Henry Fairfield Osborn, head of the department of vertebrate paleontology at New York's American Museum of Natural History, received the fossil tooth in February of that year, he would have thought it a gift from the gods—had he believed in any god at all. Marxist in his views, and a prominent member in good standing of the American Civil Liberties Union, he was aware that plans were being made by the ACLU to challenge

SYMBOLS OF EVOLUTION LACK SUBSTANCE

legislation that would forbid the teaching of evolution in American schools. He saw in the tooth precious evidence for the test case, which eventually was held in 1925 at Dayton, Tennessee (the famous Scopes 'Monkey Trial'). The trial, as it turns out, was an arranged affair, but the tooth was not brought in as evidence because dissension occurred among those who knew of its existence. ...A further search was made at Snake Creek (the site of the original discovery), And by 1927 it was concluded (albeit begrudgingly) that the tooth was that of a species of Prosthennops, an extinct genus related to the modern peccary (a wild pig). These facts were not considered generally newsworthy, but did appear in Science (see Gregory, 1927, 66:579). The fourteenth edition of *Encyclopedia Britannica* (1929, 14:767) coyly admitted that a mistake had been made and that the tooth belonged to a 'being of another order'" {42}.

NEANDERTHAL (Neandertal) and CRO-MAGNON MAN

THE POOR STEP-BROTHER ("Neandertal") vs. DAD'S FAVORITE (Cro-Magnon)

For several years, Neanderthal (also known as Neandertal) had been viewed as a more primitive predecessor to what has been considered our modern ancestor, Cro-Magnon. Science has since changed its perspective on that poor old Neandertal Man realizing now that Neandertal (and other fossils considered to be the more modern form of human beings) had been living side by side for many thousands of years by the evolutionary methods of dating. In fact, there was one set of Neandertal fossils that were dated at less than 8,000 years ago by their own dating methods. So, to state it simply, there is so much confusion and speculation at this time that Darwinians are offering up several different speculations as to why Neandertal Man just simply could not be one of us (modern Homo-sapiens).

MARVIN L. LUBENOW, in his book, *Bones of Contention*, writes about the differences of opinion and confusion as to who and what "Neandertal" Man really is:

"The older but still somewhat popular evolutionist view regarding Neandertal could be called the Neandertal phase of human evolution. It saw the Neandertals in the mainstream of the evolutionary process, moving from Homo erectus to an archaic phase of Homo sapiens to Neandertal and on to modern humans. ...A second viewpoint is that the Neandertals were absorbed by more modern Homo populations through gene migration and hybridization. Either of these views means that modern

CHAPTER 5

humans have Neandertal genes in their make-up. Two other views consider the Neandertals as an isolated side branch on the family tree. The main branch of human evolution passed by the Neandertals who ended in a European backwater. One view sees environmental factors bringing about their demise without issue. The alternate scenario, perhaps the more popular one today, holds that the Neandertals were exterminated in one way or another by more modern humans who invaded Europe and the Near East from Africa. In either of these latter views, modern humans would not be the genetic descendants of the Neandertals" {43}.

PERHAPS THE SIZE OF NEANDERTHAL'S BRAIN WOULD PROVE HIS ALLEGED MORE PRIMITIVE AND INFERIOR EVOLUTIONARY DEVELOPMENT.

I have heard and read for several years that one of the determining factors in evolutionary development, especially as it is applied to the more modern humans, such as, the Cro-Magnon Man, is that the larger the size of the skull, the larger the size of the brain capacity. In such cases, the Cro-Magnon Man should have a larger brain capacity than the lowly Neanderthal Man. Notice the comparisons that Lubenow has documented in his research:

"In seeking to establish the concept of human evolution, the evolutionist leans heavily on skull morphology and, to a lesser degree in recent years, on skull size. Both are spurious arguments and prove nothing. Typical of the charts and illustrations used by evolutionists is a display at the American Museum of Natural History in New York City. It is titled 'Increasing Brain Size' and shows an increase in brain sizes as follows:

Increasing Brain Size

Homo sapiens	1450 cc [cubic centimeters]
Neanderthal	1625 cc
Pithecanthropus [Homo erectus]	914 cc
Australopithecinae	650 cc
Gorilla	543 cc
Chimpanzee	400 cc
Gibbon	97 cc

(Bracketed material added for clarity.)

SYMBOLS OF EVOLUTION LACK SUBSTANCE

The obvious question is, What is the purpose of this display? or, What does this display say? The obvious answer, since it is a part of the museum's display on 'The Evolution of Man,' is to show that the hominid brain has enlarged by evolution over time" {44}.

Did you notice something on this chart of "Increasing Brain Size?" Neanderthal Man has a larger brain size—1625 cc—than Homo sapiens—1450 cc. If, by their own chart and standards, Cro-Magnon Man, who is listed in their own classification lists among the species of "Modern humans," is alleged to be more advanced than Neanderthal, why is Cro-Magnon's brain size less than Neanderthal's?

PERHAPS NEANDERTHAL WAS PHYSICALLY INFERIOR TO CRO-MAGNON AND LACKED THE ABILITY TO USE TOOLS.

WRONG AGAIN!

Another important detail about Neanderthals, as Lubenow points out is the fact that they appeared to be extremely muscular with more physical strength than most modern humans:

"The evidence indicates that the Neandertals were people of incredible power and strength—far superior to all but the most avid body builders of today."

"Valerius Geist (University of Calgary) says:

"Neanderthal was far more powerful than modern humans. Whereas archeologists can experimentally duplicate the wear pattern on tools such as were used by people from the Upper Paleolithic (the people that followed Neanderthal...), the wear patterns on Neanderthal's tools cannot be duplicated. We do not have the strength to do it. Neanderthal's skeleton reflects a supremely powerful musculature" {45}.

IT MAY BE, AS MUCH OF THE EVIDENCE SEEMS TO INDICATE, THAT NEANDERTHAL MAN APPEARS TO HAVE A LARGER BRAIN SIZE AND A MORE POWERFUL AND MUSCULAR BODY THAN THE MORE MODERN CRO-MAGNON MAN, PLUS, NEANDERTHAL APPEARS TO HAVE THE ABILITY TO USE TOOLS, AS DID CRO-MAGNON. SO THE ALLEGED

CHAPTER 5

DIFFERENCE HAD TO OCCUR ELSEWHERE. PERHAPS IT OCCURRED SOMEWHERE IN THE DNA?

Still unwilling to accept Neanderthal as a legitimate equal to the other recorded modern humans resulted in the 'Out of Africa' theory in 1987. Lubenow explains:

"The Out of Africa theory on the disappearance of the Neandertals exploded upon the paleontological world in 1987 when three Berkeley biochemists, Rebecca Cann, Mark Stoneking, and Allan Wilson, published a paper in Nature. ...They explored a new way of tracing human origins using tracer DNA from inside the cell called mitochondria (mtDNA). ...The original 1987 study used mtDNA from 136 women from many parts of the world having various racial backgrounds. The analysis led back to a single ancestral mtDNA molecule from a woman living in sub-Saharan Africa about 200,000 years ago. A subsequent and more rigorous 1991 study seemed to confirm and secure the theory" (pp.68, 70) {46}.

As with other attempts to sideline Neanderthal from the mainstream of modern humans, however, the biochemists ran into serious problems. Lubenow continues to explain:

"The computer program was, however, far more complicated than the biochemists realized. They did not know that the result of their single computer run was biased by the order in which the data was entered. Others have determined that with thousands of computer runs and with the data entered in different random orders, an African origin for modern humans is not preferred" {47}.

Lubenow describes how more than one authority seriously disagreed with the results of the mtDNA study. In fact, later, "one of the original researchers' admitted that the "African Eve" theory has been disproved:

"In a letter to Science, Mark Stoneking (one of the original researchers who is now at Pennsylvania State University) acknowledges that African Eve has been invalidated" {48}.

Nevertheless, this was not the end of the mtDNA argument that Neanderthals are not us (modern humans). Some evolutionists continued to tinker with the mtDNA

SYMBOLS OF EVOLUTION LACK SUBSTANCE

theory (more accurately declared a hypothesis). Then in 1997 came what Darwinists considered a more improved theory of mtDNA and Neanderthals, which BRAD HARRUB Ph.D. and BERT THOMPSON Ph.D. examine in detail in their book, *The Truth About Human Origins*, truly an excellent book for investigative research on human origins:

"Creationists accept the 'Neanderthal' species as nothing more than modern man. Evolutionists disagree, based mainly on studies regarding Neanderthal DNA. The July 11, 1997 issue of the journal Cell contained an article by Krings, et al., titled 'Neanderthal DNA sequences and the Origin of Modern Humans' (Krings, et al., 1997). In that article, Dr. Krings and his coworkers explained how they successfully extracted mitochondrial DNA (mtDNA — which resides in the cell's mitochondria or 'energy factories') from the humerus (right arm bone) of the original Neanderthal fossil discovered in 1856" {49}.

The authors then explain the controversies over Neanderthal classifications by evolutionists:

"When the first Neanderthal fossil was discovered, the creature was classified as Homo neanderthalensis, and as such was considered a separate species within the genus Homo. However, when additional evidence became available (in 1964) to suggest that Neanderthals were in fact, humans, Neanderthals were reclassified as Homo sapiens neanderthalensis (i.e., a sub-species of humans), and modern humans were given a sub-species designation as well—Homo sapiens sapiens. Now there is a clamoring among evolutionists—based on mtDNA evidence—to return to the original H. neanderthalensis designation. ...In his 2000 book, *Genes, People, and Languages*, Luigi Cavalli-Sforza, who is professor emeritus of genetics at Stanford University and the director of the International Human Genome Project, commented: 'There is a considerable difference between the mtDNA of this Neandertal and that of practically any modern human'" {50}.

A "considerable difference between" Neanderthal and modern human mtDNA? Dr. Harrub and Dr. Thompson both disagree:

"We beg to differ! The results of mtDNA research **do not** 'show clearly that Neandertal was not our direct ancestor.' A closer examination of the mtDNA

CHAPTER 5

research shows that it is not all it has been cracked up to be. The Krings study compared DNA sequences from **1669** modern humans with **one** Neanderthal. Statistically, this not only is insignificant, but also incorrect. As Lubenow wrote in regard to this mtDNA research: 'Statistics has been used to cloud the relationship between Neandertals and modern humans. It is improper to use statistical "averages" in situations where many entities are being compared with only one entity. In this case, 994 sequences from 1669 humans are compared with one sequence from one Neandertal. Thus there is no Neandertal "average," and the comparison is not valid' (1998, 12 [1]:92). The original study showed that the Neanderthal individual had a minimum of 22 mtDNA substitution differences when compared to modern humans. Yet the mtDNA substitution differences among modern humans range from 1 to 24" {51}.

Furthermore, in 1996, even stronger evidence was discovered that Neanderthals were no different from other modern humans:

"In 1996 however, researchers were forced to reevaluate their long-held views on Neanderthals, due to the discovery of five different types of musical instruments, items of personal ornamentation (similar to our jewelry), and even the first example of a Neanderthal cave painting (see Hublin, et.al,, 1996; 'Neanderthal Noisemaker,' 1996; Folger and Menon, 1997; 'Human Origins,' 1997). Furthermore, almost all anthropologists recognize burial rituals as being not just strictly associated with humans, but as a distinctly religious act as well. That being the case, the strongest evidence to date that the Neanderthals were, in fact, human, is that at four different sites where Neanderthal fossils were found, **Neanderthals and modern humans were buried together!** As Lubenow noted: 'That Neandertals and anatomically modern humans were buried together constitutes strong evidence that they lived together, worked together, intermarried and were accepted as members of the same family, clan, and community. ...If genuine mtDNA was recovered from the fossil from the Neander Valley, the results have been misinterpreted'" (1998, 12(1):89).

Harrub and Thompson's final comments include a quote from archaeologist Randall White:
"As archaeologist Randall White of New York University said of Neanderthals: 'The more this kind of evidence accumulates, the more they look like us' (as quoted in Folger and Menon, 18[1]:33). Yes, they do. And so they should!" {52}.

SYMBOLS OF EVOLUTION LACK SUBSTANCE

Finally, before I summarize, I want to include one last bit of information on Neanderthal and Cro-Magnon. (Note: I've been using Cro-Magnon as representative of the direct ancestors of modern humans that were discovered that were contemporaries of the Neanderthals). This comes from the research efforts of Marvin L. Lubenow concerning age dating and the fossil evidence. You see, Neanderthals were supposed to have died out 30,000 or more years before the arrival of modern humans. Notice what Lubenow has found recorded in the fossils.

THE ESTIMATED AGES OF "NEANDERTAL" FOSSILS COMPARED WITH "CRO-MAGNON" AND OTHER MODERN HUMANS.

On page 67, in his book *Bones of Contention*, Lubenow provides a chart of existing fossils, consisting of a list of [1]: "Fossils more modern than Neandertal"; [2]: "Neandertal fossils (partial list)" [3]: "Fossils more archaic than Neandertal."

In column [1]: "Fossils more modern than Neandertal," he lists 28 fossils; those dated as far back as approximately "200,000 y.a." [years ago] to as recent as "30,000 y.a."
In column [2]: "Neandertal fossils (partial list)," he lists 22 fossils dated from "200.000 y.a." to "30,000 y.a."

In column [3]: "Fossils more archaic than Neandertal," he lists 27 fossils dated from "200,000 y.a." to "30,000 y.a." {53}.

Keep in mind, these methods of fossil dating are suggested by evolutionists and not necessarily by all creationists. Their age-dating methods leave a lot of questions unanswered! Lubenow points out the weakness and inconsistencies in their dating system:

"It is almost universally accepted [by evolutionists] that the Neandertals became extinct—for whatever reason—between 30,000 and 35,000 y.a. ...The reasons for distancing modern humans from the Neandertals are philosophical. Since the Neandertal problem is still unsolved, the evolutionist must keep his options open. If he eventually decides that the best solution is to derive modern humans from a Neandertal stock, he must allow enough time for that to happen. ...However, there is evidence that the Neandertals persisted long after their alleged demise. The

CHAPTER 5

Neandertal skull known as Amud I from upper Galilee, Israel, was found as a burial just below the top of layer BI. If Amud I was buried into layer BI, it follows that he cannot be older than layer BI but could be younger. The radiocarbon date for upper BI is 5,710 y.a. Michael Day (British Museum—Natural History) states: 'These dates are believed to be too "young" as the result of contamination by younger carbon' (30). While it is certainly true that younger carbon compromises a radiocarbon date, this is the standard excuse given whenever a radiocarbon date is too young to fit the system. DAY GIVES NO EVIDENCE THAT YOUNG CARBON WAS PRESENT. It is understood by evolutionists that if a radiocarbon date is too young to fit the evolutionary scenario, that is PROOF ENOUGH that the sample was contaminated, since a 'good' date would unquestionably fit the scheme. …and the Neandertal Banolas mandible, found near Gerona, Spain, gave a radiocarbon date of 17,000 y.a. …Possibilities are given for the too recent date, BUT NO PHYSICAL EVIDENCE IS CITED TO INDICATE THAT THESE POSSIBILITIES ARE VALID" (emphasis added) {54}.

NO MATTER HOW HARD DARWINISTS TRY, OLD NEANDERTHAL APPEARS TO BE JUST ANOTHER ONE OF US "MODERN HUMANS!"

For further information, Marvin L. Lubenow's book, *Bones of Contention*, and Brad Harrub and Bert Thompson's book, *The Truth About Human Origins* provide several pages of valuable information about the bits and pieces of fossil discoveries relating to the origin of humanity.

There is one more symbol of alleged human evolution that needs to be examined, a fossil find so well-publicized that it is still being raved about by evolutionists, although the man who originally discovered the fossils now admits he made some mistakes in his rush to judgment.

SYMBOL #7: AFARENSIS—AL288-1 (ALSO KNOWN AS "LUCY")

Some of you may remember the discovery of "LUCY" about 30 years ago. "Lucy" was supposedly the first evidence of an upright walking "hominid" (a primate, such as an bipedal ape-like creature preceding the human species in natural selection).

SYMBOLS OF EVOLUTION LACK SUBSTANCE

The discovery gained tremendous publicity in the media and was again proclaimed to be the first substantial piece of evidence of evolution from the ape to man, the long sought-after "missing link." The discovery was made by Donald Johanson and Tom Gray in 1978, in Ethiopia. They recovered a lot of bones at the site from what was thought to be the oldest ancestor to present-day man. It turned out to be just another case of mistaken identity.

Dr. Harrub and Dr. Thompson will provide some historical information about "Lucy":

"Donald Johanson's account of the discovery of the creature now known popularly as 'Lucy' reads like a Hollywood script—filled with mystery, excitement, and emotion. ...He tells of a strong, subconscious 'urge' to go with American graduate student Tom Gray to locality 162. ...So, on November 30, 1974, Johanson (who was serving at the time as the director of the Cleveland, Ohio, Museum of Natural History) and Gray loaded up in a Land Rover and headed out to plot an area of Hadar, Ethiopia, known as 'locality 162.' After several hours of surveying...the two decided to head back. ...Johanson suggested they take an alternate route...to survey...a nearby gully. ...Buried in the sandy hillside of the slope was an arm bone—the single bone that eventually led to the unearthing of a skeleton that was nearly **40% complete**. ...It would soon become one of the most famous (and most controversial) fossils of all time, and would shake every limb on the famous hominid family tree, completely upsetting then-current theories about how man came to be bipedal. ...But as additional studies were carried out, it soon became obvious that this 'missing link' was, in fact, 'too good to be true. Dr Johanson named his find Australopithecus afarensis—thus designating it as the southern ape from the Afar depression of northeastern Ethiopia (Johanson et. al.,1978, 28:8). The creature quickly earned the nickname 'Lucy,' after the Beatles song, 'Lucy in the Sky with Diamonds.' ...The fossil, officially designated as AL288-1, consisted of skull fragments, a lower jaw, ribs, an arm bone, a part of a pelvis, a thighbone, and fragments of shinbones. It was said to be an adult, and was dated at 3.5 million years. [Johanson also found at Hadar the remains of some 34 adults and 10 infants, all of which are dated at 3.5 million years.]" {55}.

Yes, "Lucy" promised to be the "missing link" which had been and still is, according to some, the long-awaited first primate that walked on two legs just like modern

CHAPTER 5

humans, highly publicized and touted to be without question what every Darwinist had been hoping for. Harrub and Thompson describe it this way:

"Not only was this fossil find unusually complete, but it also was believed to have been from an animal that walked in an upright fashion, as well as being the oldest human ancestor—the equivalent of a grand slam in baseball" {56}.

However, there were several serious problems with "Lucy" that just didn't add up to being "the oldest human ancestor (3.5 million years)." Marvin L. Lubenow points out that there were other fossil finds that raised doubts about "Lucy" AL288-1 being in existence before modern humans.

[1] THE DISCOVERY OF HUMAN FOOTPRINTS IN TANZANIA

This is significant because it challenges the widely-publicized claim that A. afarensis (AL288-1) was the first upright-walking "human ancestor." Lubenow records the discovery and impact it created:

"Beginning in 1978, associates of Mary Leakey discovered a series of what appear to be human footprint trails at site G, Laetoli, thirty miles south of Olduvai Gorge, in northern Tanzania. The strata above the footprints has been dated at 3.6 m.y.a., while the strata below them has been dated at 3.8 m.y.a. (K-Ar). These footprint trails rank as one of the great fossil discoveries of the twentieth century. Mary Leakey told the story in the April 1979 issue of *National Geographic*. She described the footprints as 'remarkably similar to those of modern man.' Three parallel trails are seen, made by three individuals. ...The trails contain a total of sixty-nine prints extending a length of about thirty yards."

Did the "evolutionist community" change their views about "Lucy" AL288-1 as the "oldest human ancestor"? As Lubenow says, not hardly. He describes their reaction:

"Virtually everyone agrees that they are strikingly like those made by modern humans. In spite of that fact, the evolutionist community has ascribed them to the Lucy-type hominid known as Australopithecus afarensis. ...The specialist who has conducted the most extensive recent study of these footprints is Russell H. Tuttle (University of Chicago). He did so at the invitation of Mary Leakey. The footprint trails at Laetoli appear to have been made by individuals who were barefoot, probably habitually unshod. ...As a part of Tuttle's investigations he observed the Machiguenga Indians in the rugged mountains of Peru, a habitually barefoot people. More than seventy individuals from ages seven to sixty-seven, both male and female, constituted his study. He concludes: 'In sum, the 3.5 million-year-old footprint trails at Laetoli site G resemble those of habitually unshod modern humans.' ...Elsewhere Tuttle writes: 'In discernable features, the Laetoli G prints are indistinguishable from those of habitually barefoot Homo sapiens.'"

Lubenow also noted: "He is especially struck by the similarity of the Laetoli prints to those of the Machiguenga Indains: 'Casts of Laetoli G-1 and of Machiguenga footprints in moist, sandy soil further illustrate the remarkable humanness of Laetoli hominid feet in all detectable morphological features.'" {57}.

Keep in mind that the age dating system applied to these fossils is the method used by scientists who believe in evolutionary-based principles of natural selection. The evidence shows several conflicting age-dating figures which point toward a very doubtful predetermined conclusion that "Lucy" could be the first step, so to speak, from a tree-dwelling chimp-like primate to an upright walking first ancestor primate to modern Homo sapiens, man. When evolutionists have to challenge their own dating method figures (such as the 5,710 y.a. being not old enough for Neanderthal), it points toward just one conclusion: there must be something seriously wrong with their dating system. Lubenow brings out the fact that their own rules of evidence are arbitrary and subjective:

"Interpreting the Laetoli footprints is not a question of scholarship; it is a question of logic and the basic rules of evidence. We know what the human foot looks like. There is no evidence that any other creature, past or present, had a foot exactly like the human foot. We also know what human footprints look like. But we will never know for sure what australopithecine footprints look like because there is no way of associating 'beyond reasonable doubt' those extinct creatures with any fossil footprints we might discover. On the one hand, we have very positive identification: the human foot and the Laetoli footprints. On the other hand, is the total absence of the kind of information needed to make any identification of those prints with australopithecines. ...Were it not for the darkness evolution casts upon the human mind, there would be no question at all as to which category those Laetoli footprints should be assigned" {58}.

CHAPTER 5

[2] IN FACT, IT'S RATHER "HUMERUS"—"THE KANAPOI ELBOW FOSSIL"

This is one of the best cases of evidence that AL288-1 "Lucy" fossils are younger in date, according to their own dating procedures than modern man. It came about with the discovery of the fossil KP 271 (an upper arm bone). Lubenow explains:

"One of the most flagrant cases of wand waving to deflect evidence that could be embarrassing to the idea of human evolution involves a fossil found at Kanapoi, southwest of Lake Rudolf (Turkana) in northern Kenya. This fossil, known as KP 271, is the lower end of an upper arm bone (distal end of the humerus). It was found in 1965 by Bryan Patterson (Harvard University), and is in an excellent state of preservation. The most recent dating of the fossil gives it an age of 4.5 m.y.a. It thus becomes the oldest hominid fossil ever found—older than Lucy and all of the australopithecines. The question is, What is it? To answer the question of identity of KP 271, Patterson and W.W. Howells used the method of computer discriminate analysis. They compared KP 271 with the distal ends of the humeri of a modern human, a chimpanzee, and the only other fossil they had at the time: Australopithecus (Paranthropus) robustus, from Kromdraai, South Africa. Patterson and Howells published the results of their study in Science, 7 April 1967. 'In these diagnostic measurements Kanapoi Hominid 1 [the original name given to the fossil] is strikingly close to the means of the human sample.' Further computer analysis of many more measurements revealed even more dramatically the similarity of KP 271 to modern humans. Henry M. McHenry (University of California, Davis) wrote: 'The results show that the Kanapoi specimen, which is 4 to 4.5 million years old, is indistinguishable from modern Homo sapiens'" {60}.
"Modern Homo sapiens"—That's us! According to their own system of age determination, modern humans have been here for 4.5 million years! How then could "Lucy" have been the first upright, walking 'missing link' to modern man, if there is evidence that modern human beings existed before "Lucy"? There is more.

[3] "LUCY" LACKED AN "EVOLVED LARGER BRAIN"

According to Harrub and Thompson: "Prior to her discovery, evolutionists had assumed that these ape-like species had evolved larger brains, which allowed them to crawl down out of the trees and begin foraging for food on the ground. ...Lucy took this nice, neat little story and flipped it upside down. Her brain case was not enlarged. In fact, from all appearances, it was comparable in size to the common chimpanzee" {61}.

[4] "LUCY'S" PELVIS: "TOO NARROW" FOR " BIRTH PROCESS"

With further examination some scientists concluded that Lucy AL288-1 would not be able to give birth because of a narrow pelvis. Dr. Harrub and Dr. Thompson comment on the problem: "The pelvis was just too narrow to accommodate an australopithecine fetus. Hausler and Schmid noted that Lucy's pelvis was ridgeless and heart shaped—which means that "she was more likely a 'he.'" They noted:

"A female of the same species as AL288-1 would have had a pelvis with a larger sagittal diameter and a less protruding sacral promontorium. ...Overall, the broader pelvis and the more laterally oriented iliac blades of AL288-1 would produce more favourable insertion sites for the climbing muscles in more heavily built males."

Are all natural selection advocates on board with Harrub, Thompson, Hausler, and Schmid? Of course, they're not. However, as the evidence continued to mount, Johanson himself began to realize that his excitement of the possibility that he appeared to have found the ape-to-man missing link, was beginning to fade. He slowly changed his view.

[5] "LUCY'S LOCKING" WRIST POINTS TO A "KNUCKLE-WALKING" APE
Johanson's jump to preconceived conclusion, of discovering the first ape-to-man, was laid to rest by continued investigation. The most telling blow of all appears to be the fact that Lucy had a "wrist-locking type joint." Why is this such a critical piece of evidence? Harrub and Thompson explain:

"But what do Lucy's arms and legs tell us in regard to her locomotion? If she were a biped, surely her upper and lower extremities would point toward an upright stance. After all, the bone that led to Johanson's discovery of Lucy was that of an arm. Yet the bony framework that composes Lucy's wrist may be the most telling factor of all. ...Richmond and Strait discovered that knuckle-walking apes have a mechanism that locks the wrist into place in order to stabilize this joint. In their report, they noted: "Here we present evidence that fossils attributed to Australopithecus anamensis (KNM-ER-20419) and A. afarensis (AL288-1) retain

CHAPTER 5

specialized wrist morphology associated with knuckle-walking" (2000, 404:382, parenthetical item in orig.). ...Moreover, additional evidence has come to light which suggests that Lucy is little more than a chimpanzee. Johanson and his coworkers admitted in an article in the March 31, 1994 issue of Nature that Lucy possessed chimp-proportioned arm bones (see Kimbel, et. al., 1994) and that her alleged descendants (e.g., A. africanus and H. habilis) had ape-like limb proportions as well—which is a clear indication that she did not evolve into something 'more human'" {63}.

All of this, plus the fact that Australopithecines, (which includes A. afarensis-Lucy) had different ear canal structures from modern man, caused Dr. Harrub and Dr. Thompson to conclude: "All of these characteristics led inevitably to the conclusion that LUCY WAS SIMPLY A CHIMP-LIKE CREATURE. You might be asking yourself why this charade has been allowed to go on this long. The answer...can be found in Johanson's own words: **'I was trying to jam evidence of dates into a pattern that would support conclusions about fossils which, on closer inspection, the fossils themselves would not sustain** (Johanson and Edey, 1981, pp. 257, 258). He went on to admit: 'It is hard for me now to admit how tangled in that thicket I was. But the insidious thing about bias is that it does make one deaf to the cries of other evidence' (p. 277). ...Finally, in the March 1996 issue of *National Geographic*, Donald Johanson himself admitted: 'Lucy has recently been dethroned' (189[3]:117). His (and Lucy's) fifteen minutes of fame are history" (emphasis added) {64}.

SYMBOL #8: THE MILLER EXPERIMENT

If you are not familiar with the Miller Experiment back in the 1950's, allow me to explain that this was a case where a scientist named Stanley Miller received a lot of publicity on an experiment about how life had been created in a test tube. *Readers Digest* published a rather detailed article about what Miller had accomplished and what was not accomplished. LEE STROBEL, in his book, *The Case for a Creator*, gives some background on it and how the Miller Experiment had impressed him as a high school student:

"This was the most powerful picture of all—the laboratory apparatus that Stanley Miller, then a graduate student at the University of Chicago, used in 1953 to

SYMBOLS OF EVOLUTION LACK SUBSTANCE

artificially produce the building blocks of life. By reproducing the atmosphere of the primitive earth and then shooting electric sparks through it to simulate lightning, Miller managed to produce a red goo containing amino acids. The moment I first learned of Miller's success, my mind flashed to the logical implication: if the origin of life can be explained solely through natural processes, then God was out of a job!" {65}.

However, like the other Darwinian natural selection Symbols ("sacred relics") that have been investigated in detail, the Miller Experiment has serious problems. First of all, after I had finished reading the *Reader's Digest* article on Miller's discoveries I realized that what Miller had done was a perfect example of how it requires intelligent, detailed planning to have the right substances, the right power source, and perfect timing to produce these cell-like structures—it was not a chance accidental happening! Miller himself had stated that he had not actually created life, because he couldn't produce something else that was needed. Strobel's interview with Dr. Jonathan Wells began with this question:

"'What's the best scientific assessment today?' I asked Wells. 'Did Miller use the correct atmosphere or not?'

"'Well, nobody knows for sure what the early atmosphere was like, but the consensus is that the atmosphere was not at all like the one Miller used. ...Miller chose a hydrogen-rich mixture of methane, ammonia, and water vapor, which was consistent with what many scientists thought back then. But scientists don't believe that anymore. ...By the mid-1970's, Belgian biochemist Marcel Florkin was declaring that the concept behind Miller's theory of the early atmosphere "has been abandoned." Two of the leading origin-of-life researchers, Klaus Dose and Sidney Fox, confirmed that Miller had used the wrong gas mixture. And Science magazine said in 1995 that experts now dismiss Miller's experiment because "the early atmosphere looked nothing like the Miller-Urey simulation"'" {66}.

Strobel asked Dr. Wells:

"'What's the current thinking of scientists concerning the gas content of the early earth?'

CHAPTER 5

[Wells replied]: 'The best hypothesis now is that there was very little hydrogen in the atmosphere because it would have escaped into space. Instead, the atmosphere probably consisted of carbon dioxide, nitrogen and water vapor,' Wells said. 'So my gripe is that textbooks still present the Miller experiment as though it reflected the earth's early environment, when most geochemists since the 1960's would say it was totally unlike Miller's.'

Strobel then asked Dr. Wells:
"'What happens if you replay the experiment using an accurate atmosphere?'
[Wells replied]: 'I'll tell you this: you do not get amino acids, that's for sure. ... Some textbooks fudge by saying, well, even if you use a realistic atmosphere, you still get organic molecules, as if that solves the problem.'
"'Organic molecules?' I said. ...'But couldn't those be precursors to life?'
"Wells recoiled. 'That's what they sound like, but do you know what they are? Formaldehyde! Cyanide! ...They may be organic molecules, but in my lab at Berkeley you couldn't even have a capped bottle of formaldehyde in the room, because the stuff is so toxic. You open the bottle and it fries proteins all over the place, just from the fumes. It kills embryos'" {67}.

Dr. Wells summed it up clearly in the interview by stating emphatically: "The problem is you can't make a living cell," he said. "There's not even any point in

trying. It would be like a physicist doing an experiment to see if he can get a rock to fall upwards all the way to the moon. No biologist in his right mind would think you can take a test tube with those molecules and turn them into a living cell" {68}.

Jonathan Wells is certainly not alone in his conclusion. In the book, *That Their Words May Be Used Against Them*, are lists compiled by Henry M. Morris in 1997, quotes from several evolutionists who have changed some of their previous views about spontaneous generation (life from non-life). They include:

DOSE, PROFESSOR DR. KLAUS, 'The origin of Life; More Questions than Answers,' *Interdisciplinary Science Reviews*, vol. 13, no.4 (1988), pp. 348-356.

NOTE: Jonathan Wells has a Ph.D. in "molecular and cell biology from Berkeley" (Lee Strobel, *The Case for a Creator*, p. 34).

SYMBOLS OF EVOLUTION LACK SUBSTANCE

"Considerable disagreements between scientists have arisen about detailed evolutionary steps. The problem is that the principle evolutionary processes from prebiotic molecules to progenotes **have not been proven by experimentation** and that the environmental conditions under which these processes occurred are not known. Moreover, we do not actually know where the genetic information of all living cells originates, how the first replicable polynucleotides (nucleic acids) evolved, **or how the extremely complex structure-function relationships in modern cells came into existence**" (p. 348 emphasis added) {69}.

HOYLE, SIR FRED and CHANDRA WICKRAMASINGHE, *Evolution from Space* (New York: Simon & Schuster, 1984).

"The likelihood of the spontaneous formation of life from inanimate matter is one to a number with 40,000 noughts after it. ....It is big enough to bury Darwin and the whole theory of evolution. There was no primeval soup, neither on this planet nor on any other, and if the beginnings of life were not random, they must therefore have been **the product of purposeful intelligence**" (p. 148 emphasis added).

"Hoyle, Sir Fred, and Chandra Wickramasinghe, 'Where Microbes Boldly Went,' *New Scientist*, vol. 91, (August 13, 1991), pp. 412-415.

"Precious little in the way of biochemical evolution could have happened on the Earth. It is easy to show that the two thousand or so enzymes that span the whole of life could not have evolved on the Earth. If one counts the number of trial assemblies of amino acids that are needed to give rise to the enzymes, the probability of their discovery by random shufflings turns out to be less than 1 in 1040,000" {70}.

Hoyle and Wickramasinghe estimated the mathematical odds of the spontaneous generation of life from non-life "IS ONE TO A NUMBER WITH 40,000 NOUGHTS AFTER IT. ...IT IS BIG ENOUGH TO BURY DARWIN AND THE WHOLE THEORY OF EVOLUTION" (emphasis added). But, there is another reason why the evolution of life from non-life did not happen as evolutionists have postulated. It happens to be a basic scientific law, the Law of Biogenesis.

NOTE: In 1988, when Dr. Dose made these comments he was "Director, Institute for Biochemistry, Johannes Gutenberg University, West Germany."

CHAPTER 5

The Law Of Biogenesis

To my knowledge, there are few biologists who would openly deny the Law of Biogenesis, which has been consistently demonstrated time after time without fail. It has been a well-known fact of Science for over 150 years. To explain the law's impact on biological science is a microbiologist who may have the clearest explanation of the Law of Biogenesis and its history. BERT THOMPSON holds as earned Ph.D. in microbiology from Texas A&M University and is a former professor in the College of Veterinary Medicine at Texas A&M. He is the former editor of *Reason & Revelation*, a Christian evidences journal published by Apologetics Press. In his book, *The Scientific Case for Creation*, he explains the significance of the Law of Biogenesis and the effect it has on the hypothesis of spontaneous generation (which is the often repeated myth that life began by accident from non-living material):

"In the field of biology, one of the most commonly accepted and widely used laws of science is the Law of Biogenesis. This law was set forth many years ago to dictate what both theory and experimental evidence showed to be true among living organisms—that life comes only from preceding life of its own type or kind" {71}.

"Experiments that ultimately formed the basis of this law were carried out first by such men as Francesco Redi (1688) and Lazzaro Spallanzani (1799) in Italy, Louis Pasteur (1860) in France, and Rudolph Virchow (1858) in Germany. It was Virchow who documented that cells do not rise from amorphous matter, but instead come only from preexisting cells" {72}.

It is a well-documented fact established through repeated experiments that all living things (including living cells) come from preexisting life. Thompson continues to explain what was taking place through the scientific community after Virchow and Pasteur's work was completed:

"Through the years countless thousands of scientists in various disciplines have established the Law of Biogenesis as just that—a scientific law stating that life comes only from preexisting life. Interestingly, the Law of Biogenesis was established firmly in science long before the contrivance of modern evolutionary theories" {73}.

SYMBOLS OF EVOLUTION LACK SUBSTANCE

HISTORICALLY SPEAKING, one critical point which must be kept in mind is the fact that the evidence for the Law of Biogenesis was determined during the same period of history that Charles Darwin's theory of natural selection emerged. In 1859, Charles Darwin published his book *The Origin of Species*. Virchow, in 1858, and Pasteur, in 1860, had completed their well-documented experiments. It was but five years later that Louis Pasteur publicly announced that the possibility of spontaneous generation (life from non-life) was not scientifically possible. In Bert Thompson's book, *The History of Evolutionary Thought*, he records a statement made by Louis Pasteur:

"In his triumphal lecture at the Sorbonne in 1864, Pasteur said, 'Never will the doctrine of spontaneous generation recover from the mortal blow struck by this simple experiment. There is the question of so-called spontaneous generation. Can matter organize itself? In other words, are there beings that can come into the world without parents, without ancestors? ...No, today there is no circumstance known under which one could affirm that microscopial beings have come into the world without germs, without parents resembling themselves'" (p. 164) {74}.

Keep in mind, as I have stated before, I am not a scientist. But Jonathan Wells, Klaus Dose, Sir Fred Hoyle, Chandra Wickramasinghe, Bert Thompson, Rudolph Virchow, and Louis Pasteur are scientists. And as they have stated, accidental life from non-life has been scientifically proven to be impossible according to the Law of Biogenesis.

If evolution through spontaneous generation cannot start the engine of life for natural selection then the mechanism of chance comes to a direct halt. The answer to the beginning of life has to be an Intelligent Creator! This is exactly what that ancient book, the Bible has been telling us all along.

"Then God said, 'Let the earth bring forth living creatures after their kind: cattle and creeping things and beasts of the earth after their kind;' and it was so. And God made the beasts of the earth after their kind, and the cattle after their kind, and every thing that creeps on the ground after its kind; and God saw that it was good" (Genesis 1:24-25 NASB).

Chapter 6

LAWS OF PROBABILITY
TRUTH IN SCIENCE POINTS TO GOD

CHAPTER 6

A lot of you may remember the television show on Friday nights called "Numbers." It was a series about two brothers. One was an FBI agent, the other a mathematics professor. The professor used mathematical calculations to determine the probabilities of the criminal being in a certain location or committing another crime in a specific place. He used math to help his brother, the FBI agent, solve crimes. It was fascinating to watch him work the math and apply it to the crime.

The use of numbers is so commonplace it is part of everyday life. Everything we do involves us in some way with basic arithmetic. In fact, there is a specialty among professionals in the insurance industry called Actuary. In the profession it is known as Actuarial Science.

People involved in actuarial science use mathematics to analyze various risks so they can determine the probability among people, male or female, of death, auto accidents, future investments, etc., for annuity premiums, retirement programs, cash reserves and dividends.

Mathematical calculations can help determine whether life could have accidentally evolved through environmental changes and mutations or whether our being here involved someone intelligent enough to have created us.

Mathematical Probability

The Laws of Probability are a critical part of science. For example, what are the chances that life could develop from some form of non-life (possibility from atmospheric gases or crystals, etc.). DR. BERT THOMPSON, in his book, *The Scientific Case for Creation*, gives a brief history of how the "laws of probability" became an essential part of determining the reality of an Intelligent Creator and the devastating impact on the theory of accidental, natural selection:

"Over the years, investigators have elucidated successfully what today are known as the 'laws of probability.' Building upon the work of such men as Blaise Pascal, the famous French mathematician and scientist, others forged the principles that are employed today on a daily basis in almost every scientific discipline. George

SYMBOLS OF EVOLUTION LACK SUBSTANCE

Gamow was one such individual (1961). Emile Borel was another. Dr. Borel, one of the world's foremost experts on mathematical probability, formulated what scientists and mathematicians alike refer to as the basic 'law of probability"{1}.

The first question, then, is: How would mathematical probability help to determine whether life began by chance—accidental happening—of non-living matter becoming living matter and then continuing to evolve into more complex forms of life?

The next question is: If mathematically, life is too complex to have started by chance, how would mathematical probability demonstrate the reality of an Intelligent Creator (God)?

Michael J. Behe and "The Biochemical Challenge To Evolution"

Michael Behe, in his book, *Darwin's Black Box*, published in 1996, stirred up considerable controversy and anxiety among atheists and especially among Darwin's disciples in biology. Behe challenges the concept that complex life forms can be "formed by numerous, successive, slight modifications." His research has pointed out that even the more simple forms of life, such as bacteria, have extremely complex systems by which they move about, such as the "bacterial flagellum." Behe explains Darwin's own admission that his theory would prove to be false if complicated forms of life could not develop by slow, unplanned minute changes:

"Darwin knew that his theory of gradual evolution by natural selection carried a heavy burden: 'If it could be demonstrated that any complex organ existed which could not possibly have been formed by numerous, successive, slight modifications, my theory would absolutely breakdown.' It is safe to say that most of the scientific skepticism about Darwinism in the past century has centered on this requirement. ...What type of biological system could not be formed by 'numerous, successive, slight modifications'? Well, for starters, a system that is irreducibly complex. By irreducibly complex I mean a single system composed of several well-matched, interacting parts that contribute to the basic function, wherein the removal of any one of the parts causes the system to effectively cease functioning" {2}.

CHAPTER 6

Behe, in his book, makes use of a powerful example, the "BACTERIAL FLAGELLUM."

"Some bacteria boast a marvelous swimming device, the flagellum, which has no counterpart in more complex cells. In 1973 it was discovered that some bacteria swim by rotating their flagella. So the bacterial flagellum acts as a rotary propeller—in contrast to the cilium, which acts more like an oar" {3}.

Just how complex are bacterial flagellum? Far more than one might imagine.

WILLIAM A. DEMBSKI, in his book, *Intelligent Design*, explains the huge irreducibly complex hurdle for Darwin's mechanism of natural selection:

"Michael Behe's irreducibly complex biochemical systems are a case in point. ... irreducibly complex biochemical systems require numerous components specifically adapted to each other and each necessary for function. Such systems are both complex and specified, and therefore exhibit CSI. [NOTE: CSI means "Complex Specified Information," p. 127, Dembski, *Intelligent Design*]. Consider now an organism that possesses an irreducibly complex biochemical system—for definiteness let's say it is a bacterial flagellum. ...On a Darwinian view that organism evolved via selection and inheritance with modification from an organism without a flagellum. The flagellum is a complex protein machine requiring over forty proteins each necessary for function. For the Darwinian mechanism to produce the flagellum, chance modifications have to generate those various proteins and then selection must preserve them" {4}.

Dembski continues to explain why "chance modifications" are a serious drawback to bacteria acquiring a flagellum:

"But how is selection to accomplish this? Selection is nonteleological, so it cannot cumulate proteins, holding them in reserve until with the passing of many generations they're finally available to form a complete flagellum. ...No, selection can only build on partial function, gradually improving function that already exists. But a flagellum without its full complement of protein parts doesn't function at all. Consequently if selection and inheritance with modification are going to produce the flagellum, they have to do it in one generation" {5}.

SYMBOLS OF EVOLUTION LACK SUBSTANCE

According to the wishful thinking of the evolutionist who claims that all of this is possible, how do simple bacteria hang around these supposed millions of years waiting to develop some form of locomotion to reach their food supplies? To see the impossibility of this, one need only look at the math. Dembski lays it all out, pointing to the amount of "Complex Specified Information" (CSI) needed to develop this particular bacteria flagellum:

"The CSI of a flagellum far exceeds 500 bits. What's more, selection, if operating for only one generation, merely kills off organisms that lack some feature (in this case the flagellum). ...It follows that inheritance with modification has to produce a flagellum in a single generation. But this is infeasible" {6}.

Why is producing a flagellum in a single generation by chance "infeasible"? Because of the huge amount of complex information needed, the Law of Probability points out that it cannot be done! There is such a thing in mathematical probability as being "probability bound." Simply put, any event that is going to happen by chance—accidental modifications, such as flagellum—have no chance at all of happening if the amount of information and steps necessary to complete the transformation are beyond any mathematical chance of completion!

William A. Dembski, Ph.D. in mathematics, explains why:

"...A probability bound of 10-150 translates to 500 bits of information. Accordingly, specified information of complexity greater than 500 bits cannot reasonably be attributed to chance" {7}.

The "complex specified information" necessary, according to Dr. Dembski, that is needed for a bacterial flagellum to exist and provide a means of locomotion for this species of bacteria is a whole lot more than 500 bits of information. It is beyond any chance for natural selection to have accomplished this through tiny modifications, no matter how many billions of years they estimate for the age of the earth!

BERT THOMPSON, Ph.D., a microbiologist and former professor of veterinary medicine, makes it clear the effect that the laws of probability have on life's beginning:

CHAPTER 6

"There are two important issues that must be addressed in this section on statistical probability. The first is whether or not—according to accepted use of the laws of probability—the origin of life via evolutionary mechanisms is **statistically probable** in the first place. The second is whether or not such scenarios are logically possible. It is important to recognize that any event that is **logically impossible** is, by definition, probabilistically impossible on the face of it" {8}.

In other words, the Laws of Probability clearly point out whether life's beginning is "statistically" possible and "logically" possible by a chance, evolutionary mechanism (spontaneous generation). If not, then life had to begin by an Intelligent Creator!

In the last chapter, Sir Fred Hoyle and Chandra Wickramasinghe clearly state:

"The likelihood of the spontaneous formation of life from inanimate matter is one to a number with 40,000 noughts after it [NOTE: noughts are zeros]. ...It is big enough to bury Darwin and the whole theory of evolution. There was no primeval soup, neither on this planet nor on any other, and if the beginnings of life were not random, they must therefore have been the product of purposeful intelligence" (p. 148) {9}.

In his book, Dr. Thompson includes estimates from distinguished scientists such as **DR. HAROLD MOROWITZ**: "For example, Dr. Morowitz himself estimated that the probability for the chance formation of the smallest, simplest form of living organism known is one chance in $1 \times 10^{340,000,000}$ [that is, one chance out of ten followed by 340 million zeroes]" (1968, p.99) {10}.

STEPHEN C. MEYER, Ph.D., a distinguished scientist who received his Ph.D. in "the philosophy of science" from the University of Cambridge, wrote a book titled, *Signature in the Cell*, regarding: "the evidence for *Intelligent Design*." In his book, he has recorded the work of the "Wistar Institute" which began: "in Philadelphia in 1966. The conference was titled, 'Mathematical Challenges to Neo-Darwinism' and [was] ...chaired by Sir Peter Medawar, a Nobel laureate from England. ... Though the skeptics mainly expressed doubt about the role of random mutations in biological evolution, the questions they raised had equally important implications for assessing the role of chance in chemical evolutionary theories about the first life" (p. 204) {11}.

SYMBOLS OF EVOLUTION LACK SUBSTANCE

During their conference, several questions were raised which they were not able to answer concerning amino acids sequences:

"How rare, or common, are the functional sequences of amino acids among all the possible sequences of amino acids in a chain of any given length? In the late 1980's…studies were conducted in the laboratory of MIT biochemist Robert Sauer in order to investigate this question. …The results of their experiments could help determine the probability that a functional protein would arise by chance from a prebiotic soup. So what did they find? …The probability of achieving a functional sequence of amino acids in several known (roughly 100 amino acid) proteins at random is still 'exceedingly small,' about 1 chance in 1063 (to put this in perspective, there are 1065 atoms in our galaxy)" (p. 208) {12}.

A scientist by the name of Douglas Axe, Ph.D., had published, between 1996 and 2004, "a series of papers in the *Journal of Molecular Biology, Biochemistry*, and the *Proceedings of the National Academy of Sciences*. Dr. Meyer explains what Dr. Axe had accomplished in his work up to 2004:

"The results of a paper he published in 2004 were particularly telling. Axe performed a mutagenesis experiment using his refined method on a functionally significant 150-amino-acid section of a protein called betalactamase, an enzyme that confers antibiotic resistance upon bacteria…(a) the number of 150-amino-acid sequences that can perform that particular function to (b) the whole set of possible amino-acid sequences of this length. Axe estimated this ratio to be 1 to 1077" (p.210) {13}.

"In June 2007, Axe had a chance to present his findings at a symposium commemorating the publication of the proceedings from the original Wistar symposium forty years earlier. In attendance at this symposium in Boston was retired MIT engineering professor Murray Eden. …Eden had been one of the original conveners of the Wistar conference and was the one who had most forcefully explained the combinatorial problem facing neo-Darwinism. …Axe's experimental work had now confirmed Eden's initial intuition: the odd are prohibitively stacked against a random process producing functional proteins. Functional proteins are exceedingly rare among all the possible combinations of amino acids. Axe's improved estimate…has now made it possible to calculate the probability that a 150-amino-acid compound assembled by random interactions in a prebiotic soup

CHAPTER 6

would be a functional protein. ...The odds of getting even one functional protein of modest length (150 amino acids) by chance from a prebiotic soup is no better than 1 chance in 10_{164}." (pp. 211-212) {14}.

"The odds of getting even one functional protein of modest length (150 amino acids) by chance from a prebiotic soup is no better than 1 chance in 10_{164}." William A. Dembski's mathematical calculations indicate that when you reach 10_{150}, your chances are "probability bound." In other words, it's beyond any chance of happening!

"A probability bound of 10_{150} translates to 500 bits of information. Accordingly, specified information of complexity greater than 500 bits cannot reasonably be attributed to chance" (*Intelligent Design*, p.166) {15}.

BERT THOMPSON, Ph.D., in his book, *The Scientific Case for Creation*, gives some statistics from the late CARL SAGAN:

"The late Carl Sagan estimated that the chance of life evolving on any given single planet, like the earth, is one chance in $1 \times 10_{2,000,000,000}$ [that is one chance out of 1 followed by 2 billion zeroes] (1973, p.46). This figure is so large that it would take 6,000 books of 300 pages each just to write the number!" {16}.

The enormous size of these mathematical estimates for the probability of life, or the gigantic number of a chance incident that would need to have occurred just to produce a flagellum on a species of bacteria by natural selection mechanisms is beyond any chance of happening. One doesn't need a Ph.D. in Mathematical Probability to see that it is much more reasonable to believe that a super-intelligent, designing architect who the Bible refers to as "God" could have produced the intricate, complex kinds of living creatures which we observe all around us. Thompson emphasizes the fact that it is more "logical" to believe that life originated through an Intelligent Creator:

"Having addressed whether the mechanistic origin of life is **statistically possible**, let us now examine whether or not it is **logically possible**. Evolutionists are fond of churning out the gargantuan numbers...and then asserting rather matter-of-factly that 'anything can happen, given enough time.' ...However, what these same evolutionists forget is that logically such scenarios not only are improbable but impossible" {17}.

SYMBOLS OF EVOLUTION LACK SUBSTANCE

Thompson brings us back to the serious questions raised in the Wistar Institute symposium in Philadelphia in 1967, especially that raised by MURRAY EDEN concerning the question about "random, chance processes" of evolution:

"In an impressive scientific symposium held at the Wistar Institute in Philadelphia, mathematician Murray Eden addressed the idea that somehow random, chance processes can account for the ultimate successes of evolution. He said: 'It is our contention that if "random" is given serious and crucial interpretation from a probabilistic point of view, the randomness postulate is highly implausible and that an adequate scientific theory of evolution must await the elucidation of new natural laws—physical, physico-chemical and biological' (1967, p.109)" {18}.

"It is our contention that if, 'random' is given serious and crucial interpretation from a probabilistic point of view, the randomness postulate is highly implausible" (Murray Eden).

SIR FRED HOYLE and CHANDRA WICKRAMASINGHE summed it up this way in 1984:

"No matter how large the environment one considers, life cannot have had a random beginning. Troops of monkeys thundering away at random on typewriters could not produce the works of Shakespeare, for the practical reason that the whole observable universe is not large enough to contain the necessary monkey hordes, the necessary typewriters, and certainly not the waste paper baskets required for the deposition of wrong attempts. The same is true for living material. The likelihood of the spontaneous formation of life from inanimate matter is one to a number with 40,000 noughts after it. ...It is big enough to bury Darwin and the whole theory of evolution. There was no primeval soup, neither on this planet nor on any other, and if the beginnings of life were not random, they must therefore have been the product of purposeful intelligence" (p.148) {19}.

DR. HENRY M. MORRIS, in his book, *Scientific Creationism*, comments on the extremely complex "DNA Molecule" beginning with a quote from FRANK B. SAULISBURY, "who is himself an evolutionary biologist":

CHAPTER 6

"A medium protein might include about 300 amino acids. The DNA gene controlling this would have about 1,000 nucleotides in its chain. Since there are four kinds of nucleotides in a DNA chain, one consisting of 1,000 links could exist in 4^{1000} different forms. Using a little algebra (logarithms) we can see that $4^{1000}=10^{600}$. Ten multiplied by itself 600 times gives the figure 1 followed by 600 zeros! This number is completely beyond our comprehension. It seems beyond all question that such complex systems as the DNA molecule could never arise by chance, no matter how big the universe nor how long is time. The creation model faces this fact realistically and postulates a great Creator, by whom came life" (Henry M. Morris) {20}.

THE LAW OF PROBABILITY CLEARLY POINTS TO THE REALITY OF GOD

"For since the creation of the world His invisible attributes, His eternal power and divine nature, have been clearly seen, being understood through what has been made, so that they are without excuse" (Romans 1:20 NASB).

In Summary

REMEMBER, in the search for truth, I began by opening your eyes to scientific principles that have been demonstrated through countless experiments to be declared Laws of Science.

(1) THE SECOND LAW OF THERMODYNAMICS, (also known as Entropy), has demonstrated the fact that everything in the Universe, including the Sun, from which the earth draws its energy, is wearing out, running down, and losing its useful energy. This is important for two reasons.

FIRST, it indicates the Bible is correct when the God-inspired writer of Psalm 102:25-26 wrote over 2,000 years ago that the earth is wearing out:

"In the beginning you laid the foundations of the earth, and the heavens are the work of your hands. They will perish, but you remain; they will all wear out like a garment. Like clothing you will change them and they will be discarded" (Psalm 102:25-26).

SYMBOLS OF EVOLUTION LACK SUBSTANCE

SECOND, the Entropy Law establishes the fact that if the Universe is wearing out it must have had a beginning, and this is what the inspired writer of Genesis wrote in the first chapter of the Bible over 3,000 years ago:

"In the beginning God created the heavens and the earth" (Genesis 1:1).

(2) THE LAW OF CAUSE AND EFFECT (also known as Causality) has established the fact that every material effect must have a preceding, sufficient cause. For example, it is obvious that the Cliff Palace in Mesa Verde, Colorado, could not have been caused by accidental natural causes or simply popped into existence without any cause at all. It is also obvious that the complex, intricate structures, built out of rock, placed in minute detail, had to be the result of purposeful, intelligent planning and design by intelligent minds.

Michael Behe, gives a good example in William A. Dembski's book, *Intelligent Design*, using scrabble letters:

"If we turned a corner and saw a couple of scrabble letters on a table that spelled AN, we would not, just on that basis, be able to decide if they were purposely arranged. Even though they spelled a word, the probability of getting a short word by chance is not prohibitive. On the other hand, the probability of seeing some particular long sequence of Scrabble letters, such as, NDEIRUABFDMOJHRINKE, is quite small. ...Nonetheless, if we saw that sequence lined up on a table, we would think little of it because it is not specified. ...But if we saw a sequence of letters that read, say, METHINKSITISLIKEAWEASEL, we would easily conclude that the letters were intentionally arranged that way. The sequence of letters is not only highly improbable, but it also matches an intelligible English sentence. It is a product of intelligent design" (p.10, Foreword) {21}.

NOTE: Michael Behe doesn't reject natural selection completely. In his book, *Darwin's Black Box*, he made this comment: "Further, I find the idea of common descent (that all organisms share a common ancestor) fairly convincing, and have no particular reason to doubt it. ...Although Darwin's mechanism—natural selection working on variation—might explain many things, however, I do not believe it explains molecular life" (p.5) {22}.

CHAPTER 6

Dr. Bert Thompson stated that: "Everything that exists can be classified as either MATTER or MIND. There is no third alternative" (Chapter 4, end note #14).

Dr. Robert Jastrow stated that: "The Universe is the totality of all matter, animate and inanimate, throughout space and time" (Chapter 4, end note #14).

The Second Law of Thermodynamics clearly states that MATTER is not eternal. It had a beginning. Therefore, MATTER is an EFFECT not a cause. It is impossible for matter (the Universe) to have created itself. That would be something from nothing, which is both scientifically and philosophically impossible. Thus, it must by necessity infer that the only preceding sufficient cause would have to be a MIND sufficiently intelligent to cause such an effect as the Universe and a MIND that would have been in existence before the Universe began.

Atheistic Darwinists have insisted that the mind is simply a form of organized physical matter (the brain), and certainly not some form of a spiritual inner consciousness. It shook their materialistic foundation to the core, when scientists, such as Wilder Penfield, Sir Charles Sherrington, Sir Karl Popper, and Sir John Eccles declared that through scientific demonstrations they discovered that, as Norman Cousins stated after his discussions with Dr. John Eccles: "Nor was Sir John Eccles claiming too much when **he insisted that the action of nonmaterial mind on material brain has not been merely postulated but scientifically demonstrated**" (Chapter 4, end note #27).

It was Sir John Eccles' firm belief that there has to be a divine MIND that brought into focus the creation of the human brain and spirit in words that this author finds it hard to ignore:

"**We come to exist through a divine act.** That divine guidance is a theme throughout our life; at our death the brain goes, but that divine guidance and love continues. Each of us is a unique, conscious being, a divine creation. **It is the religious view. It is the only view consistent with all the evidence**" (Chapter 4, end note #28).

"And God created man in His own image, in the image of God He created Him; male and female He created them" (Genesis 1:27 NASB).

SYMBOLS OF EVOLUTION LACK SUBSTANCE

"God is spirit, and those who worship Him must worship in spirit and truth" (John 4:24 NASB).

The Law of Cause and Effect points toward a preceding, capable, uncaused First Cause. The only thing that exists outside of matter is Mind. Therefore, it would have to be a preceding, uncaused, intangible, super intelligent, Eternal Mind. The only Mind that is qualified to create such a complex Universe and humanity is God, who is Spirit. This is what the Bible has claimed for over 1,900 years:

"For every house is built by someone, but the builder of all things is God" (Hebrews 3:4 NASB).

(3) THE LAW OF BIOGENESIS has demonstrated that all life comes from preexisting life, without exception. It never, ever comes from accidental spontaneous generation! Evolution has proven to be just another human philosophy. All life on this planet came from the eternal, living Being—GOD ALMIGHTY.

All the "Symbols" of evidence for evolution that were covered here have proven to be either deliberate forgery or hoax, or sincere mistakes by scientists who prematurely jumped to conclusions that later were proven to be false. This is not to say that determined evolutionists have given up. They will continue to come up with what they believe to be new "evidences" for natural selection, just as surely as they have "new evidences" today, that have yet to be fully checked out. So the struggle for truth will continue until Jesus comes again, and then all will know the truth (Revelation 1:6-8; Acts 17:30-31; Titus 2:11-14).

(4) THE LAW OF MATHEMATICAL PROBABILITY, the fourth and final law of science used to establish the fact of the Reality of God, shows that regardless how much time passes or how many accidental mutations take place, it is mathematically impossible for life to have come into being through spontaneous generation and natural selection. The only way the Universe and all living creatures, including humanity, could have come into existence is through an intelligent, preexisting Creator capable of designing the hugely complex Universe and living organisms in ways that are still beyond all our human abilities to comprehend.

In the realm of science, William A. Dembski pointed out that any form of life that

CHAPTER 6

contains 500 bits of information is "PROBABILITY BOUND" [in math, that is 10_{150}]. Just the flagellum of a certain bacteria has more than 500 bits of information, according to Dembski (Chapter 6, end notes #5 and #6). Other scientists such as, Sir Fred Hoyle, Chandra Wickramasinghe, Stephen C. Meyer, Bert Thompson, and, Henry M. Morris concur. The extreme complexity of life is such that chance natural selection could not possibly have achieved it, no matter how much time is allowed.

Do you understand what scientists who deal in mathematical probability are telling us? "The beginnings of life were not random, they must therefore have been the product of purposeful intelligence" (Sir Fred Hoyle.) The Law of Probability clearly points to the Reality of God!

The New Testament letter to the Roman Christians by Paul, the apostle, was written over 1,900 years ago. What we know today, the writer Paul knew to be true in the first century.

"For since the creation of the world God's invisible qualities—his eternal power and divine nature—have been clearly seen, being understood from what has been made, so that men are without excuse" (Romans 1:20).

The laws of science and all studies done so far have been presented to illustrate that God has not left humanity in a world of darkness without the realization that He has revealed Himself through His creation of the Universe and life itself. It is through these subtle illuminations of evidence that even the most skeptical of truth-seekers may discover that God has declared His presence to them in areas where they least expect it.

When the Roman governor, Pontius Pilate, asked the prisoner before him, "What is truth?" (recorded in the eighteenth chapter of the Gospel of John in the New Testament), neither he nor most of the world realized that the truth of what the man, Jesus, was talking about, was a kingdom not made with tangible matter, but the eternal kingdom, which a materialist like Pilate could not comprehend because of its intangible nature. Only after Jesus' death and resurrection would the whole truth of God's purpose be known!

Chapter 7
THE HOLY INSPIRED BIBLE AND THE CANON

CHAPTER 7

After a comparison with four of the basic laws of science, it is evident that Charles Darwin's theory of natural selection (evolution) lacks the starter mechanism necessary for life to begin and the mathematical odds against it make spontaneous generation evolving upward to the first modern human both mathematically and logically impossible. Therefore, the cause of such an enormous effect as the Universe, the complex and varied plant and animal species, not to mention the miraculous creation of man with his intelligence and abilities, would of necessity demand a preceding indescribably more complex and intelligent Creator. The Bible writer, in the first chapter of the creation text, refers to this Creator as "God."

At this point I will shift into a higher gear and the focus will be on the Bible itself. How did the Bible originate? How long has it been around? How many writers were involved? How can we know these writers were inspired by an eternal, intelligent Creator? And most important of all, why was the Bible written?

The Bible

The Bible has a uniqueness that makes it different from any other book ever written. Other books have been written whose authors have made the same claim, but evidence has never been close to being as convincing as that for the Bible.

Actually, the Bible is made up of several books written by over 40 authors over a time period of about 1500 years. The authors came with different backgrounds. Some were kings, some were common folk we might today refer to as "blue collar" workers. Some were high-ranking officials in government. Others were fishermen or doctors or sheepherders. Some were scholars of higher learning. But they all had one thing in common: Their writings were uniquely inspired by God.

Another interesting fact about the Bible is that it was written by these authors in different geographical locations. Some were written in sparsely inhabited areas such as the Sinai Peninsula. Many were written in the present-day countries of Egypt, Israel, Jordan, and Iraq. Still others were written throughout Europe and Turkey. Yet in spite of this variation of sources, the central theme of the Bible remains the same. Readers will see that the writings are not the collected mutterings

THE HOLY INSPIRED BIBLE AND THE CANON

of wildly imaginative people, but will witness for themselves the inspired (God-breathed) collection of books that reveal a beautiful scheme, for lack of a better word, or determined strategy, to bring God's most complex creation—humanity—into loving fellowship with Him.

W.E. VINES, *An Expository Dictionary of Biblical Words*, by W.E. Vine, Merrill F. Unger, and William White Jr.., defines "inspiration" as used in the Bible:

"INSPIRATION OF GOD, INSPIRED OF GOD: 'THEOPNEUSTOS' [the Greek word for 'inspired'] inspired by God (Theos, God, pneo, to breathe), is used in 2-Tim. 3:16, of the Scriptures as distinct from non-inspired writings" {1}.

"All Scripture is inspired by God and profitable for teaching, for reproof, for correction, for training in righteousness;" (2 Timothy 3:16 NASB).

It is extremely vital to understanding the difference between God-breathed inspiration and human-motivated inspiration. God "breathed" His message to targeted individuals directed by Him to write. For example, according to all the credible sources of evidence we have, Moses wrote the first five books of the Bible: Genesis, Exodus, Leviticus, Numbers, and Deuteronomy. When God spoke to Moses, He didn't suggest to Moses something like: "I wish you would say something, maybe write it down, about what would be some good ideas for the people of Israel to do." Notice how God spoke to Moses:

"Then the LORD said to Moses, 'Write down these words, for in accordance with these words I have made a covenant with you and with Israel" (Exodus 34:27).

The writer of Hebrews in the New Testament explains how God spoke to humanity:

"In the past God spoke to our forefathers through the prophets at many times and in various ways" (Hebrews 1:1).

Isaiah, was a prophet of God during the reign of five kings. Here is an example of one of his God-inspired prophecies:

"The LORD said to me, 'Take a large scroll and write on it with an ordinary pen:

CHAPTER 7

Maher-Shalal-Hash-Baz. And I will call in Uriah the priest and Zechariah son of Jeberekiah as reliable witnesses for me.'" (Isaiah 8:1-2).

"Above all, you must understand that no prophecy of Scripture came about by the prophet's own interpretation." (2 Peter 1:20).

The Bible is divided into two distinct parts commonly referred to as the Old Testament and the New Testament. Every God-inspired Scripture in the Old Testament begins with Genesis and ends with Malachi. Every God-inspired Scripture in the New Testament begins with Matthew and ends with Revelation.

If you turn to the table of contents of most English versions of the Holy Bible you will find a list of all the "books" of the Old Testament and all the "books" of the New Testament, inspired by God. The reason the word "books" is found in a large percentage of translations (such as the NIV) is that the word "Bible" is derived from the Greek word "biblos" (meaning "books"). Thus, "the Bible" means "the books."

What convinced men to believe the Biblical writers were inspired with directives from a Supernatural being? The fact that the Bible could not have been written by any human being or group of human beings begins to appear in the number of scientific facts recorded in these ancient texts long before modern scientists discovered them. Here are a few examples:

1) THE SECOND LAW OF THERMODYNAMICS (Entropy) which we examined in chapter three demonstrates the fact that everything is wearing out—running down—because the Universe is using up its available energy, including the sun that provides energy for the earth and all its inhabitants. Yet we know that this evidence was written down by Biblical writers well over a thousand years before scientists in the 19th century discovered the Laws of Thermodynamics (Genesis 1:1, Psalm 102:25-27, Hebrews 1:10-12).

2) THE FIRST LAW OF THERMODYNAMICS states that there is nothing new being created in the presently-known Universe. The late Dr. HENRY M. MORRIS comments on the First Law in his book, *Many Infallible Proofs*: "The First Law of Thermodynamics, the Law of Conservation of Mass-Energy...is the most universal

THE HOLY INSPIRED BIBLE AND THE CANON

and certain of all scientific principles, and it states conclusively that, so far as empirical observation has shown, there is nothing now being created anywhere in the known universe" (p. 244, 10th printing, 1990, Master Books, P.O. BOX 727, Green Forest, AR 72638). One must ask, how did Moses know when he wrote the book of Genesis that God created the Universe and that God had completed His work? Moses wrote in Genesis 2:2: "And by the seventh day God completed His work which He had done; and He rested on the seventh day from all His work which He had done." And how did the psalmist know that the Universe is "wearing out"?

JEAN SLOAT MORTON, Ph.D., in her book, *Science in the Bible*, made this comment in the introduction of her book:

"The Bible is not primarily a book of science; it is a book of salvation, but wherever science is mentioned it is accurate. Many scientific facts, which prove the infallibility of Scripture, are tucked away in its pages. These proofs are given in nonscientific language; nevertheless, they substantiate the claims of the authenticity of the Holy Scriptures" {2}.

BERT THOMPSON, Ph.D., and BRAD HARRUB Ph.D., in their book, *Investigating Christian Evidences*, include a chapter on "Scientific Foreknowledge" in the Bible. The authors begin with this statement:

"Among the many intriguing proofs of the Bible's inspiration is its unique scientific foreknowledge. From anthropology to zoology, the Bible presents astonishingly accurate scientific information that the writers, on their own, simply could not have known" {3}.

THE SPRINGS OF THE SEA and the RECESSES OF THE DEEP: "Have you entered into the springs of the sea? Or have you walked in the recesses of the deep?" (Job 38:16 NASB).

In the book of JOB, which from the description in the text appears to be one of the oldest books of the Bible, the man Job has a similar lifestyle to Abraham, a patriarch who lived around 1900 to 2000 B.C., where one's financial standing was based upon his herds of sheep, goats, and other domestic animals. What is fascinating about the book of Job is that part of the text in which God is questioning Job about his knowledge.

CHAPTER 7

THOMPSON AND HARRUB comment on the accuracy of the writer's knowledge and as to where he got the information, regarding the ocean's "springs and "recesses":

"There is a hook-like bay on the southernmost tip of Maui that locals call La Perouse—named after the Frenchman who discovered it. Imagine scientists' surprise when they learned that, up until just a few years ago, natives from this village got their fresh water from the ocean water in this bay—without a desalinization factory. To get to the fresh water, the ancient Hawaiians (knowing that salt water was warmer and more dense than the cold, fresh water) learned how to use gourds to collect fresh water from the deep-sea springs. In fact, if you were to travel there today, you would find surfing spots on the Big island where surfers and children dive into the fresh water springs before getting out of the water, thus saving them the trouble of having to shower later. Yet thousands of years earlier, Job was asked by God (38:16), 'Hast thou entered into the springs of the sea? Or hast thou walked in the recesses of the deep?' The Hebrew word for 'recesses' (or 'trenches') refers to that which is 'hidden, and known only by investigation.' What were these 'recesses of the deep' (the Hebrew word for 'deep' is the word for seas and oceans)? Man, in previous centuries, considered the seashore as nothing but a shallow, sandy extension from one continent to another. Then, in 1873 a team of British scientists working in the Pacific Ocean found a 'recess' 5 ½ miles deep. Later, another team of researchers discovered another trench 35,800 feet deep (over 6 miles down). Trenches now are now known to exist in all three major oceans" {4}.

Obviously, Job did not know about either the fresh water "springs" or the "recesses of the deep" oceans or seas or he would have answered God when God questioned him. The writer of Job appeared to have received this by God-revealed inspiration. If not, then as Thompson and Harrub have asked: "How did Job know about these 'recesses in the deep,' when we didn't discover them for centuries? A lucky guess?" {5}.

THE PATHS OF THE SEAS: "The birds of the heavens, and the fish of the sea, Whatever passes through the paths of the seas" (Psalm 8:8 NASB).

THE HOLY INSPIRED BIBLE AND THE CANON

JEAN SLOAT MORTON, in her book, *Science in the Bible*, devoted over 260 pages to Scriptures in the Bible that have established the fact that several now-known scientific facts were mentioned in the Bible several hundreds-to-over-2000 years before scientists discovered the truths of their reality. One such case is the discovery of "the paths of the seas" mentioned in a Psalm of David, a king of Israel, who reigned about 1055 to 1015 B.C. The man responsible for this scientific discovery was MATTHEW FONTAINE MAURY. Morton describes the event:

"Matthew Fontaine Maury (1806-1873) discovered the paths of the sea by reading about them in the Psalms; he is known as the pathfinder of the seas. The verses that inspired him were Psalm 8:8, Psalm 107:23-24, and Ecclesiastes 1:8 (Ecclesiastes 1:7 in the KJV). These verses describe the paths of the sea and the water cycle. ...Maury reasoned there must be specific patterns of wind and water movement that created paths and would allow a ship to move faster in the water. He was the first to recognize that the ocean was a circulating system with interaction between wind and water. He made detailed studies of winds and currents from the ships logs. By taking advantage of these winds and currents, he plotted ship routes across the ocean. These routes form the basis of an international agreement. His work enabled shipping companies to save thousands of dollars and reduce the possibility of accidents. Maury's native state of Virginia paid a tribute to him in 1923. Monuments of Maury were placed in Richmond and Goshen, Virginia. The inscription tells how Maury was inspired by reading the Bible" {6}.

THE WATER CYCLE: "All the rivers run into the sea, Yet the sea is not full; To the place from which the rivers come, There they return again" (Ecclesiastes 1:7 New King James Version—NKJV). "If the clouds are full of rain, They empty themselves upon the earth" (Ecclesiastes 11:3a NKJV).

Morton describes the Hydrologic or Water Cycle: "The water cycle consists of three major phases: evaporation, condensation, and precipitation. Solar heat causes millions of tons of water to evaporate daily from the oceans and other streams. ... The vapor ascends into the air, but whenever the air is cooled below the saturation point, the vapor condenses to form clouds. When the clouds are full, droplets unite to form rain. 'If the clouds be full of rain, they empty themselves upon the earth' (Ecclesiastes 11:3a). When precipitation occurs, part of the water is stored as ground water, and some is utilized by plants. The balance runs off to lakes,

CHAPTER 7

ponds, rivers, and oceans; then the cycle repeats itself. ...The idea of a complete water cycle was not generally accepted until the sixteenth and seventeenth centuries. The first substantial evidence on the cycle came from experiments of Pierre Perrault and Edme Mariotte. ...Astronomer Edmund Halley also contributed valuable data to the concept of a complete water cycle. ...More than two thousand years before their discovery the Scripture indicated a water cycle in Ecclesiastes 1:7" {7}.

Morton gives additional detail on the history of the "Hydrologic" water cycle in her book on page 49. The question still continues to arise, how did the writer of Ecclesiastes know about the water cycle? Just another one of those "lucky guesses?" I don't think so.

THE EARTH IS ROUND (A "SPHERE"): "He sits enthroned above the circle of the earth, And its people are like grasshoppers. He stretches out the heavens like a canopy, And spreads them out like a tent to live in" (Isaiah 40:22). (NIV)

I don't know about you, but I have heard several people—even friends—who believe in evolution, jokingly refer to Christians as "people who believe the earth is flat" or "the flat-earth people." Then follows the usual subtle chuckling or other expressions of laughter, eye rolling, and ridicule. Because, after all, they are the more enlightened ones. They know that all people (especially Christians) before science arrived were ignorant. But, wait a minute! It wasn't the esteemed evolutionary scientists who first informed us that the earth was round. Notice what THOMPSON and HARRUB write about Isaiah 40:22:

"The Hebrew word Isaiah used for 'circle' is the word khug, which means literally something with 'roundness,' 'a sphere.' But of course, the people of Isaiah's day thought the Earth was flat. And that was the concept of many generations of people who followed Isaiah. Later, of course, it was discovered that the Earth was not flat; rather it was a khug (circle). Isaiah had been correct all along, even when the people of his day emphatically stated the opposite. How did Isaiah know the Earth to be a sphere? Just a lucky guess?

THE LIFE IS IN THE BLOOD: "For the life of the flesh is in the blood, and I have given it to you upon the altar to make atonement for your souls; for it is the blood that makes atonement for the soul." (Leviticus 17:11). (NKJV)

THE HOLY INSPIRED BIBLE AND THE CANON

Do you know how recently it was learned that "the life of the flesh is in the blood"? It was not known in President George Washington's day!

Drop down to verse 14a: "For it is the life of all flesh. Its blood sustains its life. Therefore I said to the children of Israel, 'You shall not eat the blood of any flesh, for the life of all flesh is its blood'" (NKJV)

Why did Moses stress such vital concern with blood, not only of animals but even human blood? "...for the life of all flesh is in the blood." BERT THOMPSON holds an earned Ph.D. in microbiology and taught Veterinary Medicine at Texas A & M and BRAD HARRUB who holds an earned Ph.D. in neurobiology and anatomy from the University of Tennessee Health Sciences Center in Memphis. They give detailed information on "blood cells" and "oxygen":

"Moses told the Israelites (Leviticus 17:11-14) the 'the life of the flesh is in the blood.' He was correct. Because the red blood cells can carry oxygen (due to hemoglobin in the cells) life is made possible. In fact, the human red blood cells carry, for example, approximately 270,000,000 molecules of hemoglobin per cell (see Perutz, pp. 64-65). If there were any less, there would not be enough residual oxygen to sustain life after, say, a hard sneeze or a hefty pat on the back. We know today that the 'life of the flesh is in the blood.' But we didn't know that in George Washington's day. How did the 'father of our country' die? We bled him to death (see Havron, 1981, p. 62). People felt that the blood was where evil 'vapors' were found, and that getting rid of the blood would make a person well again. Today, of course, we know that is not true. Think of how often blood transfusions have made life possible for those who otherwise would have died. Today we know the truth of the matter. How did the Biblical writer know it?" {8}.

We have just covered some of the validated facts of science that Biblical writers wrote about several hundreds to thousands of years before they were discovered by modern science and there are more not included in this book. The question remains, how could these Biblical writers have had any knowledge of the entropy of the Universe, the Earth as a sphere, the springs in the ocean, the deep trenches (recesses) on the ocean floor, the paths of the seas, or that blood sustains the life of all flesh? There are too many of these examples to be just coincidences or lucky guesses. I know skeptics will argue that there have been others who have revealed things in

CHAPTER 7

the past which have just been discovered. Perhaps if these were the only evidences of divine Biblical inspiration they might have a point. But these are just the beginning of the evidences that God had a long and detailed strategy, which is contained in the Bible, to bring all people into a relationship with Him, a purpose that remained a mystery until He brought Christ Jesus into the world. And through Christ, God made known His master plan for those who would accept it to be blessed.

This is just the beginning!

The "Canon" of The Holy Scriptures

How do we know the Biblical writers were actually inspired (God-Breathed) as the result of supernatural direction? How did a group of imperfect human beings decide what books, out of thousands of ancient writings, were actually inspired by a supernatural, super-intelligent being which today we know as "God"? At this point it is important to spend some time on what is known as the "Canon" of Holy Scriptures.

The best place to start would be with those who have spent years of research into this question. The first is NEIL R. LIGHTFOOT, Ph.D., Distinguished Professor of New Testament at Abilene Christian University, in Abilene, Texas, as he defines the meaning of the word "Canon" in his book, *How We Got the Bible*:

"The English word 'canon' goes back to the Greek word kanon and then to the Hebrew qanah. Its basic meaning is 'reed,' our English word 'cane' being derived from it. Since a reed was sometimes used as a measuring rod, the word kanon came to mean a standard or rule. It was used to refer to a list or index and when so applied to the Bible denotes the list of books which are received as Holy Scripture. Thus, if one speaks of the 'canonical' writings, one is speaking of those books which are regarded as having divine authority and which comprise our Bible" {9}.

NORMAN L. GEISLER, in the *Baker Encyclopedia of Christian Apologetics*, further defines the differences and misunderstanding of how this collection of books was determined to be God-inspired. For those raised in totally secular backgrounds, we will explain that the authenticity was determined by a group of clergy in the

THE HOLY INSPIRED BIBLE AND THE CANON

fourth century who claimed authority to establish which books were to be accepted and which were not accepted:

"**Definition of Canonicity.** The distinction between God's determination and human determination and human discovery is essential to the correct view of canonicity, and should be drawn carefully. ...In the 'Incorrect View' the authority of the Scriptures is based upon the authority of the church; the correct view is that the authority of the church is to be found in the authority of the Scriptures. ...It is God who regulated the canon; man merely recognized the divine authority God gave to it. God determined the canon, and man discovered it" {10}.

In other words, the "Synod of Hippo in A.D. 393" did not have any authority to regulate or grant the New Testament inspiration. The Holy Scriptures themselves compelled men to recognize the fact that these 27 books were God-Breathed! Neither were these men the first to recognize their divine inspiration. JOSH McDOWELL, in his book, *Evidence that Demands a Verdict*, Volume 1, lists a quote from F.F. Bruce, about the "Synod of Hippo in A.D. 393" that concurs with Geisler's definition:

"F.F. Bruce states that 'when at last a church council—The Synod of Hippo in A.D. 393—listed the twenty-seven books of the New Testament, it did not confer upon them any authority which they did not already possess, but simply recorded their previously established canonicity" 15/113 {11}.

"It is God who regulated the canon; man merely recognized the divine authority God gave to it. God determined the canon, and man discovered it" (Norman L. Geisler).

Man's discovery of the Holy Inspired Scriptures had taken place long before the meeting of the Synod of A.D. 393. However, before we look at the abundant evidence of early recognition of the New Testament, what about the Old Testament? Where does one begin to find its acceptance among early scribes as being directed by the finger of God?

CHAPTER 7

In NEIL R. LIGHTFOOT'S book, *How We Got the Bible*, among the evidences he mentions is the written testimony of the Jewish historian JOSEPHUS:

"Josephus [was] a well-known Jewish historian of the first century... In his *Against Apion*, written about A.D. 95, he defends the Jews by arguing that they possessed an antiquity unmatched by the Greeks: '...It follows that we do not possess myriads of inconsistent books, conflicting with each other. Our books, those which are justly accredited, are but twenty-two, and contain the record of all time. Of these, five are the books of Moses, comprising the laws and traditional history from the birth of man down to the death of the lawgiver. This period falls only a little short of three thousand years. From the Death of Moses until Artaxerxes, who succeeded Xerxes as king of Persia, the prophets subsequent to Moses wrote the history of the events of their own times in thirteen books. The remaining four books contain hymns to God and precepts for the conduct of human life. From Artaxerxes to our own time the complete history has been written, but has not been deemed worthy of equal credit with the earlier records, because of the failure of the exact succession of the prophets'" {12}.

The call of Moses, mentioned in Exodus chapters 3 and 4, dates from about 1491 B.C. (Ussher's estimate) to 1688 B.C. (Hales' estimate). The five books of Moses, according to Jewish tradition and the Biblical texts themselves, agree with the Historian Josephus—which also agrees with the statement Jesus made in Luke 24:44 plus several others—that Moses' writings were the beginning of the Old Testament. (The reign of Artaxerxes [King of Persia, Ezra 7:1,11] is listed by LIGHTFOOT as the years 464-424 B.C.):

"The time covered in these books is expressly limited. Josephus believed that the canon extended from Moses to Artaxerxes (464-424 B.C.). This corresponds with the Jewish belief that prophetic inspiration ceased with Malachi, who apparently was a contemporary of Ezra and Nehemiah. ...Others indeed wrote later, but their writings are not on par with the earlier writings. In other words, according to Josephus, the canon is closed" {13}.

How did the Jews regard these writings? Were they viewed as simply the wise sayings of some good men with good ideas? Think again. These books were looked upon as the sacred "Scriptures" revealed to man by Almighty God, nothing less!

THE HOLY INSPIRED BIBLE AND THE CANON

LIGHTFOOT records the sacredness with which Josephus and the Jews held these Holy "Scriptures":

"Josephus goes on to state how highly the Jews esteemed their Scriptures: 'We have given practical proof of our reverence for our own Scriptures. For, although such long ages have now passed, no one has ventured either to add, or to remove, or to alter a syllable; and it is an instinct with every Jew, from the day of his birth, to regard them as the decrees of God, to abide by them, and, if need be, cheerfully to die for them' {14}.

The Old Testament clearly has direct statements in it that point to God's directions in writing the Holy Scriptures. For example, God directed Moses to write the ten commandments as follows:

"Then the LORD said to Moses, 'Write down these words, for in accordance with these words I have made a covenant with you and with Israel'" (Exodus 34:27 NASB).

The divine authority of Moses' writings, as well as those of the prophets and the Psalms, was openly referred to by Jesus Himself shortly after His resurrection:

"He said to them, 'This is what I told you while I was still with you: Everything must be fulfilled that is written about me in the Law of Moses, the Prophets and the Psalms'" (Luke 24:44). (NIV)

Yes, indeed, Moses did prophesy about the coming of the Messiah (Christ Jesus) all the way back in the book of Genesis, right after the disobedience of the man and the woman in the Garden of Eden, and later, with Abram (Abraham) and about the tribe of Judah:

IN THE GARDEN OF EDEN: "And I will put enmity between you and the woman, and between your offspring and hers, he will crush your head, and you will strike his heel" (Genesis 3:15). (NIV)

THE PROMISE TO ABRAM (ABRAHAM): "Now the LORD had said to Abram: 'Get out of your country, From your family And from your father's house, To a land

CHAPTER 7

that I will show you. I will make you a great nation; I will bless you And make your name great; And you shall be a blessing. I will bless those who bless you, And I will curse him who curses you; And in you all the families of the earth shall be blessed'" (Genesis 12:1-3 NKJV).

THE PROMISE TO JUDAH: "The scepter will not depart from Judah, Nor the ruler's staff from between his feet, Until he comes to whom it belongs And the obedience of the nations is his" (Genesis 49:10).(NIV)

These are three deeply connected promises (prophecies) that the LORD directed Moses to write down for our learning. Later will cover their significance in more detail as to how they apply to the Messiah (Christ). These are three of the Scriptures Jesus referred to when He spoke to His disciples after His resurrection.

THE HOLY SCRIPTURES: "Jesus said to them, 'Did you never read in the Scriptures, "THE STONE WHICH THE BUILDERS REJECTED, THIS BECAME THE CHIEF CORNER STONE; THIS CAME ABOUT FROM THE LORD, AND IT IS MARVELOUS IN OUR EYES"?'" (Matthew 21:42 NASB emphasis added).

"Paul, a servant of Christ Jesus, called to be an apostle and set apart for the gospel of God—the gospel he promised beforehand through his prophets in the Holy Scriptures" (Romans 1:1-2).

Throughout the New Testament the writers consistently referred respectfully to the Old Testament writings as "the Scriptures" or "the Holy Scriptures." The "Scriptures" were considered the inspired word of God. In the words of Moses when he spoke of God's promises in Genesis 3:15, Genesis 12:1-3, and Genesis 49:10, "the LORD" already had a master plan as to how He would rescue humanity from their bondage to sin.
LIGHTFOOT, explains why the word "Scripture" is necessary to separate the uninspired writings and opinions of humans from that which came from the mind of a living God:

"Good evidence exists in the New Testament which shows that by the time of Jesus the canon of the Old Covenant had been fixed. It cannot be questioned that Jesus and his apostles time after time quote from a distinctive body of authoritative writings. They designate them as 'the Scripture' (John 7:38; Acts 8:32; Rom.4:3), 'the Scriptures' (Matt. 21:42; John 5:39; Acts 17:11), 'the Holy Scriptures' (Rom. 1:2), 'the Sacred Writings' (2 Tim. 3:15), and so forth. They often introduce their quotations with 'it is written,' that is, it stands firmly written and it is indisputably true. ...If some writings were 'Scripture,' others were not..." {15}.

Old Testament Inspiration Was Confirmed By Jesus

"'Haven't you read,' he replied, 'that at the beginning the Creator "made them male and female," and said, "For this reason a man will leave his father and mother and will be united to his wife, and the two will become one flesh"?'" (Matthew 19:4-5). (NIV)

This is a direct quotation from the first of the Old Testament books Moses wrote:

"For this reason a man will leave his father and mother and be united to his wife, and they will become one flesh" (Genesis 2:24).

"From the blood of Abel to the blood of Zechariah, who perished between the altar and the house of God..." (Luke 11:51a NASB).

The Hebrew Bible was arranged differently from the modern Biblical versions used by Christians today. Jesus, when referring to death of Zechariah, knew that the Hebrew Bible listed Chronicles as the last book in their writings. JOSH McDOWELL, in his book, Evidence That Demands a Verdict, made this comment:

"Jesus here confirms His witness to the extent of the Old Testament canon. ... Genesis was the first book in the Hebrew canon and Chronicles the last book. Jesus basically said 'from Genesis to Chronicles,' or, according to our [Biblical] order, 'from Genesis to Malachi'" {16}.

NOTE: ABEL was the first person of faith to be killed (Genesis 4:8, Hebrews 11:4). ZECHARIAH was stoned to death for prophesying about the sins of the nation of Judah (2 Chronicles 24:20-21 NASB). Zechariah was a prophet of God. He was "the son of Jehoiada the priest, and [was] put to death during the reign of Joash the king of Judah."

CHAPTER 7

NEIL R. LIGHTFOOT, in his book, *How We Got the Bible*, writes:

"We should keep in mind that the Jewish order of the Old Testament differs from ours, and that Chronicles is placed at the end of the Hebrew Bible. Thus the Old Testament Jesus knew was a collection of writings reaching from Genesis to Chronicles, with all the other books in between, a collection that embraces the same books as in our Old Testament today" {17}.

Jesus did not leave any doubt as to His authority from God. He made these statements referring to Moses' writings, the accepted canon of the Jews:

"For if you believed Moses, you would believe Me; for he wrote of Me" (John 5:46 NASB).

"He who believes in Me, as the Scripture said, 'From his innermost being shall flow rivers of living water'" (John 7:38 NASB).

In the book of Acts, the New Testament writer records an incident when a Christian named Philip came across an Ethiopian, "an important official" in charge of the "treasury of Candace, queen of the Ethiopians" who was reading from the Old Testament prophet Isaiah:

"The eunuch was reading this passage of Scripture: 'He was led like a sheep to the slaughter, And as a lamb before the shearer is silent, So he did not open his mouth'" (Acts 8:32). (NIV)
The Ethiopian was reading a passage foretelling the death of the promised Messiah (Isaiah 53:7). Isaiah was part of the Holy Scriptures that made up the Hebrew canon. The 53rd chapter of Isaiah plays a significant role in the coming of the Messiah and His future death because it identifies who He is and why He came. It is a mystery kept hidden until the proper time at the right place, fulfilled by the only one who could accomplish it.

In Matthew is recorded a very revealing statement Jesus made in His sermon on the mountain:
"Do not think that I came to destroy the Law or the Prophets. I did not come to destroy but to fulfill" (Matthew 5:17 NKJV).

THE HOLY INSPIRED BIBLE AND THE CANON

The grand, eternal part of the strategy and divine purpose of a Holy God was about to be completed just as it was foretold in prophecy from the beginning. Christ Jesus was to be the fulfillment of "the Law" (the five books of Moses) and the "Prophets'" testimony.

LIGHTFOOT listed four "conclusions" in his summary of the canon of the Old Testament, of which I wish to include the first:

"The number of books looked upon as having divine authority is carefully limited to twenty-two. By joining Ruth to Judges and Lamentations to Jeremiah, and remembering that the Jews enumerated their books differently, the twenty-two books mentioned by Josephus are the same as the thirty-nine books in our Bible today" {18}.

The Canon of the New Testament

McDOWELL, states: "The basic factor for determining New Testament canonicity was inspiration by God, and its chief test, apostolisticity" 32/181 {19}.

The apostle Paul, who wrote several of the New Testament books, wrote in his letter to the Ephesians:

"Now, therefore, you are no longer strangers and foreigners, but fellow citizens with the saints and members of the household of God, having been built on the foundation of the apostles and prophets, Christ Jesus Himself being the chief cornerstone" (Ephesians 2:19-20 NKJV).

Notice, the language Paul used to describe the Christians in Ephesus: "fellow citizens with the saints and members of the household of God." In other words, God's family (the Household of God) rested upon a "FOUNDATION!"

IN A MATERIAL SUBSTANCE, such as a building, a foundation is: "an underlying base or support: the whole masonry substructure of a building" {20}.

IN A SPIRITUAL FOUNDATION, as in Ephesians 2:20, the foundation is that of

CHAPTER 7

the "APOSTLES and PROPHETS, JESUS CHRIST Himself being the CHIEF CORNERSTONE," The CANON of God-Breathed inspiration rests upon the foundation of the testimony of the apostles who were witnesses of the living Christ and His Death, Burial, and Resurrection, including the Old Testament prophets who foretold Christ's coming and the New Testament prophets such as John in the book of Revelation.

The "CHIEF CORNERSTONE" is a spiritual symbol that underscores the strength of the foundation. As used in construction, the cornerstone was: "a stone placed at the corner, or intersecting angle, where two walls of a building come together. In Biblical times, buildings were often made of cut, squared stone. By intersecting two walls, a cornerstone helped align the whole building and tie it together" {21}. CHRIST not only gave spiritual strength to the foundation and building, He is also the true anchor for all spiritual truth!

The Testimony of the Apostles

Knowing His disciples were unprepared to handle the tremendous responsibility He was passing on to them, Jesus told them:

"I have yet many things to say to you, but you cannot bear them now. When the Spirit of truth comes, he will guide you into all the truth; for he will not speak on his own authority, but whatever he hears he will speak, and he will declare to you the things that are to come" (John 16:12-13 Revised Standard Version RSV 1971 Edition).

Thus, He promised the "Spirit of truth" would come to guide them "into all the truth!" After Jesus was gone, believers would follow the examples and teachings of the disciples (apostles):

"And they devoted themselves to the apostles teaching and fellowship, to the breaking of bread and the prayers" (Acts 2:42 RSV 1971).

The apostles' teachings came directly from the guidance of the Holy Spirit. This was the teaching they passed to those new Christian converts. The apostle Paul stated:

THE HOLY INSPIRED BIBLE AND THE CANON

"I want you to know, brothers, that the gospel I preached is not something that man made up. I did not receive it from any man, nor was I taught it; rather, I received it by revelation from Jesus Christ" (Galatians 1:11-12 NIV).

Paul made it emphatically clear that "the gospel" he preached came by the "REVELATION of JESUS CHRIST."

"Bear in mind that our Lord's patience means salvation, just as our dear brother Paul also wrote you with the wisdom that God gave him" (2 Peter 3:15 NIV).

Peter, an apostle, testifies to the fact that the apostle Paul's "wisdom" came by the inspiration of God. "God gave him" that "wisdom!"

"His divine power has given us everything we need for life and godliness through our knowledge of him who called us by his own glory and goodness" (2 Peter 1:3 NIV).

"The Revelation of Jesus Christ, which God gave Him to show to His bond-servants, the things which must shortly take place; and He sent and communicated it by His angel to His bond-servant John" (Revelation 1:1 NASB).

Early Christians Testify To the Inspired New Testament Books

As mentioned previously, the acceptance of the inspired (God-breathed) books of the New Testament was attested to long before the Synod of A.D. 393. We will list a few of the early Christians who accepted them. One of the first who testified to the acceptance of the inspiration of the books was a Christian by the name of IRENAEUS who lived within 100 years of the writing of the last book, The Revelation.

EVERETT FURGUSON, in his book, *Early Christians Speak*, lists a quotation from the writings of Irenaeus, one the most fundamental teachings of Christian belief who wrote about A.D.180:

"For the church, although dispersed throughout the whole world as far as the ends of the earth, received from the apostles and their disciples the faith in one God the

CHAPTER 7

Father Almighty, who has made the heaven, the earth, the seas, and all things in them; and in one Christ Jesus the Son of God, who was made flesh for our salvation; and in the Holy Spirit, who has proclaimed through the prophets the plans of God and the comings of Christ, both the birth from the virgin, the passion, the rising from the dead, and the bodily ascension into heaven of the beloved Christ Jesus our Lord..." {22}.

JOSH McDOWELL, in his book, Evidence That Demands a Verdict, quotes from F.F. BRUCE:

"'The importance of evidence lies in his link with the apostolic age and in his ecumenical associations. Brought up in Asia Minor at the feet of Polycarp, the disciple of John, he became Bishop of Lyons in Gaul, A.D. 180. His writings attest the canonical recognition of the fourfold Gospel and Acts, of Roman, 1 and 2 Corinthians, Galatians, Ephesians, Philippians, Colossians, 1 and 2 Thessalonians, 1 and 2 Timothy, and Titus, of 1 Peter and 1 John and of the Revelation...'" {23}.

MURATORIAN FRAGMENT: a second-century list of the accepted New Testament writings considered to be canonical (inspired by God). Although it had two books in it considered by most as not inspired, the writer of the list mentioned that fact. LIGHTFOOT explains why this has legitimate validation:

"One of these early lists is known as the Muratorian Fragment. Since its date has been unsuccessfully challenged, it remains an important second-century witness to the canon. The Fragment derives its name from L.A. Muratori, who first discovered the list and published it in the eighteenth century. ...The only books not included in the list are Hebrews, James, 1 and 2 Peter, and perhaps 3 John. ...It should be stated, however, that the Muratorian Fragment accepts two other books, the Wisdom of Solomon and the Apocalypse of Peter. The Fragment qualifies the latter by saying that 'some of our people' do not want to have it read in the church" {24}.

GARY R. HABERMAS, in his book, *The Historical Jesus*, on page 113, in a footnote at the bottom of the page, lists the date of the "Muratorian Canon (about A.D. 180)." Habermas provides other facts that reveal that even the earliest Christians accepted the "Gospel" as inspired: "In his Epistle to the Corinthians, usually dated about AD 95, CLEMENT OF ROME made an important reference to the 'Gospel,' which was the central message that the apostles had received from Jesus Christ himself and had passed on to their hearers. ...On other occasions, Clement cited various teachings of Jesus which are found in all three synoptic Gospels, introducing them as 'the words of the Lord Jesus' and 'His hallowed words'" {25}.

Habermas continues by pointing out how quickly the early Christians had already accepted the "teachings of Jesus" as canon:

"Here we have an early, first century reference either more generally to the teachings of Jesus or to the text of one or more of the canonical Gospels themselves, which were recognized in either case as the words of Jesus" {26}.

IGNATIUS clearly indicates what was the most important message of the Bible, without which the rest of the Scriptures would have no meaning or purpose. Habermas comments on Ignatius' writings:

"Ignatius, writing seven epistles around AD 110-115 on his way to Rome to suffer martyrdom, quoted the statement found in Luke 24:39 as the words of Jesus (Smyrnaeans 3)" {27}.
Here is the verse quoted by Ignatius:

"Look at my hands and my feet. It is I myself! Touch me and see; a ghost does not have flesh and bones, as you see I have" (Luke 24:39 NIV).

Why is this significant? Because this is a statement Jesus made right after His resurrection from the dead! The message of the death, burial, and resurrection is the most critical part of the Holy, inspired text of the New Testament! This is what was spoken at the very beginning when the apostles began to teach and to write. Why is this so extremely important? We need to understand what the message was that these early Christians believed, taught, and for which many suffered death.

In his book, *Early Christians Speak*, EVERETT FERGUSON records the words of IGNATIUS about what early Christians believed from the very beginning and wrote down for our benefit:

CHAPTER 7

"Be deaf whenever anyone speaks to you apart from Jesus Christ, who was of the race of David, who was from Mary, who was truly born, both ate and drank, was truly persecuted under Pontius Pilate, was truly crucified and died, with beings heavenly, earthly, and under the earth looking on, who also was truly raised from the dead, his Father raising him (Trallians 9)" {28}.

DAN BARKER, a declared atheist, in his book, *Godless*, in the sixteenth chapter titled: "Did Jesus Really Rise from the Dead?" attempts to debunk the historical fact of Christ's resurrection. Take notice of his words:

"There have been many reasons for doubting the claim, but many critical scholars today agree that the story is a 'legend.' During the 60 or 70 years it took for the Gospels to be composed, the original story went through a growth period that began with the unadorned idea that Jesus, like Grandma, had 'died and gone to heaven.' It ended with a fantastic narrative produced by a later generation of believers that included earthquakes, angels, an eclipse, a resuscitated corpse and a spectacular bodily ascension into the clouds" {29}.

Now look at a God-inspired statement from the New Testament text written by Paul the apostle just a few years after Jesus death and resurrection and understand why it is "of first importance." On this truth hangs all the credibility of Jesus Christ, His death, burial, and resurrection, not to mention the fact that this passage is a fundamental key to the validation of God's inspiration:

"Now, brothers, I want to remind you of the gospel I preached to you, which you received and on which you have taken your stand. By this gospel you are saved, if you hold firmly to the word I preached to you. Otherwise, you have believed in vain. For what I received I passed on to you as of first importance: that Christ died for our sins according to the Scriptures, that he was buried, that he was raised on the third day according to the Scriptures" (1 Corinthians 15:1-4 NIV).

Dan Barker, like other skeptics, is obviously mistaken. Perhaps his research has been limited only to those pieces of literature that dominate his own subjective viewpoint. I don't know how he missed the written testimony of the first century Christians.

THE HOLY INSPIRED BIBLE AND THE CANON

For example, in LEE STROBEL'S book, *The Case for Christ*, he interviews a well-respected Bible scholar and apologist for Christ, DR. GARY HABERMAS, PH.D., D.D., who has written several books and has debated one of the most well-known atheists in this period of history. In this interview, Lee Strobel, an investigative reporter and former atheist, discusses with Dr. Habermas the fact that 1 Corinthians 15:1-4 is the earliest statement of the traditionally accepted "creed" for the New Testament, the foundation principle "of first importance" for first-century Christians:

"That raised the question of how primitive the creed is. 'How far back can you date it?' I asked. [Habermas replied] "We know that Paul wrote 1 Corinthians between A.D. 55 and 57. He indicates in 1 Corinthians 15:1-4 that he has already passed on this creed to the church at Corinth, which would mean it must predate his visit there in A.D. 51. Therefore the creed was being used within twenty years of the Resurrection, which is quite early" {30}.

The major point here is that the canon of inspired Scriptures already included 1 Corinthians 15:1-4 "WITHIN TWENTY YEARS OF THE RESURRECTION" (emphasis added) considering that Jesus' death and resurrection took place somewhere between A.D 29 to 33, depending upon the dating of the year Jesus was born, which will be considered in more detail in another chapter.

Coming back to IGNATIUS who had written abundantly in letters at the beginning of the second century, HENRY H. HALLEY, in *Halley's Bible Handbook*, records how Ignatius considered several of the New Testament writings to be inspired of God:

"Ignatius, in his Seven letters, written about A.D. 110, during his journey from Antioch to Rome for his martyrdom, quotes from Matthew, I Peter, I John, cites nine of Paul's Epistles, and his letters bear the impress of the other three Gospels" {31}.

We could add written testimony from other early Christians, but for now this should be sufficient to demonstrate that, contrary to Mr. Barker and the opinions of other skeptics, it did not take "60 or 70 years" for Christians to develop a resurrection story. The apostles' writings on Christ's death and resurrection were considered to be factual and canonical more than 50 years before the dates Barker alleges. And the canon itself was being accepted for the most part long before A.D. 393.

CHAPTER 7

To summarize, it is a known fact that both Irenaeus and the Muratorian Fragment considered all but four or five of the New Testament Scriptures to be Inspired and accepted as canonical. Irenaeus and the Muratorian Fragment were written about A.D. 180, MORE THAN 200 YEARS BEFORE THE SYNOD OF A.D 393! In addition, Paul's Corinthian letter, contained the foundational message of the Gospel, which is the Death, Burial, and Resurrection of Jesus Christ from the dead, written perhaps less than 25 years from Jesus death and accepted as inspired Scripture by Ignatius more than 280 years before the Synod of A.D 393!

Looking back at the first half of the first century (A.D. 0 to 49), within a few years after Jesus' death and resurrection his disciples were beginning to write down everything of importance Jesus did and taught. This did not happen as the result of human recollection and memory alone. They were guided by the Holy Spirit who was directly involved in what they did, what they said, and what they wrote!
Jesus promised in John 16:12-13 that the Holy Spirit would guide them "into all truth" (NKJV). Peter stated in his second letter, 2 Peter 1:3, "...His divine power has given to us all things that pertain to life and godliness" (NKJV). The Old Testament canon was settled by the time of the Persian king Artaxerxes (464-424 B.C.). The primary message "of first importance" in the New Testament was clearly stated by the apostle Paul in his first letter to the Corinthians in the fifteenth chapter. It is the message of the gospel (good news) about the death, burial, and resurrection of Jesus Christ written A.D. 55 to 57. Ignatius recognized this message as God-Breathed in A.D. 110. Iranaeus, in A.D. 180, recognized at least 20 of the 27 books as inspired. The Muratorian Fragment (A.D. 180), recognized all but five of the New Testament books as inspired.

It should be noted that included in the Fragment are two non-inspired books, "the Wisdom of Solomon" and the "Apocalypse of Peter." Also included is the fact that "some of our people" didn't accept them as part of the canon {32}. It became evident that there were several books appearing among Christians that were not inspired. These will be covered later in more detail. They were written for the most part in the latter half of the second century, and they were beginning to cause confusion among Christians and are considered to be Apocryphal. In today's definition, the word "apocryphal" means: "of doubtful authenticity: SPURIOUS" [synonymous with fictitious] (see *Merriam Webster's Collegiate Dictionary*, 10th Edition, p 54, 1996).

THE HOLY INSPIRED BIBLE AND THE CANON

To keep an accurate perspective of what it meant for a New Testament book to be canonical (authentic and inspired by God) I close this chapter with the words of Norman L. Geisler's summary of what "Canonicity" means:

"....It is God who regulated the canon; man merely recognized the divine authority God gave to it. God determined the canon, and man discovered it" {33}.

Chapter 8

TRUTH IN BIBLICAL PROPHECY
PROMISE OF A MESSIAH KING

CHAPTER 8

Biblical prophecy not only points out the reality of God, it sends a clear message that the God of Creation had a master plan—a divine strategy to bring humanity into a loving fellowship with the Father. Watch and see the mystery unlocked in an everlasting Victory!

Ever since the fall of man and woman in the Garden of Eden those who believed in God were looking for a Messiah. The Jews believed the writings they were meticulously preserving were inspired of God, and they believed that El Shaddai, this "God Almighty" of Abraham" (formerly named Abram) would keep His covenant promises to His people (Genesis 17:1-8). These promises included a redeemer of the children of Abraham, a Messiah, a deliverer, who would restore them from their fallen state. Did they know how God would accomplish this? No, not completely. They knew a king was coming who would reign on God's throne and over His Kingdom, but they didn't know how God would bring this about.

KYLE BUTT, M.A., in a January 2006 article in *Reason & Revelation*, a journal published monthly on *Christian Evidences*, wrote on *The Predicted Messiah*. He referred to "solving the mystery of the Messiah":

"Such is the case when approaching the study of the predicted Messiah, or, as it were, when solving the mystery of the Messiah. Anyone familiar with New Testament writings is quite familiar with the term 'mystery' as it applied to God's plan for the redemption of the human race through the predicted Messiah. 26(1):1" {1}.

Kyle continues to explain how some liberal scholars have alleged that "the ancient Jewish scribes...were not really looking for a personal Messiah." But when one reads from some of these ancient scholars, they tell a different story. He quotes a respected Messianic author by the name of David Baron:

"It has been suggested that the ancient Jewish scribes, rabbis, and general population were not really looking for a personal Messiah. Eminently respected Messianic Jewish author David Baron first published his work, *Rays of Messiah's Glory*, in 1866. In that volume, Baron wrote: 'I am also aware that in recent times many intelligent Jews, backed by rationalistic, so-called Christians...deny that there is a hope of a Messiah in the Old Testament Scriptures, and assert that the prophecies on which Christians ground such a belief contain only 'vague anticipations and general hopes, but no definite predictions of a personal Messiah,' and that consequently the alleged agreement of the gospel history with prophecy is imaginary" (2000, p.16) {2}.

As David Baron stated, these are postulations based upon assumptions coming from rather liberal and somewhat skeptical Jews and apparently unconvinced "so-called Christians" that Jesus was not who He said He was—that He may have been a nice person with marvelous ideals but it is doubtful such a person could rise from the dead and be anyone's savior. Some skeptics in the past have alleged that the New Testament manuscripts and the Old Testament prophecies were not written until hundreds of years after Christ died. Some leading atheists today even claim Jesus Christ did not exist.

We know these allegations are, to put it mildly, extremely inaccurate. For example, the Isaiah Scroll found among the Dead Sea Scrolls was written at least 125 years before Jesus was even born. We'll cover the scrolls later as we get into the prophecies themselves. In fact, two formerly liberal scholars now date the New Testament writings at no later than A.D.85. Kyle Butt continues with a quote of Baron's comments on how he and other Jewish scholars still await the coming of the Messiah:

"In his statements that refute the 'non-Messianic' view of the Old Testament Scripture, Baron wrote: 'Even Maimonides, the great antagonist of Christianity, composed that article of the Jewish creed which unto the present day is repeated daily by every true Jew: "I believe with a perfect faith that the Messiah will come, and although His coming be delayed, I will await His daily appearance""" (p. 18) {3}.

Kyle Butt continues to point out that the documented evidence indicates that the Jews who reject the Biblical promise of a "personal Messiah" are, for the most part, a small minority:

"He [Baron] commented further: 'Aben Ezra, Rashi, Kimchi, Abarbanel, and almost every other respectable and authoritative Jewish commentator, although not recognizing Jesus as the Messiah, are yet unanimous that a personal Messiah is

CHAPTER 8

taught in the Old Testament Scriptures' (pp. 19-20). Baron also noted that only an 'insignificant minority of the Jews' had dared to suggest that the Old Testament lacks definitive predictions of a personal Messiah. He then eloquently stated: '[W]ith joy we behold the nation [Jews], as such, still clinging to the anchor which has been the mainstay of their national existence for so many ages—the hope of a personal Messiah, which is the essence of the Old Testament Scriptures' (p.20)" (bracket in original text) {4}.

In the article, Kyle Butt documents the writings of another Jewish writer who states that the "Rabbinical Writings" indicate an "abundance of Messianic interpretation" believing in the hope of a promised Messiah:

"In his volume, *The Messiah in the Old Testament: In Light of Rabbinical Writings*, Risto Santala wrote: 'If we study the Bible and the Rabbinic literature carefully, we cannot fail to be surprised at the abundance of Messianic interpretation in the earliest works known to us. ...The Talmud states unequivocally: "All the prophets prophesied only for the days of the Messiah"'" (1992 p. 22) {5}.

It is evident that through the ages the promise of a Messiah remained uppermost in the minds and hopes of the Jews. Certainly, the promise to Abraham to build a nation from his seed and the gift of the land of Canaan were also involved, but this was not all. Almighty God would somehow bring them a Messiah, and in the Messiah, a king! Not an ordinary king. This king would be empowered and put on the throne by the God of promise. In the book of Genesis, as see a prophecy of one "to whom it [the throne] belongs."

GENESIS 49:1,10: THE PROMISE OF A KING
Jacob's Promise (prophecy) to his son, Judah

"THEN Jacob summoned his sons and said, 'Assemble yourselves that I may tell you what shall befall you in the days to come'" (Genesis 49:1 NASB).

Jacob had twelve sons. This was more than simply a tangible man expressing his future hopes of prosperity for his sons. This came from the breath of God. After he foretold the future for his sons, Reuben, Simeon, and Levi, Jacob spoke to his son, Judah. Notice what he prophesied for JUDAH:

TRUTH IN BIBLICAL PROPHECY: PROMISE OF A MESSIAH KING

"The scepter shall not depart from Judah, Nor the ruler's staff from between his feet, Until Shiloh comes, And to him shall be the obedience of the peoples" (Genesis 49:10 NASB).

The Promise To Judah And His Descendents Is Leadership

"The SCEPTER shall not depart from JUDAH,
Nor the RULER'S STAFF from BETWEEN HIS FEET" (emphasis added)

According to *Nelson's Bible Dictionary*, the "SCEPTER" is: "the official staff of a ruler, symbolizing his authority and power. Originally the scepter was the shepherd's staff, since the first kings were nomadic princes (Micah 7:14). ...Sometimes the symbolism of a scepter refers to the Messiah who will rule from Israel, from the tribe of Judah in particular (Gen. 49:10)" {6}.

Nelson's definition is in agreement with Jewish Rabbis and commentators who understood Genesis 49:10 to be a promise of a future Messianic Ruler.

KYLE BUTT, in his article, makes further comments on Genesis 49:10:

"In regard to specific Old Testament prophecies, a plethora of rabbinical commentary verifies that the nation of Israel certainly had in view a coming Messiah. Concerning Genesis 49:10, the noted author Aaron Kligerman wrote: 'The rabbis of old, though not agreeing with each other as to the meaning of the root Shiloh, were almost unanimous in applying the term to the Messiah' (1957, pp. 19-20). Immediately after this statement, Kligerman listed the Targum Onkelos, Targum Jerusalem, and the Peshito all as referring to Genesis 49:10 as a Messianic prophecy pointing toward an individual, personal Messiah (p.20)" {7}.

Again, the "staff"—the symbolic expression of leadership: "...nor the RULER'S STAFF from between his feet..."

For example, before Israel had a king, we see the authority of the staff when Moses stretched out his staff, striking "the dust of the earth, that it may become gnats through all the land of Egypt" (Exodus 8:16-24). The gnats, and later other insects,

CHAPTER 8

overwhelmed the Egyptians. There is no question that the "staff" in Moses hand signified that he was leader of the Israelites, demonstrated by the miraculous power of God.

Genesis 49:10 specifies it will be the tribe of Judah! "Until Shiloh comes..."

I looked up the word "Shiloh" in the *Gesenius Hebrew-English Lexicon to the Old Testament*, translated by Samuel P. Tregelles. According to TREGELLES, the meaning of the word is: "(1) tranquility, rest; ...This power of the word seems to be that which it has in the much discussed passage, Gen. 49:10, 'The scepter shall not depart from Judah ...until tranquility shall come, and the peoples shall obey him (Judah). Then let him bind,' etc.; i.e. Judah shall not lay down the scepter of the ruler, until his enemies be subdued, and he shall rule over many people; an expectation belonging to the kingdom of the Messiah, who was to spring from the tribe of Judah. Others whom I followed...render it the peaceable one, peace-maker; either understanding the Messiah...or Solomon. ...The ancient versions take...to him in this sense, "until he shall come to whom the scepter, the dominion belongs" i.e. Messiah" {8}.

The AMPLIFIED BIBLE translates Genesis 49:10 as the second interpretation mentioned by Tregelles: "The scepter or leadership shall not depart from Judah, nor the ruler's staff from between his feet until Shiloh [the Messiah, the peaceful One] comes to Whom it belongs, and to Him shall be the obedience of the people."

THIS IS ABOUT ONE INDIVIDUAL PERSON: "HIS FEET"—"TO HIM."

The understanding of Tregelles and many rabbinic scholars is that
this text is speaking about a future Messiah!

The message is simple and clear. Moses' prophecy in Genesis 49:10 specifies that the ruler ("Shiloh") will come through the tribe of Judah. "The scepter shall not depart from Judah...Until Shiloh ("the peaceful one") comes," and this is definitely indicating it is going to be one single individual ("...And to Him shall be the obedience of the peoples."). Tregelles and the rabbinic scholars agree that this text is Messianic.

TRUTH IN BIBLICAL PROPHECY: PROMISE OF A MESSIAH KING

From this point, we are going to take a historical leap from about 1500 B.C. to about 1000 B.C. to a young man from the tribe of Judah anointed by the prophet Samuel to become God's chosen king to replace Saul (who had disobeyed God's commands after defeating the Amalekites; 1 Samuel 15:1-23). That man was David:

"The LORD said to Samuel, 'How long will you mourn for Saul, since I have rejected him as king over Israel? Fill your horn with oil and be on your way; I am sending you to Jesse of Bethlehem. I have chosen one of his sons to be king'" (1 Samuel 16:1).

DROP DOWN TO VERSES 12-13:

"So he sent and had him [David] brought in. He was ruddy, with a fine appearance and handsome features. Then the LORD said, 'Rise and anoint him; he is the one.' So Samuel took the horn of oil and anointed him in the presence of his brothers, and from that day on the Spirit of the LORD came upon David in power. Samuel then went to Ramah" (1 Samuel 16:12-13 NIV).

After rejecting Saul as king, the LORD sent Samuel to see Jesse of Bethlehem. The LORD rejected seven of Jesse's sons, but there was still one more named David who was out tending sheep. Samuel sent for him: "Then the LORD said: 'Rise and anoint him; he is the one.'" Samuel's anointing David demonstrated to everyone present that he was the one chosen by God to replace Saul as king.

After Saul's death (Saul was from the tribe of Benjamin), David, who was from the "house of Judah" and had been anointed beforehand, became king of Israel (2 Samuel 2:4-7).

"David was thirty years old when he became king, and he reigned forty years. In Hebron he reigned over Judah seven years and six months, and in Jerusalem he reigned over all Israel and Judah thirty-three years" (2 Samuel 5:4-5).
David and the tribe of Judah are critical links in the mystery of our LORD'S master plan to bring redemption and pardon to all of humanity.

"Now therefore thus you shall say to my servant David, 'Thus says the LORD of hosts, I took you from the pasture, from following the sheep, that you should be prince over my people Israel;'" (2 Samuel 7:8 Revised Standard Version-RSV).

CHAPTER 8

DROP DOWN TO VERSES 11-12:

"...from the time that I appointed judges over my people Israel; and I will give you rest from all your enemies. Moreover the LORD declares to you that the LORD will make you a house. When your days are fulfilled and you lie down with your fathers, I will raise up your offspring after you, who shall come forth from your body, and I will establish his kingdom" (2 Samuel 7:11-12 RSV).

NOW DROP DOWN TO VERSE 16:

"And your house and your kingdom shall be made sure for ever before me; your throne shall be established for ever'" (2 Samuel 7:16 RSV 1971).

This is a promise made by "the LORD" to David through the prophet Nathan, a special message for the king. This is part of the continued unveiling of God's Master Plan.

NOTICE WHAT HAS BEEN UNCOVERED SO FAR:

Point #1: The LORD Himself "will make you [King David] a house." (Nathan was not talking about a residential building but a linage of descendants.)

Point #2: David's "house" was the tribe of JUDAH. (David's father, JESSE, was from BETHLEHEM.)

Point #3: David's "offspring" from David's linage, his "THRONE" and His "KINGDOM," would be "ESTABLISHED FOR EVER."

Note 1 Kings 2:12: "Then Solomon sat on the throne of his father David; and his kingdom was firmly established" (NKJV).
NOTICE- When Solomon took over as ruler of the nation of Israel he sat on the "THRONE of his father DAVID." The rulership continued through the linage of DAVID from the TRIBE OF JUDAH, through Rehoboam, Asa, Jehoshaphat, Jehoram, Ahaz, Hezekiah, Manasseh, Amon, Josiah, and Zedekiah.

The book of Psalms contains several poetic writings from the pen of King David.

TRUTH IN BIBLICAL PROPHECY: PROMISE OF A MESSIAH KING

Some of these were prophetic, pointing to the Messiah. Such are the words found in the 132nd Psalm:

"The LORD swore an oath to David, a sure oath that he would not revoke: 'One of your own descendants I will place on your throne…" (Psalm 132:11 NIV).

Jesus Christ is the fulfillment of this Scripture and of 2 Samuel 7:12: "I will raise up your offspring after you…and I will establish his kingdom." We also see this in the New Testament in Acts chapter two, but before we move to the New Testament there are two other prophetic Scriptures that are important in order to understand how God brought about the establishment of a Messiah king just as He had promised.

"But you, Bethlehem Ephrathah, though you are small among the clans of Judah, out of you will come for me one who will be ruler over Israel, whose origins are from old, from ancient times" (Micah 5:2 NIV).

"BETHLEHEM" comes into the Messianic word-picture again. JESSE, the father of DAVID was from Bethlehem (1 Samuel 16:1). DAVID, the son of Jesse, was from Bethlehem. JESSE and DAVID were from the "CLANS OF JUDAH." From DAVID'S LINAGE would come a "RULER OVER ISRAEL" "WHOSE ORIGINS ARE FROM OLD [FROM ANCIENT TIMES]" (emphasis added).

"Thy throne O God is forever and ever; A scepter of uprightness is the scepter of Thy kingdom. Thou hast loved righteousness and hated wickedness; Therefore God, Thy God, has anointed Thee With the oil of joy above Thy fellows" (Psalm 45:6-7 NASB).

We have looked at some critical prophecies in the Old Testament. Now it is time to look at their fulfillment and the impact the ancient prophecies have on confirming the truth in Biblical Scriptures. Truth is what we are looking for because truth has genuine value. Unproven speculations are worthless.

NOTE: If you have an New International Version Bible you may have a footnote at the bottom of the page that reads: "Or from days of eternity." The New American Standard Bible reads: "from the days of eternity." The New King James Version reads: "from everlasting."

CHAPTER 8

After reading the prophecies—plus other Old Testament Scriptures—we have just covered, if you were looking for a Messiah who would become king, what would you look for? A Messiah king that would be coming through the linage of the tribe of Judah, according to Genesis 49:10.

Let's begin in the New Testament with the Gospel of Matthew, chapter one. Matthew lists the genealogy of the man Jesus Christ, a Jew. To the Jew this would be crucial in the identification of the Messiah. If someone claimed to be the Messiah and was not from the tribe of Judah, he was not the Messiah king promised by God Almighty:

"A record of the genealogy of Jesus Christ the son of David, the son of Abraham: Abraham was the father of Isaac, Isaac the father of Jacob, Jacob the father of Judah and his brothers, Judah the father of Perez and Zerah, whose mother was Tamar, Perez the father of Hezron, Hezron the father of Ram" (Matthew 1:1-3).

DROP DOWN TO VERSES 6-7:

"...and Jesse the father of King David. David was the father of Solomon, whose mother had been Uriah's wife, Solomon the father of Rehoboam, Rehoboam the father of Abijah, Abijah the father of Asa" (Matthew 1:6-7).

NOW LOOK AT VERSE 16:

"...and Jacob the father of Joseph, the husband of Mary, of whom was born Jesus, who is called Christ" (Matthew 1:16 NIV).

The English word "Christ" is from the Greek word "Christos" meaning "anointed." Remember, in 1 Samuel 16:12-13 David was anointed with oil by the prophet Samuel, signifying that David was chosen to be king by God {9}.

In Hebrew the word for "the anointed" is "Mashiach," the "anointed one," the Messiah (W.E. Vine, p. 9) {10}.

IN MATTHEW CHAPTER ONE THERE ARE FIVE SIGNIFICANT FACTS

NOTE: For a more detailed explanation, read W.E. Vine, Merrill F. Unger & William White Jr., *An Expository Dictionary of Biblical Words*, p.182 (1984).

TRUTH IN BIBLICAL PROPHECY: PROMISE OF A MESSIAH KING

Fact #1: This is the genealogical record of Jesus Christ, Son of "King David" (v. 1).

Fact #2: Notice this is the linage of JUDAH (v. 3).

Fact #3: It includes JESSE (of BEHLEHEM) (v. 6).

Fact #4: It includes KING DAVID, Solomon, and Rehoboam (v. 6-7).

Fact #5: It includes Jacob, Joseph's father. Joseph was "the husband of Mary, of whom was born Jesus, who is called CHRIST" (v. 16 emphasis added).

In the Gospel of John chapter one and again in John chapter four, John used the word "Messiah" instead of Christ.

"He first found his own brother Simon, and said to him, 'We have found the Messiah' (which is translated, the Christ)" (John 1:41 NKJV).

"The [Samaritan] woman said, 'I know that Messiah' (called Christ) is coming. When he comes, he will explain everything to us' Then Jesus declared, 'I who speak to you am he'" (John 4:25-26 NIV).

JESUS made a bold claim to the Samaritan woman that HE WAS THE MESSIAH: "I WHO SPEAK TO YOU AM HE" (emphasis added).

According to Micah 5:2, the promised "ruler over Israel" was to come from the town of Bethlehem.

"NOW after Jesus was born in Bethlehem of Judea in the days of Herod the king, behold, magi from the east arrived in Jerusalem, saying, 'Where is He who has been born King of the Jews? For we saw His star in the east, and have come to worship Him'" (Matthew 2:1-2).

This deeply disturbed King Herod, because Herod was extremely paranoid of anyone appearing to take over his throne. EVERETT FERGUSON, in his book, *Backgrounds of Early Christianity*, made this comment:

NOTE: "Messias (pronounced Mess-see-as), the Greek form of Messiah, is used in this instance in, John 1:41; and John 4:25; according to the *Holman Bible Dictionary*, p. 957 {11}.

CHAPTER 8

"Though it may be true that Herod was an extremely able ruler, it is also true that he was intensely jealous of his position. He killed the two sons of Mariamne when his suspicions were aroused that they might become the rallying point for Jewish patriotism. Mariamne herself was killed when his mind was poisoned against her by his sister" {12}.

"And when Herod the king heard it, he was troubled, and all Jerusalem with him. And gathering together all the chief priests and scribes of the people, he began to inquire of them where the Christ was to be born. And they said to him, 'In Bethlehem of Judea, for so it has been written by the prophet, 'AND YOU, BETHLEHEM, LAND OF JUDAH, ARE BY NO MEANS LEAST AMONG THE LEADERS OF JUDAH; FOR OUT OF YOU SHALL COME FORTH A RULER, WHO WILL SHEPHERD MY PEOPLE ISRAEL'" (Matthew 2:3-6 NASB).

The scribes and chief priests knew the prophecy of Micah 5:2 had predicted the coming of the "Ruler" who would come forth out of "Bethlehem" from the tribe of "Judah." Now in Herod's hearing the testimony of the "magi" who were drawn to Judea by the "star in the east" to search for the new-born "King of the Jews" brought the prophecy to life. The scribes, chief priests, and Herod, who was paranoid of a usurper come to take away his throne, his power, and his honor, knew the prophecy of Micah had been FULFILLED!
NOTE: The word, "magi," according to *Holman's Bible Dictionary*, refers to a group of "Eastern wise men, priests, and astrologers expert in interpreting dreams and other 'magic arts'...Men whose interpretation of the stars led them to Palestine to find and honor Jesus, the newborn King (Matthew 2)" {13}.

The Census of Caesar Augustus and the Birth of Jesus

"NOW it came about in those days that a decree went out from Caesar Augustus, that a census be taken of all the inhabited earth [i.e., the Roman Empire]. This was the first census taken while Quirinius was governor of Syria. And all were proceeding to register for the census, everyone to his own city. And Joseph also went up from Galilee, from the city of Nazareth, to Judea, to the city of David, which is called Bethlehem, because he was of the house and family of David" (Luke 2:1-4 NASB).

TRUTH IN BIBLICAL PROPHECY: PROMISE OF A MESSIAH KING

Caesar Augustus ruled the Roman Empire from B.C. 31 to A.D. 14. During his reign he ordered that a census be taken of the whole empire of Rome. It is not hard to see God's providential planning in providing a reason by "decree" for bringing Mary, who was pregnant with God's only Son, with Joseph, to Joseph's home town of Bethlehem. This was not an accident. It was part of the divine purpose of God.

Critics have raised the issue that Luke's accuracy should be called into question on two points:

First, skeptics have called into question Luke's statement that people would be required to return to their ancestral home. However, evidence has been found that it was a requirement under Roman rule. MERRILL F. UNGER, in his book, *Archaeology and the New Testament*, mentions the discovery of an edict of enrollment:

"Supporting also the now widely admitted possibility that Luke's census may have involved the return of everyone to his ancestral home is the evidence from periodic enrollments in Egypt which were conducted on a fourteen-year cycle and were by households. ...The edict in question is that of G. Vibius Maximus, prefect of Egypt and dated 104 A.D. 'Since the enrollment by households is approaching, it is necessary to command all who for any reason are out of their own district to return to their own home, in order to perform the usual business of the taxation...' In addition a letter from the late third century contains a request that the writer's sister endeavor to enroll for him but if that is not possible, to let him know that he may come and do it himself. 'To my sister, lady Dionysia, from Pathermouthis, greeting. As you sent me word on account of the enrollment about enrolling yourselves, since I cannot come, see whether you can enroll us. Do not then neglect to enroll us, me and Patas; but if you learn you cannot enroll us, reply to me and I will come...'" {14}.

Second, if Quirinius was not governor at that time that would mean Luke, the Gospel writer, was mistaken and inaccurate concerning the date of Jesus' birth. Not only that, but it also raises the question about whether Jesus is the Messiah of prophecy. Again, as the result of archaeological discoveries, Luke's accuracy has been verified. UNGER [MERRILL F. UNGER, TH.D., PH.D., Professor at Dallas Theological Seminary] lists the evidence in support of Luke's account in the Second Chapter of his Gospel:

CHAPTER 8

"The solution to this vexing problem [of whether Quirinius was actually governor of Syria when Jesus was born] is that Quirinius apparently was twice associated with the government of the province of Syria. Sir William Ramsey accepted the inscriptional evidence contained in Titulus Tiburtinus, construing the words 'iterum Syriam,' i.e. 'a second time Syria' to refer to Quirinius. Likewise the inscriptions of Aemilius Secundus (Lapis Venetus) mentions P. Sulpicius Quirinius in connection with the census (perhaps the first). But Ramsey has adduced additional inscriptional evidence that Quirinius commanded the Homanadensian campaign as legate of Syria between 12 and 6 B.C. Ramsey's inscription, discovered at Antioch of Pisidia in 1912 and dated 10-7 B.C., refers to Gaius Coristanius Fronto as 'prefect of P. Sulpicius Quirinius duumvir.' Another inscription from the village of Hissardi close to Antioch discovered by Ramsey mentions the same man, Gaius Coristanius Fronto, 'as prefect of P. Sulpicius Quirinius duumvir' and prefect of M. Servilius.' Thus Quirinius and Servilius were governing the two adjoining provinces, Syria-Cilicia and Galatia, around the year 8 B.C., when the First Census was made' ... says Ramsey" {15}.

GARY R. HABERMAS, in his book, *The Historical Jesus*, made these comments: "Therefore, while some questions have been raised concerning the events recorded in Luke 2:1-5, archaeology has provided some unexpected and supportive answers. Additionally, while supplying the background behind these events, archaeology also assists us in establishing several facts. (1) A taxation census was a fairly common procedure in the Roman Empire and it did occur in Judea, in particular. (2) Persons were required to return to their home city in order to fulfill the requirements of the process. (3) These procedures were apparently employed during the reign of Augustus (37 BC- AD 14), placing it well within the general time frame of Jesus birth" {16}.

Let's continue to read in Luke chapter two, verses 4-6:

"And Joseph also went up from Galilee, from the city of Nazareth, to Judea, to the city of David, which is called Bethlehem, because he was of the house and family of David, in order to register, along with Mary, who was engaged to him, and was with child. And it came about that while they were there, the days were completed for her to give birth" (Luke 2:4-6 NASB).

TRUTH IN BIBLICAL PROPHECY: PROMISE OF A MESSIAH KING

LOOK AT THE TIMING OF THE EVENTS. Augustus ordered a CENSUS be taken throughout the Roman Empire. EVERY SUBJECT was ordered to return "TO HIS OWN CITY." Because of this, it was necessary for JOSEPH to RETURN to BETHLEHEM with MARY, who was about to "GIVE BIRTH." WHY? Because JOSEPH BELONGED TO THE LINEAGE OF "THE HOUSE and FAMILY OF DAVID." Here in "BETHLEHEM" JESUS was BORN (emphasis added).

Is this just a coincidence, or could it be the fulfillment of a divine purpose, according to Moses' prophecy in Genesis 49:10 and Micah's prophecy in Micah 5:2?

Before reaching a final conclusion, read from the book of Acts chapter two. An event that took place during a large gathering 50 days after the Passover, a day called (in verse one) "Pentecost." This was an event in Jerusalem where "Jews... devout men, from every nation under heaven" (v. 5) heard a small group of "Galileans" (v. 7 NASB) speak to them in their "own language to which we were born."(v.8) This was a supernatural event. (NASB)

The man about whom they were making bold proclamations is "Jesus of Nazareth" (v. 22). They were talking about a king who was now sitting upon the "THRONE of DAVID" (NKJV).

"For You will not leave my soul in Hades, Nor will You allow Your Holy One to see corruption" (Acts 2:27).

DROP DOWN TO VERSES-29-31:

"Men and brethren, let me speak freely to you of the patriarch David, that he is both dead and buried, and his tomb is with us to this day. Therefore, being a prophet, and knowing that God had sworn with an oath to him that of the fruit of his body, according to the flesh, He would raise up the Christ to sit on his throne, he, foreseeing this, spoke concerning the resurrection of the Christ, that His soul was not left in Hades, nor did His flesh see corruption" (Acts 2:29-31 NKJV).

NOTE: The word "Pentecost," according to W.E. Vine, Merrill F. Unger & William White Jr., *An Expository Dictionary of Biblical Words*, means: "PENTEKOSTOS" "an adjective denoting fiftieth, is used as a noun with 'day' understood i.e., the fiftieth day after the Passover, counting from the second day of the Feast (Acts 2:1; 20:16; 1 Corinthians 16:8)" {17}.

CHAPTER 8

REMEMBER THE PROPHECY that NATHAN brought to DAVID the KING, in 2 Samuel 7:12? "When your days are fulfilled and you lie down with your fathers, I will raise up your offspring after you, who shall come forth from your body, and I will establish his kingdom." Then in verse 16 he continued: "And your HOUSE and YOUR KINGDOM...YOUR THRONE SHALL BE ESTABLISHED FOR EVER" (RSV 1971 emphasis added).

AGAIN, IN PSALM 132:11; the psalmist wrote: "The LORD swore an oath to DAVID... 'ONE OF YOUR OWN DESCENDANTS I WILL PLACE ON YOUR THRONE...'" (emphasis added).

What Peter is referring to is the prophecy of David which Peter quoted in Acts 2:27: "Nor will you allow Your Holy One to see corruption" (NASB) (referring to the resurrection of Christ which we will come back to later). But what is necessary to point out at this time is that "CHRIST" is now SITTING and does REIGN upon the THRONE OF DAVID just as GOD promised through the prophets.

Keeping in mind the promise concerning JUDAH that "the scepter shall not depart from Judah...until Shiloh comes" (or as the NIV reads: "until he comes to whom it belongs"), one can begin to see that all these prophetic writings are unveiling a divinely complex mystery about a strategy that supersedes human intelligence. No mere human would have thought of this. Human limitations would not accept the humiliation of silently submitting to the ridicule and derogatory accusations involved in the rejection of one's peers nor knowingly submit to the unmerciful beatings and pain of an exceedingly lengthy, tortuous death without knowing the final outcome. It could only have come from God!

Now, to complete the first part of the mystery concerning the prophecies of the "THRONE," the "KINGDOM" and "THE SCEPTER," Hebrews 1:8-9 records: "But about the Son he says, 'Your throne, O God, will last for ever and ever, and righteousness will be the scepter of your kingdom. You have loved righteousness and hated wickedness; Therefore God, your God, has set you above your companions by anointing you with the oil of joy."(NIV)

The "Son" the Hebrew writer is referring to is Jesus Christ. The "SON" (Jesus Christ), is sitting on the "THRONE."

TRUTH IN BIBLICAL PROPHECY: PROMISE OF A MESSIAH KING

"Your throne, O God, will last for ever and ever" (v. 8).

The "SCEPTOR" of "RIGHTEOUSNESS" is the SCEPTOR of the SON'S "KINGDOM":

"...and righteousness will be the scepter of your kingdom" (v. 8).

The "SCEPTOR" has remained with the tribe of "JUDAH," fulfilling the prophecy in GENESIS 49:10.

In his letter to the Colossian Christians, Paul the apostle reminds the "saints and faithful brethren in Christ who are in Colossae:" that they were in the kingdom of Christ "the Son" (Colossians 1:2 NASB).

"He has delivered us from the power of darkness and conveyed us into the kingdom of the Son of His love" (Colossians 1:13 NKJV).

John, the apostle, writing from the island of Patmos, affirms the fact that Christ now reigns upon the throne of the kingdom of God:

"...Jesus Christ, the faithful witness, the first-born of the dead, and the ruler of the kings of the earth. To Him who loves us, and released us from our sins by His blood, and He has made us to be a kingdom, priests to His God and Father; to Him be the glory and the dominion for ever and ever. Amen" (Revelation 1:5b-6).

DROP DOWN TO VERSE 9:

"I, John, your brother and fellow partaker in the tribulation and kingdom and perseverance which are in Jesus, was on the Island called Patmos, because of the word of God and the testimony of Jesus" (Revelation 1:9 NASB).

NOTE: The writer of the Hebrew letter in verses 8-9 is quoting from the prophecy in Psalm 45:6-7: "Your throne O God, will last for ever and ever; a scepter of justice will be the scepter of your kingdom. You love righteousness and hate wickedness; therefore God, your God, has set you above your companions by anointing you with the oil of joy," pointing out that the "SON" (JESUS CHRIST), has fulfilled this prophecy! (NIV)

CHAPTER 8

Peter declared to the crowds of Jews who were gathered in Jerusalem on the day of Pentecost: "…that God had promised him [David] on oath that he would place one of his descendants on his throne. Seeing what was ahead, he spoke of the resurrection of the Christ. …Therefore let all of Israel be assured of this: God has made this Jesus, whom you crucified, both Lord and Christ" (Acts 2:30-31, 36 NIV).

Fulfilling the prophecy of Moses in Genesis 49:10, the Scepter did not depart from the tribe of Judah until Christ came, "to whom it belongs" (Amplified Bible). The prophecies in 2 Samuel 7:8,11-12, 16; Psalm 132:11; and Micah 5:2; that David's kingdom and his throne would be occupied by David's descendants and by Jesus Christ Himself has been completed.

Are there critics who deny the fact that Christ reigns over His kingdom today? Of course there are, but their allegations have no Biblical support. Are there critics who deny that Jesus Christ is the promised Messiah? Of course! There are some who even deny that Jesus Christ ever existed, much less rose from the dead. There will always be those who refuse to accept Jesus in any way, shape, or form. However, as one will see in the following chapters, the evidence for Jesus as the resurrected Messiah, Lord, and God is overwhelming. We will see why this is so critical for everyone who lives on this earth.

Chapter 9

MESSIAH ARRIVES
PROMISES FULLFILLED CHIRST IS KING

CHAPTER 9

THE PROBABILITY OF CHANCE FULFILLMENT
(Based upon the principles of Mathematical Probability)

What would be the chances of someone showing up in the first century and by accidental coincidence fulfilling the Old Testament prophecies? There are some who believe Jesus' arrival and fulfillment of prophecy was just coincidental, an accidental, chance happening.

JOSH McDOWELL, in his book, Evidence That Demands a Verdict, lists 61 prophecies fulfilled in Christ's coming and death. He gives an example of skepticism typical to critics' objections to these facts:

"'Why you could find some of these prophecies fulfilled in Kennedy, King Nasser, etc., replies the critic.' **Answer:** Yes, one could possibly find one or two prophecies fulfilled in other men, but not all 61 major prophecies!" {1}.

In a previous chapter, the value of mathematical probability was used to demonstrate that life itself, from the simplest forms up, could not have come into being by accidental chance. Life had to begin by the design of an intelligent Creator. In the same way, the chances that any finite human being could by accidental coincidence fulfill all the intricate and detailed prophecies concerning the Messiah are beyond the limits of mathematical probability.

McDowell quotes the mathematical probabilities given by Peter Stoner:

"The following probabilities are taken from Peter Stoner in Science Speaks to show that coincidence is ruled out by the science of probability. Stoner says that by using the modern science of probability in reference to eight prophecies... 'We find that the chance that any man might have lived down to the present time and fulfilled all eight prophecies is 1 in 10_{17}.' That would be 1 in 100,000,000,000,000,000. In order to help us comprehend this staggering probability, Stoner illustrates it by supposing that 'we take 10_{17} silver dollars and lay them on the face of Texas. They will cover all of the state two feet deep. Now mark one of these silver dollars and stir the whole mass thoroughly, all over the state. Blindfold a man and tell him that he can travel as far as he wishes, but he must pick up one silver dollar and say that this is the right one" {2}.

MESSIAH ARRIVES: PROMISES FULLFILLED CHRIST IS KING

With just eight Messianic prophecies, we can see that for one man to fulfill these prophecies by accidental chance or coincidence lacks any reasonable probability unless the prophets were directed by the mind of God. But let's not stop there. McDowell lists the chance probability given by Stoner for the fulfillment of 48 prophecies:

"Stoner considers 48 prophecies and says, '…We find the chance that any one man fulfilled all 48 prophecies to be 1 in 10_{157}'" {3}.

Concerning the Law of Mathematical Probability covered in Chapter Six remember that WILLIAM A. DEMSKI, Ph.D., in his book, *Intelligent Design*, stated:

"A probability bound of 10-150 translates to 500 bits of information. Accordingly, specified information of complexity greater than 500 bits cannot reasonably be attributed to chance" {4}.

It is pretty obvious that 10_{157} is greater than 10_{150}. Any accidental chance event with the mathematical probability of 150 zeros after it is considered by Dr. Demski as "probability bound" which means no human being could by accident or by some coincidence fulfill all of 48 Messianic prophecies Stoner mentioned. It had to be a complex, detailed strategy designed by an Almighty God! Finite human beings were, and are now, incapable of accomplishing what Jesus Christ has accomplished.

Are these just wild, imaginative figures produced by unqualified people who want to produce the appearance of authenticity but lack scientific substantiation? NO, absolutely not! According to an associate of the "American Scientific Affiliation" whom McDowell quotes in his book, Evidence That Demands a Verdict:

"H. Harold Hartzler, of the American Scientific Affiliation, Goshen College, in the foreword of Stoner's book writes: 'The manuscript for Science Speaks has been carefully reviewed by a committee of the American Scientific Affiliation members and by the executive council of the same group and has been found, in general, to be dependable and accurate in regard to the scientific material presented. The mathematical analysis included is based upon principles of probability which are thoroughly sound and Professor Stoner has applied these principles in a proper and convincing way" {5}.

CHAPTER 9

For the next part of the study on Messianic prophecy, we will go back in the historical time scale to the beginning, shortly after the Creation of man and woman.

The Covenant Between the First Human (Adam), and God

"The LORD God took the man and put him in the Garden of Eden to work it and take care of it. And the LORD God commanded the man, 'You are free to eat from any tree in the garden; but you must not eat from the tree of the knowledge of good and evil, for when you eat of it you will surely die'" (Genesis 2:15-17).

The Creator made a covenant (a binding agreement) with the man whom He appointed as caretaker ("to take care of") the Garden of Eden. Within this covenant was a large but flexible range of duties; to name all of the creatures God had created and to be caretaker of the garden with the right to eat of everything in the garden except one particular tree, "the tree of the knowledge of good and evil," one of two trees in the center of the garden with the potential for huge impact upon humanity:

"And the LORD God made all kinds of trees grow out of the ground—trees that were pleasing to the eye and good for food. In the middle of the garden were the tree of life and the tree of the knowledge of good and evil" (Genesis 2:9).

There was one law, concerning one tree, which held serious consequences for both man and woman:

"…but you must not eat from the tree of the knowledge of good and evil, for when you eat of it you will surely die" (Genesis 2:17).

You see, the first man (Adam) and woman (Eve) were created and brought to life in a state of innocence. They had no conception of what was good and what was evil. This was all new to them. The only thing they knew for sure is they were not to eat from that tree. This became the first human experience with Law—THE LAW OF SIN AND DEATH!

Beginning in chapter three, another creature, "the serpent," enters the scene. The Bible states he was "crafty" (the RSV 1971 uses the word "subtle").

MESSIAH ARRIVES: PROMISES FULLFILLED CHRIST IS KING

"Now the serpent was more crafty than any beast of the field which the LORD God had made. And he said to the woman, 'Indeed, has God said, "You shall not eat from any tree of the garden"?'" (Genesis 3:1 NASB).

Let's begin by clarifying who the "serpent" really was. He was not simply the garden variety snake one finds in nature. He is the enemy of God Almighty. He has waged a war against the Creator since the beginning. In the last book of the Bible John, the writer, quite clearly reveals his identity:

"And there was war in heaven. Michael and his angels fought against the dragon, and the dragon and his angels fought back. But he was not strong enough, and they lost their place in heaven. The great dragon was hurled down—that ancient serpent called the devil or Satan, who leads the whole world astray. He was hurled to the earth, and his angels with him" (Revelation 12:7-9 NIV).

There is a war going on. It is not easily recognizable with the naked eye, but it can be seen in the lives of human beings. It may begin with envy or jealousy, vicious deceitful attacks of one person upon another's character. The hatred increases into violence and murder. The war affects politics and nations. It is spiritual warfare, an intangible battle between intangible forces. Difficult to detect with our tangible nature alone, it must be recognized through our intangible spirit, the inward man or woman. One must become aware of the enemy and how the "dragon," "that ancient serpent," "the devil or Satan," operates. Jesus points him out quite unmistakably:

"You are of your father the devil, and the desires of your father you want to do. He was a murderer from the beginning, and does not stand in the truth, because there is no truth in him. When he speaks a lie, he speaks from his own resources, for he is a liar and the father of it" (John 8:44 NKJV).

Deceit is a very strong weapon used by "the devil" to bring about his ultimate goal. He did not appear to formerly innocent woman (Eve) in his spiritual form; instead he used the camouflage of one of nature's creatures, something the woman would be accustomed to in the garden, to present himself. Notice Satan's first tactic—the half-lie:

CHAPTER 9

"Indeed has God said, 'You shall not eat from any tree of the garden'? And the woman said to the serpent, 'From the fruit of the trees of the garden we may eat; but from the fruit of the tree which is in the middle of the garden, God has said, "You shall not eat from it or touch it, lest you die."' And the serpent said to the woman, 'You surely shall not die! For God knows that in the day that you eat from it your eyes will be opened, and you will be like God, knowing good and evil.'" (Genesis 3:1-5 NASB).

The serpent (Satan) lies to the woman, "You surely shall not die!" For it is understood from what the LORD God distinctly told the man, "FOR IN THE DAY THAT YOU EAT FROM IT YOU SHALL SURELY DIE" (Genesis 2:17 emphasis added).

Next he tells her she will be able to know good and evil and that would put her on a level with her Creator because she "will be like God."

"When the woman saw that the tree was good for food, and that it was a delight to the eyes, and that the tree was desirable to make one wise, she took from its fruit and ate; and she gave also to her husband with her, and he ate" (Genesis 3:6 NASB).

Sin Destroys Innocence—Result: Spiritual & Physical Death

"Then the eyes of both of them were opened, and they knew that they were naked; and they sewed fig leaves together and made themselves loin coverings. And they heard the sound of the LORD God walking in the garden in the cool of the day, and the man and his wife hid themselves from the presence of the LORD God among the trees of the garden. Then the LORD God called to the man, and said to him, 'Where are you?' And he said, 'I heard the sound of Thee in the garden, and I was afraid because I was naked; so I hid myself.' And He said, 'Who told you that you were naked? Have you eaten from the tree of which I commanded you not to eat?'" (Genesis 3:7-11 NASB).

It was obvious that both man and woman had eaten from the forbidden tree of knowledge. First, they were hiding. Why would they be hiding unless something they did was wrong? They were always in God's presence before without this sudden appearance of fear. Second, they knew something they had not realized

MESSIAH ARRIVES: PROMISES FULLFILLED CHRIST IS KING

before—they were naked—to which God asked the obvious question: "Who told you that you were naked? Have you eaten from the tree of which I commanded you not to eat?" The jig was up. By their actions and the man's reply, they were exposed in their own disobedience to their Creator. It is interesting to note that human nature has not changed. Notice how the man passes the responsibility and blame on to the woman:

"Then the man said, 'The woman whom you gave to be with me, she gave me of the tree, and I ate'" (Genesis 3:12 NKJV).

The woman points to the serpent as the culprit, which of course, he was, as the instigator, But neither man nor woman was absolved of their responsibility to obey God regardless of the serpent (Satan's) conspiracy against God Almighty. The result was as the LORD God had promised:

"…In the day that you eat of it you shall surely die" (Genesis 2:17b NKJV).

DEATH has always been one of the least understood subjects, especially as it is used in the Bible. Generally speaking, worldview perspective of death is of a physical nature. Man dies. He is buried. That's the end of it. But that is only one part of it. There are two distinct parts of a human being. One part is the physical body, which includes the brain. The Body is tangible. We can see, feel, and touch it. The other part is intangible. It is the spiritual part of man. It is referred to by one Biblical writer as the "inward man." In Genesis, when God told the man if he disobeyed he (Adam) would "surely die" it was the truth. Both man and woman suffered death that day. How? The Scriptures state that Adam and Eve were still alive after they ate from the tree of knowledge of good and evil. The death they suffered as the result of their sin was spiritual death:
"Surely the arm of the LORD is not too short to save, nor his ear too dull to hear. But your iniquities have separated you from your God; your sins have hidden his face from you, so that he will not hear" (Isaiah 59:1-2 NIV).

"As for you, you were dead in your transgressions and sins" (Ephesians 2:1 NIV).

The LORD, their creator, made it clear to the first man and woman that when they broke the Law of Sin and Death they would surely die, and die they did on the very

CHAPTER 9

day they disobeyed Him. Their sin "SEPARATED" them from their LORD and they were "DEAD" in their "TRANSGRESSIONS AND SINS." This is SPIRITUAL DEATH. While their outward physical bodies remained alive, the inward man and woman were separated from their God spiritually. However, the consequences of their disobedience also brought about their eventual physical death:

"Then the LORD God said, 'Behold, the man has become like one of Us, knowing good and evil; and now, lest he stretch out his hand and take also from the tree of life, and eat, and live forever therefore the LORD God sent him out from the Garden of Eden, to cultivate the ground from which he was taken" (Genesis 3:22-23 NASB).

"Then the dust will return to the earth as it was, and the spirit will return to God who gave it" (Ecclesiastes 12:7 NASB).

"Furthermore, we have had human fathers who corrected us, and we paid them respect. Shall we not much more readily be in subjection to the Father of spirits and live?" (Hebrews 12:9 NKJV).

"Therefore we do not lose heart. Even though our outward man is perishing, yet the inward man is being renewed day by day" (2 Corinthians 4:16 NKJV).

Remember there were two trees in the middle of the garden (Genesis 2:9). One was the forbidden tree of knowledge of good and evil. For man to eat of it would bring spiritual death—separation from God. To eat of the other, the tree of life, would give man eternal life. When man and woman disobeyed God they were denied access to eternal life. The tangible outward man and woman then suffered eventual physical death. The Human body was created from the dust of the ground (Genesis 2:7). When the outward man suffers physical death the body ("the dust") returns "to the earth as it was." The inward man—"the spirit"—returns "to God who gave it" (Ecclesiastes 12:7).

Dr. John Eccles, quoted in the previous chapter (The Law of Cause and Effect), made this statement when speaking about the inward spiritual man:

"Each of us is a unique, conscious being, a divine creation. It is the religious view. It is the only view consistent with all the evidence" (The Intellectuals Speak Out About God, p. 50, 1984).

MESSIAH ARRIVES: PROMISES FULLFILLED CHRIST IS KING

Death came into the world because of sin. Man was created with a free will. He could choose to obey God and live, or he could choose to disobey God and suffer death. The Creator in His wisdom knew this. In fact, even before man and woman were created, God had a plan to save humanity:

"Praise be to the God and Father of our Lord Jesus Christ, who has blessed us in the heavenly realms with every spiritual blessing in Christ. For he chose us in him before the creation of the world to be holy and blameless in his sight" (Ephesians 1:3-4a).

PLEASE NOTE: "Every spiritual blessing [IS] IN CHRIST." When did God, our Creator decide to do this? Answer: "For HE CHOSE US IN HIM [CHRIST] BEFORE THE CREATION OF THE WORLD" to be holy and blameless in his [God's] sight" (emphasis added). This plan was already decided in the foresight that humanity might make the wrong choice—which they did. Praise God our Father, and Christ Jesus our Lord, that the way for our salvation was provided BEFORE WE WERE EVEN CREATED!

The Divine Strategy For Human Salvation

"And I will put enmity Between you and the woman, And between your seed and her seed; He shall bruise you on the head, And you shall bruise him on the heel" (Genesis 3:15 NASB).
Remember what Jesus said to Pontius Pilate, in their dialogue when Pilate was questioning Jesus, his prisoner? "Jesus answered, 'You are right in saying I am a king. In fact, for this reason I was born, and for this I came into the world, to testify to the truth. Everyone on the side of truth listens to me.' 'WHAT IS TRUTH?' Pilate asked" (John 18:37b-38a emphasis added).

In the humanist perspective, truth is relative. Truth has no meaning, no substance, no absolutes, unless, of course, it is something the humanist/atheist believes to be true, such as, evolution. The truth that Jesus brings is not accepted by the humanist/atheist because it is spiritual. Humanists are materialists. They find it hard to conceive of anything they cannot see, touch, or feel. Neither could Pilate.

CHAPTER 9

"The truth" testified to by Jesus Christ is far deeper and more complex than superficial materialists can comprehend. You see, Jesus Christ is the fulfillment of Genesis 3:15 because this is where the prophecy of the promised Messiah began:

To the "serpent" which is Satan, God said: "And I will put enmity between you (Satan) and the woman, And between your seed and her seed" (Genesis 3:15a NASB).

In order for the reader to grasp what has happened in the past and what is happening today, let's take another look at the last book in the Bible, Revelation:

"And there was war in heaven. Michael and his angels fought against the dragon, and the dragon and his angels fought back. But he was not strong enough, and they lost their place in heaven. The great dragon was hurled down—that ancient serpent called the devil or Satan, who leads the whole world astray. He was hurled to the earth, and his angels with him" (Revelation 12:7-9).

This is the war—the "enmity" between Satan and "the woman" and "her seed," which is Jesus Christ (the Messiah) that Moses wrote about in Genesis 3:15b:

"He shall bruise you on the head, And you shall bruise Him on the heel" (NASB).

Picture this in your mind: In order for Christ, "the seed" of woman, to "bruise" "the head" of Satan, the serpent, He must step on the serpent's head. This is a crushing blow, rendering the serpent helpless, because the power of this death-dealing serpent is his head. The bruising of Jesus' heel is superficial and temporary.

KYLE BUTT, M.A., wrote an article in the January 2006, publication of *Reason & Revelation*, titled "*The Predicted Messiah*," mentioned in the previous chapter. His article gives some unique insights into the Messianic promise of Genesis 3:15:

"Into this scene of shame and sin, God brought judgment upon all parties involved. Death would be the consequence of this sinful action, as well as increased pain in childbirth for the woman and increased hardship and toil for the man. Yet in the midst of God's curse upon the serpent, He included a ray of glorious hope for humanity. To the serpent He said: 'And I will put enmity between your seed and her seed; He shall bruise your head, and you shall bruise

MESSIAH ARRIVES: PROMISES FULLFILLED CHRIST IS KING

his heel' (Genesis 3:15). This brief statement made by God to the serpent concerning the seed of woman is often referred to as the protevangelium" {6}.

"PROT," according to Webster's Collegiate Dictionary: "prot- or proto-…. Gk prot- proto-…1a: first in time <protohistory>"…{7}.

"EVANGELIUM," Webster's Collegiate Dictionary, "evangel…evangelium fr. Gk euangelion good news, gospel" {8}.

Jewish and Christian scholars agree that Genesis 3:15 is predicting a future Messiah. The Scripture not only promises a Messiah (Hebrew—"mashiach"), it gives the assurance of a Savior who will be victorious over Satan. Butt continues, quoting from some noted authorities:

"The Jewish scholar, Aaron Kligerman, noted that three things stand out in this first prediction of the Messiah, 'namely that the Deliverer must be—(A) of the seed of woman and (B) That He is to be temporarily hindered and (C) Finally victorious" (1957, p.13, italics in original).

Butt continues with other quotations, such as that of Charles A. Briggs:

"Of the protevangelium, Charles A. Briggs, in his classic work, Messianic Prophecy, noted: 'Thus we have in this fundamental prophecy explicitly a struggling, suffering, but finally victorious human race, and implicitly struggling, suffering and finally victorious son of woman, a second Adam, the head of the race. …The protevangelium is a faithful miniature of the entire history of humanity, a struggling seed ever battling for ultimate victory…until it is realized in the sublime victories of redemption' (1988 reprint, p. 77)" {9}.

How many Scriptures in the Old Testament actually prophesy a future Messiah who would deliver Israel from bondage? And what will happen to the Gentiles? To the Jews, in general, this was a mystery. KENNY BARFIELD, in his book, *The Prophet Motive*, lists the names of Bible scholars who have done extensive study in Messianic prophesy:

NOTE: According to W.E. Vine's, Merrill F. Unger's, William White Jr.'s, Dictionary of Biblical Words, Hebrew "mashiach" means: "anointed one; Messiah" (p. 246 1984) {10}.

CHAPTER 9

"Admittedly, some prophetic strokes are barely distinguishable. Others stand out in bold relief. Even scholars cannot be certain they have correctly isolated each reference to the coming Messiah. At one end of the spectrum stands the venerable and meticulous 19th century scholar Alfred Edersheim. ...Using his Jewish background as a foundation, Edersheim cataloged 456 references from the Old Testament that early rabbinical sources labeled as 'Messianic.'... Pierson, while not claiming his list to be complete, identified more than 300 predictions regarding the Messiah taken from the Old Testament. Likewise, without claiming an encyclopedic listing, James E Smith itemized 72 prophecies he claimed were fulfilled by Jesus of Nazareth. J. Barton Payne of Covenant Theological Seminary listed 127 predictions, drawn from approximately 3,000 verses of scripture as future references to the Messiah" {11}.

JOSH McDOWELL, in his book, Evidence That Demands a Verdict, lists 61 Messianic prophecies (pp. 144-166, 1979). With a little more research one could find even more Biblical scholars with lists of the number of Old Testament Messianic prophecies, each probably varying to some degree. However, it is easy to see that there are several, more than enough to establish the fact that the basic theme of the Old Testament is to point out how humans by themselves could not keep from disobeying their Creator's commands, being flawed and falling prey to their accuser and the forces of darkness. It would take a perfect human being to defeat Satan, and this is the One whom the Old Testament prophets predicted would come! {11}.

It is not the intention of this author to list all the known Scriptures of the coming Savior, but the prophecies the reader will see in this book are more than enough to leave no doubt as to who this Messiah is and how He alone, above all the people who have inhabited this earth, was able not only to defeat Satan, but also to free every human being from bondage to Satan.

To begin unfolding the mystery—the veiled divine agenda to bring this about—requires a leap in history from the fall of man and woman and the promise of hope of final victory through the seed of woman to a point in history about 2,000 years later, the call of Abram (later known as Abraham).

Abram, the son of Terah, was living in Haran, which appears to have been in the northern part of the area referred to as "the land of Canaan" (Genesis 11:31-32) when "the LORD" spoke to him:

MESSIAH ARRIVES: PROMISES FULLFILLED CHRIST IS KING

"Now the LORD had said to Abram: Get out of your country, From your family And from your father's house, To a land that I will show you. I will make you a great nation; I will bless you And make your name great; And you shall be a blessing. I will bless those who bless you, And I will curse him who curses you; And in you all the families of the earth shall be blessed" (Genesis 12:1-3 NKJV).

This promise is divided into two parts. In other words, as described by HOMER HAILEY, this is a "TWO-FOLD PROMISE" {13}.

THE FIRST PART, verses 1 and 2, is that the nation of Abraham's seed would grow and increase into a sizeable nation in Egypt. They would leave Egypt and move to the land of Canaan where they would dwell on the land promised by God in Genesis 12:6-7:

"Abram passed through the land to the place of Shechem, as far as the terebinth tree of Moreh. And the Canaanites were then in the land. Then the LORD appeared to Abram and said, 'To your descendants I will give this land.' And there he built an altar to the LORD, who had appeared to him" (NKJV).

THE SECOND PART is found in the last twelve words of verse three: "And in you all the families of the earth shall be blessed."

This promise goes a lot farther and deeper than the building of the nation of Israel. It is a promise that would be fulfilled 2,000 years later. The Messiah would come through the "SEED" and "DESCENDANTS" of ABRAHAM! (God changed Abram's name to Abraham in Genesis 17:5.)

The same promise was made to Abraham's descendant, Jacob:

"Also your descendants shall be as the dust of the earth; you shall spread abroad to the west and the east, to the north and the south; and in you and in your seed all the families of the earth shall be blessed" (Genesis 28:14 NKJV).

The Promise of the Messiah continues to unfold;

CHAPTER 9

(1) He would come from the seed of woman.
(2) He would come through the seed of Abraham.
(3) He would come through the seed of Jacob (Israel).
(4) He would be wounded by Satan (the serpent).
(5) He would "crush" the head of the serpent, in other words he would render the serpent (Satan) POWERLESS.

From Abraham, we take another leap forward into the historical period of the prophet ISAIAH. Isaiah's prophecies continued through the reigns of four kings of Judah; Uzziah, Jotham, Ahaz, and Hezekiah, who died about 698 B.C. This would mean that Isaiah's prophetic writings took place from about 750 B.C. until after 698 B.C.

Isaiah's writings are loaded with Messianic prophecies that predict the Messiah's coming, His Deity, and His death. According to KYLE BUTT, Jewish scholars, generally speaking, are in agreement:
"Concerning the book of Isaiah and the predictive, Messianic prophecy contained within it, Santala stated: 'The Messianic nature of the book of Isaiah is so clear that the oldest Jewish sources, the Targum, Midrash and Talmud, speak of the Messiah in connection with 62 separate verses'" (1992, pp. 164-165)" {14}.

Key among them is ISAIAH 7:14; "Therefore the Lord himself will give you a sign: The virgin will be with child and will give birth to a son, and will call him Immanuel." (NIV)

Point #1: "The Lord...will give you a SIGN..." (A "sign" as used in Isaiah 7:14 is something that will give validation as to the truth of the prophet's message, such as a miraculous, supernatural event.

Point #2: The SIGN will be a "VIRGIN WITH CHILD."

Point #3: The virgin's child will be male: "A SON."

Point #4: "IMMANUEL" gives meaning as to who this Son is. It points to His Deity: "GOD WITH US."

NOTE: NIV Footnote reads: "Immanuel means God with us."

MESSIAH ARRIVES: PROMISES FULLFILLED CHRIST IS KING

In the 9th chapter, Isaiah's prophetic writings provide more about the "SON" who was to come, a "SON" who will be more than just another man:

"For to us a child is born, to us a son is given, and the government will be on his shoulders. And he will be called Wonderful Counselor, Mighty God, Everlasting Father, Prince of Peace. Of the increase of his government and peace there will be no end. He will reign on David's throne and over his kingdom, establishing and upholding it with justice and righteousness from that time on and forever. The zeal of the Lord Almighty will accomplish this" (Isaiah 9:6-7).

ISAIAH PREDICTS:
    This Son will rule: "The government will be on his shoulders."
    This Son will be Divine: "Mighty God."
    This Son will be called: "Prince of Peace."
    This Son: "…will reign on David's throne and over his kingdom,"
    This Son's Government will be Eternal: "There will be no end."

The next series of prophesies predict the suffering and death of the Messiah, then His triumph over Satan through His death and resurrection. The nature of these prophecies also brought a confusing picture to the minds of the Jews. A triumphant king? Yes. But a king that is to suffer and die as a servant? No. This couldn't be the king who would triumph and restore the kingdom to Israel. If there was to be a suffering servant then he must be someone else. Perhaps there would be two Messiahs. In his article, Kyle Butt comments on the misconceptions of the Jews of Old Testament times and rabbinical thought today:

"Throughout the Old Testament, various Messianic passages refer to a majestic, glorious King who will reign over a never-ending kingdom. Yet, at the same time, other Messianic prophecies depict a suffering Messiah who will bear the guilt and sin of the entire world. Because these two aspects of Messianic prophecy seem contradictory, many in the ancient Jewish community could not understand how such diverse prophetic sentiments could be fulfilled in a single individual. Due to this conundrum, ancient and modern Jews have posited the idea that two Messiahs would come: one would be the suffering Servant, while the other would be the glorious King. …Jewish rabbi Robert M. Cohen stated: 'The rabbis saw that scripture portrayed two different pictures of King Messiah. One would conquer and reign and bring Israel back to the land by world peace and bring the fullness of

CHAPTER 9

obedience to the Torah. They called him Messiah ben David. The other picture is of a servant who would die and bear Israel's sin that they refer to as the "leprous one" based on Isaiah 53 (n.d.; see Parsons, 2003-2006)." {15}.

Isaiah Chapter 53 is one of the major prophecies that will be covered in this chapter. Many Jews see in Isaiah 53 a suffering servant sent to die for the sins of Israel, but this suffering servant would be more than this. He would also become the King who would reign on David's throne. As Kyle Butt continues to point out in the article, they fail to see that the two they envision are actually ONE:

"However, the dual Messianic idea failed to comprehend the actual nature of Messianic prophecy, and missed a primary facet of the Messianic personality: that the Messiah would be both a suffering Servant and a majestic King" (emphasis in article) {16}.

The 22ND PSALM

The Hebrew Old Testament was divided into three major divisions.
    (1). The Law (the five books of Moses)
    (2). The Prophets (both major and minor)
    (3). The Writings (in which the Psalms are included)

The Psalms are considered poetic in nature; yet the Psalms include some definite Messianic prophecies. One is the 22nd Psalm. This Psalm is attributed to King David:

"For the choir director; upon Aijeleth Hashshahar. A Psalm of David. MY God, my God, why hast thou forsaken me? Far from my deliverance are the words of my groaning. O my God, I cry by day, but Thou dost not answer; And by night, but I have no rest. Yet Thou art holy, O Thou who art enthroned upon the praises of Israel. In Thee our fathers trusted; They trusted, and Thou didst deliver them. To Thee they cried out, and were delivered; In Thee they trusted, and were not disappointed. But I am a worm, and not a man, A reproach of men, and despised by the people. All who see me sneer at me; They separate with the lip, they wag the

MESSIAH ARRIVES: PROMISES FULLFILLED CHRIST IS KING

head, saying, 'Commit yourself to the LORD; Let Him deliver him; Let Him rescue him, because He delights in him.' Yet Thou art He who didst bring me forth from the womb; Thou didst make me trust when upon my mother's breasts. Upon Thee I was cast from birth; Thou hast been my God from my mother's womb. Be not far from me, for trouble is near; For there is none to help. Many bulls have surrounded me; Strong bulls of Bashan have encircled me. They open wide their mouth at me, As a ravening and a roaring lion. I am poured out like water, And all my bones are out of joint; My heart is like wax; It is melted within me. My strength is dried up like a potsherd, And my tongue cleaves to my jaws; And Thou dost lay me in the dust of death. For dogs have surrounded me; A band of evil doers has encompassed me; They pierced my hands and my feet. I can count all my bones. They look, they stare at me; They divide my garments among them, And for my clothing they cast lots" (Psalm 22:1-18 NASB).

After reading the text of the 22nd Psalm, one can see why the Jews could see the picture of a suffering servant in prophecy. To them this was not a prophecy of victory and royalty. David, who was both prophet and king, has given us a detailed word picture of the Messiah's suffering:

v. 1: He is forsaken of God.
v. 6: He is scorned and "despised."
v. 7: They "sneer" at Him. They wag (shake) their heads.
v. 16: He is encircled by "evil doers." His "hands" and "feet" are pierced.
v. 18: They divide His "garments" and "cast lots" for them.

At this point, let's leap ahead from King David another 200 years to a man we've already referenced who lived and prophesied during the reign of four kings. His name is Isaiah.

ISAIAH CHAPTER 53

"He grew up before him like a tender shoot, and like a root out of dry ground. He had no beauty or majesty to attract us to him, nothing in his appearance that we should desire him. He was despised and rejected by men, a man of sorrows, and familiar with suffering. Like one from whom men hide their faces he was despised,

CHAPTER 9

and we esteemed him not. Surely he took up our infirmities and carried our sorrows, yet we considered him stricken by God smitten by him, and afflicted. But he was pierced for our transgressions, he was crushed for our iniquities; the punishment that brought us peace was upon him, and by his wounds we are healed. We all, like sheep, have gone astray, each of us has turned to his own way; and the LORD has laid on him the iniquity of us all" (Isaiah 53:2-6 NIV).

DROP DOWN TO VERSE 9:

"He was assigned a grave with the wicked, and with the rich in his death, though he had done no violence, nor was any deceit in his mouth" (Isaiah 53:9 NIV).

The message of the Messiah's affliction, suffering, and death is clearly visible in the 53rd chapter of Isaiah. The prediction this prophesy makes is pretty obvious. I want to point out the reason for which He died and the ones with whom He was associated in His death and burial:
v. 5-6: "He was pierced for our transgressions, He was crushed for our iniquities; …the LORD has laid on Him the iniquity of us all."
v. 9: "He was assigned a grave with the wicked, and with the rich in His death…"

In the previous prophecies, attention was centered on pointing to the Messiah's coming as a king: "the government will be on His shoulders. …He will reign on David's throne and over his kingdom…" (Isaiah 9:6-7). In these last prophecies our attention is centered on the suffering servant who would die for humanities' sins. He would be "pierced for our transgressions" (Isaiah 53:5).

The next prophecy speaks of life after death: the 16th Psalm, another Psalm of David. Notice how the Psalmist describes his faith and hope of his own resurrection, but also that of the LORD'S "Holy One":

"Therefore my heart is glad, and my glory rejoices; My flesh also will rest in hope. For you will not leave my soul in Sheol, Nor will you allow your Holy One to see corruption" (Psalm 16:9-10 NKJV).

The last three Scriptures point out so clearly the hope of David and every believer in God—that our failures and iniquities will not be held against us forever. Someone

MESSIAH ARRIVES: PROMISES FULLFILLED CHRIST IS KING

was coming to suffer for our transgressions, our sins. They would all be "LAID ON HIM" and all humanity could look forward to a resurrection from the dead. Not only that, BUT MOST IMPORTANTLY, GOD WOULD NOT LET HIS "HOLY ONE" SEE DECAY!

The next step in our search for truth will be to answer the critical skepticism of the dubious critics in the past. Some allege that prophecies such as Isaiah's are too recent for predictive validation or that Moses did not actually write the first five books of the Bible or other allegations. Therefore, the next chapter will look at the evidence of truth that is available to us.

Chapter 10

THE SUBTLE RESISTANCE OF THE SKEPTICS
THE NOT-SO-SUBTLE WAR AGAINST JESUS CHRIST

CHAPTER 10

This chapter is dedicated to answering many critics of the Biblical writers, from those who question the authorship of Moses, David, and Isaiah, to those that doubt Luke's accuracy of First Century, historical background and the time of Jesus' birth. Also, I will address the views of 20th and 21st century critics, from those that openly deny Biblical inspiration to those who now refuse to believe that Jesus Christ was a living historical person. Books, documentaries, and motion pictures are being produced constantly by people using shallow and inaccurate data designed to raise doubt in the majority of people in our culture who lack knowledge of ancient history and Biblical fundamentals.

Christianity and Jesus Himself have been under attack by some scholars who are sincere yet mistaken and by others who appear to have dubious ulterior motives. This has been going on since the first century. Some methods have been subtle while others are openly hostile, raising vicious accusations both of Jesus' disciples and of Jesus Himself regarding their moral character and motives.

The fundamental departure between Bible-believing scholars who accept a supernatural, intelligent Creator and unbelieving Biblical scholars who accept only secular, natural results is the fact that the unbelieving biblical critics will not consider anything that is not tangible. Believing Bible scholars comprehend the existence of an intangible, eternal, intelligent, supernatural Mind by whom all things came to exist. Secular Bible critics recognize only materialism. In their minds, matter is the only thing that exists. This form of criticism has been referred to as "Higher Criticism."

JOSH McDOWELL, in his book, *A Ready Defense*, explains the division between Higher and Lower Criticism:

"Lower criticism is identified with textual criticism since textual criticism is foundational to all other forms of biblical criticism. Textual criticism seeks to determine the original wording of the biblical text, especially since we do not have the original documents (called 'autographs') themselves."

From this point, "higher criticism" takes over. McDowell explains:

"Building upon…textual criticism, **higher criticism** uses other means to evaluate the text which lower criticism establishes as the most authentic version of the original."

THE SUBTLE RESISTANCE OF THE SKEPTICS

McDowell continues:

"Higher criticism can be divided into two broad disciplines, historical criticism and literary criticism. **Historical criticism**...addresses such questions as: (1) When and where was it written? (2) Who wrote it? (3) What circumstances surrounded the author or authors? (4) To whom was it written?"

What developed from "historical criticism," was an even more scrutinizing method, known as "source criticism." This method was used by a group of skeptical Bible scholars to cast implications of doubt upon the reliability of the Holy Scriptures. McDowell explains the impact it had upon the authorship of Moses:

"Source criticism emerged to a position of prominence among higher critics in the eighteenth century as many critical scholars rallied around the 'documentary hypothesis" {1}.

The "Documentary Hypothesis" of Julius Wellhausen (1844-1918)

What do we know about Wellhausen? NORMAN L.GEISLER, in his book, *Baker Encyclopedia of Christian Apologetics*, gives some background of his life:

"Julius Wellhausen (1844-1918) was a German Bible scholar known as the father of modern biblical criticism. ...He studied at Gottingen and taught at Gottingen, Griefswald, Halle, Marburg and finally returned to Gottingen as historian, philologist, and master of Hebrew, Aramaic, Syriac, and Arabic. ...Wellhausen was influenced by W.F.G. Hegel and Wilhelm Vatke, who applied the Hegelian dialectic of historical development to the development of the religion of Israel. From this platform Wellhausen developed the documentary hypothesis" {2}.

JOSH McDOWELL, in his book, *More Evidence That Demands a Verdict*, describes what the "documentary hypothesis" implies:
"Julius Wellhausen in 1895 added the finishing touches to a hypothesis which is prevalent in modern biblical circles. The hypothesis is known as the Documentary Hypothesis (JEDP hypothesis). Using literary criticism as its basis for argument, this hypothesis sets forth the idea that the Pentateuch (Genesis to Deuteronomy) was not written by Moses, as the Bible claims, but was completed years after Moses died" {3}.

CHAPTER 10

What are the implications of this type of modern biblical criticism? It raises serious questions as to divine inspiration and the credibility of Jesus Himself.

McDowell continues to explain:

"Those adhering to the Documentary Hypothesis teach that the first five books of the Bible were written close to one thousand years after Moses' death and were the result of a process of writing, rewriting, editing and compiling by various anonymous editors or redactors" {4}.

Previously, Bible scholars, as a general rule, accepted the Biblical claims that Moses was the author of the Pentateuch, guided by direct inspiration of God. The impact on modern Bible scholarship of the Documentary Hypothesis is probably more than most of us fully understand. My own personal experience comes from smatterings of conversations with Bible scholars with whom I have been associated who have just completed higher education, having received Doctorates in Theology or those who are currently studying in liberal theological universities working toward higher degrees in education. The conversation might go something like this: "Well, God probably inspired them to write it [the Pentateuch], but it just wasn't written by one man (of course, meaning Moses)."

NORMAN L. GEISLER, in the *Baker Encyclopedia of Christian Apologetics*, describes the "result" of the Documentary Hypothesis:

"The result is the famous J-E-P-D theory of the authorship of the Pentateuch. According to this theory, Moses did not write the Pentateuch (Genesis-Deuteronomy), as both Jewish and Christian scholars have held through the centuries. Rather, it was written by a number of persons over a long period. These documents are identified as:
1. the Jehovist or Yahwist (J), ninth century B.C.;
2. the Elohist (E), eighth century B.C.;
3. the Deuteronomist (D), ca. the time of Josiah, 640-609 B.C., and
4. the Priestly (P), ca. fifth century B.C.

The Pentateuch was a mosaic put together from different authors who can be identified partly by their various uses of Jehovah (Yahweh), or Elohim for God or by references to the work of the priests (P) or the laws (D). One or more 'redactors' or editor/compilers brought together all of this evolutionary development within

THE SUBTLE RESISTANCE OF THE SKEPTICS

the religious history of Israel. Wellhausen assumes that there is a 'popular religion' of Israel which must be discovered among the many impositions by later redactors, and when this religion is discovered it reveals its form at each stage in the evolutionary development" {5}.

There are serious implications involved in the Documentary Hypothesis. It clearly implies that Moses did not write the five books of the Pentateuch: Genesis, Exodus, Leviticus, Numbers, and Deuteronomy. It is easy for someone to say, "Well, perhaps Moses didn't write these books, but I believe God inspired the writers that did." In my own limited capacity, I recognize some serious problems with the Documentary Hypothesis.

1. It denies the Holy Scripture's testimony that Moses wrote the five books of the Law.

GENESIS is the First Book of the Law. It is true that Moses' name is not mentioned in Genesis. However, two prophetic Scriptures in Genesis verify that Moses was the author:

"I will put enmity between you and the woman, and between your seed and her seed; he shall bruise your head, and you shall bruise his heel" (Genesis 3:15 RSV 1971).

NOTE: "The Hegelian Dialectic of historical development" is the philosophy of "Georg Wilhelm Friedrich Hegel (1770-1831). Many things could be said about Hegel's influence on civilization in both political and religious philosophy. Hegel's philosophy influenced the development of fascism in Europe and Wellhausen's worldview of evolution in the religion of Israel. In his book, *Western Civilizations*, EDWARD McNALL BURNS, describes "The central doctrine of Hegel's philosophy":

"The central doctrine of Hegel's philosophy is the idea of purposive evolution. He regarded the universe as in a condition of flux, with everything tending to pass over into its opposite. In particular, each institution or social or political organism grows to maturity, fulfills its mission, and then gives way to something different. But the old itself is never entirely destroyed; the clash of opposites results eventually in a fusion, in the creation of a new organism made up of elements taken from the two opposites themselves. Then the process is repeated over and over again with each new stage representing an improvement over that which has gone before. But Hegel's conception of evolution was not mechanistic. He believed the whole process to be guided by the universal reason or God. Evolution, he maintained, is the unfoldment of God in History. Further, he argued that the war of opposites would ultimately lead to a beneficent goal. This goal he described as the perfect state, in which the interests of every citizen would be perfectly blended with the interests of society. …Hegel worshipped the state in a much more ecstatic fashion than did any of the other Romantic Idealists. He held that true liberty consists in subjection to political society, and that the individual has no rights which the state is bound to respect; for without the state the individual would be nothing but an animal. 'The State is the Divine Idea as it exists on earth'" {6}

CHAPTER 10

"The scepter shall not depart from Judah, nor the ruler's staff from between his feet, until he comes to whom it belongs; and to him shall be the obedience of the peoples" (Genesis 49:10 RSV 1971).

JESUS the Messiah, shortly after His resurrection from the dead, clearly testified that Moses prophesied about Him in Genesis:

"Then he said to them, 'These are my words which I spoke to you, while I was still with you, that everything written about me in the Law of Moses and the prophets and the psalms must be fulfilled" (Luke 24:44 RSV 1971).

2. It denies the truth of the claims Jesus made when He stated that Moses wrote about Him.
"If you believed Moses, you would believe me, for he wrote of me. But if you do not believe his writings, how will you believe my words?" (John 5:46-47 RSV 1971).

This is where the credibility of Jesus Christ was and still is being challenged. It was challenged by skeptical Jews during the first century while Jesus was living and fulfilling His ministry on earth. It was being challenged by Wellhausen and others who denied supernaturalism in 1895. It is still being challenged by skeptics who question Moses' and Christ's credibility to an even stronger degree today. By their accusations they have subtly alleged that Moses' writings were not inspired by any supernatural God.

3. It indirectly accuses the alleged writers (whom they claim wrote the books instead of Moses) of being liars because the text states that Moses wrote all the Law, including the Ten Commandments:
"Then the LORD said to Moses, 'Write down these words, for in accordance with these words I have made a covenant with you and with Israel.' So he was there with the LORD forty days and forty nights; he did not eat bread or drink water. And he wrote on the tablets the words of the covenant, the Ten Commandments" (Exodus 34:27-28 NASB).

4. All five books of the Law declare directly or indirectly that Moses was the author:

THE SUBTLE RESISTANCE OF THE SKEPTICS

GENESIS: In Genesis 3:15 & Genesis 49:10 Moses prophesied about the coming of the Messiah (Christ) and Jesus Himself testified: "If you believed Moses, you would believe me, for he wrote of me" (John 5:46 RSV 1971).

EXODUS: "Then the LORD said to Moses, 'Write down these words, for in accordance with these words I have made a covenant with you and with Israel.' So he was there with the LORD forty days and forty nights; he did not eat bread or drink water. And he wrote on the tablets the words of the covenant, the Ten Commandments" (Exodus 34:27-28 NASB).

In Mark 12:26 Jesus reminded the Jewish Sadducees of what "the book of Moses" recorded in (Exodus 3:6, 15): "But concerning the dead, that they rise, have you not read in the book of Moses, in the burning bush passage, how God spoke to him, saying, 'I am the God of Abraham, the God of Isaac, and the God of Jacob'? (Mark 12:26 NKJV)

LEVITICUS: "Now the LORD called to Moses, and spoke to him from the tabernacle of meeting, saying, 'Speak to the children of Israel, and say to them: "When any one of you brings an offering to the LORD, you shall bring your offering of the livestock—of the herd and of the flock"'" (Leviticus 1:1-2 NKJV).

"And the LORD spoke to Moses, saying, 'Speak to the children of Israel, and say to them: "The feasts of the LORD, which you shall proclaim to be holy convocations, these are My feasts"'" (Leviticus 23:1-2 NKJV).

NUMBERS: "NOW the LORD spoke to Moses in the Wilderness of Sinai, in the tabernacle of meeting, on the first day of the second month, in the second year after they had come out of the land of Egypt, saying: 'Take a census of all the congregation of the children of Israel, by their families, by their fathers' houses, according to the number of names, every male individually'" (Numbers 1:1-2 NKJV).

CHAPTER 10

"At the LORD'S command Moses recorded the stages in their journey. This is their journey by stages" (Numbers 33:2 NIV).

DEUTERONOMY: The Law of the Blessings and the Curses in chapters 28-31

"These are the terms of the covenant the LORD commanded Moses to make with the Israelites in Moab, in addition to the covenant he had made with them at Horeb" (Deuteronomy 29: 1 NIV).

NOTICE THIS "COVENANT" WAS "IN ADDITION TO THE COVENANT HE HAD MADE WITH THEM AT HOREB (Mount Sinai).

"So Moses wrote this law and gave it to the priests, the sons of Levi, who carried the ark of the covenant of the LORD, and to all the elders of Israel" (Deuteronomy 31:9 NASB).

The written declaration of Jesus that Moses wrote about him and that He came to fulfill the things that were written about Him in Genesis ("the Law of Moses") needed to be fulfilled. The written declaration in the other four books of the Law is that Moses was their author. Either the supposed J.E.P.D. writers were lying or Wellhausen was seriously in error in his hypothesis.

The allegation of Wellhausen and those that adhere to his philosophy is perfectly clear—the five books of the Pentateuch: Genesis Exodus, Leviticus, Numbers and Deuteronomy—were written by people who were trying to deceive the Israelites living in the land of Canaan, the Jews after Israel and Judah divided, the Jews living during Christ's lifetime. It also alleges that Jesus Christ was Himself deceived or that He was promoting the fabrication of Moses' authorship and the historical time frame in which these five books were written.

The preceding written testimony of the five books of Law points to the fact that Moses was specifically designated and commanded by God to write the books of the Law. This is not all. Other Old Testament writers and New Testament writers along with some Hebrew historians and Christians living after the Death and Resurrection of Christ also make it clear that Moses was the accepted author.

THE SUBTLE RESISTANCE OF THE SKEPTICS

JOSHUA: "Then Joshua built an altar to the LORD, the God of Israel, in Mount Ebal, just as Moses the servant of the LORD had commanded the sons of Israel, as it is written in the book of the law of Moses, an altar of uncut stones, on which no man had wielded an iron tool; and they offered burnt offerings on it to the LORD, and sacrificed peace offerings" (Joshua 8:30-31 NASB).

1 KINGS: "...and observe what the LORD your God requires: Walk in his ways, and keep his decrees and commands, his laws and requirements, as written in the Law of Moses, so that you may prosper in all you do and wherever you go" (1 Kings 2:3 NIV).

2 KINGS: "Yet he did not put the sons of the assassins to death, in accordance with what is written in the Book of the Law of Moses where the LORD commanded: 'Fathers shall not be put to death for their children, nor children put to death for their fathers; each is to die for his own sins'" (2 Kings 14:6 NIV).

1 CHRONICLES: "And the Levites carried the ark of God upon their shoulders with the poles, as Moses had commanded according to the word of the LORD" (1 Chronicles 15:15 RSV 1971).

2 CHRONICLES: "And Jehoi'ada posted watchmen for the house of the LORD under the direction of the Levitical priests and the Levites whom David had organized to be in charge of the house of the LORD, to offer burnt offerings to the LORD, as it is written in the law of Moses, with rejoicing and with singing, according to the order of David" (2-Chronicles 23:18 RSV 1971).

NOTE: This was part of the Law given to Moses by "the LORD" in Numbers 4:1-15. Notice how it begins: "The LORD said to Moses and Aaron..." (v. 1 RSV 1971). This is a direct Inspiration from "the LORD!"

CHAPTER 10

EZRA: "Then arose Jeshua the son of Jo'zadak, with his fellow priests, and Zerub'babel the son of She-al'ti-el with his kinsmen, and they built the altar of the God of Israel, to offer burnt offerings upon it, as it is written in the law of Moses the man of God" (Ezra 3:2 RSV 1971).

NEHEMIAH: "AND all the people gathered as one man at the square which was in front of the Water Gate, and they asked Ezra the scribe to bring the book of the law of Moses which the LORD had given to Israel" (Nehemiah 8:1 NASB).

DANIEL: "All Israel has transgressed thy law and turned aside, refusing to obey thy voice. And the curse and oath which are written in the law of Moses the servant of God have been poured out upon us, because we have sinned against him" (Daniel 9:11 RSV 1971).

It is interesting to note that four of the books Moses wrote had written testimony in them that Moses received direct inspiration from "the LORD" God. Genesis' authorship by Moses is verified by Jesus Christ in the New Testament gospel of Luke (Luke 24:44), and John's gospel (John 5:46-47). From about 1500 B.C. onward no one, including Joshua, ever mentioned another author, such as J. or E.,P., or D. From the time of Joshua, a contemporary of Moses whose historical recordings of the taking of the promised land dated about 1450-1443 B.C., onward to the historical time of Ezra and Nehemiah (458-400 B.C.), it is always—always—spoken of as "the law of Moses" or "the book of the law of Moses" or "the law in the book of Moses" (2 Chronicles 25:4). There is no mention whatsoever of other sources as being the authentic authors of the Pentateuch. There have been skeptics of the accuracy, inspiration, and authorship of the Bible, at least since Benedict Spinoza (1632-1677) and probably before, who may have never expressed their philosophy in public. As NORMAN GEISLER has commented: "Spinoza became one of the first modern intellectuals to engage in systematic higher criticism of the Bible. ...Spinoza's naturalism led him to conclude that Moses could not have written many passages in the Pentateuch" {7}.

NOTE: Daniel is referring back to the Blessing and the Curse (Deuteronomy 28:1-2, 15).

THE SUBTLE RESISTANCE OF THE SKEPTICS

When God breathed His New Covenant message into the writers of the New Testament Scriptures Gospel writers did not fail to recognize the fact that Moses was the former God-directed lawgiver:

MATTHEW: "And Jesus said to him, 'See that you tell no one; but go your way, show yourself to the priest, and offer the gift that Moses commanded [referring to Deuteronomy 24:8], as a testimony to them" (Matthew 8:4 NKJV).

MARK: "But concerning the dead, that they rise, have you not read in the book of Moses, in the burning bush passage, how God spoke to him, saying, 'I am the God of Abraham, the God of Isaac, and the God of Jacob'?" (Mark 12:26 NKJV).

LUKE: "And when the days for their purification according to the law of Moses were completed, they brought Him up to Jerusalem to present Him to the Lord" (Luke 2:22 NASB).

JOHN: "For the law was given through Moses; grace and truth came through Jesus Christ" (John 1:17).

"[Phillip to Nathaniel] We have found the one Moses wrote about in the Law, and about whom the prophets also wrote—Jesus of Nazareth, the son of Joseph" (John 1:45b).

Matthew, Mark, and John were Jews living under the Law of Moses until the advent of Christ's Death, burial, and resurrection when Jesus fulfilled the Law of Moses, the prophets, and the Psalms (Luke 24:44).

HISTORICAL EVIDENCE
(Separate from the Canon of the Holy Scriptures)

Moses' authorship was accepted by the Jewish historian Josephus:

CHAPTER 10

FLAVIUS JOSEPHUS (A.D. 37-100): An important Jewish historian of the first century, who left us with several confirming historical records about the canon of the Old Testament, Jesus Christ, and James the brother of Jesus. Josephus affirms the authorship of Moses, of whom he wrote:

"For we have not an innumerable multitude of books among us, disagreeing from and contradicting one another, [as the Greeks have,] but only twenty-two books, which contain the records of all the past times; which are justly believed to be divine; and of them **five belong to Moses, which contain his laws and the traditions of the origin of mankind till his death**" (emphasis added) {8}.

This is not all Josephus wrote about the Old Testament books. More will follow later, but first let's have a look at some of the other early Jewish writers.

JOSH McDOWELL, in his book, *More Evidence That Demands a Verdict*, lists the Talmud, Mishnah, and Philo among others who maintain the "Jewish Tradition" that Moses was the author of the Pentateuch:

"2C. THE TALMUD, (Baba Bathra, 146), a Jewish commentary on the Law (Torah), dating from about 200 B.C., and the MISHNAH, (Pirqe Aboth, 1,1), a rabbinic interpretation and legislation dating from about 100 B.C., both attribute the Torah to Moses.

"3C. Likewise, PHILO, the Jewish philosopher-theologian born approximately 20 A.D. held Mosaic authorship: 'But I will…tell the story of Moses as I have learned it, both from the sacred books, the wonderful monuments of his wisdom which he has left behind him, and from some of the elders of the nation' 51/279" {9}. Skeptics critical of Moses' authorship refuse to accept anything that suggests or implies a supernatural occurrence.

To accept Moses' authorship of Genesis means to accept the supernatural inspiration of the book of Genesis, since it includes thousands of years of Bible history of events and people who lived long before Moses' birth. Jews and Christians accept Moses as the author of Genesis precisely because they believe in divine (God-breathed) inspiration. It wasn't necessary for Moses to have been with Adam, Noah, or Abraham because Almighty God could have directly inspired Moses to write

THE SUBTLE RESISTANCE OF THE SKEPTICS

about the creation and the flood, possibly during the same period when Moses wrote the covenant written at Sinai (Horeb), or later, when he recorded the covenant written in the land of Moab: "besides the covenant he made with them at Horeb" (Deuteronomy 29:1b NASB).

For the same reasons, the plagues of blood, frogs, flies, livestock, hail, locusts, darkness, the death of the firstborn of Egypt, the parting of the Red Sea and all of the other supernatural events the Bible records will not be accepted because they defy the philosophy of materialistic naturalism, which denies any historic event or anything else that is supernatural. Paul the apostle wrote in his second letter to Timothy regarding how Timothy had learned the Holy Scriptures (2 Timothy 1:5) since early youth from his faithful Jewish grandmother Lois and his mother Eunice. About the Scriptures, Paul wrote:

"…from childhood you have known the sacred writings which are able to give you the wisdom that leads to salvation through faith which is in Christ Jesus. All Scripture is inspired by God and profitable for teaching, for reproof, for correction, for training in righteousness; that the man of God may be adequate, equipped for every good work" (2 Timothy 3:15-17 NASB).

Here are a list of authors who give an excellent, meticulously detailed refutation and rejection of the Documentary Hypothesis:

MORE EVIDENCE THAT DEMANDS A VERDICT, (1975) JOSH McDOWELL. This book devotes over 100 pages to the evidence for Mosaic authorship for the first five books of the Old Testament, plus the lack of evidence from Wellhausen and others for their JEPD "Hypothesis" (a hypothesis means it's hypothetical—no evidence).
A READY DEFENSE, (1992) The Best of Josh McDowell, Compiled by BILL WILSON. This book devotes 24 pages to the Documentary Hypothesis and condensed evidence for the rejection of it. There are over 490 pages dedicated to the defense of the Christian faith.

EVIDENCE FOR CHRISTIANITY, (2006) JOSH McDOWELL. This contains over 100 pages of evidence against the Documentary Hypothesis in a book of over 740 pages of: "Historical Evidences for The Christian Faith."

CHAPTER 10

BAKER ENCYCLOPEDIA of CHRISTIAN APOLOGATICS (1999) NORMAN L. GEISLER. In the 841 pages of this encyclopedia is a vast assortment of facts relating to Christian evidences. Geisler gives an excellent rebuttal to the seven basic arguments opposing Moses' authorship of the Pentateuch, plus some detailed information on Julius Wellhausen called "the father of modern biblical criticism," not to mention several pages on "Bible Criticism" explaining and refuting the various allegations against the God-breathed inspiration of the Holy Scriptures.

I have three other books by Geisler in my library, some from which I will be quoting later.

In my opinion, the efforts to cast unfounded allegations which appear to be intended to diminish one's faith in the fact that God did indeed direct Moses to write the first five books—Genesis, Exodus, Leviticus, Numbers, and Deuteronomy—have gathered no substantial evidence to assert that four or more writers—"J.E.P.D."— recorded and put together the Pentateuch long after Moses' death. It is, as stated, a "Hypothesis."

In Summary, looking at the evidence found in Old and New Testament Scriptures and in the writings of early Jewish historians, theologians, and commentaries, there is no reasonable evidence to indicate there were other writers who compiled the Pentateuch at much later dates.

Moses' authorship is verified throughout the Scriptures. Genesis is substantiated as Moses' writings by Jesus Christ, the Son of God (Luke 24:44; John 5:46-47). The Old Testament Scriptures in Exodus, Leviticus, Numbers, Deuteronomy, Joshua, 1 Kings, 2 Kings, 1 Chronicles, 2 Chronicles, Ezra, Nehemiah, and Daniel testify that Moses was the inspired author (Exodus 34:27-28; Leviticus 23:1-2; Numbers 33:2; Deuteronomy 31:9; Joshua 8:30-31; 1 Kings 2:3; 2 Kings 14:6; 1 Chronicles 15:15; 2 Chronicles 23:18; Ezra 3:2; Nehemiah 8:1; Daniel 9:11). The New Testament Gospel writers—Matthew, Mark, Luke, and John—testified that Moses was the author of "The Law of Moses" (Matthew 8:4; Mark 12:26; Luke 2:22; John 1:17, 45).

THE SUBTLE RESISTANCE OF THE SKEPTICS

The Jewish Historian Josephus, the Jewish commentary the Talmud, and the Jewish philosopher/theologian Philo, all believed and accepted Moses as the divinely-inspired author of the five books of Law.

It wasn't until more than 3,000 years later when Julius Wellhausen became the primary founder of the "Documentary Hypothesis" that a group of skeptics challenged the authenticity of the God-breathed inspiration of the Holy Scriptures. Wellhausen and associates decided they knew more than Jesus, the Son of God, about who wrote the Law of Moses. This could be the reason why Wellhausen's allegations are still considered to be a "HYPOTHESIS"!

The Book of Isaiah under Anti-Supernaturalistic Scrutiny

It should come as no surprise that the Book of Isaiah, one of the foremost books of Messianic prophecy, should be brought into question by the skeptical eyes of those who will not accept any type of supernatural event, especially events that point out the future arrival of a promised Messiah. Thus, the authority of the divine inspiration of the prophet Isaiah has inevitably been challenged! If there truly is a Messiah then there truly is a decision that needs to be made about what is truth! Jesus' statement to Governor Pontius Pilate when He was brought before him was this: "You say correctly that I am a king. For this reason I have been born, and for this I have come into the world, to bear witness to the truth. Everyone who is of the truth hears My voice" (John 18: 37b); to which Pilate asks the question which still has to be answered by every person living today: "**What is Truth?**" (John 18:38a NASB).

The challenges by the skeptics are two-fold. First, the authentic date for the book of Isaiah is in question. Second, allegations have been made that more than one author was involved.

Since Isaiah, "the son of Amoz" (Isaiah 1:1), was not around in the nineteenth century to defend and substantiate his prophecies, "anti-supernatural" scholars sprung forth to provide their own interpretation of what occurred. As one investigates the prophetic writings in the book of Isaiah, the deeply Messianic nature of the book provides a rather clear motive for challenging the authority of Holy Scripture by those who rebel against it. One cannot read the 53rd chapter of Isaiah without

CHAPTER 10

recognizing its detailed prediction of the death of Christ.

KENNY BARFIELD, in his book, *The Prophet Motive*, dismantles their thinly concealed ulterior motives:

"The traditional view among Jews and early Christians places the composition of Isaiah during the prophet's lifetime (in the eighth century B.C.). The superscription (1:1) avows the book to be the inspired product of Isaiah ben Amoz. This view dominated thinking until the nineteenth century. Then, bolstered by a surge of anti-supernatural critics, scholars splintered the book into various strands. They held each to be the work of different authors. The more common scheme attributes much of chapters 1-39 to Isaiah ben Amoz with chapters 40-66 to an unknown later prophet. Others subdivide the second section into 'Second Isaiah' (40-55) and 'Third Isaiah' (56-66). Still others claim additional editors, or redactors, shared in shaping the final version" {10}.

Barfield describes three motives for the revisionists to make allegations of a much later date for Isaiah:

"Three reasons support the critic's position. First, the times offered safe haven to those who denied the prophets intended to predict future occurrences. Clearly, if the prophets did not foretell events, the highly accurate description of history had to be written after the event. Second, scholars detected a stylistic distinction between chapters 1-39 and chapters 40-66. They assumed these divergent styles and subjects meant different authors. ...Third, critics argued 'Second Isaiah' often demands a setting during the Babylonian exile while much of the opening chapters demands a setting in Palestine. Again, critics assume the impossibility of 'looking into the future'" {11}.

There is ample evidence that the prophecies of Isaiah were written during the time when Isaiah claimed they were written:

"THE vision of Isaiah the son of Amoz, concerning Judah and Jerusalem which he saw during the reigns of Uzziah, Jotham, Ahaz, and Hezekiah, kings of Judah" (Isaiah 1:1 NASB).

THE SUBTLE RESISTANCE OF THE SKEPTICS

Hezekiah's Reign

Hezekiah, the fourth king Isaiah mentioned in chapter 1:1, reigned from about 726 to 716 B.C. (2 Kings 20:1-18). Isaiah was with Hezekiah (in about 712 B.C.) during his illness and recovery when God added fifteen years to his life.

Sennacherib, King Of Assyria, Invaded Judah

"NOW it came about in the fourteenth year of king Hezekiah, Sennacherib king of Assyria came up against all the fortified cities of Judah and seized them. And the king of Assyria sent Rabshakeh from Lachish to Jerusalem to king Hezekiah with a large army. And he stood by the conduit of the upper pool on the highway of the fuller's field" (Isaiah 36:1-2 NASB).

Hezekiah Sends for Isaiah the Prophet

"AND when king Hezekiah heard it, he tore his clothes, covered himself with sackcloth and entered the house of the LORD. Then he sent Eliakim who was over the household with Shebna the scribe and the elders of the priests, covered with sackcloth, to Isaiah the prophet, the son of Amoz" (Isaiah 37:1-2 NASB).

Dickson's New Analytical Bible, Old Testament Chronology, p. 1454 lists the historical date of Sennacherib's Invasion of Judah at 701 B.C. {12}.

The historian, Edward McNall Burns, in his book, *Western Civilizations*, estimates the reign of the Assyrian King, Sennacherib, at 705-681 B.C.:

"Their empire reached its height in the eighth and seventh centuries under Sargon II (722-705 B.C.), Sennacherib (705-681), and Assurbanipal (668-626)" {13}.

Continuing to help pin-point the historical dates of Isaiah as author of the complete book, there is corroborating evidence in archeology.

CHAPTER 10

MERRILL F. UNGER, in his book, *Archeology and the Old Testament*, offers substantial support to the testimony of Isaiah the prophet concerning the invasion of Sennacherib's Assyrian army into Judah:

"The early years of Sennacherib, accordingly, seemed to Hezekiah propitious for rebelling against Assyria, and the strong and godly ruler of Judah did not hesitate to do so. The Assyrian king in 701 B.C. launched his great western campaign to punish Hezekiah and other recalcitrants and bring them back under the Assyrian yoke. This important undertaking is not only graphically described in the Bible but is also recorded in the annals of Sennacherib which were recorded on clay cylinders or prisms. The final edition of these annals is found on the so-called Taylor prism of the British Museum and a copy on a prism in the Oriental Institute of the University of Chicago. 'As for Hezekiah, the Jew, who did not submit to my yoke, 46 of his strong walled cities, as well as the small cities in their neighborhood, which were without number, by escalade and by bringing up siege engines, by attacking and storming on foot, by mines, tunnels and breaches, I besieged and took 200,150 people...male and female, horses, mules, asses, camels, cattle and sheep, without number I brought away from them and counted as spoil. Himself, like a caged bird, I shut up in Jerusalem, his royal city'" {14}.

There are three important pieces of evidence found in King Sennacherib's own testimony:

1. Hezekiah is mentioned by name in the prism as the king who refused to submit to the Assyrian yoke at this point in history, thus giving strong incentive for the Assyrian king's invasion of Judah. King Hezekiah's reign in history is verified in 701 B.C.

2. Isaiah the prophet, son of Amoz, is verified as being present with Hezekiah when Sennacherib invades Judah in 701 B.C. throughout Old testament Scriptures:

"NOW it came about in the fourteenth year of King Hezekiah, Sennacherib king of Assyria came up against all the fortified cities of Judah and seized them" (Isaiah 36:1 NASB).

THE SUBTLE RESISTANCE OF THE SKEPTICS

"And when king Hezekiah heard it, he tore his cloths, covered himself with sackcloth and entered the house of the LORD. Then he sent Eliakim who was over the household with Shebna the scribe and the elders of the priests, covered with sackcloth, to Isaiah the prophet, the son of Amoz" (Isaiah 37:1-2 NASB).

2 Chronicles and 2 Kings also record the historical event and Isaiah's presence with Hezekiah (2 Chronicles 32:1-2, 20; 2 Kings 18:13-14; 2 Kings 19:1-2). Most reliable sources claim the author was Ezra, the priest and scribe (Ezra 7:11-12). These sources include the Jewish Talmud, most Jewish writers, and early Christian writers. The two books of Chronicles were written between 430-400 B.C. According to Josephus, the first century Jewish historian, all of the Old Testament was completed by the time of the Persian king, Artaxerxes (465-424 B.C.) which basically agrees with the Talmud and other scholars.

Biblical skeptics do not seriously challenge the authenticity of Isaiah chapters 1-39. It is the most critical part of Isaiah, chapters 40-66, they allege were written by someone else at a much later date. It is in this section, chapter 53, where he predicts with great detail the future death of the Messiah. Therefore, the authenticity of the passage must be discredited.

The providential power of God and His ability to control nations for His own purpose is beyond our human capacity to fully comprehend. He has raised up people throughout history since the beginning of creation to achieve His eternal purpose. His divine strategy is the salvation of all of humanity, regardless of their flaws, if they will accept His Messiah, His Son, with a willingness to put their complete trust in Him, the Savior the Father sent into the world (John 1:1-14). In chapters 44 and 45 of Isaiah, the prophet, through the inspiration of God, reveals the destiny of two nations and a ruler whom He will use to free the nation of Judah and to rebuild the temple in Jerusalem:

"This is what the LORD says—your Redeemer, who formed you in the womb: 'I am the LORD, who has made all things, who alone stretched out the heavens, who spread out the earth by myself…" (Isaiah 44:24 NIV).
DROP DOWN TO VERSE 28:

"…who says of Cyrus, 'He is my shepherd and I will accomplish all that I please; he will say of Jerusalem, 'Let it be rebuilt,' and of the temple, 'Let its foundations

CHAPTER 10

be laid'" (Isaiah 44:28 NIV).

"This is what the LORD says to his anointed, to Cyrus, whose right hand I take hold of to subdue nations before him and to strip kings of their armor, to open doors before him so that gates will not be shut..." (Isaiah 45:1 NIV).

Isaiah prophesied during the reign of King Hezekiah. Hezekiah's reign ended, according to the chronologists, from about 697 B.C. to about 687 B.C., and Isaiah's Biblical prophesies appear to have ended during the reign of Hezekiah. You see, Cyrus, king of Persia, sometime during the first year of his reign, about 536 B.C., made the proclamation that he had been given divine authority by Almighty God to build the temple in Jerusalem (Ezra 1:1-4). This took place about 151 to 161 years after Isaiah's predictive prophecy.

According to the first century Jewish historian, FLAVIUS JOSEPHUS, Cyrus the king, knew about Isaiah's prophecy and had read it himself:

"This was known to Cyrus by his reading the book which Isaiah left behind him of his prophecies; for this prophet said that God had spoken thus to him in a secret vision: 'My will is, that Cyrus, whom I have appointed to be king over many and great nations, send back my people to their own land, and build my temple.' This was foretold by Isaiah one hundred and forty years before the temple was demolished" {15}.

NOTE: The fall of Jerusalem and the destruction of the temple by the Babylonians took place in 587 B.C. Isaiah had written the prophecy of Cyrus, appointed by God to see that the temple was rebuilt, during Hezekiah's reign which began about 727 B.C. Add the 140 years that Josephus stated to the time when the prophecy was fulfilled and you come up with 727 B.C.!
The book of 2 Chronicles is part of the historical grouping of the Old Testament. The 36th chapter of 2 Chronicles also records how Cyrus was "stirred up" by "the LORD" to rebuild the temple in Jerusalem:

"Now in the first year of Cyrus king of Persia, that the word of the LORD by the

THE SUBTLE RESISTANCE OF THE SKEPTICS

mouth of Jeremiah might be fulfilled, the LORD stirred up the spirit of Cyrus king of Persia, so that he made a proclamation throughout all his kingdom, and also put it in writing, saying, 'Thus says Cyrus king of Persia: All the kingdoms of the earth the LORD God of heaven has given me. And He has commanded me to build Him a house at Jerusalem which is in Judah. Who is among you of all His people? May the LORD his God be with him, and let him go up!'" (2 Chronicles 36: 22-23 NKJV).

JEREMIAH, the prophet living in Jerusalem before and during the siege of Jerusalem, foretold Judah's fall to king Nebuchadnezzar of Babylon in 587 B.C. and also predicted its return from captivity back to the land (Jeremiah 30:1-3).

JOSEPHUS, the historian who recorded the proclamation of Cyrus for the temple to be rebuilt, also stated that all the Old Testament, including 2 Chronicles, was completed by the time king Artaxerxes ruled Persia:

"For we have not an innumerable multitude of books among us, disagreeing from and contradicting one another, [as the Greeks have,] but only twenty-two books, which contain the records of all the past times…"

NOTE: The English Bible arranges the Old Testament into 39 books. The Jewish historian Josephus lists only 22 books. Why the difference? The books in the Hebrew Bible are grouped in different order and some are condensed into one book.

The Hebrew Bible will group their books in this arrangement:

1. The 5-books of Law (Pentateuch)
    Genesis, Exodus, Leviticus, Numbers, Deuteronomy..................................5

2. The Prophets
    Former Prophets—Joshua, Judges, 1 & 2-Samuel, 1 & 2 Kings..................4
    Latter Prophets—Isaiah, Jeremiah, Ezekiel, the Book of the Twelve..........4
    (minor prophets)
    [NOTE: 1&2 Samuel counted as one Book; 1&2 Kings
    counted as one Book; the 12 minor prophets counted as one Book]

3. The Writings

CHAPTER 10

> Psalms, Proverbs, Job, Song of Solomon, Ruth, Lamentations,
> Ecclesiastes, Esther, Daniel, Ezra-Nehemiah, 1 & 2 Chronicles............11
> [NOTE: Ezra/Nehemiah counted as one Book;
> 1&2 Chronicles as one Book]

TOTAL...**24**

This brings the count of the number of books a lot closer, but there is still a difference of two books. I think perhaps NORMAN L. GEISLER may have the answer in his *Baker Encyclopedia of Christian Apologetics* concerning Josephus' historical testimony about the Hebrew Canon:

"Testimony to the Canon. Josephus supports the Protestant view of the canon of the Old Testament against the Roman Catholic view, which venerates the Old Testament Apocrypha. ...He even lists the names of the books, which are identical with the thirty-nine books of the Protestant Old Testament. He groups the thirty-nine into twenty-two volumes to correspond with the number of letters in the Hebrew alphabet" {16}.

Now continuing on with Josephus historical testimony:

"...which are justly believed to be divine; and of them five belong to Moses, which contain his laws and the traditions of the origin of mankind till his death. This interval of time was little short of three thousand years; but as to the time from the death of Moses till the reign of Artaxerxes king of Persia, who reigned after Xerxes, the prophets, who were after Moses, wrote down what was done in their times in thirteen books. The remaining four books contain hymns to God, and precepts for the conduct of human life" {17}.

The allegations of the skeptics that the latter part of Isaiah's prophecies were written by someone else at a much later historical date are now beginning to show serious flaws.

The Persian king, Artaxerxes, reigned from 465 to 424 B.C., therefore, by this time the Hebrew Canon was complete. Not only did Josephus leave written testimony about Cyrus having read Isaiah's prophecy, in the first years of his reign (536 B.C.), we have historical evidence that the Old Testament Canon had been completed at least 400 years before the arrival of the Messiah, Christ Jesus. Both of the Persian

THE SUBTLE RESISTANCE OF THE SKEPTICS

Kings are confirmed by Ezra:
"NOW in the first year of Cyrus king of Persia, that the word of the LORD by the mouth of Jeremiah might be fulfilled, the LORD stirred up the spirit of Cyrus king of Persia, so that he made a proclamation throughout all his kingdom, and also put it in writing…" (Ezra 1:1a NKJV).

"Now after these things, in the reign of Artaxerxes king of Persia, Ezra the son of Seraiah, the son of Azariah, the son of Hilkiah…" (Ezra 7:1 NKJV).

There were two other prophets living during the 8th century B.C.

KENNY BARFIELD, in his book, *The Prophet Motive*, comments on the writings of Micah and Amos with similar backgrounds to Isaiah:

"Much of Isaiah's material closely parallels writings of Amos and Micah, both of whom wrote during the eighth century B.C. When compared to these early prophets, Isaiah plainly shares both a common background and common experiences. Since most scholars accept an early origin for both books, it is contradictory to deny a comparable early origin to Isaiah" {18}.

This is especially significant, since it was Micah who prophesied the specific place of Messiah's birth from the lineage of Judah: "whose origins are from old, from ancient times." Micah, in the first chapter, claims his divinely inspired predictions were made during the reigns of "Jotham, Ahaz, and Hezekiah" (Micah 1:1).

"But you, Bethlehem Ephrathah, though you are small among the clans of Judah, out of you will come for me one who will be ruler over Israel, whose origins are from of old, from ancient times" (Micah 5:2 NIV).

It was 700+ years later when the birth of Jesus Christ was recorded in Matthew 2:1-6. The Messiah had arrived as promised. None of the critics seem to challenge Micah, a contemporary of Isaiah, like they challenge Isaiah chapters 40-66. Perhaps this is because of the detailed death of the Messiah predicted in Isaiah chapter 53.

CHAPTER 10

The Dead Sea Scrolls' Testimony of Isaiah's Early Prophecies

The problems created for materialists (who are unwilling to accept any supernatural event) by the discovery of the Dead Sea Scrolls are demonstrated in two critical areas. First is the date established of the Isaiah scroll found among the Old Testament copies and how these manuscripts were esteemed among the Essenes, a monastic community isolated in an area very close to the Dead Sea. Second is the astonishing accuracy demonstrated when the Isaiah scroll was compared to the Hebrew Masoretic text of the 10th century A.D.

KENNY BARFIELD, in his book, *The Prophet Motive*, claims the "anti-supernatural" establishment cannot substantiate their rejection of Isaiah's prophecies:

"Since the anti-supernatural barrage fails to justify banishing either predictive prophecy or the supernatural from the prophecies of Isaiah, we may now turn to several reliable witnesses who place the manuscript's origin years before many of its predictions came to pass" {19}.

JAMES C. VANDERKAM, a professor of Hebrew Scriptures at the University of Notre Dame, was part of an international organization involved with translating and editing the unpublished Dead Sea Scrolls. In his book, *The Dead Sea Scrolls Today*, he describes how the scrolls, such as the Isaiah Scroll from cave one, were methodically dated using three different methods:

1) "Paleography is the study of ancient scripts or the ways in which scribes shaped the letters of the texts they were writing or copying. Styles of letter formation change over time. By observing the changes, the paleographer can determine roughly where on the line of development a particular document belongs" (emphasis added) {20}.

2) "Accelerator Mass Spectrometry...One external control is now available for the first time—accelerator mass spectrometry (AMS), a more refined form of carbon-14 dating" (emphasis added) {21}.

THE SUBTLE RESISTANCE OF THE SKEPTICS

3) "Internal Allusions...A third means for obtaining a general idea of when the scrolls were written is provided by references in them to known individuals...or peoples. If a text names a recognizable individual, then it could not have been written before that person's lifetime" (emphasis added) {22}.

On page 18, Vanderkam's book provides a table detailing the three methods used to date the Isaiah Scroll "IQIsaa" in Cave one:

"Internal [Allusions] Date..125-100 B.C.
"Paleographical Date..335-327 B.C.
"AMS Date..202-107 B.C." {23}.

According to the three different methods used to determine the date of the Isaiah Scroll found in Cave One, the age could be as old as 335 B.C. or as recent as 100 B.C. Since AMS (Carbon-14) dating and Internal Allusions dating seem to suggest a period of 202 B.C. to 100 B.C., rather than engaging in dispute about the validity of the earlier dates, it seems to me, as to some of the Biblical scholars, prudent to settle on the latest date for this great manuscript, and that would be the year 100 B.C.

Barfield explains why:

"The Isaiah Scroll, found at Qumran and said by most authorities to be a copy of an earlier manuscript of the prophet's work, gives the best evidence on the age of the book. Scholars set 200 B.C. as the earliest verifiable date for the scroll's composition, with 100 B.C. the 'best guess.' If copies found at Qumran date from the early second century [100 to 199 B.C.], the original should be much older" {24}.

In other words, no matter how you slice it, the Qumran copy of Isaiah had to be a copy of a much older manuscript, but whether the skeptic believes that or not, the fact that most all the scholars who worked on the Isaiah Scroll state that this copy was written at least 100+ years before the death of the Messiah, Christ Jesus, the details involved in His death are far too numerous for this to be just a lucky coincidence.

CHAPTER 10

Stylistic Differences In the Book of Isaiah

The third major argument used to promote the allegation of two separate authors for the Book of Isaiah is the claim of distinct stylistic differences between chapters 1-39 and 40-66. Realistically, this shouldn't surprise us because Isaiah's prophetic ministry lasted throughout the period of four kings of Judah (Isaiah 1:1), mentioned earlier in this chapter. The writings of authors—both secular and theological—may change somewhat if they have been writing for a long period of time.

I have authored two other books. My first was a novel written as a humorous parody using a mythical, symbolic story about three salesmen who started three businesses that impacted two small towns in two different states, with outlandish results. Thirteen years after that I published an amusing parody with a more realistic story with a serious message about our culture today. Now I am writing again, and the style of this book is much different from either of the other two. Therefore, I have no problem with a supposed different style of writing if the message demanded a different approach.

NORMAN L. GEISLER, Ph.D., a distinguished apologetic writer of several books, some co-authored with other writers, in his book, *Baker Encyclopedia of Christian Apologetics*, commented on the allegations that Isaiah did not write chapters 40-66 because they were written by someone else after the time when Cyrus reigned in Persia. Geisler provides a logical response to the assertions that writing styles differ between the first 39 chapters and later ones:

"The difference in words and style of writing between the two sections of the book has been used by critical scholars to substantiate their claim that there are at least two different books. However, these differences are not as great as has been claimed. ...No author writes in exactly the same style using precisely the same vocabulary when writing about different subject matter. Nevertheless, a number of phrases found in both sections attest to the unity of the book. For example, the title 'the Holy one of Israel' is found twelve times in chapters 1 through 39 and fourteen times in 40 through 66" {25}.

THE SUBTLE RESISTANCE OF THE SKEPTICS

Geisler then lists the examples of six Scriptures in Isaiah to show the similarity between chapters 1 through 39 and 40 through 66. See the similarities in the following verses:

Compare "Your hands are full of blood" (Isaiah 1:15b) with "For your hands are defiled with blood" (Isaiah 59:3).

Compare "In that day the Lord Almighty will be a glorious crown, a beautiful wreath for the remnant of his people" (Isaiah 28:5) to "You will be a crown of splendor in the Lord's hand, a royal diadem in the hand of your God" (Isaiah 62:3).

Compare "Water will gush forth in the wilderness and streams in the desert" (Isaiah 35:6b) and "I will make rivers flow on barren heights and springs within the valleys. I will turn the desert into pools of water; and the parched ground into springs" (Isaiah 41:18) {26}.

BARFIELD, like Geisler, does not see stylistic differences as a legitimate reason for assuming a different author at later dates for chapters 40-66:

"Stylistic evaluations for most writers yield major differences between earlier materials and those written much later. Since Isaiah's prophetic career touched five decades, differences in his writing style ought to be detectable. I sense shifts in my style between this book and earlier efforts even though less than five years separate them" {27}.

THE FINAL POINT OF TRUTH which becomes essential to the validation of Isaiah as being the sole author of the book of Isaiah rests in the testimony of the promised Messiah when He sat in the synagogue on the Sabbath in His hometown where He had grown up and every adult knew Him and His family:

"He went to Nazareth, where he had been brought up, and on the Sabbath day he went into the synagogue, as was his custom. And he stood up to read. The scroll of the prophet Isaiah was handed to him. Unrolling it, he found the place where it is written: 'The spirit of the Lord is on me, because he has anointed me to preach good

CHAPTER 10

news to the poor. He has sent me to proclaim freedom for the prisoners and recovery of sight for the blind, to release the oppressed, to proclaim the year of the Lord's favor.' Then he rolled up the scroll, gave it back to the attendant and sat down. The eyes of everyone in the synagogue were fastened on him, and he began by saying to them, 'Today this scripture is fulfilled in your hearing'" (Luke 4:16-21).

The prophecy of Isaiah that Jesus had just quoted was from the sixty-first chapter of "the scroll of Isaiah" (Isaiah 61:1-2) that had been in that synagogue before the time when Jesus returned to Nazareth to proclaim to the people sitting in that synagogue that He was the fulfillment of the prophecy in Isaiah.

IF Isaiah did not write the sixty-first chapter, Jesus appeared to be unaware of that because He accepted what was considered by the Jews as "The Scroll of the Prophet Isaiah" (v. 17a).

IF Jesus knew Isaiah didn't write chapter sixty-one He would have been concealing a fraud, and He would have been a false Messiah.

IF Isaiah did not write chapter sixty-one it would mean that not only Jesus, the synagogue Jews, and also Luke, the one who penned the Gospel of Luke, received false information from "those who from the first were eye witnesses and servants of the word" (Luke 1:2). Luke claimed to have "investigated everything from the beginning" (Luke 1:1-3), which would mean that either he was sloppy in his investigation or he was involved in a conspiracy to deceive along with all the rest of the disciples. You would think someone, somewhere, would have uncovered the plot and revealed the real author because every one of them—the Jews, Jesus Christ, His disciples, and Luke—appear to have accepted chapter sixty-one as the authentic prophecy of Isaiah.

IF this was not Isaiah's prophecy it would imply that there was a giant conspiracy that involved thousands of scribes who refused to identify the real author.

Every adult human being living on this earth today must decide for themselves, as did those in Nazareth, standing in the synagogue, whether Jesus—that son of Joseph, the carpenter, whom they had watched grow up, who claimed to have fulfilled the prophecy of Isaiah 61:1-2—is the promised Messiah. Jesus knew this was the prophecy of Isaiah and not some other unknown author. Jesus also knew

THE SUBTLE RESISTANCE OF THE SKEPTICS

that Isaiah prophesied (in the 53rd chapter) His future death in minute detail. The overwhelming amount of evidence points clearly to the fact that Isaiah did write all the prophecies in his book, from chapter one through chapter sixty-six.

David's authorship of the 22nd & the 16th Psalm Questioned

One thing you can be sure of: Anything that would add credibility to the Messianic message of the Bible, whether Old Testament or New Testament, has been and will continue to be severely scrutinized beyond reason, especially if it clearly confirms— with established proof—the arrival, death, and resurrection of the promised Messiah. The denial of Moses' inspired authorship of the five books of Law and his Messianic prophecies in Genesis has been proven to be without substance. The allegation of multiple writers for the Book of Isaiah has shown to be lacking verifiable evidence. Everything points to the fact that Isaiah was the sole inspired author. There will probably be other attempts to discredit both Moses and Isaiah, perhaps being instigated at this present time. However, I have no doubt they will all eventually be proven to be without merit.

The attack on King David is somewhat different. The assertion by historical revisionists is that the existence of David, the king, lacks any type of historical evidence. In other words, David was just a mythical legend made up to provide a King Arthur-like figure, a hero from Israel's past. David's place in Messianic prophecy is critical to the New Testament writers' proclamation of Christ's lineage, death, and resurrection.

RANDALL PRICE, in his book, *The Stones Cry Out*, explains the cynic's accusations and the final results of years of historical research.

The Search for the Historical King David

"With such an emphasis on David in the Scriptures, it may come as a surprise to many to learn that until recently all books dealing with the history of the Holy Land had to admit that no trace of David had ever appeared in archaeological record. … This lack of evidence led many critical scholars to doubt that a historical David had

CHAPTER 10

ever existed. Historical revisionists (or minimalists) argued that the 'David Myth' had been a literary invention drawn from various heroic traditions to explain the formation of Israel's monarchy. In one development of this myth, according to the critics, a priestly school surrounding the Temple had sought a theological basis for their own concept of divine government. This was the concept of an ideal king (David) set against an imperfect king (Saul). According to the critics, Saul, of course, did not exist either, but served with David as contrasting theological models of man's choice (Saul) versus God's choice (David)" {28}.

These allegations of doubt brought forth by several critical scholars, a prominent authority of biblical archaeology, and historical revisionists created a serious challenge to the authenticity of several critical parts of the Messianic message presented in the New Testament. If David is just a myth, and Jesus' disciples continually refer to Jesus Christ as from the lineage of some king named David claiming that Jesus fulfilled some mythical king's prophecies about His death and resurrection, then neither the Old nor the New Testament would have any purposeful meaning to anyone! It would be just another fairy tale to read to little children.

So why hasn't historical evidence been discovered? The period of David's and Solomon's reigns was Israel's heyday. The territory they controlled covered from the brook of Egypt (Wadi-el-Arish) in the south to the banks of the Euphrates River in the north. Price gives some reasonable explanations why finding archaeological evidence is so difficult:

"One major reason for the lack of evidence may simply be that so little has actually been excavated in the areas related to their reigns. Israel is one gigantic tel, and in places like Hebron and Jerusalem, where the most evidence for this period would be expected, competing religious claims and political unrest make access to some of the most promising sites virtually impossible to archaeologists. ...at the southern wall of the Temple Mount, archaeologists have uncovered only a small section of a building that is datable to the time of Solomon. In general, thousands of years of later occupations cover most of the site. ...One reason few written records are found is because the Israelites...wrote most of their court documents and other records on scrolls of perishable papyrus. Papyrus was both more efficient and less costly than other forms of writing material" {29}.

THE SUBTLE RESISTANCE OF THE SKEPTICS

Although few and far between because of the difficulties in finding areas that can be excavated, some archaeological sites have been uncovered: "Israeli archaeologist Ronny Reich uncovered in the southern area of David's City an immense stone structure thought to be a defensive tower" {30}.

The Discovery of the Tel Dan Stele

The credibility of the allegation by revisionists of a "David Myth" experienced a serious setback from the discovery of an inscription that mentioned the "House of David." Randall Price gives the details of the discovery of more solid evidence of the reality of King David:

"Despite the excavations that have revealed an established Israelite presence in the Holy Land near the time of David—and have even uncovered structures in the City of David related to his time—critics continued to hold fast to the David Myth because no specific mention of David had ever surfaced in such excavations. However, these critics were forced to reconsider their opinions based on new evidence that was unearthed in 1993. The challenge to these revisionists came from a nearly 3000-year-old monumental inscription (stele) written on black basalt by one of Israel's foreign enemies. Discovered at the northern Israelite site of Tel Dan, this startling inscription includes the words 'House of David.' The archaeologist who made this discovery is Professor Avraham Biran, director of the Nelson Glueck School of Biblical archaeology of the Hebrew Union College. The House of David Stele crowned 27 years of archaeological discoveries at Tel Dan, the site in northern Israel where the stele was found" {31}.

The date the stele was inscribed has been estimated from the latter half of the 9th century to the beginning of the 8th century. According to Price, Professor Biran appears to have narrowed down the historical date during the period of an Aramean king, Hazael:

"Professor Biran has more precisely dated the inscription to the time of the Aramean usurper Hazael, whom he believes authored the inscription. ...Told by the prophet Elisha that he would be king, he murdered the king of Aram, Hadad-'izr, and reigned between 842-800 B.C. After he ascended to the throne, he immediately went to war

CHAPTER 10

against Israel, Judah, and Philistia. The Biblical record indicates that he decimated Israel's army and turned both it and Philistia into vassal (subservient) states (2 Kings 10:32-33; 12:17). Judah also seems to have shared this same fate (2 Kings 12:17-18). Professor Biran thinks that the House of David Stele was erected as a memorial to these deeds, and was probably written in the latter part of Hazael's reign. The line that contains the reference to the House of David (line 9) is in the context of the slaying of the Israelite and Judean kings" {32}.

Price explains: "The term House of David is a dynastic title implying that if there was a 'House of David' there must have been a David" {33}.

We find the term "House of David" in the following scriptures:

"So Jonathan made a covenant with the house of David, saying, 'May the LORD call David's enemies to account'" (1 Samuel 20:16 NIV).

[Concerning the division of Judah and Israel] "Now it came to pass when all Israel heard that Jeroboam had come back, they sent for him and called him to the congregation, and made him king over all Israel. There was none who followed the house of David, but the tribe of Judah only" (1 Kings 12:20 NKJV).

[A "man of God" sent a message to Jeroboam] "Then he cried out against the altar by the word of the LORD, and said, 'O altar, altar! Thus says the LORD: 'Behold, a child, Josiah by name shall be born to the house of David; and on you he shall sacrifice the priests of the high places who burn incense on you, and men's bones shall be burned on you'" (1 Kings 13:2 NKJV).

Notice how the words **"house of David"** in these Scriptures refer to the lineage of King David and his descendents who would rule Judah. The dynasty began with David and his son Solomon, who became king after David, followed by Rehoboam, the son of Solomon, who became king after Solomon's death.
GARY K. BRANTLEY, in his book, *Digging for Answers*, agrees with Professors Biran and Price in their conclusions that the Tel Dan Stele is definitely referring to the Biblical King David, about whom so much has been written:

"Avraham Naveh, Biran's paleographer, translated this latter phrase 'House of

THE SUBTLE RESISTANCE OF THE SKEPTICS

David.' Such a translation has tremendous implications for biblical history. If the name 'David' actually appears in this ancient inscription, it provides extra-biblical confirmation of the actual existence of David, known only from biblical sources to this point. ...This would undermine the position of scholars who deny that David was an actual historical figure. Even more remarkable is the fact that his name appears in the familiar phrase 'House of David.' Given the date of the stela, this serves to confirm the biblical usage of this designation (cf. 1 Kings 12:19; 14:8; Isaiah 7:2; et. al.)" {34}.

Brantley's conclusion is that this inscription is another important witness of the Bible's credibility:

"Thus, the translation 'House of David' actually is based on a solid linguistic foundation. No doubt, analysis of, and debate over, the stela will continue for some time. It appears quite certain, however, that the name 'David' has been found in a ninth-century B.C. text other than the Bible. That important fact is yet another ancient witness to biblical credibility" {35}.

Simply put, the allegations of several authors of the five books of Moses and the prophecies of Isaiah, and the allegation of a "David-Myth" are without merit.

As I bring this chapter to its conclusion, it becomes necessary to point out why these charges must be addressed. There are three significant prophesies in Genesis, three in Isaiah, and two in the Psalms that point out how the ultimate victory of the family of God over the forces of darkness is through Christ and in

Christ. It is a mystery kept hidden from the very foundation of the world, but is now revealed to us through Jesus Christ.

When Pontius Pilate questioned that man accused of being an imposter with the intent to usurp the throne and overthrow the power of Rome and Caesar (John 19: 12-13), the man named Jesus replied: " Every one who is of the truth hears my voice." Pilate's response? "What is truth?" It has been the purpose of this author to present to you the truth of Jesus Christ, from the reality of God to the Victory in Christ Jesus (John 18:38 RSV 1971).

NOTE: The Tel Dan Stele has been dated by archaeologists as a 9th century B.C. inscription.

CHAPTER 10

"For he has made known to us in all wisdom and insight the mystery of his will, according to his purpose which he set forth in Christ as a plan for the fullness of time, to unite all things in him, things in heaven and things on earth" (Ephesians 1:9-10 RSV1971).

Chapter 11

MESSIAH HAS ARRIVED
CHRIST'S PROMISES AND DEATH

"Blessed be the God and Father of our Lord Jesus Christ, who has blessed us with every spiritual blessing in the heavenly places in Christ, just as He chose us in Him before the foundation of the world, that we should be holy and without blame before Him in love" (Ephesians 1:3-4 NKJV).

CHAPTER 11

In the ninth chapter of this book there were seven major prophecies concerning the coming Messiah, of His ministry on earth, His rejection and death, and His resurrection. In this chapter, we shall see the fulfillment of these prophecies and the promises He made concerning His resurrection, and the promises He made to each one of us who truly put our faith and trust in Him.

You see, our Creator was not caught off guard and unaware when the adversary, Satan, appeared in the form of a serpent in the garden back at the beginning of human history and conspired through deception to bring about the death and separation of humanity from their Creator God.

The adversary, your accuser, has never given up his agenda of overthrowing our God and positioning himself as ruler of the universe. Our God and Father knew this; therefore, He instigated His master plan "before the foundation of the world" and "chose us" (in Christ) "that we should be holy and without blame before Him in love" (Ephesians 1:4 NKJV).

The Supernatural Conception of the Messiah—Jesus Christ

Jesus Christ's Lineage from Abraham, through David, through Joseph, by the Holy Spirit, is detailed in the book of Matthew:

"A record of the genealogy of Jesus Christ of the son of David, the son of Abraham: Abraham was the father of Isaac, Isaac the father of Jacob, Jacob the father of Judah and his brothers" (Matthew 1:1-2 NIV).

Remember, Jacob had promised his son, Judah, that the scepter and ruler would come through the tribe of Judah "until he comes to whom it belongs," which Moses had prophesied in Genesis 49:10.

BACK TO CHRIST'S GENEALOGY, DROP DOWN TO VERSE 6:

"...and Jesse the father of King David. David was the father of Solomon, whose mother had been Uriah's wife" (Matthew 1:6 NIV).

MESSIAH HAS ARRIVED: CHRIST'S PROMISES AND DEATH

Remember that after David's death, Solomon sat on David's throne (1 Kings 2:12).

NOW LOOK AT VERSE 16:

"…and Jacob the father of Joseph, the husband of Mary, of whom was born Jesus, who is called Christ" (Matthew 1:16 NIV).

This completes the picture of Messiah's line from Abraham through the tribe of Judah, through the lineage of Kings David and Solomon, all the way to the promised Messiah, Jesus Christ.

DROP DOWN TO VERSES 18-23:

"This is how the birth of Jesus Christ came about: His mother Mary was pledged to be married to Joseph, but before they came together, she was found to be with child through the Holy Spirit. Because Joseph her husband was a righteous man and did not want to expose her to public disgrace, he had in mind to divorce her quietly. But after he had considered this, an angel of the Lord appeared to him in a dream and said, 'Joseph son of David, do not be afraid to take Mary home as your wife, because what is conceived in her is from the Holy Spirit. She will give birth to a son, and you are to give him the name Jesus, because he will save his people from their sins.' All this took place to fulfill what the Lord had said through the prophet: 'The virgin will be with child and will give birth to a son, and they will call him "Immanuel" — which means, 'God with us'" (Matthew1:18-23 NIV).

There is no doubt that Jesus' conception in Mary, a virgin (Luke 1:27), was a supernatural event of specific purpose. Remember that the prophet Isaiah had written:

"Therefore the Lord himself will give you a sign…" This word, **"sign"** (from the Hebrew word 'oth') as it is used in Isaiah 7:14 means a miraculous, supernatural occurrence that will verify what will happen, leaving no doubt that the event comes from God Himself! Matthew, the inspired writer of the Gospel that bears his name, quotes from the prophecy of Isaiah:

"Therefore the Lord himself will give you a sign: The virgin will be with child and

CHAPTER 11

will give birth to a son, and they will call him Immanuel [Isaiah 7:14]—which means, 'God with us'" (Matthew 1:22 NIV).

Isaiah, through the God-breathed inspiration from God, recorded the promise and prediction about 700 years before Jesus was born. Matthew, a Jew, knew the significance of this prophecy being fulfilled by the Holy Spirit's supernatural power.

Mary's Son Will Reign On David's Throne Forever

"Then the angel said to her, 'Do not be afraid, Mary, for you have found favor with God. And behold, you will conceive in your womb and bring forth a Son, and shall call His name Jesus. He will be great, and will be called the Son of the Highest; and the Lord God will give Him the throne of His father David. And He will reign over the house of Jacob forever, and of His kingdom there will be no end'" (Luke 1:30-33 NKJV).

"God With Us"—"The Word Was God"—"Became Flesh"—"Among Us"

"In the beginning was the Word, and the Word was with God, and the Word was God. He was in the beginning with God. All things were made through Him, and without Him nothing was made that was made" (John 1:1-3).

DROP DOWN TO VERSE 14:

"And the Word became flesh and dwelt among us, and we beheld His glory, as of the only begotten of the Father, full of grace and truth" (John 1:14 NKJV).

The fact that Jesus Christ was brought into this world was not an afterthought. It was and always has been the eternal purpose of God "before the foundation of the world." It was in the mind of God, the Father, before the creation of the heavens and the earth, before the creation of man, to send the Word who "became flesh and dwelt among us."

MESSIAH HAS ARRIVED: CHRIST'S PROMISES AND DEATH

In the beginning Satan, in the form of a serpent, was successful in causing the woman and man to break God's covenant of the tree of the knowledge of good and evil. When they sinned they suffered death, thus being separated from God and separated from the tree that provided eternal life. In the war between God and Satan, it appeared the forces of darkness had won an important victory through the power of death. At first it seems impossible for human intelligence to comprehend, to understand the master plan our Creator had already laid out in the first prophecy of His eternal strategy:

"And I will put enmity Between you and the woman, And between your seed and her seed; He shall bruise you on the head, And you shall bruise him on the heel" (Genesis 3:15 NASB).

Imagine a powerful snake confronting the "seed" of woman. The victorious outcome would result in the bruising. The power of the serpent is in the head, whether to bite with a venomous poison like a viper or to grab hold of the victim with those long curved teeth like a python until the coils have constricted the life out of him. If the seed of woman were to step on the head of the serpent with a crushing blow, the teeth and the poison of the snake would be rendered useless. This is what the prophecy means. The Messiah would render Satan's power of death to be of no avail (powerless)!

But what about the damage (bruise) to be inflicted upon "the heel" of "her seed" (the seed of woman)? What would be the outcome of that bruising? If you were to kill a snake by stomping on the head you might actually bruise your heel, especially if you were barefoot or had on a pair of shoes with thin soles. You would heal from the wound, but the snake would be dead and powerless to harm anyone. So how does this play out in the history of humankind? Read the following passages as the mystery begins to unfold:

"A Child" — "A Son" — "Will Be Born" — "Mighty God" — "Peace"

"For a child will be born to us, a son will be given to us; And the government will rest on His shoulders; And His name will be called Wonderful Counselor, Mighty God, Eternal Father, Prince of Peace. There will be no end to the increase of His

CHAPTER 11

government or of peace, On the throne of David and over His kingdom, To establish it and to uphold it with justice and righteousness From then on and forevermore. The zeal of the Lord of hosts will accomplish this" (Isaiah 9:6-7 NASB).

Previously, in chapter eight, we saw how the Scriptures point out that Jesus, the Messiah, now reigns on the throne of David as king over His kingdom forevermore (Acts 2:27-31; Hebrews 1:8-12). Yet the scripture points out that there was to be an injury to the coming Messiah (the seed of woman). How could this be if Christ is now reigning supreme? Where was the injury (that "bruise…on the heel")?

"The Fulness Of The Time Came"—"Her Seed"—"Born Of A Woman"

"But when the fullness of the time came, God sent forth His Son, born of a woman, born under the Law" (Galatians 4:4 NASB).

This birth is different from any other human birth. Why? The conception in Mary was not a natural event between man and woman. Mary's child was conceived by the Holy Spirit, making it a supernatural conception! This is why Paul wrote that Jesus was: **"born of a woman."**

According to Moses' prophecy in Genesis 3:15; the war ("enmity") being waged is between the seed of Satan ("between your seed") and the seed of woman ("her seed"). When Jesus came into the world, the world did not recognize or accept Him. That is why John wrote in his gospel:

"He was in the world, and though the world was made through him, the world did not recognize him. He came to that which was his own, but his own did not receive him" (John 1:10-11 NIV).

Paul explained it this way:

"Your attitude should be the same as that of Christ Jesus: Who, being in very nature God, did not consider equality with God something to be grasped, but made himself nothing, taking the very nature of a servant, being made in human likeness. And

MESSIAH HAS ARRIVED: CHRIST'S PROMISES AND DEATH

being found in appearance as a man, he humbled himself and became obedient to death—even death on a cross!" (Philippians 2:5-8 NIV).

Jewish Scholars Envisioned Two Messiahs

A Messiah who is King and God and also a servant who would suffer death on a cross? How could this be? This was, and still is, a conflicting frustration to Jewish scholars. In their minds this had to be two separate Messiahs. KYLE BUTT and ERIC LYONS, in their book, *Behold! The Lamb of God*, comment on how Jews could not grasp how this could all be in one Messiah:

"Throughout the Old Testament, various Messianic passages refer to a majestic, glorious king who will reign over a never-ending kingdom. Yet, at the same time, other Messianic prophesies depict a suffering Messiah who will bear the guilt and sin of the entire world. Because these two aspects of Messianic prophecy seem contradictory, many in the ancient Jewish community could not understand how such diverse prophetic sentiments could be fulfilled in a single individual. Due to this conundrum, ancient and modern Jews have posited the idea that two Messiahs would come: one would be the suffering Servant, while the other would be the glorious King" {1}.

Butt and Lyons cite different sources for their conclusion. John Ankerberg, John Weldon, and Walter Kaiser, in their book, The Case for Jesus the Messiah, wrote of the difficulties of Jewish rabbis trying to understand how the triumphant victorious King of prophecy could be a subjugated, tormented person who would suffer the pangs of death:

"[T]hey (early Jewish rabbis) could not reconcile the statements that so clearly spoke of a suffering and dying Messiah with those verses in other passages that spoke of a triumphant and victorious Messiah. What is important to note is that they did recognize that both pictures somehow applied to the Messiah. But they assumed it was impossible to reconcile both views in one person. Rather than seeing one Messiah in two different roles, they saw two Messiahs—the suffering and dying Messiah, called 'Messiah ben Joseph,' and the victorious conquering Messiah, called 'Messiah ben David'" (1989, pp. 57-58 parentheses in text).

CHAPTER 11

The other source Butt and Lyons listed, Jewish rabbi Robert H. Cohen, gave the following explanation:

"The rabbis saw that scripture portrayed two different pictures of King Messiah. One would conquer and reign and bring Israel back to the land by world peace and bring the fullness of obedience to the Torah. They called him Messiah ben David. The other picture is of a servant who would die and bear Israel's sin that they could refer to as the 'leprous one' based on Isaiah 53 (Cohen, n.d.; also see Parsons, 2003-2006)" {2}.

David S. Ariel, in his book, What Do Jews Believe? also mentions the conflicting problems among rabbis "of the Mishnah and Talmud" of a Messiah that dies:

"The rabbis of the Mishnah and Talmud speculated on the nature of the messianic era, but no systematic theory emerged. Some rabbis predicted that the messianic era would begin with catastrophic events, while others thought events would unfold in a more rational sequence. It became increasingly difficult to reconcile the contradictory views on the events leading up to the arrival of the Messiah. One solution to this problem was the introduction of the idea that there are really two messianic figures. The first, Messiah son of Joseph (ben Yosef), follows the arrival of Elijah but he himself dies before the messianic era begins. The second, Messiah son of David, is the figure who concludes the process, restores the Davidic throne, and ushers in the end of days" {3}.

Butt and Lyons points out that Jewish scholars in general fail to connect "the themes of suffering and regal authority." It remains a mystery to them how God would bring about what they assumed would be a triumphant king restoring the kingdom of Israel as a nation:

"It is evident, from the rabbinical view of two Messiahs, that the themes of suffering and regal authority were so vividly portrayed in Old Testament Messianic prophecy that both themes demanded fulfillment. To suggest two Messiah's provided such a fulfillment. However, the dual Messianic idea failed to comprehend the actual nature of Messianic prophecy, and missed a primary facet of the Messianic personality" {4}.

MESSIAH HAS ARRIVED: CHRIST'S PROMISES AND DEATH

"Light" (Verses) "Darkness"

"In Him was life, and the life was the light of men. And the light shines in the darkness, and the darkness did not comprehend it" (John 1:4-5 NASB).

Here is where the opposition begins. In Christ Jesus ("the Word") there is "life." The "life" in Christ is "the light of men." When Jesus came, the "light" was shining in the "darkness" but "the darkness did not comprehend it." His purpose for coming into the world was not understood by those living in darkness. To them it was a mystery, a mystery (to defeat the forces of darkness) that even His foremost adversary (Satan) did not fully comprehend.

DROP DOWN TO VERSES 9-11:

"There was the true light which, coming into the world, enlightens every man. He was in the world, and the world was made through Him, and the world did not know Him. He came into His own, and those who were His own did not receive Him" (John 1:9-11).

Why would John, the gospel writer, claim that "the world" which the "Word" Himself created would refuse to receive Him? True, some did receive Him, such as His chosen apostles and other disciples, but as a whole, the remainder of the Jews rejected Him. Were they not expecting a Messiah? Yes, they were. Remember in Matthew chapter two when the wise men from the east came looking for the newborn "king of the Jews"? King Herod asked the scribes and chief priests about where the Messiah would be born. The religious elite knew a Messiah ("a ruler who will shepherd my people Israel" Matthew 2:6) would come from Bethlehem. They were expecting Him, a majestic ruler who would restore the kingdom of Israel like their ancestors had in the 'good-old-days' when David ruled Israel. But this was not to be. What the Jews expected was not what they saw and experienced.

DROP DOWN TO VERSE 14:

"And the Word became flesh, and dwelt among us, and we beheld His glory, glory as of the only begotten from the Father, full of grace and truth" (John 1:14 NASB).

CHAPTER 11

God became one of us. He became "God with us" in human flesh, unlike anything else that has ever happened.

DROP DOWN TO VERSES 19-28:

When priests and Levites questioned John the Baptist on who he was he told them he was neither the Christ nor Elijah. His mission was to baptize and prepare the way for the Christ. "These things took place in Bethany beyond the Jordan, where John was baptizing" (John 1:28 NASB).

"The next day he saw Jesus coming to him, and said, 'Behold, the Lamb of God who takes away the sin of the world!" (John 1:29 NASB).

"Behold, the Lamb of God who takes away the sin of the world!"

Think back to the prophecy of Isaiah chapter 53:

"All of us like sheep have gone astray, Each of us has turned to his own way; But the LORD has caused the iniquity of us all To fall on Him. He was oppressed and He was afflicted, Yet He did not open His mouth; Like a lamb that is led to slaughter, And like a sheep that is silent before its shearers, So He did not open His mouth" (Isaiah 53:6-7 NASB emphasis added).

Through divine inspiration, John the Baptist knew that Jesus was someone special; anointed by the Father to do something no human being alone could possibly do: that is, someone ordained who "takes away the sin of the world!" All through history, from the very beginning immediately after the fall of man and woman in the garden, Moses prophesied that the seed of woman would bruise His heel (Genesis 3:15). In the children of Israel's release from their bondage to Egypt, the blood of a lamb without defect had to be spread over the lintel and two door posts (the door frame) that led to the outside of the house. This was called "the Passover lamb:

"Your lamb shall be without blemish, a male of the first year. You may take it from the sheep or from the goats" (Exodus 12:5 NKJV).

MESSIAH HAS ARRIVED: CHRIST'S PROMISES AND DEATH

DROP DOWN TO VERSES 21-23:

"Then Moses called for all the elders of Israel and said to them, 'Pick out and take lambs for yourselves according to your families, and kill the Passover lamb. And you shall take a bunch of hyssop, dip it in the blood that is in the basin, and strike the lintel and the two door posts with the blood that is in the basin. And none of you shall go out of the door of his house until morning. For the LORD will pass through to strike the Egyptians; and when He sees the blood on the lintel and on the two door posts, the LORD will pass over the door and not allow the destroyer to come into your houses to strike you" (Exodus 12:21-23 NKJV).

The "destroyer" struck all of the Egyptian firstborn with death. The firstborn of the Israelites were saved by the blood of the Passover lamb. The Egyptian Pharaoh released the Israelites from their bondage.

"Behold! The Lamb Of God"

"This is He on behalf of whom I said, 'After me comes a Man who has a higher rank than I, for He existed before me'" (John 1:30 NASB).

After His baptism by John the Baptist (Luke 3:21-22), Jesus left the area of the Jordan River, where He was led by the Holy Spirit to a wilderness area called "the desert" (Luke 4:1), where, after 40 days of not eating, at the point of severe hunger, He was tempted by the adversary, Satan himself. In one of these temptations Satan enticed the Son of God with the opportunity for power and wealth. This particular temptation reveals the intended conspiracy of the devil:

"The devil led him up to a high place and showed him in an instant all the kingdoms of the world. And he said to him, 'I will give you all their authority and splendor, for it has been given to me, and I can give it to anyone I want to. So if you worship me, it will all be yours.' Jesus answered, 'It is written: "Worship the Lord your God and serve him only"'" (Luke 4:5-8 NIV).

Jesus' reply is found written in the Holy Scriptures in Deuteronomy 6:13. It is the power of what is written in the word of God that Jesus used to overcome: "It is

CHAPTER 11

written…" Satan's motive remains what it always has been, to rule the universe, including God Almighty! The very offer of all the kingdoms [IF] Christ (the anointed) "Word" through whom all things were created, would "worship" Satan, reveals his conceit and arrogance. When this failed, the devil left until he could find a more "opportune time" (Luke 4:13 NIV).

In 1 Timothy 3:6 Paul wrote concerning requirements for "overseers" (elders). One of these is: "He must not be a recent convert, or he may become conceited and fall under the same judgment as the devil."

After withstanding the challenging temptations by the devil, Jesus returned to the area of Galilee, gaining a reputation as a teacher in their synagogues and throughout the area. He then returned to His hometown of Nazareth, located about 15 miles west of the Jordan River. This is where Jesus was raised from a small child until He became an adult. It was here in this small town where most everyone knew Him that He revealed to them He was the promised Messiah. He did this by entering the local synagogue where He read from the Holy Scriptures the prophecy of Isaiah in Chapter sixty-one, the nature of His purpose and why He was the fulfillment of that prophecy. Notice their reaction afterward:

"And He came to Nazareth, where He had been brought up; and as was His custom, He entered the synagogue on the Sabbath, and stood up to read. And the book of the prophet Isaiah was handed to Him. And He opened the book, and found the place where it was written, 'THE SPIRIT OF THE LORD IS UPON ME, BECAUSE HE ANOINTED ME TO PREACH THE GOSPEL TO THE POOR. HE HAS SENT ME TO PROCLAIM RELEASE TO THE CAPTIVES, AND RECOVERY OF SIGHT TO THE BLIND, TO SET FREE THOSE WHO ARE DOWNTRODDEN, TO PROCLAIM THE FAVORABLE YEAR OF THE LORD.' And He closed the book, and gave it back to the attendant, and sat down; and the eyes of all in the synagogue were fixed upon Him. And He began to say to them, 'Today this Scripture has been fulfilled in your hearing.' And all were speaking well of Him, and wondering at the gracious words which were falling from His lips; and they were saying, 'Is this not Joseph's son?'" (Luke 4:16-22 NASB).

MESSIAH HAS ARRIVED: CHRIST'S PROMISES AND DEATH

The Synagogue

The synagogue was a local place to assemble and worship. Usually every Jewish town or community had at least one. Nazareth was no exception. According to the *Holman Bible Dictionary*: "Jewish sources indicate that a synagogue was to be established wherever there were as many as ten Jewish men. The principle meeting was on the Sabbath. A typical service consisted of the recitation of the Shema (confession of faith in one God), prayers, Scripture readings from the Law and the Prophets, a sermon, and a benediction. …They often appointed a ruler of the synagogue…a layman who cared for the building and selected those who participated in the service. The ruler was assisted by an attendant. One of his duties was to deliver the sacred scrolls to those who read and return them to the special place where they were kept (Luke 4:17, 20)" {5}.

I want to focus attention on ten extremely critical words in verse 18:

"HE HAS SENT ME TO PROCLAIM RELEASE TO THE CAPTIVES…"

What captives? Where are they? Who does He mean? Those Jews who have been imprisoned by the Romans? What does He mean by this statement? Jesus was quoting from the prophet Isaiah (Isaiah 61:1-2). He had grown up among these people. They knew He was the son of the local carpenter, but they didn't know who He really was. Therefore, when He told them, **"Today this Scripture has been fulfilled in your hearing…" they did not understand!** (emphasis added).

One of the problems lay in who this hometown boy had as a father:

"Is this not Joseph's son?" (Luke 4:22 NASB).

You see, Joseph was a carpenter, a 'blue collar' worker (Matthew 13:55). They knew His mother ("Mary") and His brothers ("James, Joses, Simon, and Judas"). There were no religious leaders among them. Carpenters were considered skilled craftsmen, with their ability to work with their hands, to make furniture, cut down trees, build door frames, etc., but never as educated scribes, rabbis or priests, certainly not like the celebrated and respected Gamaliel who was a member of the

CHAPTER 11

Sanhedrin and a doctor of the Law (Acts 5:34; Acts 22:3). Jesus was a carpenter's son. Thus, as custom would have it, He would have been instructed in the blue collar work of carpentry without any formal education in the Law or the writings of the prophets.

Jesus recognized their rejection. "And He said, 'Truly I say to you, no prophet is welcome in his home town'" (Luke 4:24). After He rebuked them for their unbelief they threw Him out of the synagogue and drove Him out of town with intention of killing Him, but He was able to escape from the lynch mob (Luke 4:24-30).

The hostility continued to grow between Jesus and religious elite among the Jews. One incident clearly clarifies how the Pharisees, reputedly strict according to the Law, continued to question Jesus about His authority and His claim to equal God, the Father. Their ultimate purpose was to discredit Him, or if necessary, to kill him. Such an incident took place at a time when Jesus was in Jerusalem in the Temple area.

Jesus Accused of Having a Demon

"To the Jews who had believed him, Jesus said, 'If you hold to my teaching, you are really my disciples. Then you will know the truth, and the truth will set you free.' They answered him, 'We are Abraham's descendants and have never been slaves of anyone. How can you say that we shall be set free?' Jesus replied, 'I tell you the truth, everyone who sins is a slave to sin'" (John 8:31-34 NIV).

DROP DOWN TO VERSES 39-42:

"'Abraham is our father,' they answered. 'If you were Abraham's children,' said Jesus, 'then you would do the things Abraham did. As it is, you are determined to kill me, a man who has told you the truth that I heard from God. Abraham did not do such things. You are doing the things your own father does.' 'We are not illegitimate children,' they protested. 'The only Father we have is God himself'" (John 8:39-41 NIV).

MESSIAH HAS ARRIVED: CHRIST'S PROMISES AND DEATH

The confrontation continues to point out the smoldering hostility between the Jews and Jesus, their promised Messiah. It increases until finally it ignites sparks of violence:

"Jesus said to them, 'If God were your Father, you would love me, for I came from God and now am here. I have not come on my own; but he sent me'" (John 8:42 NIV).

Jesus understood where the hostility was coming from. These people were living in darkness. They were in bondage to a different father, the prince of darkness. Jesus then told them the truth which they were not ready to accept.

DROP DOWN TO VERSES 44-47:

"You belong to your father, the devil, and you want to carry out your father's desire. He was a murderer from the beginning, not holding to the truth, for there is no truth in him. When he lies, he speaks his native language, for he is a liar and the father of lies. Yet because I tell you the truth, you do not believe me! Can any of you prove me guilty of sin? If I am telling the truth, why don't you believe me? He who belongs to God hears what God says. The reason you do not hear is that you do not belong to God" (John 8:44-47 NIV).

Jesus' words cut right to the reality of the problem. They were in bondage to the instigator of evil, the prince of this world, the devil, "the father of lies", who through deceit brought about the sin that separated man and woman from their Creator in the beginning (Genesis 3:1-15). This is why Christ (the anointed), the Son of God, came—to free all who would listen to Him from their bondage to sin!

Satan had been waiting for an "opportune time" to bring about his ultimate desire, to defeat the purpose of God. Here is that moment. Sensing the hostility of his people (those who live in darkness), the devil motivated the Jews to bring condemning accusations against their own Messiah:

"The Jews answered him, 'Aren't we right in saying that you are a Samaritan and demon-possessed?' (John 8:48 NIV).

CHAPTER 11

The "Samaritan" was considered to be a heretical mongrel by Jews. They were openly hostile to any type of relationship with Samaritans, which was clearly noticeable as far back as the Persian Empire when Ezra and Zerubbabel returned to rebuild the Temple in Jerusalem. Samaritans were referred to by Ezra even then as "the enemies of Judah and Benjamin" (Ezra 4:1-17). Hostilities continued to increase so that by the time Nehemiah came to Jerusalem a man named Sanballat stirred up violence to prevent the repair of the city walls (Nehemiah 4:1-21).

Word must have gotten around about when Jesus traveled through Samaria and stopped to visit with a Samaritan woman (John 4:1-42). This was unheard of in Jesus' time. Influenced by Satan, whom they unwittingly served, the Pharisees unjustly accused Jesus of being "demon-possessed." That is not at all surprising. Satan is also known as the "accuser" (Revelation 12:7-12). When Jesus healed a man who was demon-possessed He was accused of using "Beelzebub, the prince of demons" (Matthew 12:22-28).

In John 8:56-59, the debate continued, steadily increasing in polarization and hostility. The breaking point came when Jesus said in verse 56: "Your father Abraham rejoiced at the thought of seeing my day; he saw it and was glad." The Jews retorted:

"'You are not yet fifty years old, and you have seen Abraham!'" (John 8:57 NIV).

Then Jesus stated quite directly to them in words they could not misunderstand: "'I tell you the truth,' Jesus answered, 'before Abraham was born, I am!'" (John 8:58 NIV).

"I AM!" Those were the words declared to Moses by God when Moses asked the name of the One setting the Israelites free from bondage to the Egyptians. Their conversation went like this:

"'…The God of your fathers has sent me to you,' and they ask me, 'What is his name?' Then what shall I tell them?' God said to Moses, 'I AM WHO I AM. This is what you are to say to the Israelites: "I AM has sent me to you."'" (Exodus 3:12-14 NIV).

MESSIAH HAS ARRIVED: CHRIST'S PROMISES AND DEATH

The Jews knew exactly what Jesus was telling them, He was the great "I AM," the eternal God, who created "all things" (John 1:3). He was deity in the flesh, standing before them. Because He had said this, and they didn't believe Him: "...they picked up stones to kill Him" (John 8:59). His enemies were determined to get rid of Him one way or another. Their enmity had now developed into a conspiracy to violently eliminate Him, especially after the incident at Bethany.

The Death of Lazarus—The Miracle of his Resurrection

A friend of Jesus named Lazarus became seriously ill and died. Jesus returned to Bethany, about two miles from Jerusalem, four days after his burial. Jesus approached to the tomb: "Now it was a cave, and a stone was lying against it. Jesus said: 'Remove the stone.'" Martha, Lazarus' sister, reminded Jesus that after four days Lazarus body was in a state of decay. The stone was removed: "And Jesus raised His eyes, and said, "Father I thank Thee that Thou heardest Me" (from John 11:17-41 NASB).

"'And I knew that Thou hearest Me always; but because of the people standing around I said it, that they may believe that Thou didst send Me.' And when He had said these things, He cried out with a loud voice, 'Lazarus, come forth.' He who had died came forth, bound hand and foot with wrappings; and his face was wrapped around with a cloth. Jesus said to them, 'Unbind him and let him go.' Many therefore of the Jews, who had come to Mary and beheld what He had done, believed in Him. But some of them went away to the Pharisees, and told them the things which Jesus had done" (John 11:42-46 NASB).

Did the miraculous raising of Lazarus from the dead convince everyone? No, it did not. The New Testament Scriptures record over thirty miracles Jesus performed, many in front of large crowds of people. From the water turned into wine at the wedding feast (John 2:1-11), His first miracle, to the event where He fed 5,000 men plus women and children (Matthew 14:13-23; Mark 6:33-45), to restoring the sight of a man who was blind from birth (John 9:1-41), and yes, even to the miraculous bringing of Lazarus back to life after he had been dead for four days, none of these happenings convinced everyone in the crowds that Jesus was indeed the Messiah. "Some of them went away to the Pharisees, and told them the things which Jesus

CHAPTER 11

had done" (John 11:46). This brought about His ultimate condemnation from the religious elite in Jerusalem:

"Therefore the chief priests and the Pharisees convened a council, and were saying, 'What are we doing? For this man is performing many signs. If we let Him go on like this, all men will believe in Him, and the Romans will come and take away both our place and our nation.' But a certain one of them, Caiaphas, who was high priest that year, said to them, 'You know nothing at all, nor do you take into account that it is expedient for you that one man should die for the people, and that the whole nation should not perish.' Now this he did not say on his own initiative; but being high priest that year, he prophesied that Jesus was going to die for the nation, and not for the nation only, but that He might also gather together into one the children of God who are scattered abroad. So from that day on they planned together to kill Him. Jesus therefore no longer continued to walk publicly among the Jews, but went away from there to the country near the wilderness, into a city called Ephraim; and there He stayed with the disciples." (John 11:47-54 NASB).

The religious authorities knew Jesus had accomplished many miracles seen by thousands, even some who were present at that council meeting. They knew Jesus had predicted the most astounding miracle of all — His resurrection from the dead — many days in advance (John 2:19; Matthew 16:21; Matthew 27:62-65).

So why was Jesus' death so necessary for the high priest and the rest of the prominent Jewish religious elite?

First, He represented a threat to their power and prestige: in other words, their job security. If the Romans perceived Jesus to be a threat to the political peace in Jerusalem and the surrounding areas and the high priest and the Sanhedrin Council were thought to be behind Jesus, the Jewish elite feared they would be removed from office and the nation itself would be in danger of destruction.

Second, since several of the prominent rabbis and others, including Caiaphas the high priest, thought there might be two Messiahs with Jesus representing the suffering servant, the religious elite could be patient and wait for the Majestic King who would restore the kingdom back to Israel as it was under David's and Solomon's reigns.

MESSIAH HAS ARRIVED: CHRIST'S PROMISES AND DEATH

Third, and most important, the high priest and most of the prominent religious authorities failed to grasp that Jesus Christ would also prove to be their king and their high priest after the order of Melchizedek, both king and priest during Abraham's lifetime (Genesis 14:18; Hebrews 7:17). The death and resurrection of Christ was the most important part of God's ultimate strategy to be fulfilled, to save not only the Jews, but all people everywhere throughout the earth for all time (John 3:16-17).

Jesus spoke clearly, about His death and the casting out of Satan

"'Now is the judgment of this world; now the ruler of this world will be cast out. And I, if I am lifted up from the earth, will draw all peoples to Myself.' This He said, signifying by what death He would die" (John 12:31-33 NKJV).

This is why He came! To those such as the high priest and religious authorities, yes and even to "the ruler of this world" (Satan), it would appear that the death of Christ Jesus would be an end to their problem. Things would continue as normal. The religious elite would maintain their positions of authority and the devil would still have control over them and would keep his power of death over all those who continued to live in darkness.

The Arrest—the Trial—the Conviction—the Crucifixion

"Now when the devil had ended every temptation, he departed from Him until an opportune time" (Luke 4:13 NKJV).

THE MOST "OPPORTUNE TIME" CAME JUST BEFORE THE PASSOVER:

"Now the feast of Unleavened Bread drew near, which is called Passover. And the chief priests and the scribes sought how they might kill Him, for they feared the people. **Then Satan entered Judas, surnamed Iscariot, who was numbered among the twelve.** So he went his way and conferred with the chief priests and captains, how he might betray Him to them. And they were glad, and agreed to give him money. So he promised and sought opportunity to betray Him to them in the absence of the multitude" (Luke 22:1-5 NKJV emphasis added).

CHAPTER 11

Satan had found the opportunity and the one who would betray Jesus, Judas Iscariot. He was the one who pilfered their money box (John 12:1-6). There is no question that the devil had been influential in promoting the Jews' intent to murder Jesus.

The Arrest

"When he had finished praying, Jesus left with his disciples and crossed the Kidron Valley. On the other side there was an olive grove, and he and his disciples went into it. Now Judas, who betrayed him, knew that place, because Jesus had often met there with his disciples. So Judas came to the grove, guiding a detachment of soldiers and some officials from the chief priests and Pharisees. They were carrying torches, lanterns and weapons. Jesus, knowing all that was going to happen to him, went out and asked them, 'Who is it you want?' 'Jesus of Nazareth,' they replied. 'I am he,' Jesus said. (And Judas the traitor was standing there with them.) When Jesus said, 'I am he,' they drew back and fell to the ground" (John 18:1-6 NIV).

DROP DOWN TO VERSES 12-14:

"Then the detachment of soldiers with its commander and the Jewish officials arrested Jesus. They bound him and brought him first to Annas, who was the father-in-law of Caiaphas, the high priest that year. Caiaphas was the one who had advised the Jews that it would be good if one man died for the people" (John 18:12-14 NIV).

Why did they take Jesus to Annas first and not Caiaphas, the high priest? The answer lies in the historical/political background of the first century under Roman rule in the area of Palestine. There are four men who held an enormous impact on the events that took place during Jesus trial: Annas, Caiaphas, Pontius Pilate, and Sejanus. One can see the hand of God in His foresight to send His Son, Christ Jesus, into people's lives at this particular point in history and why God let the "ruler of this world," who reigns over the "world forces of this darkness" (John 12:31; Ephesians 6:10-12) influence and manipulate both the religious authorities in Jerusalem and the Roman governor, Pilate, to bring about the Crucifixion death of the promised Messiah.

MESSIAH HAS ARRIVED: CHRIST'S PROMISES AND DEATH

EVERETT FERGUSON, in his book, *Backgrounds of Early Christianity*, describes how the political forces in power had a lot to do with the appointment of the high priest and why Annas had a large influence over the Jewish religious community:

"The office of high priest was inherited according to the Old Testament, but Hellenistic kings were accustomed to removing and appointing priests as political favors or in response to bribes (as the Seleucids did in Jerusalem on the eve of the Maccabean revolt). Herod the Great and his Roman successors changed high priests with some frequency—there were twenty-eight from Herod to A.D. 70. The family of Annas (who was high priest A.D. 6-15), however furnished eight of the high priests…" {6}.

Annas was actually removed from the official office of high priest as the result of political interference by a Roman official, according to RONALD F. YOUNGBLOOD, F.F. BRUCE, and R.K. HARRISON, editors of *Nelson's New Illustrated Bible Dictionary*:

"ANNUS…[was] one of the high priests at Jerusalem, along with CAIAPHAS, when John the Baptist began his ministry, about A.D. 26 (Luke 3:2). Quirinius, governor of Syria, appointed Annas as high priest about A.D. 6 or 7. Although Annas was deposed by Valerius Gratus, the Procurator of Judea, about A.D. 15, he was still the most influencial of the priests and continued to carry the title high priest (Luke 3:2; Acts 4:6). After his removal, Annas was officially succeeded by each of his five sons, one grandson, and his son-in-law CAIAPHAS, the high priest who presided at the trial of Jesus. …Jesus was first taken to Annas, who then sent Jesus to Caiaphas (John 18:13,24)" (pp. 77-78) {7}.

CAIAPHAS, the son-in-law of Annas, presided over the Sanhedrin Council at the trial of "Jesus of Nazareth" (John 18:5). According to Ferguson, Caiaphas presided as high priest for quite some time, longer than the other appointed high priests of the first century:

"The man who held the office the longest in the first century was Joseph Caiaphas, son-in-law of Annas, who officiated from A.D. 18 to 36. The Sanhedrin, the council of the seventy presided over by the high priest, had considerable, if limited, authority over internal affairs" {8}.

CHAPTER 11

SEJANUS was the prefect of the Praetorian Guard. He had enormous political power and authority under the emperor, Tiberius. Everett Ferguson describes what part Sejanus indirectly had in the conviction and crucifixion death of Christ:

"Sejanus was anti-Jewish; Pontius Pilate, governor of Judea at the time of Jesus' crucifixion, was one of his appointees. Pilate's dealing with the Jews may reflect the varying fortunes of his sponsor in Rome" {9}.

PONTIUS PILATE was the appointed provincial governor of Judea during the time of Jesus' ministry and death. Ferguson explains the advantage of having Sejanus as his patron and the later disadvantage which crept up during the trial of Jesus:

"The best known of the early governors…is one of most interest to readers of the Gospels, Pontius Pilate (A.D. 26-36). Pilate had a powerful patron in Rome in Sejanus, prefect of the praetorian guard; and Pilate's change from arrogance toward the Jews in his early years as governor to deference at the trial of Jesus may be due to Sejanus' fall from power. He was the first of the governors seriously to antagonize the Jewish populace" {10}.

The Trial

"Then the detachment of soldiers with its commander and the Jewish officials arrested Jesus. They bound him and brought him first to Annas, who was the father-in-law of Caiaphas, the high priest that year" (John 18:12-13 NIV).

Annas interrogates Jesus:

"Meanwhile, the high priest questioned Jesus about his disciples and his teaching. 'I have spoken openly to the world,' Jesus replied. 'I always taught in synagogues or at the temple, where all the Jews come together. I said nothing in secret. Why question me? Ask those who heard me. Surely they know what I said.' When Jesus said this, one of the officials nearby struck him in the face. 'Is this the way you answer the high priest?' He demanded. 'If I said something wrong,' Jesus replied, 'testify as to what is wrong. But if I spoke the truth, why did you strike me?' Then Annas sent him, still bound, to Caiaphas the high priest" (John 18:19-24 NIV).
Annas was still recognized as the religious authority by the people while his son-in-

MESSIAH HAS ARRIVED: CHRIST'S PROMISES AND DEATH

law, Caiaphas, was recognized by the Roman authorities as high priest. Thus Luke refers to this historical period as being: "during the high priesthood of Annas and Caiaphas" (Luke 3:2a). After being questioned by Annas, Jesus was then taken to appear before Caiaphas and the Sanhedrin Council:

"While I was with you daily in the temple, you did not lay hands on Me; but this hour and the power of darkness are yours" (Luke 22:53 NASB).

The Beginning of a "Kangaroo Court"

"And those who had seized Jesus led Him away to Caiaphas, the high priest, where the scribes and the elders were gathered together" (Matthew 26:57 NASB).

DROP DOWN TO VERSES 59-61:

"Now the chief priests and the whole Council kept trying to obtain false testimony against Jesus, in order that they might put Him to death; And they did not find any, even though many false witnesses came forward. But later on two came forward" (Matthew 26:59-61 NASB).

I refer to this trial as a "kangaroo court" because obviously the prosecutors are looking for only one answer, one verdict: Guilty! Regardless of what the truth is, after specifically looking for false witnesses to bring testimony against Him, they were unable to find anything they could charge Jesus with, until finally they did find two who may or may not have misunderstood what Jesus had meant after they asked for a sign of authority when He cleaned out the Temple of money-changers and merchants selling sheep, oxen, and doves because the temple He was speaking about was "the temple of His body" (John 2:18-22 NASB).

The Trial Continues with their testimony:

"But later two men came forward, and said, 'This man stated, "I am able to destroy the temple of God and to rebuild it in three days."' And the high priest stood up and

---

NOTE: "**Kangaroo court** ...1:a mock court in which the principles of law and justice are disregarded or perverted" (*Merriam Webster's Collegiate Dictionary, Tenth Edition*, p.637, 1996) {11}.

CHAPTER 11

said to Him, 'Do you make no answer? What is it that these men are testifying against you?' But Jesus kept silent. And the high priest said to Him, 'I adjure you by the living God, that you tell us whether You are the Christ, the Son of God.' Jesus said to him, 'You have said it yourself; nevertheless I tell you, hereafter you shall see THE SON OF MAN SITTING AT THE RIGHT HAND OF POWER, and COMING ON THE CLOUDS OF HEAVEN.' Then the high priest tore his robes, saying, 'He has blasphemed! What further need do we have of witnesses? Behold, you have now heard the blasphemy; what do you think?' They answered and said, 'He is deserving of death!' Then they spat in His face and beat Him with their fists; and others slapped Him" (Matthew 26:61b-67 NASB).

Now they have it. He declared it just as they said it with the question:

"TELL US YOU ARE THE CHRIST, THE SON OF GOD." And Jesus answered: "YOU HAVE SAID IT YOURSELF" (emphasis added). There was no need to find someone to perjure himself with false testimony. No need to pursue the question of what He meant when He stated in John 2:19: "Destroy this temple, and I will raise it again in three days." They didn't believe Him when He told them: "...before Abraham was born, I AM." They didn't believe Him when He worked miracles right in front of the eyes of several witnesses, including some of the Pharisees, but they claimed it was "by the prince of demons that he drives out demons" (Matthew 9:32-34). Their verdict: "He is deserving of death!"

Then they brought Jesus before Pontius Pilate, the governor appointed by Sejanus, the powerful prefect of the Praetorian Guard who was hostile toward Jews, and Pilate himself was not that friendly to the Jewish authorities.

Jesus on Trial Before Pilate

"Then the whole body of them arose and brought Him before Pilate. And they began to accuse Him, saying, 'We found this man misleading our nation and forbidding to pay taxes to Caesar, and saying that He Himself is Christ, a King.' And Pilate asked Him, saying, 'Are You the King of the Jews?' And He answered him and said, 'It is as you say.' And Pilate said to the chief priests and the multitudes, 'I find no guilt in this man.' But they kept on insisting, saying, 'He stirs up the people, teaching all over Judea, starting from Galilee, even as far as this place.' But when Pilate heard it, he asked whether the man was a Galilean. And when he learned that He belonged to Herod's jurisdiction, he sent Him to Herod, who himself also was in Jerusalem at that time" (Luke 23:1-7 NASB).

Jesus was a serious political problem for Pilate. Trouble had been brewing in Rome between the emperor Tiberius and Sejanus, Pilate's sponsor. EVERETT FERGUSON describes how the fall of Sejanus may have affected Pilate's final decision:

"Although a brilliant military commander, Tiberius had grown bitter and melancholy by the time he became emporer. ...Tiberius disliked the trappings of power, and although he professed a desire for the senate to have freedom, its own debasement under the long rule of Augustus and Tiberius isolation from it (from A.D. 26 he lived on Capri and did not attend another meeting of the senate) strained relations between them. This isolation plus the oppressive practices of Sejanus, the prefect of the praetorian guard...gave to the senatorial class the black picture of Tiberius that is reflected in Tacitus. Tiberius allowed Sejanus to exercise effective power, but Sejanus finally overreached himself and Tiberius in a counterplot had him executed in A.D. 31" {12}.

The fact that Jesus was a Galilean gave Pilate what appeared to be an easy out of a situation he evidently wanted no part of. Therefore, why not send him to Herod Antipas, the tetrarch of Galilee and Perea, both of which were small districts in first century Palestine? Galilee was directly north of Jerusalem; Perea was northeast. Herod Antipas, a son of Herod the Great, had been responsible for the execution of John the Baptist.

Jesus Interrogated by Herod Antipas

This was an opportunity Herod had been waiting for—perhaps to see a miracle: "Now when Herod saw Jesus, he was exceedingly glad; for he had desired for a long time to see Him, because he had heard many things about Him, and he hoped to see some miracle done by Him. Then he questioned Him with many words, but He answered him nothing. And the chief priests and scribes stood and vehemently accused Him. Then Herod with his men of war, treated Him with contempt and

CHAPTER 11

mocked Him, arrayed Him in a gorgeous robe, and sent Him back to Pilate. That very day Pilate and Herod became friends with each other, for previously they had been at enmity with each other" (Luke 23:8-12 NKJV).

Pilate and Herod now had something in common—a political problem with no satisfactory solution. Herod looked for amusement from what he thought was a very strange magician, but Jesus wouldn't even answer any of Herod's questions, much less perform a miracle. Therefore, after treating their promised Messiah with contempt and ridicule, Herod and his soldiers sent Jesus back to Pilate. After this incident, Pilate and Herod, who had previously been enemies, became friends.

Jesus' Final Trial Before Pilate

Herod apparently wanted no part of executing this man, so he did what most politicians do when presented with an opportunity to not be involved with the final outcome. He sent Jesus back to Pilate. The New Testament offers four accounts of the trial before Pontius Pilate—in Matthew 27:11-27; Mark 15:1-16; Luke 23:13-23; John 18:28-40; 19:1-16. Pilate's dilemma is magnified by the advice of his wife:

"While Pilate was sitting on the judge's seat, his wife sent him this message: 'Don't have anything to do with that innocent man, for I have suffered a great deal today in a dream because of him'" (Matthew 27:19 NIV).

"Pilate called together the chief priests, the rulers and the people, and said to them, 'You brought me this man as one who was inciting the people to rebellion. I have examined him in your presence and have found no basis for your charges against him. Neither has Herod, for he sent him back to us; as you can see, he has done nothing to deserve death'" (Luke 23:13-15 NIV).

Pilate had intentions of releasing Jesus. The fact that Herod didn't officially condemn Him added weight to Pilate's opinion that Jesus had committed no crime worthy of capital punishment. If Herod had thought Jesus guilty of sedition, he would have taken political advantage of the situation to rid Rome of a potential uprising, thus gaining some added kudos from Rome over Pilate because Pilate

MESSIAH HAS ARRIVED: CHRIST'S PROMISES AND DEATH

hadn't handled the situation but passed the buck to Herod. But Herod did not. Instead, he sent this unwanted problem back to Pilate.

In this final scene portrayed in the word pictures of the Gospel writers of Matthew, Mark, Luke, and John, the vicious intent of the religious elite that dominated the religious/political culture, especially in Jerusalem during this period of history, is clearly visible. Mark's Gospel records the final trial before Pilate, beginning with a custom at the time of the Passover feast. The Roman governor in charge would release a Jewish prisoner of the Jews' own choosing (Mark 15:6-16). Matthew, likewise, records the final interrogation before Pilate just before the traditional release of a prisoner (Matthew 27:11-31). Luke records the incident after Pilate had sent Jesus to Herod and Herod sent Him back, where the remainder of the trial takes place with the assembly of the principle Jewish authorities standing before the governor (Luke 23:13-25). Pay special attention to the Gospel of John's record of what took place as Jesus and an accused prisoner stand before Pilate prior to the prisoner release ritual:

"Pilate then went back inside the palace, summoned Jesus and asked him, 'Are you the king of the Jews?'
"'Is that your own idea,' Jesus asked, 'or did others talk to you about me?'
"'Am I a Jew?' Pilate replied. 'It was your people and your chief priests who handed you over to me. What is it you have done?'
"Jesus said, 'My kingdom is not of this world. If it were, my servants would fight to prevent my arrest by the Jews. But now my kingdom is from another place.'
"'You are a king, then!' said Pilate.
"Jesus answered, 'You are right in saying I am a king. In fact, for this reason I was born, and for this I came into the world, to testify to the truth. Everyone on the side of truth listens to me.'
"'What is truth?' Pilate asked. With this he went out again to the Jews and said, 'I find no basis for a charge against him. But it is your custom for me to release to you one prisoner at the time of the Passover. Do you want me to release "the king of the Jews?"
"They shouted back, 'No, not him! Give us Barabbas!' Now Barabbas had taken part in a rebellion" (John 18:33-40 NIV).
It is important to note that Jesus did not respond nor reply to the charges when false witnesses were brought against Him and when He was accused of claiming He

CHAPTER 11

would destroy the Temple in Jerusalem and raise it up again in three days. Jesus remained silent. Why He did not answer these erroneous charges? He was fulfilling what the prophet Isaiah had predicted: "He was oppressed and He was afflicted, Yet He did not open His mouth" (Isaiah 53:7a NASB).

The very people who postured themselves as God's chosen leaders were debasing themselves morally to the point of calling for the release of a man who was a known insurrectionist and murderer! These men were the highest ranking of Jerusalem's own religious and political authorities—the high priests Annas and Caiaphas, the highly-touted scribes who were interpreters of the Law, and other men considered Jewish authorities.

Pontius Pilate, on the other hand, had two conflicting pressures to deal with. First is the fact that this man had committed no crime that violated Roman law. In fact, even Pilate's wife sent a message "saying, 'Have nothing to do with that righteous Man; for last night I suffered greatly in a dream because of Him'" (Matthew 27:19b NASB). Second, during this historical period a serious problem had developed in Rome. The once politically powerful Sejanus, Pilate's sponsor, had fallen from power and Tiberius had executed him. This would have put Pilate in a position where he believed his governorship was in a precarious situation. If Pilate's decision concerning the Jesus incident caused violence and rioting in Jerusalem this would not look good in Rome even if it was the right thing to do.

Pilate would have to have known this. Therefore, after brutally scourging the Son of God, he made efforts to release him (John 19:1-5), but he was faced with a hostile mob demanding the innocent Man's death. Here is what took place:

"Pilate therefore said to Him, 'You do not speak to me? Do You not know that I have authority to release You, and I have authority to crucify You?'

NOTE: The Gospel writer Luke informs us that Barabbas was what one would refer to today as a terrorist: "With one voice they cried out, 'Away with this man! Release Barabbas to us!' (Barabbas had been thrown into prison for an insurrection in the city, and for murder)" (Luke 23:18-19 NIV).

MESSIAH HAS ARRIVED: CHRIST'S PROMISES AND DEATH

"Jesus answered, 'You would have no authority over Me, unless it had been given you from above; for this reason he who delivered Me up to you has the greater sin.'"
"As a result of this Pilate made efforts to release Him, but the Jews cried out saying, **'If you release this Man, you are no friend of Caesar; everyone who makes himself out to be a king opposes Caesar.'**
"When Pilate therefore heard these words, he brought Jesus out, and sat down on the judgment seat at a place called The Pavement, but in Hebrew, Gabbatha.
"Now it was the day of preparation for the Passover; it was about the sixth hour. And he said to the Jews 'Behold your King!'
"They therefore cried out, 'Away with Him, away with Him, crucify Him!'
"Pilate said to them, 'Shall I crucify your King?'
"The chief priests answered, 'We have no king but Caesar.'
"So he then delivered Him to them to be crucified" (John 19:10-16 NASB emphasis added).

Pontius Pilate was no friend of the Jews, politically or religiously. Thus, his decision to compromise what he knew was true, that Jesus was an innocent Man, apparently went against his own principles. Everett Ferguson comments on Pilate's decision to pacify the Jews:

"The best known of the early governors…is the one of most interest to readers of the Gospels, Pontius Pilate (A.D. 26-36). Pilate had a powerful patron in Rome in Sejanus, prefect of the praetorian guard; and Pilate's change from **arrogance toward the Jews in his early years as governor to deference at the trial of Jesus may be due to Sejanus' fall from power**" {13}.

"What Is Truth?"

This is the question Pilate asked Jesus after the Son of God said: "Everyone on the side of truth listens to me" (John 18:37-38). Pontius Pilate's confusion in understanding the reality of truth differs little from later historical figures such as Darwin, Huxley, Dewey, and Dawkins, because humanism and pride causes their perception of reality to center on who they believe to be most important—themselves. They—not God—are the center of reality and there is no room for God because everything is viewed from materialistic assumptions. Materialists have

CHAPTER 11

little or no understanding of Spiritual truth, and because they either lack or refuse to accept Spiritual truth, they have difficulty seeing the reality of truth in history and science, let alone the reality of God taking on human flesh and becoming a servant in order that He might suffer extreme humiliation, physical beatings and scourging, and die a cruel, torturous cross. They see no value in this. They see failure and defeat, nothing that would instill human pride. Yet, to everyone's amazement, this human event in history brought about the greatest victory of all!

Christ Jesus the Eternal Hope For Humanity Fulfilled Every Messianic Prophecy

[1] THE 1st PROPHECY: In Genesis 3:15 Moses records the prophecy that Messiah would come from the Seed of Woman. This was fulfilled in Mary's conception:

"This is how the birth of Jesus Christ came about: His mother Mary was pledged to be married to Joseph, but before they came together, she was found to be with child through the Holy Spirit" (Matthew 1:18 NIV).

"But when the fullness of the time had come, God sent forth His Son, born of a woman, born under the law" (Galatians 4: 4 NKJV).

Okay, so how does this differ from any other pregnancy of a woman before she had sexual relations with her husband? By that time in history, pregnancy probably had occurred to numerous unmarried women, and a few perhaps that were pledged to marry. The difference lies in the fact that this pregnancy came about through Supernatural Intervention. God, the Holy Spirit, was involved in the conception. The inspired Scriptures state the birth in this manner: **"God sent forth His Son, born of a woman!"** This inspired statement leaves Joseph, Mary's husband, completely out of the picture because this conception and birth was brought about by God alone!

[2] THE 2nd PROPHECY: Isaiah 7:14 states, "Therefore the Lord Himself will give you a **sign**: Behold, the virgin shall conceive and bear a Son, and shall call His name Immanuel" (NKJV emphasis added). NOTE: In Hebrew "Immanuel" is literally "God with us.)

MESSIAH HAS ARRIVED: CHRIST'S PROMISES AND DEATH

Isaiah's prophecy was fulfilled with Mary's divine conception:

The angel told Joseph (Mary's betrothed husband) that the conception was by the Holy Spirit: "'And she [Mary] will bring forth a Son, and you shall call His name Jesus, for He will save His people from their sins.' So all this was done that it might be fulfilled which was spoken by the Lord through the prophet, saying; 'Behold, the virgin shall be with child, and bear a Son, and they shall call His name Immanuel,' which is translated, 'God with us'" (Matthew 1:21-23 NKJV).

A "SIGN" in the Scriptures indicates something out of the ordinary. A young woman becoming pregnant has always been a common, everyday occurrence. But if the Scripture states this will be "a sign," then this is special; this is something beyond the norm; it is Supernatural! It means God is directly involved with the outcome. Isaiah's prophecy was fulfilled in the first century when a virgin named Mary became pregnant with a child by the Holy Spirit!

"And Mary said to the angel, 'How can this be, since I am a virgin?' And the angel answered and said to her, 'The Holy Spirit will come upon you, and the power of the Most High will overshadow you; and for that reason the holy offspring shall be called the Son of God'" (Luke 1:34-35 NASB).

The Gospel writers Matthew and Luke make it very clear that the birth of Jesus was not an ordinary event. It was Supernatural: **"for that reason the holy offspring shall be called the Son of God."**

[3] THE 3rd PROPHECY is in Genesis 12:3b. Moses wrote of the promise to Abram (later in Genesis 17:5 changed by the LORD to Abraham): "And in you all the families of the earth shall be blessed" (NASB).

IN OTHER WORDS: ALL THE NATIONS SHALL BE BLESSED IN ABRAHAM. Paul the apostle wrote to the Christians in Galatia: "And the Scripture foreseeing that God would justify the Gentiles by faith, preached the Gospel beforehand to Abraham, saying, 'ALL THE NATIONS SHALL BE BLESSED IN YOU.' So then those who are of faith are blessed with Abraham, the believer" (Galatians 3:8-9 NASB).

CHAPTER 11

DROP DOWN TO VERSE-14:

"...in order that in Christ Jesus the blessing of Abraham might come to the Gentiles, so that we might receive the promise of the Spirit through faith" (Galatians 3:14 NASB).

The Blessing to All Nations Was Fulfilled "in Christ Jesus"

[4] THE 4th PROPHECY is in Genesis 28:14b. Moses wrote of the promise made to Jacob: "All peoples on earth will be blessed through you [Jacob] and your offspring."

God's prophecy to Jacob recorded by MOSES of the blessing that would come through Jacob's "offspring" was shown to be fulfilled in the genealogy of Jesus Christ:

"A record of the genealogy of Jesus Christ the son of David, the son of Abraham: Abraham was the father of Isaac, Isaac the father of Jacob, Jacob the father of Judah and his brothers..." (Matthew 1:1-2 NIV emphasis added).

[5] THE 5th PROPHECY is in Genesis 3:15. Here lies the hidden strategy of a merciful God:
CRUSHING (BRUISING) THE HEAD OF THE SERPENT
STRIKING (BRUISING) THE HEEL OF THE WOMAN'S OFFSPRING:

In the New International Version it reads: "And I will put enmity between you and the woman, and between your offspring and hers; he will crush your head, and you will strike his heel."

In the New King James Version it reads: "And I will put enmity between you and the woman, And between your seed and her Seed; He shall bruise your head, And you shall bruise His heel."

MESSIAH HAS ARRIVED: CHRIST'S PROMISES AND DEATH

The "Lord God" Will Defeat ("Crush") the Power of Satan By the Crucifixion of His Son (God's Concealed Strategy). The fulfillment of God's Promise to Defeat Satan (the serpent) and Render his Power Useless Rests in the Crucifixion! Jesus' heel was bruised when He struck the serpent's (Satan's) head but the serpent was then powerless to strike or deceive.

In John 8:44, Jesus, the Son of God, had a confrontation with the seed of their (the Jewish religious leaders') father, the devil (the serpent in Genesis chapter 3): "You are of your father the devil, and you want to do the desires of your father. He was a murderer from the beginning, and does not stand in the truth, because there is no truth in him. Whenever he speaks a lie, he speaks from his own nature; for he is a liar, and the father of lies" (NASB).

This is a clear example of the "enmity" between Jesus and Satan's seed (the Jews who wanted to destroy Jesus' influence or kill Him, whichever achieved their purpose). Later, both Satan and his seed believed they had achieved this when Jesus, the Son of God, was crucified. Satan may have believed he had won the war, but in reality he had lost.

"They took Jesus therefore, and He went out, bearing His own cross, to the place called the Place of a Skull, which is called in Hebrew, Golgotha. There they crucified Him, and with Him two other men, one on either side, and Jesus in between" (John 19:17-18 NASB).

"He Himself likewise also partook of the same, that through death He might render **powerless him who had the power of death, that is, the devil**" (Hebrews 2:14b NASB).

In the next two prophetic Scriptures we will see the prophecies made by two separate and distinct men that lived about 300 years apart in history which foretold in intricate detail the death of the promised Messiah. Little did the religious elite in power during the first century in Jerusalem realize they not only did not rid themselves of that troublesome outsider, but this was only the beginning!

"A Psalm of David. My God, my God, why hast Thou forsaken me? Far from my deliverance are the words of my groaning" (Psalm 22:1 NASB).

CHAPTER 11

[6] THE 6th PROPHECY is the words cried out in anguish by Jesus the Messiah, which fulfilled David's prophecy made about 1,000 years before the death of Christ Jesus:

"And about the ninth hour Jesus cried out with a loud voice, saying, 'ELI, ELI, LAMA SABACHTHANI?' that is, 'MY GOD, MY GOD, WHY HAST THOU FORSAKEN ME?' (Matthew 27:46 NASB).

FORSAKEN BY GOD? How could this be? Wasn't Jesus the Son of God? Yes, He was. Most unbelievers would look at this as the words of a Man who claimed to be the Son of God—in fact, claimed He was the "I AM," the Creator Himself—unable even to prevent an angry mob from hanging Him on a cross. What they didn't understand then, and still don't today, is that it had to be this way. Jesus' own disciples, dejected and feeling lost and defeated, came to understand this after His resurrection. Christ Jesus, God's anointed Savior of humanity, had to become a curse for us:

"All who rely on observing the law are under a curse, for it is written: 'Cursed is everyone who does not continue to do everything written in the Book of the Law.' Clearly no one is justified before God by the law, because, 'The righteous will live by faith.' The law is not based on faith; on the contrary, 'the man who does these things will live by them.' Christ redeemed us from the curse of the law by becoming a curse for us, for it is written: 'Cursed is everyone who is hung on a tree.' He redeemed us in order that the blessing given to Abraham might come to the Gentiles through Christ Jesus, so that by faith we might receive the promise of the Spirit" (Galatians 3:10-14 NIV).
The Jews who relied on the Law (of Moses) were under a curse because they were not able to keep every law perfectly as it was written. Christ became a curse, forsaken by God, in order to redeem all those who lived under the law. It is by faith that both Jews and Gentiles can receive the blessing of Abraham.

There is more yet to learn, but this is sufficient to understand why Jesus had to be forsaken by God to complete His eternal purpose.

"All who see me mock me; they hurl insults, shaking their heads: 'He trusts in the LORD;   let the LORD rescue him. Let him deliver him, since he delights in him'" (Psalm 22:7-8 NIV).

MESSIAH HAS ARRIVED: CHRIST'S PROMISES AND DEATH

[7] THE 7th PROPHECY is David pointing out in detail the cruel, vindictive mockery and insults that would be heaped upon the promised Messiah. Notice how the Gospel writer Matthew records this in the 27th chapter at the scene of the crucifixion. Jerusalem's religious elite, blinded and manipulated by the prince of darkness to accomplish his agenda, the death of the Son of God, mock and insult him:

"In the same way the chief priests, the teachers of the law and the elders mocked him. 'He saved others,' they said, 'but he can't save himself! He's the King of Israel! Let him come down now from the cross, and we will believe in him. He trusts in God. Let God rescue him now if he wants him, for he said, "I am the Son of God"'" (Matthew 27:41-43 NIV).

"Those who passed by hurled insults at him, shaking their heads and saying, 'So! You who are going to destroy the temple and build it in three days, come down from the cross and save yourself!' In the same way the chief priests and the teachers of the law mocked him among themselves. 'He saved others,' they said, 'but he can't save himself!'" (Mark 15:29-32 NIV).

Both Matthew and Mark clearly point out how David's prophecy in the 22nd Psalm has been fulfilled. How would David know what would historically take place about a thousand years later unless he was Inspired by God to write this?

[8] THE 8th PROPHECY leaves no doubt about the fact that David was Predicting the Crucifixion Death of the Messiah, which was historically fulfilled when Christ Jesus' hands were nailed to that Cross:

"For dogs have surrounded me; A band of evildoers has encompassed me; **They pierced my hands and my feet**" (Psalm 22:16 NASB emphasis added).

"And when they had crucified Him, they divided up His garments among themselves, casting lots…" (Matthew 27:35 NASB).

"And they crucified Him, and divided up His garments among themselves, casting lots for them, to decide what each should take" (Mark 15:24 NASB).

CHAPTER 11

"And when they came to the place called The Skull, there they crucified Him and the criminals, one on the right and the other on the left" (Luke 23:33 NASB).

"They took Jesus therefore, and He went out, bearing His own cross, to the place called the Place of a Skull, which is called in Hebrew, Golgotha. There they crucified Him, and with Him two other men, one on either side, and Jesus in between" (John 19:17-18 NASB).

There is no question Biblically, prophetically, or historically, that Jesus the Christ was indeed crucified, having His hands and His feet pierced when the Roman soldiers hung Him on the cross.

For skeptics to deny this is to deny one of the most well-established facts in ancient historical records. Yet in spite of the evidence, some still deny it.

Dan Barker, an avowed atheist, in his book, *Godless*, states that he doubts the historical existence of the Jesus of the Bible:

"But when I became a freethinker, I did decide to look it up and was very surprised at what I found—or more precisely, at what I didn't find. I am now convinced that the Jesus story is a combination of myth and legend, mixed with a little bit of real history unrelated to Jesus" [p.251] {14}.

Contrary to what Dan Barker may believe, the evidence for the crucifixion death of Jesus Christ is overwhelmingly established by those who knew Jesus personally and by a surprising number of neutral and hostile witnesses with no ulterior reason to support His existence other than the fact that Jesus Christ did exist and did indeed die on the cross. To deny the fact that Jesus died on the cross in the first century would be like denying the assassination death of President John Fitzgerald Kennedy.

Hostile Roman and Jewish Historical Records

"CORNELIUS TACITUS (ca. AD 55-120) was a Roman historian who lived through the reigns of over a half dozen Roman emperors. ...Tacitus is best known for two works—the Annals and the Histories. ...The Annals covers the period from Augustus' death in AD 14 to that of Nero in AD 68," as recorded by GARY R. HABERMAS.

MESSIAH HAS ARRIVED: CHRIST'S PROMISES AND DEATH

HABERMAS, in his book, *The Historical Jesus*, states: "Tacitus recorded at least one reference to Christ and two to early Christianity, one in each of his major works. The most important one is that found in the Annals, written about AD 115." The following was recounted concerning the great fire in Rome during the reign of Nero:

"Consequently, to get rid of the report, Nero fastened the guilt and inflicted the most exquisite tortures on a class hated for their abominations, called Christians by the populace. Christus, from whom the name had its origin, suffered the extreme penalty during the reign of Tiberius at the hands of one of our procurators, Pontius Pilatus, and a most mischievous superstition, thus checked for the moment, again broke out not only in Judaea, the first source of the evil, but even in Rome, where all things hideous and shameful from every part of the world find their centre and become popular" {15}.

This is only part of Tacitus' historical record, but is enough to point out that even the historians who were hostile to Christianity admitted that Christ ("Christus") was a real historical person who lived and was put to death by Pontius Pilate ("Pilatus"). For more details on Tacitus' negative report on Christianity, read *The Historical Jesus*, by Gary R. Habermas, who holds a Ph.D. from Michigan State University. His book will provide the reader with many more historical details concerning Christ. Habermas points out several details of evidence from Tacitus' reference to Christ:

"(1) Christians were named for their founder, Christus (from the Latin), (2) who was put to death by the Roman procurator Pontius Pilatus (also Latin), (3) during the reign of emperor Tiberius (AD 14-37). (4) His death ended the 'superstition' for a short time, (5) but it broke out again, (6) especially in Judea, where the teaching had its origin" {16}.

Hostile Historical Account about Jesus in the Jewish Talmud

KYLE BUTT and ERIC LYONS, in their book, *Behold! The Lamb of God*, mention historical data written by Jewish rabbis about 200 A.D. called the "Talmud":

CHAPTER 11

"On the eve of the Passover Yeshu was hanged. For forty days before the execution took place, a herald went forth and cried, 'He is going forth to be stoned because he has practiced sorcery and enticed Israel to apostasy. ...But since nothing was brought forward in his favor he was hanged on the eve of the Passover" (Shachter 43a).

The Somewhat More Neutral Historical Records of Josephus

FLAVIUS JOSEPHUS was a first century Jewish historian. His name is well-known among noted skeptics and atheists as well as Christian apologists. His writings have stirred up controversy because of one critical historical record that

Josephus did include about the historical Christ. Actually, Josephus mentioned Christ twice in his writings as a historical figure but only one of these has been actively contested, primarily by skeptics and liberal theologians. GARY R. HABERMAS, in his book, *The Historical Jesus*, presents an interesting word portrait of the historian Josephus:

"Jewish historian Flavius Josephus was born in AD 37 or 38 and died in AD 97. He was born into a priestly family and became a Pharisee at the age of nineteen. After surviving a battle against the Romans, he served commander Vespasian in Jerusalem. After the destruction of Jerusalem in AD 70, he moved to Rome, where he became the court historian for emperor Vespasian. The Antiquities, one of Josephus major works, provides some valuable but disputed evidence concerning Jesus. Written around AD 90-95, it is earlier than the testimonies of the Roman historians" {18}.

The historical records of Josephus are particularly bothersome to skeptics in general because they point out the fact that Josephus' records were written less than 70 years after the death of Jesus Christ. WILLIAM WHISTON, in his translation of *The Life and Works of Flavius Josephus*, has translated Josephus' historical records where he twice mentions Jesus. Here is one where James, the Lord's brother, is also mentioned:

NOTE: "Yeshu or Yeshua is the Hebrew spelling equivalent to the name Jesus" {17}.

MESSIAH HAS ARRIVED: CHRIST'S PROMISES AND DEATH

"So he assembled the sanhedrin of judges, and brought before them the brother of Jesus, who was called Christ, whose name was James, and some others" (Bk. 20, Ch. 9) {19}.

Concerning the death of Jesus, here is a quotation from an Arabic manuscript, with comments by Habermas:

"In 1972 Professor Schlomo Pines of the Hebrew University in Jerusalem released the results of a study on an Arabic manuscript containing Josephus statement about Jesus: ...'At this time there was a wise man who was called Jesus. His conduct was good and (he) was known to be virtuous. And many people from among the Jews and the other nations became his disciples. Pilate condemned him to be crucified and to die'" {20}.

There is more of this text that will be mentioned in the next chapter. However, the point that needs to be asserted here is the fact that Josephus knew about a living historical person named Jesus, "a wise man" with good conduct and many disciples who was put to death by "Pilate" and was "crucified." This much is certainly in agreement with the earlier accounts by the four gospel writers—Matthew, Mark, Luke, and John.

Although Josephus was a Jew, his writings do not appear to extend favoritism to Jews or Christians. One reason for his subtle neutrality might be the fact that he gained favor with the Roman commander, Vespasian.

Kyle Butt and Eric Lyons provide circumstantial evidence for this:

"When Jerusalem rebelled against the Roman authorities, he [Josephus] was given command of the Jewish forces in Galilee. After losing most of his men, he surrendered to the Romans. He found favor in the man who commanded the Roman army, Vespasian, by predicting that Vespasian soon would be elevated to the position of emperor. Josephus prediction came true at Vespasian's inauguration in A.D. 69. After the fall of Jerusalem, Josephus assumed the family name of the emperor (Flavius) and settled down to live a life as a government pensioner. It was during these latter years that he wrote *Antiquities of the Jews* between September 93 and September 94 (Bruce, 1960, pp.102-104). ...His contemporaries viewed his career indignantly as one of traitorous rebellion to the Jewish nation (Bruce, 1960, p. 103)" {21}.

CHAPTER 11

Under the circumstances it would be politically expedient for Josephus to remain neutral to any controversy that would cause him to lose favor and endanger his position as historian for the Roman emperor.

Four friendly witnesses who lived with Jesus for about three years, two hostile witnesses who acknowledge Jesus' historical existence, and one neutral witness that wrote about Jesus on two occasions, all left historical records of His death. Without a doubt, Jesus' death on the cross fulfilled David's prophecy of the Messiah's death by crucifixion (Psalm 22:16).

---

[9] THE 9th PROPHECY has particular significance because of David's intricate details regarding the dividing of Messiah's garments and the casting of lots for them at His crucifixion:

"They divide my garments among them, And for my clothing they cast lots" (Psalm 22:18 NASB).

All four Gospels make note of this occurrence at Jesus crucifixion (Matthew 27:35; Mark 15:24; Luke 23:34; and John 19:23-24), but it is John who personally witnessed Jesus' death at the cross and who Jesus asked to take care of Mary, His mother (John 19:26-27). It is John that makes specific reference to the fact that dividing the garments and casting lots for them was the specific fulfillment of Psalm 22:18:

"The soldiers therefore, when they had crucified Jesus, took His outer garments and made four parts, a part to every soldier and also the tunic; now the tunic was seamless, woven in one piece. They said therefore to one another, 'Let us not tear it, but cast lots for it, to decide whose it shall be'; that the Scripture might be fulfilled, 'THEY DIVIDED MY OUTER GARMENTS AMONG THEM, AND FOR MY CLOTHING THEY CAST LOTS'" (John 19:22-24 NASB).

NOTE: "The casting of lots" was a method of using "objects of unknown shape and material…to determine the divine will. …The awful picture of soldiers casting lots for Jesus' garments was this kind of 'fair play' use of lots (Mt. 27:35)" (*Holman's Bible Dictionary*, p.896) {22}.

MESSIAH HAS ARRIVED: CHRIST'S PROMISES AND DEATH

John, the writer of the fourth Gospel, is openly declaring that what happened when Jesus was nailed to the cross is exactly what David had prophesied, about a thousand years before Jesus' birth!

In the 53rd chapter of Isaiah there are two more very significant prophecies that were fulfilled which need to be disclosed. They openly reveal why it was necessary for God to come in human form:

ISAIAH'S PROPHECIES IN THE 53rd CHAPTER ARE A CLEAR WORD-PICTURE OF THE SUFFERING SERVANT. THIS IS HOW JOHN THE BAPTIST DECRIBED JESUS TO TWO OF HIS DISCIPLES:

"BEHOLD, THE LAMB OF GOD!" (John 1:36b NASB emphasis added).
"For He shall grow up before Him as a tender plant, And as a root out of dry ground. He has no form or comeliness; And when we see Him, There is no beauty that we should desire Him. He is despised and rejected by men, A Man of sorrows and acquainted with grief. And we hid, as it were, our faces from Him; He was despised, and we did not esteem Him. Surely He has born our griefs And carried our sorrows; Yet we esteemed Him stricken, Smitten by God, and afflicted. But He was wounded for our transgressions, He was bruised for our iniquities; The chastisement for our peace was upon Him, And by His stripes we are healed. All we like sheep have gone astray; We have turned, every one, to his own way; And the LORD has laid on Him the iniquity of us all" (Isaiah 53:2-6, 9 NKJV).

The Bruising of the Seed of the Woman

[10] THE 10th PROPHECY provides the Eternal Master Strategy our Creator devised to complete His Master Plan to be victorious over Satan (the adversary) and to provide every human being the opportunity to be free from their bondage to the devil:

"But He was wounded for our transgressions, He was bruised for our iniquities; The chastisement for our peace was upon Him, And by His stripes we are healed" (Isaiah 53:5-6 NKJV emphasis added).

CHAPTER 11

In the Gospel of John 19:1: "So then Pilate took Jesus and scourged Him." The scourging method used by the Romans is something no man or woman should ever have to go through. *Nelson's New Illustrated Bible Dictionary* describes "the whip" and the method used for this type of punishment:

"The whip used for this type of punishment consisted of a handle to which one or more leather cords or thongs were attached. Some times these cords were knotted or weighted with pieces of metal or bone to make the whip more effective as a flesh-cutting instrument" {23}.

Why did Jesus voluntarily suffer the indignation, humiliation, extremely torturous suffering, and death, having been forsaken by God, in order to become a curse for us by hanging on a tree? The answer is pointed out in a clear, self-evident motive — to be "bruised for our iniquities," not His!
"You see, at just the right time, when we were still powerless, Christ died for the ungodly. Very rarely will anyone die for a righteous man, though for a good man someone might possibly dare to die. But God demonstrates his own love for us in this: while we were still sinners, Christ died for us" (Romans 5:6-8 NIV).

"For to this you were called, because Christ also suffered for us, leaving us an example, that you should follow His steps: Who committed no sin, Nor was deceit found in His mouth"; who, when He was reviled, did not revile in return; when He suffered, He did not threaten, but committed Himself to Him who judges righteously; who Himself bore our sins in His own body on the tree, that we, having died to sins, might live for righteousness — by whose stripes you were healed" (1 Peter 2:21-24 NKJV).

Here is your answer: God, the "Word" (John 1:1-3), "at just the right time" came down, took the form of a human being, lived His entire life without sin, "bore our sins in His own body"..."by whose stripes you were healed!" The motivation was LOVE:

"But God demonstrates his own love for us in this: while we were still sinners, Christ died for us" (Romans 5:8 NIV).

No finite human being could have accomplished this:

MESSIAH HAS ARRIVED: CHRIST'S PROMISES AND DEATH

"…For all have sinned and fall short of the glory of God" (Romans 3:23 NASB).

It took our God, full of love, willing to send His own Son, who lived without sin, to die for an unworthy, sinful humanity. Why did it have to be done this way? The answer is found in the New Testament letter to the Hebrews. Under the Old Covenant, the high priest would enter the second division of the temple "once a year" to offer the blood of "goats and bulls"…"for himself and for the sins of the people." Christ the Messiah offered His blood: "but through His own blood, He entered the holy place once for all, having obtained **eternal redemption**." …"How much more will the blood of Christ, who through the eternal Spirit **offered Himself without blemish to God**…" (Hebrews 9:2-14a NASB).

"Since then the children share in flesh and blood, He Himself likewise also partook of the same, that through death He might render powerless him who had the power of death, that is, the devil; and might deliver those who through fear of death were subject to slavery all their lives" (Hebrews 2:14-15 NASB).

DEATH is the "BRUISE" the Messiah would suffer, and in doing this, He rendered Satan (the devil) powerless to hold any human being in "SLAVERY" under the penalty of death, because the captives who put their trust in Christ Jesus are FREE from the Law of Sin and Death:

"Therefore, there is now no condemnation for those who are in Christ Jesus, because through Christ Jesus the law of the Spirit of life set me free from the Law of sin and death" (Romans 8:1-2).

Why is the fulfillment of the Tenth Prophecy so critically necessary to bring about the defeat of Satan? First, because Christ Jesus' death on the cross **rendered Satan "powerless" to hold anyone who put their faith in Christ Jesus in bondage to the Law of Sin and Death!** This strategic step in the master-plan of our Creator is a critical part of what the Holy Scriptures reveal is "of first importance" (1 Corinthians 15:3). BUT there is one more critical point that must be made. In fact, Paul, the inspired writer of the two letters to the Corinthian Christians, made this pivotal observation in the fifteenth chapter of the first letter:

"If only for this life we have hope in Christ, we are to be pitied more than all men" (1 Corinthians 15:19 NIV).

CHAPTER 11

The assurance of our hope and our freedom from bondage to the Law of sin and death lies in the Messiah's resurrection from the dead. If Christ has not sinned Satan's power of death cannot hold Him! Therefore, Christ Jesus must demonstrate His power over death by rising from the dead, and this is what He did!

There is another prophecy that was fulfilled regarding the Messiah's death:

"He was assigned a grave with the wicked, and with the rich in his death" (Isaiah 53:9a NIV).

[11] THE 11th PROPHECY consists of two events that were fulfilled with the death of the Messiah (Christ Jesus).
"He was assigned a grave with the **wicked**" (Isaiah 53:9a emphasis added).

"In the same way the **robbers** who were crucified with him also heaped insults on him" (Matthew 27:44 NIV emphasis added).

"They crucified two robbers with him, one on his right and one on his left" (Mark 15:27 NIV).

That criminal's belief in his Messiah Christ Jesus and his repentance of his criminal acts freed him from his sin and bondage to Satan when Jesus died on that cross. Truly, he was with Christ in paradise.

"...and with the rich in his death" (Isaiah 53:9a emphasis added).

"As evening approached, there came a **rich man** from Arimathea, named Joseph, who had himself become a disciple of Jesus. Going to Pilate, he asked for Jesus' body, and Pilate ordered that it be given to him. Joseph took the body, wrapped it in a clean linen cloth, and placed it in his own new tomb that he had cut out of the rock. He rolled a big stone in front of the entrance to the tomb and went away" (Matthew 27:57-60 NIV emphasis added).

Eleven prophecies, concerning the arrival of the Messiah and His death by crucifixion have been fulfilled in minute detail. Prophets such as Moses, David, and Isaiah, by God-breathed inspiration, covered an expanse of over 1,400 years of

MESSIAH HAS ARRIVED: CHRIST'S PROMISES AND DEATH

history. There is no way this could have been a coincidence of happenings. The most important prophecy of them all will be covered in its fulfillment in the next chapter in a divine demonstration of power!

NOTE: One of the criminals repented:

"Then he said, 'Jesus, remember me when you come into your kingdom.' Jesus answered him, 'I tell you the truth, today you will be with me in paradise'" (Luke 23:42-43 NIV).

Chapter 12

THE DEATH, BURIAL & RESURRECTION OF CHRIST: HISTORICAL FACT

"Paul, a bondservant of Jesus Christ, called to be an apostle, separated to the gospel of God which He promised before through His prophets in the Holy Scriptures, concerning His Son Jesus Christ our Lord, who was born of the seed of David according to the flesh, and declared to be the Son of God with power according to the Spirit of holiness, by the resurrection from the dead" (Romans 1:1-4 NKJV).

CHAPTER 12

Everything written in the Holy Scriptures rests on one historical fact: the resurrection of Jesus Christ from the dead. If the man Jesus, who claimed to be the promised Messiah, did not rise from the dead as He declared He would, if the fulfillment of the promises written through the prophets that God's Messiah would indeed rise from the dead never happened, then nothing else in this book of the Holy Scriptures has anything to offer to anyone at anytime anywhere in history! The words would be just lofty platitudes of nothingness. How tragically sad it would be for all the people who suffered humiliating persecution for their trusting allegiance to someone that could not fulfill what he declared he would do. Then Pontius Pilate's ultimate question would remain unanswered:

"What is Truth?"

GARY R. HABERMAS has spent over twenty years of historical research on the resurrection of Jesus Christ. He has a Ph.D. from Michigan State University. His background and research in apologetics and the philosophy of religion clearly qualifies him as one of the foremost authorities on the historical reality of Jesus Christ and the historical evidence for His resurrection. After every attempt by the Jewish and Roman authorities to prevent it, and after all the skeptics throughout history up to this present day who refuse to accept it, the fact of Christ's resurrection stands confirmed above all efforts to deny it:

"Of all these subjects, the resurrection of Jesus is like a many-faceted diamond. Turned one way, it is the very center of the Christian Gospel. From another angle, it is the best-attested miracle-claim in Scripture (or any other 'holy book,' for that matter). Turned again, it provides an evidential basis for Christian theism. Further, in the New Testament it is a bridge to almost every major doctrine in the Christian faith, as well as being related to multiple areas of Christian practice" {1}.

Habermas dedicated over 300 pages in his book, *The Historical Jesus*, to the abundant historical evidences for the reality of the Son of God, His life among humanity, His historic resurrection from the dead, and the impact it has upon every human being.

The resurrection is the key to the valid appeal of the New Testament. It is, as the

THE DEATH, BURIAL & RESURRECTION OF CHRIST: HISTORICAL FACT

Holy Scriptures most openly declare, "of first importance." The New Testament writer Paul the apostle knew that without the raising of Christ Jesus from the dead everything else had little meaning, much less his own testimony to that fact:

"And if Christ has not been raised, our preaching is useless and so is your faith. More than that, we are then found to be false witnesses about God, for we have testified about God that he raised Christ from the dead. But he did not raise him if in fact the dead are not raised. For if the dead are not raised, then Christ has not been raised either. And if Christ has not been raised, your faith is futile; you are still in your sins. Then those also who have fallen asleep in Christ are lost. **If only for this life we have hope in Christ, we are to be pitied more than all men**" (1Corinthians 15:14-19 NIV emphasis added).

EVERETT FERGUSON, in his book, *The Church of Christ*, points out that this is the "message of the church":

"There had to be a commission to give the church a mission. There had to be a message for the church to proclaim. This gave the church a purpose. The resurrected Jesus gave the 'great commission' to his disciples to preach the gospel (Mark 16:15-16) of forgiveness of sins (Luke 24:47) and make disciples of all nations (Matthew 28:19). Paul understood the task of the proclaimers of the message about Christ (Romans 10:13-17) in terms of Isaiah 52:7—'How beautiful upon the mountains are the feet of the messenger who announces peace, who brings good news [gospel], who announces salvation, who says to Zion, 'Your God reigns.' The gospel that brings salvation centers on the facts of Jesus' death, burial, and resurrection (1 Corinthians 15:1-4)" {2}.

"Now, brothers, I want to remind you of the gospel I preached to you, which you received and on which you have taken your stand. By this gospel you are saved, if you hold firmly to the word I preached to you. Otherwise, you have believed in vain" (1 Corinthians 15:1-2 NIV).

This "gospel" is the most fundamental message of truth!

"For what I received I passed on to you as of first importance: that Christ died for our sins according to the Scriptures, that he was buried, that he was raised on the third day according to the Scriptures" (1 Corinthians 15:3-4 NIV).

CHAPTER 12

What does the word "gospel" mean?

W.E. VINE, MERRILL F. UNGER, & WILLIAM WHITE, Jr. in their book, An Expository of Biblical Words, defines "gospel" as from the Greek word "EUANGELION...originally denoted a reward for good tidings; later, the idea of reward dropped, and the word stood for the good news itself. The Eng. Word gospel, i.e. good message, is the equivalent of euangelion (Eng., evangel)" (p. 497, 1984, Thomas Nelson, Inc., Publishers, Nashville, Tennessee).

What is the "good news," in other words, the "good message"?

"For what I received I passed on to you as of first importance: that Christ died for our sins according to the Scriptures, that he was buried, that he was raised on the third day according to the Scriptures" (1 Corinthians 15:3-4 NIV).

This is the "GOOD NEWS"! Paul writes that he "RECEIVED" the good news from Christ Jesus who appeared to him on the way to Damascus and from the other apostles and disciples such as Ananias (Acts 9:17-19; Acts 22:12-16), Please notice what he writes next: "I passed [this] on to you AS OF FIRST IMPORTANCE..."

What is it that is "of first importance," Paul?

"That [Christ] died for our sins"..."that [Christ] was buried, that [Christ] was raised from the dead according to the Scriptures!"

This is what was prophesied by Moses, David, and Isaiah in the Holy Scriptures. Jesus Himself stated, after His resurrection from the dead when He appeared to His disciples:

"This is what I told you while I was still with you: everything must be fulfilled that is written about me in the Law of Moses, the prophets and the Psalms" (Luke 24:44 NIV).

In other words, Jesus died to free humanity from their sins and bondage to Satan (the devil) who held the power of death (Hebrews 2:14). Even though Jesus was

THE DEATH, BURIAL & RESURRECTION OF CHRIST: HISTORICAL FACT

buried, death could not hold Him because Jesus did not sin. Therefore, since death could not hold Him, Christ Jesus rose from the dead triumphant:

"Therefore, we are ambassadors for Christ, as though God were entreating through us; we beg you on behalf of Christ, be reconciled to God. He made Him who knew no sin to be sin on our behalf, that we might become the righteousness of God in Him" (2 Corinthians 5:20-21 NASB).

"Since then we have a great high priest who has passed through the heavens, Jesus the Son of God, let us hold fast our confession. For we do not have a high priest who cannot sympathize with our weaknesses, but one who has been tempted in all things as we are, yet without sin" (Hebrews 4:14-15 NASB).

"And God raised Him up again, putting an end to the agony of death, since it was impossible for Him to be held in its power" (Acts 2:24 NASB).

Christ Jesus lived His entire life, taking the form of a human being to serve His Father and humanity, without falling victim to the devil's power of death because Jesus did not sin. Death had no power to hold Him in bondage. Jesus was the "lamb of God," whom John the Baptist testified, "takes away the sin of the world" (John 1:29) and the suffering servant who offered Himself upon the cross as a sacrifice and a curse to free all of humanity from bondage to "the law of sin and death" (Romans 8:1-2). Jesus Christ reigns today as both king and high priest:

"This Melchizedek was king of Salem and priest of God Most High. He met Abraham returning from the defeat of the kings and blessed him, and Abraham gave him a tenth of everything. First, his name means 'king of righteousness'; then also, 'king of Salem' means 'king of peace.' Without father or mother, without genealogy, without beginning of days or end of life, like the Son of God he remains a priest forever" (Hebrews 7:1-3 NIV).

DROP DOWN TO VERSES 11-12:

"If perfection could have been attained through the Levitical priesthood (for on the basis of it the law was given to the people), why was there still need for another priest to come—one in the order of Melchizedek, not in the order of Aaron? For

CHAPTER 12

when there is a change of the priesthood, there must also be a change of the law" (Hebrews 7:11-12 NIV).

Very little is known about Melchizedek and his unique position as both king and priest in the Holy Scriptures. What we do know is that Melchizedek is mentioned in Genesis 14:18 as "king of Salem" and "priest of God Most High" and in Psalm 110:4, a psalm of King David, Hebrews 5:6; Hebrews 6:20; and Hebrews 7:1-21 describe Melchizedek as "without father or mother," beginning or end of life, and like Jesus Christ.

DROP DOWN TO VERSES 15-17:

"And what we have said is even more clear if another priest like Melchizedek appears, one who has become a priest not on the basis of a regulation as to his ancestry but on the basis of the power of an indestructible life. For it is declared: 'You are a priest forever, in the order of Melchizedek'" (Hebrews 7:15-17; ref. Psalm 110:4).

Like Melchizedek, Christ Jesus, the Son of God, has "the power of an indestructible life." He is the "I AM," the Eternal God. He is "the Word" who created "all things… that has been made" (Hebrews 7:16; John 8:58; John 1:1-3).

DROP DOWN TO VERSES 22-27:

"Because of this oath, Jesus has become the guarantee of a better covenant. Now there have been many of those priests, since death prevented them from continuing in office; but because Jesus lives forever, he has a permanent priesthood. Therefore he is able to save completely those who come to God through him, because he always lives to intercede for them. Such a high priest meets our need—one who is holy, blameless, pure, set apart from sinners, exalted above the heavens. Unlike the other high priests, he does not need to offer sacrifices day after day, first for his own sins, and then for the sins of the people. He sacrificed for their sins once for all when he offered himself" (Hebrews 7:22-27 NIV).

Jesus the high priest guarantees humankind a better covenant, because he was raised from the dead by the power of God. He lives forever—a "permanent" high priest. He is unlike Aaron and all the high priests that followed him, who were mortal.

THE DEATH, BURIAL & RESURRECTION OF CHRIST: HISTORICAL FACT

When they died another high priest took their place. Aaron and every high priest after him had to first offer a sacrifice for his own sins, then an offering for the people:

"Moses said to Aaron, 'Come to the altar and sacrifice your sin offering and your burnt offering and make atonement for yourself and the people; sacrifice the offering that is for the people and make atonement for them, as the LORD has commanded'" (Leviticus 9:7 NIV).

Jesus is without sin ("blameless"). Therefore, the offering of His body on the cross provides a permanent offering for all sins eternally, for everyone who would put their trust in Jesus Christ! This wasn't a spur of the moment decision made in the first century to cover things that were going wrong. It was planned by our Creator from the beginning:

"You see, at just the right time, when we were still powerless, Christ died for the ungodly" (Romans 5:6 NIV).

The Ultimate Demonstration of Love

"But God demonstrates His own love toward us, in that while we were still sinners, Christ died for us. Much more then, having now been justified by His blood, we shall be saved from wrath through Him" (Romans 5:8-9 NKJV).

It is hard for most people to imagine how anyone so powerful, so intelligent, and so meticulous with the capacity to create a universe that is still beyond human comprehension, could have the patience and love to put up with rebellious, arrogant, and corrupt human beings to the point of sending His own Son, who was willing to come and die for us with no thought of receiving just compensation for His sacrifice. It is a beautiful story, with the promise of a beautiful victory in Christ—UNLESS it is just a mythical story made up by some gullible people worshipping some delusional man. You see, there were some even during the life of Christ's apostles that did not believe in any sort of resurrection:

CHAPTER 12

"Now if Christ is preached that He has been raised from the dead, how do some among you say that there is no resurrection of the dead?" (1 Corinthians 15:12 NKJV).

Today that fact has not changed. There will always be some who will not accept the resurrection of Jesus Christ as historical fact. It is not the purpose of this author to question their motives or sincerity, only to point out the preponderance of evidence that has accumulated concerning Christ's resurrection.

Dan Barker, a former evangelist, now atheist, in his book, *Godless*, suggests that he, along with other "critical scholars," has established that the original story changed over many decades:

"There have been many reasons for doubting the claim, but many critical scholars today agree that the story is a 'legend.' During the 60 to 70 years it took for the Gospels to be composed, the original story went through a growth period that began with the unadorned idea that Jesus, like Grandma, had 'died and gone to heaven.' It ended with a fantastic narrative produced by a later generation of believers that included earthquakes, angels, an eclipse, a resuscitated corpse and a spectacular bodily ascension into the clouds. The earliest Christians believed in the 'spiritual' resurrection of Jesus. The story evolved over time into a 'bodily' resurrection" {3}.

The book was, of course, praised by leading skeptics such as the late Christopher Hitchens, Richard Dawkins, Oliver Sacks, Michael Shermer, and Robert Sapolsky. That is not surprising since they have similar points of view. However, the evidence leads the truth-seeker in an entirely different direction.

NORMAN L. GEISLER and FRANK TUREK, in their book, *I Don't Have Enough Faith to be an Atheist*, reject the allegation that the New Testament documents as "legend":

"**The New Testament Story Is Not a Legend**—The New Testament documents were written well within two generations of the events by eyewitnesses or their contemporaries, and the New Testament storyline is corroborated by non-Christian writers. In addition, the New Testament mentions at least 30 historical figures who have been confirmed by sources outside the New Testament. Therefore, the New Testament story cannot be a legend" {4}.

THE DEATH, BURIAL & RESURRECTION OF CHRIST: HISTORICAL FACT

In their book, Geisler and Turek have written over 400 pages on the subject of apologetics in refutation of atheistic arguments against the authenticity of the New Testament message of the resurrection of Christ from the dead. I also believe that when we have read the evidence for ourselves the rational conclusion is yes, indeed, Christ Jesus did rise from the dead, and He is our Lord and our God!

First, the allegation that it was not until the second generation after Christ that His disciples manufactured the idea that Jesus was raised from the dead has been shown to be inaccurate, at best. Historical evidence confirms an early date. The *Baker Encyclopedia of Christian Apologetics*, by NORMAN L. GEISLER, mentions the work of Jose O'Callahan, who translated a fragment of Mark's Gospel in 1972:

"The New Testament Fragments? Jose O'Callahan, a Spanish Jesuit paleographer, made headlines around the world in 1972 when he announced that he had translated a piece of the Gospel of Mark on a DSS fragment. [NOTE: DSS refers to the Dead Sea Scrolls.] This was the earliest known piece of Mark. Fragments from cave 7 had previously been dated between 50 B.C. and A.D. 50 and listed under 'not identified' and classified as 'Biblical Texts.' O'Callahan eventually identified nine fragments. The center column in the following chart uses the numbering system established for manuscripts. For example, '7Q5' means fragment 5 from Qumran cave 7.

Mark 4:28	7Q6?	A.D. 50
Mark 6:48	7Q15	A.D. ?
Mark 6:52, 53	7Q5	A.D. 50
Mark 12:17	7Q7	A.D. 50
Acts 27: 38	7Q6?	A.D. 60
Romans 5:11, 12	7Q9	A.D. 70+
1 Timothy 3:16; 4:1-3	7Q4	A.D. 70+
2 Peter 1:15	7Q10	A.D. 70+
James 1:23,24	7Q8	A.D. 70+

{5}.

Objections to O'Callahan's dates were made by skeptics and probably still are. Even conservative Christian scholars were hesitant to put much faith in O'Callahan's discoveries at the beginning. Perhaps it just appeared to be too good to be true, because this would mean that Mark's Gospel was being circulated within 25 years

CHAPTER 12

after the death of Jesus. The Essene community at Qumran existed during the same period of history as Christ and His disciples. It would make sense that some of the Essenes, would be curious to look into the writings of their contemporaries. They had a large collection of the Old Testament Scriptures among other ancient writings of their own. Later, in the same book, Geisler writes that now there is "growing acceptance of earlier New Testament dates":

"Acceptance of Early Dates. There is a growing acceptance of earlier New Testament dates, even among some critical scholars. Two illustrate this point, former liberal William F. Albright ...wrote, 'We can already say emphatically that there is no longer any solid basis for dating any book of the New Testament after about A.D. 80, two full generations before the date between 130 and150 given by the more radical New Testament critics of today" (Recent Discoveries in Bible Lands, 136). Elsewhere Albright said, 'In my opinion, every book of the New Testament was written by a baptized Jew between the forties and the eighties of the first century (very probably sometime between about A.D. 50 and 75)' ('Toward a More Conservative View 3)" {6}.

Geisler continues to explain how the "Qumran Community" evidence helped to convince Albright of earlier New Testament dating:

"Thanks to the Qumran discoveries, the New Testament proves to be in fact what it was formerly believed to be: the teaching of Christ and his immediate followers between cir. 25 and cir. 80 A.D.' (From Stone Age to Christianity, 23)" {7}.

Geisler continues to point out how even the "radical critic" John A.T. Robinson changed his assessment of New Testament reliability:

"John A.T. Robinson...wrote a revolutionary book titled *Redating the New Testament*, in which he posited revised dates for the New Testament books that place them earlier than the most conservative scholars ever held. Robinson places Matthew at 40 to after 60, Mark at about 45 to 60, Luke at before 57 to after 60, and John at from before 40 to after 65. This would mean that one or two Gospels could have been written as early as seven years after the crucifixion. At the latest they were all composed within the lifetimes of eyewitnesses and contemporaries of the events" {8}.

THE DEATH, BURIAL & RESURRECTION OF CHRIST: HISTORICAL FACT

IGNATIUS (A.D. 70-110): "Be deaf whenever anyone speaks to you apart from Jesus Christ, who was of the race of David, who was from Mary, who was truly born, both ate and drank, was truly persecuted under Pontius Pilate, was truly crucified and died, with beings heavenly, earthly, and under the earth looking on, who also was truly raised from the dead, his Father raising him. (Trallians 9)" {9a}.

The previous quotation from Ignatius was from EVERETT FERGUSON'S book, *Early Christians Speak*, p. 23, on "The Faith Preached and Believed" by Christians during the latter part of the first century and early second century. Dr. Everett Ferguson has served as Professor of Bible at Abilene Christian University since 1962. As of 1996, he was professor emeritus in its college of Biblical Studies. He has done extensive research into the background of early Christianity and its teachings, such as his books, *Early Christians Speak*, and *Backgrounds of Early Christianity*.

POLYCARP, according to GEISLER and TUREK, was a disciple of John the apostle:

"John who obviously knew all of the apostles, had a disciple named Polycarp (A.D. 69-155), and Polycarp had a disciple named Irenaeus (130-202). Polycarp and Irenaeus collectively quote 23 of the 27 New Testament books as if they are authentic—and in some cases they specifically say they are authentic" {9b}.

CLEMENT OF ROME, according to GARY R. HABERMAS, wrote a revealing document about "AD 95" that authenticates the God-inspired first letter of the apostle Paul to the Corinthians, written about A.D. 55, only about 40 years after 1 Corinthians was written:

"The Apostles received the Gospel for us from the Lord Jesus Christ; Jesus Christ was sent forth from God. So then Christ is from God, and the Apostles are from Christ. Both therefore came of the will of God in the appointed order. Having therefore received a charge, and having been fully assured through the resurrection of our Lord Jesus Christ and confirmed in the word of God with full assurance of the Holy Ghost, they went forth with the glad tidings that the kingdom of God should come. So preaching everywhere in country and town, they appointed their first-fruits, when they had proved them by the Spirit, to be bishops and deacons unto them that should believe" [Footnote 3: "Clement of Rome, Corinthians, 42"].

CHAPTER 12

Habermas makes the reader aware of certain meticulous facts in Clement of Rome's document. Here are three of them:

"In this passage, Clement of Rome claims several facts. (1) The gospel or good news of the kingdom of God was the major Christian message. (2) This gospel had been given to the apostles by Jesus himself even as it came from God. (3) Jesus' resurrection provided the assurance of the truthfulness of these teachings" [p.230] {10}.

"NOW I make known to you, brethren, the gospel which I preached to you, which also you received, in which also you stand" (1 Corinthians 15:1 NASB).

"For I delivered to you as of first importance what I also received, that Christ died for our sins according to the Scriptures, and that He was buried, and that He was raised on the third day according to the Scriptures" (1 Corinthians 15:3-4 NASB).

Jesus' crucifixion death, burial, and resurrection took place about A.D. 27 at the earliest. According to GARY R. HABERMAS, in his interview by LEE STROBEL, in his book, *The Case for Christ*, Habermas related these facts:

"We know that Paul wrote 1 Corinthians between A.D. 55 and 57. He indicates in 1 Corinthians 15:1-4 that he has already passed on this creed to the church at Corinth, which would mean it must predate his visit there in A.D. 51. Therefore the creed was being used within twenty years of the resurrection, which is quite early" {11}. Clement of Rome stated in his document, Corinthians, about A.D. 95, that "the Gospel" which Paul confirmed "as of first importance" is the death, burial, and resurrection of Jesus Christ has been "fully assured through the resurrection of our Lord Jesus Christ" within 40 years after Paul's first letter to the Corinthians! The reality of the historical Christ and His resurrection was preached, written, and distributed to all the Christians living in the first century!

The Dead Sea Scrolls had nine fragments of the New Testament among them. Some, such as Mark, have been dated at A.D. 50, others at A.D. 60 to A.D. 70+, indicating that copies of the New Testament were circulating around Palestine within 27 years

THE DEATH, BURIAL & RESURRECTION OF CHRIST: HISTORICAL FACT

of the Resurrection. New Testament scholars such as William F. Albright and John A.T. Robinson confirm much earlier dates for the composition of the New Testament.

Geisler and Turek's "Table 14.2," indicate that Irenaeus "(c 130-202)" considered 17 of the 27 New Testament Scriptures "as authentic," which means to the average reader, they were considered as divinely inspired by God who directly communicated His message to the writers of the New Testament {13}.

For further and more complete information, a list of authors and books which can be purchased at most Christian bookstores and some secular bookstores will be furnished at the end of this book. By the end of this chapter the evidence presented should be enough to establish the fact that the New Testament has a huge foundation of evidence supporting its accuracy both in historical and textual content.

In order that a clear and explanatory word-picture be presented for the evidence surrounding the historical resurrection of Christ, let's begin with the events presented in the New Testament concerning the background leading up to the resurrection.

[1] Roman Authorities Involved in the Crucifixion and Burial:

All four of the Gospel writers testify that it was Roman soldiers that took Jesus away to be crucified (Matthew 27:27-31; Mark 15:16-20; Luke 23:26-36; John 19:16-23).

Three of the Gospel writers confirm there was a Roman Centurion in charge of the crucifixion (Matthew 27:54; Mark 15:39, 44-45; Luke 23:47).

After Jesus' body was placed in a tomb belonging to Joseph from Arimathea the chief priests and Pharisees requested that Pilate, the governor, place a guard of soldiers at the tomb to prevent the disciples from stealing the body and claiming Jesus rose from the dead. Pilate provided a Roman guard unit which came and sealed the stone over the entrance (Matthew 27:62-68).

NOTE: Read *Baker Encyclopedia of Christian Apologetics*, by Norman L. Geisler, pages 188 and 529 (1999) {12}.

CHAPTER 12

A Roman "Centurion" was an officer who was in command of a unit of 100 soldiers, known as a "century." EVERETT FERGUSON, in his book, *Backgrounds of Early Christianity*, informs us that the Roman "legion" consisted of "sixty centurions" who were a critically essential part of the Roman military machine:

"A legion was divided into ten cohorts of six centuries (one hundred men) each. It was commanded by a legate (normally of senatorial rank), with six tribunes serving as staff officers. The most important tactical officers in the legion were the sixty centurions (six in each of the cohorts), each of whom commanded a century. These were the professionals in the army, commonly promoted from the ranks" {14}.

A Roman "Guard" unit: In Matthew chapter twenty-seven, when Pilate provided the Jewish authorities with "a guard": "You have a guard; go your way, make it as secure as you know how" (v. 65), he was not referring to the Jewish temple guards or to one solitary Roman soldier. He was referring to a Roman guard unit, which would consist of a "4-to-16-man security force." JOSH McDOWELL, in his book, *A Ready Defense*, compiled by BILL WILSON, explains the usual procedure:

"A Roman guard unit was a 4-to-16-man security force. Each man was trained to protect six feet of ground. The 16 men in a square of 4 on each side were supposed to be able to protect 36 yards against an entire battalion and hold it. Normally what they did was this: 4 men were placed immediately in front of what they were to protect. The other 12 were asleep in a semi-circle in front of them with their heads pointing in. ...Every 4 hours another unit of 4 was awakened" {15}.

[2] The Roman Seal Meant it Was "Off Limits" to the Public:

When there is a serious crime committed at a certain house or business, the police will close the area to the public by placing a ribbon of bright yellow tape around the immediate area, such as the house or building where the crime took place. During the first century, under Roman rule, the placing of an official authorized seal meant only an authorized Roman official could enter the area. McDowell and Wilson point out the method and legality attached to the seal:

"After the guard inspected the tomb and rolled the stone in place, a cord was stretched across the rock. This was fastened at either end with sealing clay. Finally, the clay packs were stamped with the official signet of the Roman governor" {16}.

THE DEATH, BURIAL & RESURRECTION OF CHRIST: HISTORICAL FACT

McDowell and Wilson emphasize the reason that Roman authority was involved:

"To authenticate something simply means to prove that it is real or genuine. So this seal on Jesus tomb was a public testimony that Jesus body was actually there. In addition, because the seal was Roman, it verified the fact that His body was protected from vandals by nothing less than the power and authority of the Roman Empire" {17}.

[3] Joseph of Arimathea Received Permission to Bury Jesus:

All four Gospel writers testify that it was Joseph of Arimathea who received permission from Pilate to take the body of Jesus for burial (Matthew 27:57-60; Mark 15:42-46; Luke 23:50-54; John 19:38-42).

All four Gospel writers specify that Joseph wrapped Jesus body in linen cloth (Matthew 27:59; Mark 15:46; Luke 23:53; John 19:40).
All four Gospel writers specify that Joseph laid Jesus' body in a tomb (Matthew 27:60; Mark 15:46; Luke 23:53; John 19:41).

Three of the Gospel writers specify that the tomb was cut out of rock (Matthew 27:60; Mark 15:46; Luke 23:53).

One More Fact Needs to be Pointed Out.

[4] Three of the Gospel Writers Record the Fact that Women had Witnessed the Burial at the Tomb Before the Resurrection (Matthew 27:61; Mark 15:47; Luke 23:55).

The Historical Resurrection of the Messiah Christ Jesus

[1] The Day the Resurrection took place

All four Gospel writers testify that it took place on the first day of the week:
Matthew 28:1a: "After the Sabbath, at dawn on the first day of the week…"
Mark 16:2a: "Very early on the first day of the week…"
Luke 24:1a: "On the first day of the week…"
John 20:1a: "Early on the first day of the week…"

CHAPTER 12

[2] The Time of Day

All four Gospel Writers record that it took place early in the morning:
Matthew 28:1a: "After the Sabbath, at dawn…"
Mark 16:2a: "Very early on the first day of the week, just after sunrise…"
Luke 24:1a: "On the first day of the week, very early in the morning…"
John 20:1a: "Early on the first day of the week, while it was still dark…"

[3] The First Witnesses of the Resurrection were Women (NASB):

All four Gospel writers point out that Mary Magdalene was among the first of the women to see the empty tomb:
Matthew 28:1-8: "Mary Magdalene and the other Mary came to look at the grave."
Mark 16:1: "And when the Sabbath was over, Mary Magdalene and Mary the mother of James, and Salome…"
Luke 24:10: "Now they were Mary Magdalene and Joanna and Mary the mother of James; also the other women with them…"
John 20:1: "Now on the first day of the week Mary Magdalene came early to the tomb…"

[4] The Stone that Covered the Tomb Entrance had been Removed (NASB):

All four Gospel writers report that the stone which covered the entrance to the tomb had been "rolled away from the tomb" (Matthew 28:1-2; Mark 16:1-4; Luke 24:1-2; John 20:1).
NOTE: The women were concerned because the stone was very large and heavy (Matthew 27:60; Mark 16:3-4).

[5] Jesus' First Appearances were to the Women (NKJV):

NOTE: All four Gospel writers indicate there was a group of women that saw the empty tomb, early that morning (Matthew 28:1; Mark 16:1; Luke 24:1,10; John 20:1-2) — Mary Magdalene, Mary the mother of James, Salome, Joanna, plus there appear to have been other women also (Luke 24:10). John 20:2b: "…we do not know…" "WE" indicates there was more than one woman.

THE DEATH, BURIAL & RESURRECTION OF CHRIST: HISTORICAL FACT

Try to mentally visualize what had taken place early in the morning on that first day of the week when the women arrived at the tomb as you read Matthew's account:

"Now after the Sabbath, as the first day of the week began to dawn, Mary Magdalene and the other Mary came to see the tomb. And behold, there was a great earthquake; for an angel of the Lord descended from heaven, and came and rolled back the stone from the door, and sat on it. His countenance was like lightning, and his clothing as white as snow. And the guards shook for fear of him, and became like dead men" (Matthew 28:1-5).

What took place that morning was an overpowering supernatural event. Picture the Roman guards watching this happening before them. The ground was shaking; this almost blinding appearance of angels with supernatural strength roll back that huge stone covering the tomb entrance, then sit upon it. The guards were paralyzed with fear! They couldn't move. All they could do was watch it happening before their very eyes.

"But the angel answered and said to the women, 'Do not be afraid, for I know that you seek Jesus who was crucified. He is not here; for He is risen, as He said. Come, see the place where the Lord lay. And go quickly and tell His disciples that He is risen from the dead, and indeed He is going before you into Galilee; there you will see Him. Behold, I have told you" (Matthew 28:6-7).

Before continuing with the text there are some things that need to be pointed out. (1) The tomb was now open for the women to enter. (2) The angel from heaven clearly testified: "He is not here; for He has risen…" (3) The angel wanted them to see where Jesus had been lying. The angel may have wanted them to see the grave clothes (the linen cloths) still lying there (John 20:3-7).

"So they went out quickly from the tomb with fear and great joy, and ran to bring His disciples word. And as they went to tell His disciples, behold, Jesus met them, saying, 'Rejoice!' So they came and held Him by the feet and worshipped Him. Then Jesus said to them, 'Do not be afraid. Go and tell My brethren to go to Galilee, and there they will see Me'" (Matthew 28:1-10).

CHAPTER 12

It appears that the women separated sometime after seeing the empty tomb. Mary Magdalene may have left the other women to tell Peter and John while the other women heard the testimony of the angel then left to tell the other disciples. It appears that all of the disciples were not in one place at that particular time (Luke 24:13-15).

Notice the Language and the Timing of the Events:

"Now on the first day of the week Mary Magdalene went to the tomb early, while it was still dark, and saw that the stone had been taken away from the tomb. Then she ran and came to Simon Peter, and to the other disciple, whom Jesus loved, and said to them, "They have taken away the Lord out of the tomb, and WE do not know where they have laid Him" (John 20:1-2 NKJV emphasis added).

Mary Magdalene apparently left before she saw and heard the angels declaring Jesus has risen from the dead. However, we know that she had gone to the tomb with the other women, because she said in verse two: "WE" [plural means more than one] "do not know where they have laid Him." Therefore the other women had to be with her at the tomb.

Peter and John Visit the Empty Tomb For Themselves:

"Peter therefore went out, and the other disciple, and were going to the tomb. So they both ran together, and the other disciple outran Peter and came to the tomb first. And he, stooping down and looking in, saw the linen cloths lying there; yet he did not go in. Then Simon Peter came, following him, and went into the tomb; and he saw the linen cloths lying there, And the handkerchief that had been around His head, not lying with the linen cloths, but folded together in a place by itself" (John 20:3-7 NKJV).

It is important to note that if the disciples had stolen Jesus' body while the guards were supposedly sleeping, as the Jewish authorities claimed, they wouldn't have stopped to unwrap the linen cloths and pull off the handkerchief from around His head before they took off with the body (Matthew 28:11-15).

NOTE: Psalm 16:10 prophesied the Messiah would rise from the dead. In John 2:19-22 Jesus Himself said He would rise from the dead. But neither the Psalm nor Jesus' promise were understood until after His resurrection (John 20:19-22; Luke 24:36-46; Acts 2:24-32).

THE DEATH, BURIAL & RESURRECTION OF CHRIST: HISTORICAL FACT

"Then the other disciple, who came to the tomb first, went in also; and he saw and believed. For as yet they did not know the Scripture, that He must rise again from the dead. Then the disciples went away again to their own homes" (John 20: 8-10).

The Gospel of Mark claims that Jesus "appeared first to Mary Magdalene (Mark 16:9). This would indicate that Jesus appeared to the other women after that incident.

Jesus Appears to Mary Magdalene Who Remained at The Tomb (NKJV):

After Peter and John (the "disciple whom Jesus loved") left the area and returned to their homes, Mary remained by the tomb. Emotionally upset, not knowing what had happened to Jesus' body, she then noticed "two angels":

"But Mary stood outside by the tomb weeping, and as she wept she stooped down and looked into the tomb. And she saw two angels in white sitting, one at the head and the other at the feet, where the body of Jesus had lain. Then they said to her, 'Woman, why are you weeping?' She said to them, 'Because they have taken away my Lord, and I do not know where they have laid Him.' Now when she had said this, she turned around and saw Jesus standing there, and did not know that it was Jesus. Jesus said to her, 'Woman, why are you weeping? Whom are you seeking?' She, supposing Him to be the gardener, said to Him, 'Sir, if you have carried Him away, tell me where you have laid Him, and I will take Him away.' Jesus said to her, 'Mary!' She turned and said to Him, 'Raboni!' (which is to say, Teacher). Jesus said to her, 'Do not cling to Me, for I have not yet ascended to My Father; but go to My brethren and say to them, "I am ascending to My Father and your Father, and to My God and your God.' Mary Magdalene came and told the disciples that she had seen the Lord, and that He had spoken these things to her" (John 20:11-18 NKJV).

The Women's Testimony of What Happened Was Not Accepted

"When they came back from the tomb, they told all these things to the Eleven and to all the others. It was Mary Magdalene, Joanna, Mary the mother of James, and the others with them who told this to the apostles. But they did not believe the women, because their words seemed to them like nonsense" (Luke 24: 9-11).

CHAPTER 12

The first witnesses of Jesus' resurrection were women! If the Gospel writers—Matthew, Mark, Luke, and John—were making up a story about the Son of God rising from the dead after His crucifixion, they would have selected men for witnesses, not women! EVERETT FERGUSON explains why, in his book, *Backgrounds of Early Christianity*:

"Jewish women were not as restricted in public appearance as Greek women but did not have the freedom of first-century Roman Women. The Jewish woman was the mistress of the home, but was not qualified to appear as a witness in court and was exempt from fulfilling religious duties that had to be performed at stated times (because her first duties were to her children and the home and she might not be in the required state of ritual purity). Household duties included grinding flour, cooking, laundry, making beds, and spinning wool. ...The woman's influence in the family was considered greater than the man's" {18}.

No Jewish man living in Judea in the first century would logically have contrived a story where women would have been considered in equal status with men as legal witnesses. It was just not done! Only God would have considered women's testimony as equal with men. Remember, when the Father sent His Son into the world, His physical birth was through a woman, not a man (Galatians 4:4). Therefore, the first witnesses and testimony of women in itself indicates that Jesus' resurrection was not a hoax or a myth, but a well-thought-out plan to demonstrate the power of God over sin and death. It was a Supernatural Event! It was also an historical event.

|6| Jesus Appeared to Peter Later the Same Day (NASB):

Two disciples had just returned to meet with the others and tell them about how Jesus had appeared to them late that afternoon (verses 24-29) and also that Jesus had appeared to Peter that same day:

"And they said to one another, 'Were not our hearts burning within us while He was speaking to us on the road, while He was explaining the Scriptures to us?' And they arose that very hour and returned to Jerusalem, and found gathered together the eleven and those who were with them saying, 'The Lord has really risen, and has appeared to Simon'" (Luke 24:32-34).

THE DEATH, BURIAL & RESURRECTION OF CHRIST: HISTORICAL FACT

Paul the apostle writes on how he first received the gospel message of the death, burial, and resurrection of Christ:

"For I delivered to you as of first importance what I also received, that Christ died for our sins according to the Scriptures, and that He was buried, and that He was raised on the third day according to the Scriptures, and that He appeared to Cephas, then to the twelve" (1 Corinthians 15:3-5).

The number of appearances continues to increase as the day progresses. Two disciples separated from the rest were walking on the road to a village called "Emmaus." As they traveled, they ran into what appeared to be a stranger to the region. They did not realize until later who the person was they were talking with.

[7] Jesus Appeared to Cleopas and Another Disciple the Same Day (NASB):

"And behold, two of them were going that very day to a village named Emmaus, which was about seven miles from Jerusalem. And they were conversing with each other about all these things which had taken place. And it came about that while they were conversing and discussing, Jesus Himself approached, and began traveling with them. But their eyes were prevented from recognizing Him. And He said to them, 'What are these words that you are exchanging with one another as you are walking?' And they stood still, looking sad" (Luke 24:13-17).

To understand what was taking place, these two disciples had been separated from the rest of the group at that time. Yet they knew that some of the women had reported the empty tomb and visions of angels who said Jesus was alive. Assuming that everyone in Jerusalem had heard about this, in answer to this unrecognized stranger, they asked, in essence:

"Where Have You Been?"

"And one of them, named Cleopas, answered and said to Him, 'Are you the only one visiting Jerusalem and unaware of the things which have happened here in these days?' And He said to them, 'What things?' And they said to Him, 'The things about Jesus the Nazarene, who was a prophet mighty in deed and word in the sight

CHAPTER 12

of God and all the people, and how the chief priests and our rulers delivered Him up to the sentence of death, and crucified Him. But we were hoping that it was He who was going to redeem Israel. Indeed, besides all this, it is the third day since these things happened" (Luke 24:18-21).

Notice that Cleopas and the other disciples had expected Jesus to reign over Israel as the promised majestic king. They still did not have a clear vision of Jesus as the suffering servant who would die for all humanity to free everyone who put their trust in Him from bondage to the law of sin and death (Romans 8:1-4).

In verses 22 through 24 they told about how some of their women went to the tomb, discovered it empty, seeing: "a vision of angels," who said Jesus was alive, causing some of the men to see for themselves that the tomb was empty, "...but him they did not see."

Here is Jesus' reply:

"And He said to them, 'O foolish men and slow of heart to believe in all that the prophets had spoken!'" (Luke 24:25).

Had they not read that the prophet in the 53rd chapter of Isaiah had written about Him? "As a result of the anguish of His soul, He will see it and be satisfied; By His knowledge the Righteous One, My Servant, will justify the many, As He will bear their iniquities" (Isaiah 53:11).

He continued: "'Was it not necessary for the Christ to suffer these things and to enter into His glory?' And beginning with Moses and with all the prophets, He explained to them the things concerning Himself in all the Scriptures" (Luke 24:26-27).

In verses 28 and 29, as they approached the village of Emmaus, they invited Jesus to stay with them since evening was approaching, which He did.

NOTE: "Cephas" is the Greek word for "Peter" (Galatians 2:14 NASB). The New King James Version reads "Cephas." The New International Version reads "Peter."

THE DEATH, BURIAL & RESURRECTION OF CHRIST: HISTORICAL FACT

"And it came about that when He had reclined at the table with them, He took the bread and blessed it, and breaking it, He began giving it to them. And their eyes were opened and they recognized Him; and He vanished from their sight" (Luke 24:30-31).

Why were they not able to recognize Jesus when they saw Him walking and talking with them on the road? The answer appears to be a supernatural one. The Gospel of Mark helps to clear this up:

"And after that, He appeared in a different form to two of them, while they were walking along on their way to the country. And they went away and reported it to the others, but they did not believe them either" (Mark 16:12-13).

This appearance is beyond any secular and materialist understanding, because Jesus (our God who lived among men [John 1:1-14]) is above the natural fleshly world of man. The God who created the universe and all things in it could appear to any human being with a totally different-looking human body just like He did with the two disciples walking to Emmaus.

NOW LET'S GO BACK TO LUKE 24:33-35:

"And they arose that very hour and returned to Jerusalem, and found gathered together the eleven and those who were with them saying, "The Lord has really risen, and has appeared to Simon." And they began to relate their experiences on the road and how He was recognized by them in the breaking of the bread" (Luke 24:33-35).

After all the appearances that happened on the first day of the week, there is still more. First, however, the text in Luke chapter twenty-four does mention that "the eleven" were present when the disciples from Emmaus met where they were "gathered together" (Luke 24:33). That means the apostle Thomas had to have been present when they arrived. However, it seems to indicate that Thomas left the gathering while they were discussing the events. The Gospel of John points out that Thomas was not there when Jesus made His appearance to the disciples in the evening of the first day:

CHAPTER 12

"When therefore it was evening, on that day, the first day of the week, and when the doors were shut where the disciples were, for fear of the Jews, Jesus came and stood in their midst, and said to them, 'Peace be with you'" (John 20:19).

DROP DOWN TO VERSE 24:

"But Thomas, one of the twelve, called Didymus, was not with them when Jesus came" (John 20:24).

Thomas did not see Jesus until eight days later (John 20:26 NASB).

[8] Jesus' Appears to the Disciples with Thomas Absent:
This took place again on the first day of the week (NASB):

"And while they were telling these things, He Himself stood in their midst. But they were startled and frightened and thought that they were seeing a spirit. And He said to them, 'Why are you troubled, and why do doubts arise in your hearts? See My hands and My feet, that it is I Myself; touch Me and see, for a spirit does not have flesh and bones as you see that I have.' [And when He had said this, He showed them His hands and His feet.] And while they still could not believe it for joy and were marveling, He said to them, 'Have you anything here to eat?' And they gave Him a piece of broiled fish; and He took it and ate it before them. Now He said to them, 'These are My words which I spoke to you while I was still with you, that all things which are written about Me in the Law of Moses and the Prophets and the Psalms must be fulfilled.' Then He opened their minds to understand the Scriptures, and He said to them, 'Thus it is written, that the Christ should suffer and rise again from the dead the third day'" (Luke 24:36-46).

From the fall of man in the beginning, Moses prophesied the Messiah was coming (Genesis 3:15; Genesis 49:10). From the prophesies of the Psalmists, it was foretold the Messiah was coming (Psalm 22:1-18; Psalm 16:9-10). From the Prophesies of Isaiah and Micah, it was foretold the Messiah would be both a suffering servant and a majestic king who would die for humanity's sins (Isaiah 53:1-12; Isaiah 9:6-7; Micah 5:2).

"Thus it is written, that the Christ should suffer and rise again from the dead the third day" (Psalm 16:10; Matthew 16:21).

THE DEATH, BURIAL & RESURRECTION OF CHRIST: HISTORICAL FACT

This appearance by Jesus was recorded in John's Gospel with specific detail regarding His hands and His side:

"When therefore it was evening, on that day, the first day of the week, and when the doors were shut where the disciples were, for fear of the Jews, Jesus came and stood in their midst, and said to them, 'Peace be with you.' And when He had said this, He showed them both His hands and His side. The disciples therefore rejoiced when they saw the Lord. Jesus therefore said to them again, 'Peace be with you; as the Father has sent Me, I also send you.' And when He had said this, He breathed on them, and said to them, 'Receive the Holy Spirit. If you forgive the sins of any, their sins have been forgiven them; if you retain the sins of any, they have been retained. But Thomas, one of the twelve, called Didymus, was not with them when Jesus came" (John 20:19-24 NASB).

[9] The Appearance to the Disciples with Thomas Present:

"Now Thomas (called Didymus), one of the Twelve, was not with the disciples when Jesus came. So the other disciples told him, 'We have seen the Lord!' But he said to them, 'Unless I see the nail marks in his hands and put my finger where the nails were, and put my hand into his side, I will not believe it.' A week later his disciples were in the house again, and Thomas was with them. Though the doors were locked, Jesus came and stood among them and said, 'Peace be with you!' Then he said to Thomas, 'Put your finger here; see my hands. Reach out your hand and put it into my side. Stop doubting and believe.' Thomas said to him, 'My Lord and my God!' Then Jesus told him, 'Because you have seen me, you have believed; blessed are those who have not seen and yet have believed'" (John 20:24-30 NIV).

There are some critical points that need to be made here on this text. Since Thomas had not seen Jesus alive after His resurrection as the others had he was not willing to accept what was, in his mind, 'hearsay' evidence. What Thomas wanted was empirical evidence! In other words, Thomas wanted to see and experience Jesus. Not only that, he wanted to touch Him personally. Thomas wanted to touch the nail wounds in Jesus' hands and the wound in His side. What these other disciples told him would not do! However, once he saw the risen Christ, touched Him and talked with Him, Thomas declared the message of truth which all of humanity must come to realize: "My Lord and My God!"

CHAPTER 12

We know that not everyone could have been there when the apostles and the disciples saw the risen Christ with their own eyes. What about those living in other nations at that time? What about those living in the centuries following, up to the present? How many billions of people have not been able to empirically witness the resurrected Christ? That is why, after satisfying Thomas's need for empirical evidence, our Lord and our God made this fundamental statement of truth:

"Then Jesus told him, 'Because you have seen me, you have believed; blessed are those who have not seen and yet have believed' (John 20:29 NIV).

You see, it was absolutely necessary for Christ Jesus to make empirical appearances to His apostles such as Thomas and the other disciples. Our God and Creator has always provided empirical evidences of supernatural events that have an impact on humanity when it was absolutely necessary for His purposes. He did this for Moses and the nation of Israel when He brought them out of bondage on many occasions. He provided the prophets with miracles when needed to prove beyond doubt that He was Almighty God (Exodus 12:29-36; 1 Kings 18:16-46). God the Father gave the miracle, a supernatural event. Yet it was also an historical event to demonstrate that He has fulfilled His eternal purpose with power (Romans 1:1-4)!

BUT what about those who have not seen? What about the Jews living in the first century who did not empirically witness the miracles of the past? This is the message that our Lord Jesus had for the Jews and for us today:

In Luke 16:19-31 Jesus tells the story of two men. One extremely wealthy, the other a homeless beggar named Lazarus camped right outside the rich man's gate. The wealthy man knew about Lazarus because he mentions him later in this text. Both of them died, but their destinations were not the same. Lazarus was carried by angels to a place of paradise by Abraham's side. The rich man was taken to a place the Scripture refers to as "hell" (the Greek word is "Hades") where he was "in torment" and "fire."

There was a "chasm" between the rich man and Lazarus with Abraham (v. 22-26). The rich man began to think about his five brothers still alive on earth and he requested a favor from Abraham to send Lazarus to his brothers:

THE DEATH, BURIAL & RESURRECTION OF CHRIST: HISTORICAL FACT

"He answered, 'Then I beg you, father [Abraham], send Lazarus to my father's house, for I have five brothers. Let him warn them, so that they will not also come to this place of torment.' Abraham replied, 'They have Moses and the Prophets; let them listen to them.' 'No, father Abraham,' he said, 'but if someone from the dead goes to them, they will repent.' He said to him, 'If they do not listen to Moses and the Prophets, they will not be convinced even if someone rises from the dead'" (Luke 16:27-31 NIV).

"Jesus did many other miraculous signs in the presence of his disciples, which are not recorded in this book. But these are written that you may believe that Jesus is the Christ, the Son of God, and that by believing you may have life in his name" (John 20:30-31 NIV).

There are some key principles of truth brought out in these two texts. The first is that even a miraculous event such as someone returning from the dead may not convince some people that this is a message coming directly from God. The Jews of the first century had either read or heard from their parents that God freed Moses and the people of Israel from Egyptian bondage through a series of miracles. It had been written down in Holy Scripture for over a thousand years, including the miracles of the prophets. Yet the fact is that many of the Jewish religious elite did not believe the miracles Jesus performed right in front of their eyes (Matthew 12:22-24). The same Jewish authorities also refused to believe Moses and the Prophets when they witnessed Jesus their Messiah fulfilling their prophecies right in front of their eyes. Therefore, Jesus made this point very clear:

"If they do not listen to Moses and The Prophets, they will not be convinced even if someone rises from the dead" (Luke 16:31 NIV).

John's Gospel records several "miraculous signs," including four appearances of Jesus after His resurrection, but John did not record all the events or resurrection appearances Jesus made. The other Gospels record some John didn't mention. The other gospels did not mention some that John recorded, such as that certain appearance to the disciples when Thomas was present "a week later" (John 20:24-28).

"But these are written that you may believe that Jesus is the Christ, the Son of God, and that by believing you may have life in his name."

CHAPTER 12

As the evidence continues to build, I want the reader to keep these principles in mind. There are some who will refuse to believe and accept Christ Jesus as their Lord and God regardless of the amount of evidence presented. But for those who are searching for truth, the evidence will expand their faith. It will compel them to put their trust in the only Redeemer who can offer them a release from their sins and free them from the bondage of slavery to their accuser, Satan, who is the ruler of the forces of darkness.

[10] Jesus' Appearance to His disciples at The Sea of Galilee (NKJV):

In John 21:1-14, John records this third appearance of Christ to His disciples after His resurrection from the dead.

"After these things Jesus showed Himself again to the disciples at the Sea of Tiberias [a large lake about 70 miles north of Jerusalem also called the Sea of Galilee], and in this way He showed Himself. Simon Peter, Thomas called the Twin, Nathanael of Cana in Galilee, the sons of Zebedee, and two others of His disciples were together. Simon Peter said to them, 'I am going fishing.' They said to him, 'We are going with you also.' They went out and immediately got into the boat, and that night they caught nothing. But when morning had now come, Jesus stood on the shore; yet the disciples did not know that it was Jesus. Then Jesus said to them, 'Children, have you any food?' They answered Him, 'No.' And He said to them, 'Cast the net on the right side of the boat, and you will find some.' So they cast, and now they were not able to draw it in because of the multitude of fish. Therefore that disciple whom Jesus loved said to Peter, 'It is the Lord!' Now when Simon Peter heard that it was the Lord, he put on his outer garment (for he had removed it), and plunged into the sea. But the other disciples came in the little boat (for they were not far from land, but about two hundred cubits), dragging the net with fish. Then, as soon as they had come to land, they saw a fire of coals there, and fish laid on it, and bread. Jesus said to them, 'Bring some of the fish which you have just caught.' Simon Peter went up and dragged the net to land, full of large fish, one hundred and fifty three; and although there were so many, the net was not broken. Jesus said to them, 'Come and eat breakfast.' Yet none of the disciples dared ask Him, 'Who are you?'—knowing that it was the Lord. Jesus then came and took the bread and gave it to them, and likewise the fish. This is now the third time Jesus showed Himself to His disciples after He was raised from the dead" (John 20:30-31).

THE DEATH, BURIAL & RESURRECTION OF CHRIST: HISTORICAL FACT

Before continuing on, there are some points of evidence that need to be covered.

Point Number One: The historical facts that validate Christ's Resurrection from the Dead begin with Jesus' Death and Burial, such as, [1] The Roman authorities involved; [2] The Roman seal meant the tomb was off limits to the public; [3] Joseph of Arimathea buried Jesus in his own tomb; [4] Three Gospel writers record that women were present and did witness the burial of Jesus at the tomb before His resurrection.

Point Number Two: All the evidence after the above are historically recorded facts of Jesus Christ's resurrection from the dead, such as [1] through [10]. Proceeding from this point onward there will be the inclusion of several more historical facts, including not only the Biblical New Testament record, but also first and second century Christians who left written testimony of the historical truth of the Resurrection. Both neutral and hostile historians left written historical records of Jesus' Death and His resurrection.

All the incidents so far have indicated that Jesus' appearances did not have the questionable array of seeing His face formed by the clouds or leaving the impression with observers of a brief confrontation that they thought they saw someone that looked like Jesus who vanished into thin air. In these appearances they not only saw Jesus, they held conversations with Him and on several occasions they spent considerable time with Him, some even touched Him, and ate with Him. As we proceed further the evidence continues to mount.

NOW LET'S GO BACK TO JOHN 21:1-14:

This appearance took place at the Sea of Tiberias (also known as the Sea of Galilee) sometime after the other appearances recorded by John. There were seven disciples present on this occasion. At Peter's suggestion, they decided to go out in the boat to catch some fish. The first part of the trip was a bust. They stayed out on the lake all night with no results. In the morning, there was Jesus standing on the shore. They did not recognize Him until Jesus said: "Children have you any food?" They answered "No." (v. 4-5). When Jesus told them to "cast the net on the right side of the boat," they did, and the net was packed with fish. It was at this point John ("the disciple whom Jesus loved") told Peter, "It is the Lord." Hearing this, Peter "plunged

CHAPTER 12

into the sea"… and "the other disciples came in the little boat…dragging the net with fish" (v. 7-8). Jesus already had a fire going with fish and bread "laid on it."

NOTICE the event and what John recorded in this appearance:

1. Once the disciples were on the beach they were able to witness with their own eyes that the person who told them where to catch the fish and who was preparing breakfast was Jesus Himself.

2. Jesus remained with these seven disciples for a long period of time. They knew it was Jesus whom they were talking with, and had long conversations with Him.

3. Jesus not only prepared breakfast, He also ate with them. Therefore, this appearance was not a hallucination. Seven witnesses saw Jesus, talked with Him, and ate with Him. To say this was not an actual historical event defies reason.

The next series of appearances is not necessarily in any historical order except the last appearance when Jesus was lifted up and ascended into heaven and His final appearance to Saul of Tarsus (the apostle Paul). The New Testament has recorded these appearances; therefore I will record them for the reader in this book.

[11] The Appearance Jesus made to The Eleven in Galilee (NASB):

"But the eleven disciples proceeded to Galilee, to the mountain which Jesus had designated. And when they saw Him, they worshipped Him; but some were doubtful. And Jesus came up and spoke to them, saying, 'All authority has been given to Me in heaven and on earth. Go therefore and make disciples of all the nations, baptizing them in the name of the Father and the Son and the Holy Spirit, teaching them to observe all that I commanded you; and lo, I am with you always, even to the end of the age" (Matthew 28:16-20)

[12] Jesus' Final Appearance to His disciples before His Ascension (NASB):

In Acts 1:1-11 the inspired writer for the Book of The Acts of the Apostles makes it clear that Jesus appeared alive to His disciples on several occasions for over a month.

THE DEATH, BURIAL & RESURRECTION OF CHRIST: HISTORICAL FACT

"The first account I composed, Theophilus, about all that Jesus began to do and teach, until the day when He was taken up, after He had by the Holy Spirit given orders to the apostles whom He had chosen" (Acts 1:1-2).

"To these He also presented Himself alive, after His suffering, by many convincing proofs, appearing to them **over a period of forty days**, and speaking of the things concerning the kingdom of God" (Acts 1:3).

The appearances and events that took place after Jesus rose from the dead were several, and they were convincing: "…appearing to them over a period of forty days."

"And gathering them together, He commanded them not to leave Jerusalem, but to wait for what the Father had promised, 'Which,' He said, 'you heard of from Me'" (Acts 1:4).

Jesus proceeded to tell them they would soon be "baptized with the Holy Spirit not many days from now" (v. 5-8).

"And after He had said these things, He was lifted up while they were looking on, and a cloud received Him out of their sight. And as they were gazing intently into the sky while He was departing, behold, two men in white clothing stood beside them; And they also said, 'Men of Galilee, why do you stand looking into the sky? This Jesus, who has been taken up from you into heaven, will come in just the same way as you have watched Him go into heaven'" (Acts 1:9-11).

Other Appearances of Jesus recorded in the New Testament are found in Paul the apostle's letter to the Corinthians:

[13] Jesus' Appearance to Over 500 Witnesses at One Event:

"After that, he appeared to more than five hundred of the brothers at the same time, most of whom are still living, though some have fallen asleep" (1 Corinthians 15:6-8 NIV).

NOTE: The opening two verses of this text indicate that the author was in all probability Luke (compare Luke 1:1-4).

CHAPTER 12

The fact that Jesus rose from the dead could have been checked out to see if Paul was telling the truth. Most of those 500 witnesses were still alive at the time of Paul's writing. They could have been questioned by the principle authorities—Jewish or Roman—or anyone else wanting more proof that Jesus rose from the dead.

[14] Jesus Appearance to James, the Former Skeptic:

"Then he appeared to James..." (1-Corinthians 15:7a NIV).

James was Jesus' half-brother in the same household with Mary, the same mother. James knew his brother pretty well. At least he thought he did. While Jesus was alive, James had serious doubts about Jesus being the promised Messiah. In fact, on one occasion in the Gospel of John chapter seven, His brothers—James included—asked Jesus why He didn't go and perform miracles to: "...show yourself to the world." John then writes: "For even his own brothers did not believe in him" (John 7:1-5). After Jesus appeared to James alive after His crucifixion and burial, James became a believer. He remained with his mother, Mary, and his other brothers after the resurrection (Acts 1:14). Later he is mentioned by Paul as a leader in the church in Jerusalem (Galatians 1:18-19; Galatians 2:9).

[15] Jesus Final Appearance to One Openly Hostile to Christians:

"...and last of all he appeared to me also, as to one abnormally born. For I am the least of the apostles and do not even deserve to be called an apostle, because I persecuted the church of God" (1 Corinthians 15:8-9 NIV).

This is the written testimony of Paul the apostle (formerly Saul of Tarsus) who was part of the mob that stoned Stephen (Acts 7:57-59; Acts 8:1-3). Jesus' appearance to him took place on the road to Damascus. Saul had been given authority from the high priest in Jerusalem to arrest any that professed to be a Christian: "who belonged to the Way," and take them back to Jerusalem. The risen Christ appeared to him in a blazing light from heaven that left Saul blind. It was there that Jesus spoke:

"Saul, Saul, why do you persecute me?"
"Who are you Lord?" Saul asked.

THE DEATH, BURIAL & RESURRECTION OF CHRIST: HISTORICAL FACT

"I am Jesus whom you are persecuting," he replied. "Now get up and go into the city and you will be told what you must do" (ref Acts 9:1-6 NIV).

In Damascus a disciple named Ananias came to Saul and his sight was restored and he was baptized. From that time onward Saul (later called Paul the apostle) began preaching in the synagogues "that Jesus is the Son of God." Later, he also spoke to the Gentiles (Acts 9:11-20 NIV).

Keep in mind, some of the fifteen New Testament texts mentioned in Scripture may have occurred at the same time as some of the other appearances mentioned. For example, NORMAN L. GEISLER and FRANK TUREK list twelve appearances on page 303: "THE ORDER OF THE TWELVE APPEARANCES OF CHRIST" (Table 12.1) in their book, *I Don't Have Enough Faith to Be an Atheist* {19}.

JOSH McDOWELL lists twelve appearances plus three more—to Stephen, Paul, and John:

"The appearances of Christ in the lives of individuals:
To Mary Magdalene, John 20:14, Mark 16:9
To women returning from the tomb, Matthew 28:9,10
To Peter later in the day, Luke 24:34, 1 Corinthians 15:5
To the Emmaus disciples, Luke 24:13-33
To the apostles, Thomas absent, Luke 24:36-43; John 20:19-24
To the apostles, Thomas present, John 20:26-29
To the seven by the lake of Tiberias, John 21:1-23
To a multitude of 500-plus believers on a Galilean mountain, 1 Corinthians 15:6
To James, 1 Corinthians 15:7
To the eleven, Matthew 28:16-20; Mark 16:14-20; Luke 24:33-52; Acts 1:3-12
At the ascension, Acts 1:3-12
To Paul, Acts 9:3-6; 1 Corinthians 15:8
To Stephen, Acts 7:55
To Paul in the temple, Acts 22:17; 23:11
To John on Patmos, Revelation 1:10-19"
This list of appearances from Evidence That Demands A Verdict, Volume I, by Josh McDowell, p.224, (1972, 1979) {20}.

CHAPTER 12

Each of the fifteen New Testament records which I listed mention detailed historical evidence of Christ's resurrection from the dead. The four Gospel writers were consistent on the basic fundamental facts pertaining to the accuracy of their statements:

1. All four Gospel writers testify the resurrection took place on the first day of the week (Matthew 28:1a; Mark 16:2a; Luke 24:1a; John 20:1a).
2. All four Gospel writers record that the resurrection took place early in the morning (Matthew 28:1a; Mark 16:2a; Luke 24:1a; John 20:1a).
3. All four Gospel writers state that one of the first of the women to witness the resurrection was Mary Magdalene (Matthew 28:1-8; Mark 16:1; Luke 24:10; John 20:1).
4. All four Gospel writers report that the stone that covered the tomb entrance had been removed (Matthew 28:1-2; Mark 16:1-4; Luke 24:2; John 20:1).
5. All four Gospel writers confirm that the tomb was empty (Matthew 28:5-6; Mark 16:5-6; Luke 24:3; John 20:1-2).
6. All four Gospel writers attest that the body of Jesus was gone (Matthew 28:5-6; Mark 16:1; Luke 24:6-10; John 20:1-2).
7. All four Gospel writers affirm that Jesus rose from the dead (Matthew 28:5-6; Mark 16:5-6; Luke 24:5-7; John 20:1-8).

Further factual information is noted by the Gospel writers:

8. The fact that Jesus appeared first to the women and not to the men. If the men who were Jesus' disciples had made up the story that Jesus rose from the dead they would never have written that the women were the first to have seen Jesus alive. The Jews would never have accepted it because women were not considered reliable witnesses. Notice when the women told the disciples they saw Jesus alive: "…they did not believe the women" (Luke 24:9-11 NIV).

9. The fact that the linen clothes and the handkerchief were deliberately removed and placed in separate areas of the tomb. If Jesus' body had been stolen by the disciples as the chief priests paid the Roman guards to say, there would be no logical reason to take the time to remove grave cloths there, which would increase the risk of being caught rather than to get the body out of the tomb as quickly as possible and discard the grave cloths later.

THE DEATH, BURIAL & RESURRECTION OF CHRIST: HISTORICAL FACT

10. The fact that Jesus had appeared alive after His death not just once, but several times to His disciples. He appeared to His brother James who was previously skeptical of Jesus being the promised Messiah. When He appeared to His disciples, Jesus spent several hours with them, talking to them, where they could touch Him and eat meals with Him, such as the breakfast He prepared on the beach at the Sea of Tiberias. Jesus appeared to over 500 people at one time, and as Paul stated, most of them were still alive when the record was written. Therefore, if anyone wanted to verify the record they could ask the living witnesses. Paul, the inspired author of 1 Corinthians, was a former enemy and persecutor of Christians until Jesus appeared to him and he was converted to Christ (Luke 24:36-43; John 21:1-14; 1 Corinthians 15:6-8).

11. The fact that Jesus' appearances to His disciples left no doubt that He had risen from the dead. "…to whom He also presented Himself alive after His suffering by many infallible proofs, being seen by them during forty days and speaking of the things pertaining to the kingdom of God" (Acts 1:3 NKJV).

12. The fact that on the day of Pentecost (fifty days after Passover when Jesus was buried in the tomb), Peter and the rest of the disciples began to preach that Jesus is Lord and had risen from the grave to several thousand Jews gathered on that occasion neither Roman nor Jewish authorities challenged their claims. They remained silent. If Jesus' body were still in that tomb all they would have to do was to show the public the body still lying in the tomb! They did not do this! Why? Because Jesus had risen from the dead and they knew it, so they remained silent!

The extreme importance of the resurrection of Christ Jesus cannot be over emphasized! It is the indispensable foundation and climax to everything that happened throughout both the Old Testament and the New Testament of the Holy Scriptures!

After Jesus had driven out the sacrificial animals and scattered the coins of the money changers from the temple, the Jews demanded a "miraculous sign" to demonstrate His authority for His actions. Jesus replied: "Destroy this temple and I will raise it again in three days." He was referring to His resurrection from the dead. That was to be the Messiah's final, miraculous demonstration of who He was and why He came! The apostle Paul, in his inspired letters to the Romans and to the Corinthians, emphasized this fact so clearly it could not be misunderstood.

CHAPTER 12

"Paul, a servant of Christ Jesus, called to be an apostle and set apart for the gospel of God—the gospel he promised beforehand through his prophets in the Holy Scriptures regarding his Son, who as to his human nature was a descendant of David, and who through the Spirit of holiness was declared with power to be the Son of God by his resurrection from the dead: Jesus Christ our Lord" (Romans 1:1-4 NIV).

"…and who through the Spirit of holiness was declared with power to be the Son of God by his resurrection from the dead: Jesus Christ our Lord."

"For what I received I passed on to you as of first importance: that Christ died for our sins according to the Scriptures, that he was buried, that he was raised on the third day according to the Scriptures."

Here is something to consider: If Jesus did not rise from the dead and the men who wrote the Gospel accounts along with Peter and Paul continued to make false claims to the public that Jesus was the Way to eternal life, their followers would not have continued to follow them. Yet they did! The generations of Christians from John's disciples onward continued to emphatically proclaim the same Gospel Message: "that Christ died for our sins"…"that he was buried"…"that he was raised on the third day."

GARY HABERMAS, a prominent author and debater, has researched in meticulous detail the words of the early Christians who openly declared their belief and assurance in the death, burial, and resurrection of Christ. In his book, *The Historical Jesus*, he describes Clement of Rome, a Christian writer from "about AD 95":

"One of the most important apostolic documents, Clement of Rome's letter to the Corinthian church is generally considered to be the earliest extra-New Testament Christian writing. Clement was the leading elder in the church at Rome and wrote Corinthians about AD 95 to help end a dispute…at Corinth" {21}.

"Although Corinthians is largely doctrinal and moral in nature, it contains at least one important historical reference to Jesus and earliest Christianity: 'The Apostles received the Gospel for us from the Lord Jesus Christ; Jesus Christ was sent forth from God. So then Christ is from God, and the Apostles are from Christ. Both therefore came of the will of God in the appointed order. Having therefore received

THE DEATH, BURIAL & RESURRECTION OF CHRIST: HISTORICAL FACT

a charge, and having been fully assured through the resurrection of our Lord Jesus Christ and confirmed in the word of God with full assurance of the Holy Ghost, they went forth with the glad tidings that the kingdom of God should come. So preaching everywhere in country and town, they appointed their first-fruits, when they had proved them by the Spirit, to be bishops and deacons unto them that should believe' (Clement of Rome, Corinthians, 42)."

Clement of Rome's writing took place perhaps during or just a few years after the apostle John wrote the last book in the New Testament, the book of Revelation. John wrote the Apocalypse (Revelation) sometime during his exile on the Island of Patmos or immediately thereafter (Revelation 1:9), which most scholars believe was during the reign of the Roman emperor Domitian (A.D. 81-96). This would indicate that Clement of Rome wrote Corinthians while John was still alive. Most scholars estimate the date Revelation was written to be about A.D. 95-96. Habermas points out that the validity of Christ's resurrection was the "early doctrinal proclamation" commonly taught throughout the early church:

"This certification of a chain of authority from God to Jesus to the apostles to the early Christian elders is interesting not only in that it was the basis for early doctrinal proclamation and church organization. Additionally, Clement of Rome anchors this authority in the belief that Jesus was raised from the dead and in the Scripture. A miraculous event in history was thus taken as the basic sign of authority behind the preaching of the earliest Christian message" {22}.

EVERETT FERGUSON, in his book, *Early Christians Speak*, includes a quote from the writings of Ignatius, another early Christian who wrote about 20 to 25 years after Clement of Rome, that Jesus "was truly raised from the dead":

"Be deaf whenever anyone speaks to you apart from Jesus Christ, who was of the race of David, who was from Mary, who was truly born, both ate and drank, was truly persecuted under Pontius Pilate, was truly crucified and died, with beings heavenly, earthly, and under the earth looking on, who also was truly raised from the dead, his Father raising him (Trallians 9)" {23}.

"Jesus Christ…who was truly born…was truly persecuted under Pontius Pilate, was truly crucified and died…who also was truly raised from the dead, his Father raising him" (Ignatias, Trallians 9).

CHAPTER 12

Habermas gives some historical background on Ignatius, a prominent figure in the church in Antioch, and emphasizes the foundational necessity of the resurrection which was "the chief sign for believers":

"As Bishop of Antioch and a leader in the early church, Ignatias was condemned to death in Rome. On the way to his execution he addressed seven letters to six churches and one individual (Polycarp). These letters are early witnesses to Christian Doctrine and to early church hierarchy, being written about AD 110-115. They also contain several historical references to Jesus" {24}.

Habermas points out how Ignatias continues to emphasize the hope that lies in Christ Jesus through the resurrection:

"Be ye fully persuaded concerning the birth and the passion and the resurrection, which took place in the time of the governorship of Pontius Pilate; for these things were truly and certainly done by Jesus Christ our hope (Ignatias, Magnesians, II)" {25}.

Middle way through the second century, an apologist who wrote frequently in defense of the Gospel was a man named Justin. In his first defense of the Gospel, he wrote what had been declared by earlier Christians all of the way back to the apostles and their immediate disciples. Ferguson, in his book, *Early Christians Speak*, has recorded these words of Justin:

"In the books of the prophets we found proclaimed beforehand that Jesus our Christ would come, would be born through the virgin, become man and heal every sickness and disease, raise the dead, be hated and unrecognized, and be crucified, and die and be raised again, and ascend into heaven, who is and is called the Son of God, and that certain men would be sent by him to every race of men to preach these things (Apology I, 31:7)" {26}.

Ferguson writes a brief description and background of Justin Martyr on p.241:

"Born a pagan in Samaria, converted at Ephesus (perhaps), and a Christian teacher in Rome; the most important of the second-century Apologists; known as "Martyr" from the manner of his death" {27}.

THE DEATH, BURIAL & RESURRECTION OF CHRIST: HISTORICAL FACT

Habermas records the date of Justin Martyr's First Apology, and to whom it was addressed:

"In his First Apology, written soon after AD 150 and addressed chiefly to Emperor Antoninus Pius, Justin Martyr refers to various aspects of the life of Jesus" {28}.

One cannot help but realize that the most important doctrine of Christianity is the historical and supernatural fact of the resurrection of Jesus Christ.

Continuing to trace back through early Christian writings, this fundamental truth cannot be ignored. JOSH McDOWELL, in his book, Evidence for Christianity, refers to the writings of Polycarp, whom W.J. Sparrow-Simpson quotes:

"The Epistle of S. Polycarp to the Philippians (about A.D. 110) the writer speaks of our Lord Jesus Christ having 'endured to come so far as to death for our sins, whom God raised, having loosed the pains of death…raised our Lord Jesus Christ from the dead and gave Him glory and a throne'…" {29}.

Another early Christian, according to Ferguson, was an early apologist named Irenaeus, "Bishop of Lyons in Gaul":

"Bishop of Lyons in Gaul…about 180 wrote in defense of the orthodox Christian faith against Gnosticism" {30}.

"Jesus the Son of God…the passion, the rising from the dead, and the bodily ascension into heaven of the beloved Christ Jesus our Lord" {31}.

Next we move ahead to a Christian who lived and wrote sometime in the late second century or early third century named Tertullian. According to Tertullian, the message of Christ's death and resurrection was still the main fundamental doctrine of faith. Ferguson mentions his written testimony:

"[He was] brought down into the virgin Mary by the spirit and power of God the Father, was made flesh in her womb and was born from her as Jesus Christ…was nailed to the cross, was resurrected on the third day" (Prescription of Heretics 13)" {32}.

CHAPTER 12

According to Ferguson, Tertullian was the: "First major Christian author in Latin; from Carthage, lived about 155 to 222; in his later years associated with the Montanists" {33}.

The Gospel: "...as of first importance":

"For what I received I passed on to you as of first importance: that Christ died for our sins according to the Scriptures, that he was buried, that he was raised on the third day according to the Scriptures" (1 Corinthians 15:3-4 NIV).

This is the Gospel message by which every believing and trusting Christian is saved (1 Corinthians 15:2; Romans 1:16). This was the message that was preached from the day of Pentecost onward throughout the New Testament (Acts 2:22-32; Romans 1:1-4; 1 Corinthians 15:1-4; Ephesians 2:5-6; 1 Peter 1:3; Revelation 1:4-18).

This is the same Gospel message that was preached, taught, and recorded in the writings of the early Christians from A.D. 95 to A.D. 200:

CLEMENT OF ROME: "...fully assured through the resurrection of our Lord Jesus Christ" (A.D. 95-96).
POLYCARP: "...raised our Lord Jesus Christ from the dead" (about A.D. 110).
IGNATIUS: "...and the passion and the resurrection...were truly and certainly done by Jesus Christ our hope" (A.D. 110-115).
JUSTIN MARTYR: "...and be crucified and die and be raised again" (A.D. 150).
IRENAEUS: "...Jesus the Son of God...the passion, the rising from the dead, and the bodily ascension into heaven" (about A.D. 180).
TERTULLIAN: "...Jesus Christ...was nailed to the cross, was resurrected on the third day" (about A.D. 200+).

A Neutral Jewish Historian's Historical Evidence about the Christ

FLAVIUS JOSEPHUS, a Jewish Historian who wrote during the latter part of the first century, has provided two distinct references to the historical reality of Jesus, whom His disciples believed was the promised Messiah, called "Christ." The first, was the reference to the death of James. Josephus begins with his assessment of a newly appointed high priest, named "Ananus":

THE DEATH, BURIAL & RESURRECTION OF CHRIST: HISTORICAL FACT

"But this younger Ananus...took the high priesthood, was a bold man in his temper, and very insolent; he was also of the sect of the Sadducees. ...when, therefore, Ananus was of this disposition, he thought he had now a proper opportunity [to exercise his authority]. Festus was now dead, and Albinus was but upon the road; so he assembled the Sanhedrin of judges, and brought before them the brother of Jesus, who was called Christ, whose name was James, and some others...and when he had formed an accusation against them as breakers of the law, he delivered them to be stoned" {34}.

However, several of the most influential Jewish citizens believed he overstepped his authority by assembling a Sanhedrin without Albinus's consent, and reported it to Albinus. Albinus was not happy and threatened to punish Ananus. The result:

"...on which king Agrippa took the high priesthood from him, when he had ruled but three months, and made Jesus, the son of Damneus, high priest" (Antiquities Book. 20, Chapter 9) {35}.

"Jesus" was a common name given to several Jews. What is important to note is the fact that this text clearly points out that Jesus "who was called Christ" is a real historical person, not a myth. The text specifies what is written in the New Testament, that Jesus had a brother named James, further identifying the historical reality of Jesus the Christ.

The life of Flavius Josephus is unique in many ways. He actually took part in the Jewish rebellion against Roman occupation which began about A.D. 66. He lived through a losing effort in a major battle during the war in which he surrendered. Later in his career he became a historian for the Roman emperor. Habermas supplies some of the details:

"Jewish historian Flavius Josephus was born in AD 37 or 38 and died in AD 97. He was born into a priestly family and became a Pharisee at the age of nineteen. After surviving a battle against the Romans, he served commander Vespasian in Jerusalem. After the destruction of Jerusalem in AD 70, he moved to Rome, where he became the court historian for emperor Vespasian. The Antiquities, one of Josephus' major works, provides some valuable but disputed evidence concerning Jesus. Written around AD 90-95, it is earlier than the testimonies of the Roman historians. Josephus speaks about many persons and events of first century Palestine and makes two references to Jesus" {36}.

CHAPTER 12

The first reference mentions the death of James, the half brother "of Jesus, who was called Christ," covered previously. It is the second reference to Christ that has caused controversy:

"Now there was about this time Jesus, a wise man, if it be lawful to call him a man; for he was a doer of wonderful works, a teacher of such men as receive the truth with pleasure. He drew over to him both many of the Jews and many of the Gentiles. He was [the] Christ. And when Pilate, at the suggestion of the principal men amongst us, had condemned him to the cross, those that loved him at the first did not forsake him; for he appeared to them alive again the third day; as the divine prophets had foretold these and ten thousand other wonderful things concerning him. And the tribe of Christians, so named from him, are not extinct at this day" (Antiquities, 18:3) {37}.

LEE STROBEL, an investigative journalist, in his book, *The Case for Christ*, had an interview with Edwin Yamauchi, an impressive scholar with "masters and doctoral degrees in Mediterranean studies from Brandeis University." Strobel goes on to mention:

"He has been awarded eight fellowships from the Rutgers Research Council, National Endowment for the Humanities, the American Philosophical Society, and others. He has studied twenty-two languages, including Arabic, Chinese, Egyptian, Russian, Syriac, Ugaritic, and even Commanche" {38}.

During the interview, the question came up about Josephus and what has been referred to as: "Testimonium Flavianum." Strobel then asked the question about Josephus and Christ's resurrection:
"I knew too that this passage was among the most hotly disputed in ancient literature because on its surface it appears to provide sweeping corroboration of Jesus' life, miracles, death, and resurrection. But is it authentic? Or has it been doctored through the years by people favorable to Jesus?" {39}.

Dr. Yamauchi was quite familiar with the controversy. Here was his reply to Strobel:

"'Scholarship has gone through three trends about it,' he said. 'For obvious reasons, the early Christians thought it was a wonderful and thoroughly authentic attestation of Jesus and his resurrection. They loved it. Then the entire passage was questioned by at least some scholars during the enlightenment. But today there's a remarkable consensus among both Jewish and Christian scholars that the passage as a whole is authentic, although there may be some interpolations.'"

Strobel then asked Yamauchi to explain what he meant by "Interpolations." Yamauchi explained:

"'That means early Christian copyists inserted some phrases that a Jewish writer like Josephus would not have written'" {40}.

Dr. Yamauchi explains there seem to be three probable interpolations in the text:

"…'if indeed one ought to call him a man…' This implies Jesus was more than human, which appears to be an interpolation.'…But then there's this unambiguous statement, 'He was the Christ…' That seems to be an interpolation. …Then there's this phrase: 'On the third day he appeared to them restored to life.' Again, this is a clear declaration of belief in the Resurrection, and thus it's unlikely that Josephus wrote it" {41}.

These are three phrases that appear questionable because an early Christian named Origin, about A.D. 230, wrote that Josephus never claimed to have any belief that Jesus was the promised Messiah:

"This James was of so shining a character among the people…that Flavius Josephus, when, in his twentieth book of the Jewish Antiquities…on account of what they had dared to do to James, the brother of Jesus, who was called Christ; and wonderful it is, that while he did not receive Jesus for Christ, he did nevertheless bear witness that James was so righteous a man" {42}.

However, about A.D. 324, Eusebius made the comment: "However, it may not be amiss, if, over and above, we make use of Josephus the Jew for a further witness; who, in the eighteenth book of his Antiquities, when he was writing the history of what happened under Pilate, makes mention of our Savior in these words" {43}.

Eusebius then proceeds to quote the entire text of Josephus, including the three later-to-be-considered-questionable phrases, which indicates Eusebius accepted it as it originally appeared {43}.

CHAPTER 12

There is more to be considered. Habermas comments on an Arabic manuscript, which contains this passage of Josephus, only it is worded differently from the text that Whiston translated:

"In 1972 Professor Schlomo Pines of the Hebrew University in Jerusalem released the results of a study on an Arabic manuscript containing Josephus' statement about Jesus. It includes a different and briefer rendering of the entire passage, including changes in the key words listed above" {44}.

"At this time there was a wise man who was called Jesus. His conduct was good and (he) was known to be virtuous. And many people from among the Jews and the other nations became his disciples. Pilate condemned him to be crucified and to die. But those who had become his disciples did not abandon his discipleship. They reported that he had appeared to them three days after his crucifixion, and that he was alive; accordingly he was perhaps the Messiah, concerning whom the prophets have recounted wonders."

"Of the three disputed portions, none remains unchanged. The initial problematic 'if it be lawful to call him a man' has been dropped completely, recounting only that Jesus was a wise man. The words 'he was a doer of wonderful works' have also been deleted. Instead of the words 'He was (the) Christ' we find 'he was perhaps the messiah.' The phrase 'he appeared to them the third day' now reads 'they (the disciples) reported that he had appeared to them,' which is an entirely true statement which was voiced by the first century eyewitnesses. Lastly, the statement that 'the divine prophets had foretold these and ten thousand other wonderful things concerning him' has been drastically reduced to 'concerning whom the prophets have recounted wonders,' which concerns the messiah and possibly not even Jesus, according to Josephus. Therefore, while some words are completely deleted, others are qualified by 'perhaps' and 'reported.' There are some good reasons why the Arabic version may indeed be the original words of Josephus before any Christian interpolations" {45}.

"There are some good reasons why the Arabic version may indeed be the original words of Josephus before any Christian interpolations" (Gary R. Habermas).

NOTE: The "key words" refers to the alleged Christian interpolations.

THE DEATH, BURIAL & RESURRECTION OF CHRIST: HISTORICAL FACT

After reading the observations and comments made by Dr. Edwin Yamauchi, in Lee Strobel's book, *The Case for Christ*, and Dr. Gary R. Habermas, in his book, *The Historical Jesus*, plus historical accounts of Jesus in Flavius Josephus translated by William Whiston, I find several historical facts which are presented by Josephus for which there should be no critical objection. First, and extremely important, the text in Antiquities 18:3 is a legitimate historical incident recorded by a Neutral Historian. The written testimony of Origin, about A.D. 230 who stated that Josephus "...did not receive Jesus for Christ," designates Josephus as neither a Christian nor a hostile witness. He was neutral!

Next I want to include some "historical facts" Habermas has stated which can be known from Josephus in Antiquities 18:3:

"What historical facts can be ascertained from the deleted and altered portions of Josephus' statement such as those changes made in the Arabic version? (1) Jesus was known as a wise and virtuous man, one recognized for his good conduct. (2) He had many disciples, both Jews and Gentiles. (3) Pilate condemned him to die, (4) with crucifixion explicitly being mentioned as the mode. (5) The disciples reported that Jesus had risen from the dead and (6) that he had appeared to them on the third day after his crucifixion. (7) Consequently, the disciples continued to proclaim his teachings" {46}.

Remember the Two Hostile Historical Accounts of Jesus Death:

In chapter eleven, there was the confirmation from the Roman Historian Cornelius Tacitus, about A.D. 115, and the Jewish rabbis' historical confirmation around A.D. 200 in the Talmud. Tacitus recorded that "Christus" (Christ) was put to death by "the extreme Penalty" (Crucifixion) by Pontius Pilate during the reign of Tiberius. The Talmud recorded that "Yeshu" (Christ) was "hanged" (crucified) "on the eve of the Passover."

Both these hostile historians confirmed what Josephus had written about Jesus' death and crucifixion. All three of these historical records corroborate what The New Testament has written about Christ's death and resurrection. Not only that, there are the testimonies of the early Christians—Clement of Rome A.D. 95-96, Polycarp A.D. 110, Ignatius A.D. 110-115, Justin Martyr A.D. 150, Irenaeus A.D. 180, and then Tertullian A.D. 200.

CHAPTER 12

"But in fact Christ has been raised from the dead" (1 Corinthians 15:20a RSV).

So what is the significance of all this? In other words, what is your point, author? It is simply this: Christ Jesus' death, burial, and resurrection is the final demonstration that God, through our Lord Jesus Christ, has given those who put their trust in Him until death, an eternal triumph over sin and death!

The apostle Paul explains this so clearly:

"When the perishable has been clothed with the imperishable, and the mortal with immortality, then the saying that is written will come true: 'Death has been swallowed up in victory'"

"Where, O death, is your victory?
Where, O death, is your sting?'

"The sting of death is sin, and the power of sin is the law. But thanks be to God! He gives us the victory through our Lord Jesus Christ. Therefore, my dear brothers, stand firm. Let nothing move you. Always give yourselves fully to the work of the Lord, because you know that your labor in the Lord is not in vain" (1 Corinthians 15:54-58 NIV).
What more can I, an "ignoramus," add to what the inspired Paul has written? That eternal plan of creation, love, mercy, and grace, is far beyond what I, an ordinary man, could ever have imagined! It is a victory provided for me and for any other flawed human being who could never have deserved it or worked it out on their own merit.

"Praise be to the God and Father of our Lord Jesus Christ, who has blessed us in the heavenly realms with every spiritual blessing in Christ" (Ephesians 1:3 NIV).

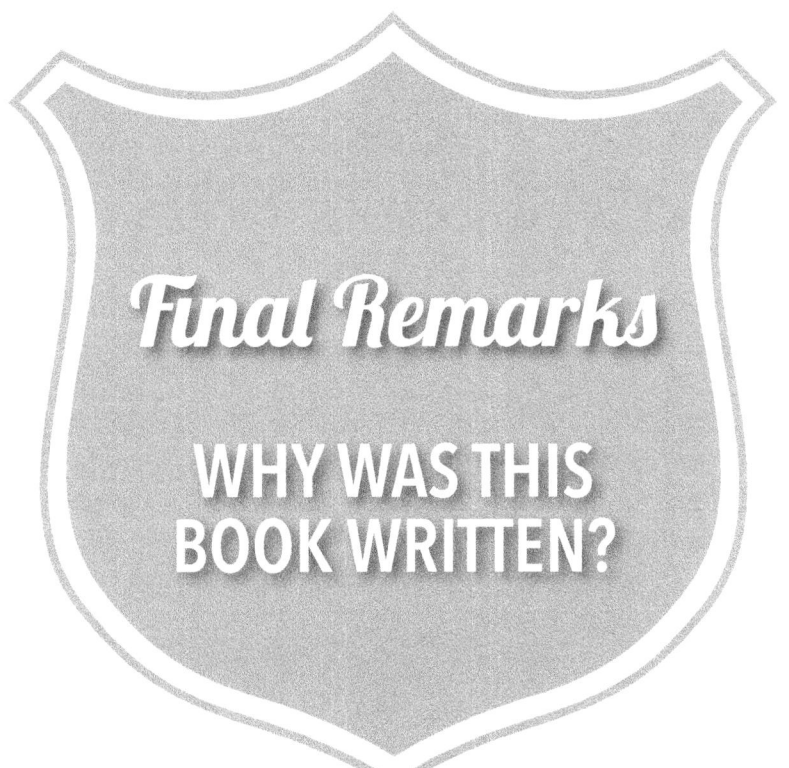

WHY WAS THIS BOOK WRITTEN?

In conclusion, all this material has been accumulated and placed in a book so readers may reach their own conclusions about the Reality of God and the Victorious Resurrected Christ. But there is more to it than that. It is to encourage each individual reader to develop a strong, heartfelt urge to search out the truth and to follow the truth.

What is Truth?

"Jesus answered, 'I am the way and the truth and the life. No one comes to the Father except through me'" (John 14:6 NIV).

In John 11:23-44; Jesus demonstrated to His disciples that He is the Son of God by raising Lazarus from the dead:

"Jesus said to her, 'I am the resurrection and the life. He who believes in Me, though he may die, he shall live. And whoever lives and believes in Me shall never die. Do you believe this?' She said to Him, 'Yes, Lord, I believe that You are the Christ, the Son of God, who is to come into the world'" (John 11:25-27).

Drop down to verses 43-44:

"Now when He had said these things, He cried out with a loud voice, 'Lazarus, come forth!' And he who had died came out bound hand and foot with graveclothes, and his face was wrapped with a cloth. Jesus said to them, 'Loose him, and let him go' (John 11:43-44 NKJV).

Romans 5:8 confirms: "But God **demonstrates** His own love toward us, in that while we were yet sinners, Christ died for us" (NASB).

God the Father has demonstrated ("declared with power") to everyone who lived and has read the gospel message in the Holy Scriptures that Jesus Christ is the Son of God by His resurrection from the dead:

"...the gospel he promised beforehand through his prophets in the Holy Scriptures regarding his Son, who as to his human nature was a descendant of David, and who

FINAL REMARKS

through the Spirit of holiness was declared with power to be the Son of God by his resurrection from the dead: Jesus Christ our Lord" (Romans 1:2-4 NIV).

In Romans 1:16; Paul wrote: "I am not ashamed of the gospel, because it is the power of God for the salvation of everyone who believes: first for the Jew, then for the Gentile." Believing in the gospel of Christ the Son of God is more than just an intellectual acknowledgement.

You see, to truthfully, sincerely believe in the resurrected Christ means that one must be willing to demonstrate that belief. W.E. Vine, Merrill F. Unger, and William White Jr., in their book, *An Expository Dictionary of Biblical Words*, explain the meaning of the Greek word "pisteuo" found in the Greek text in Romans 1:16 for the English word "belief": "to believe, also to be persuaded of, and hence, to place confidence in, to trust, signifies, in this sense of the word, reliance upon, not mere credence" (W.E. Vine, M. A., Merrill F. Unger, Th. M., Th. D., Ph.D., William White Jr., Th. M., Ph.D., p.108, *An Expository Dictionary of Biblical Words*, Thomas Nelson Publishers, Nashville (1984).

"PISTEUO" is a verb! It denotes action! To illustrate this belief as action, there is an excellent example in the second chapter of Acts where the Jews for the first time heard the Gospel message:

"Therefore let all the house of Israel know assuredly that God has made this Jesus, whom you crucified, both Lord and Christ. Now when they heard this, they were cut to the heart, and said to Peter and the rest of the apostles, 'Men and brethren what shall we do?' Then Peter said to them, 'Repent, and let every one of you be baptized in the name of Jesus Christ for the remission of sins; and you shall receive the gift of the Holy Spirit'" (Acts 2:36-38 NKJV).

Drop down to verse 41:

"Then those who gladly received his word were baptized; and that day about three thousand souls were added to them" (Acts 2:41 NKJV).

Paul the apostle explains more elaborately in his letter to the Romans how faith (belief in Christ Jesus) is demonstrated by one's actions:

WHY WAS THIS BOOK WRITTEN?

"But what does it say? 'The word is near you; it is in your mouth and in your heart,' that is, the word of faith we are proclaiming: That if you confess with your mouth, 'Jesus is Lord,' and believe in your heart that God raised him from the dead, you will be saved. For it is with your heart that you believe and are justified, and it is with your mouth that you confess and are saved" (Romans 10:8-10 NIV).

For further explanation, here is the Amplified Bible's version of Roman 10:10: "For with the heart a person believes (adheres to, trusts in and relies on Christ) and so is justified (declared righteous, acceptable to God), and with the mouth he confesses— declares openly and speaks out freely his faith—and confirms [his] salvation."

When a person is willing to demonstrate his/her belief in Christ with action by openly speaking out about his/her faith in Christ, the Scripture declares that person is "justified" (declared righteous) before God!

Paul writes that one's demonstration of faith is actually a spiritual demonstration of their belief in the Gospel message of first importance: that Christ Died, was Buried, and was Raised from the Dead (1 Corinthians 15:3-4).

In Romans he writes:

"Or do you not know that all of us who have been baptized into Christ Jesus have been baptized into His death? Therefore we have been buried with Him through baptism into death, in order that as Christ was raised from the dead through the glory of the Father, so we too might walk in newness of life" (Romans 6:3-4 NASB).

And in Colossians he reaffirms:
"...having been buried with him in baptism... [you are] raised with him through your faith in the power of God, who raised him from the dead..." (Colossians 2:12 NIV).

Baptism is an immersion, a burial in water, an open demonstration of one's faith in the death, burial, and resurrection of Christ Jesus, being set free from the Law of Sin and Death, living a New Life in Christ Jesus and having the gift of the Holy Spirit who will live in us to direct us to a holy life in Christ (Romans 8:1-2; Ephesians 1:13-14; Colossians 3:1-14).

FINAL REMARKS

"Where, O death, is your victory?
Where O death, is your sting?
The sting of death is sin, and the power of sin is the law, But thanks be to God! He gives us the victory through our Lord Jesus Christ" (1 Corinthians 15:55-57 NIV).

I bring this book to a close. This is where I leave you, the reader, time to think. Where do you go from here?

Having read this book and the Holy Scriptures, what choice will you make?

NOTES

NOTES

CHAPTER 2

1. W.E. Vine, M.A., Merrill F. Unger, Th.M., Th.D., Ph.D., William White, Jr., Th.M., Ph.D., (1984), *An Expository Dictionary of Biblical Words*, p. 1171, Thomas Nelson Publishers, Nashville, Camden, New York.
2. Norman L. Geisler, (1999), Baker Encyclopedia of Christians Apologetics, p. 224, Baker Books, Grand Rapids, Michigan 49516
3. Bert Thompson, Ph.D., (1981), *The History of Evolutionary Thought*, pp. 28-29, Apologetics Press Inc.
4. John C. Whitcomb, Jr., Th.D., Henry M. Morris, Ph.D., (1967), *The Genesis Flood*, p. 95, Baker Book House, Grand Rapids, Michigan.
5. Ibid., p. 96.
6. Ibid.
7. Bert Thompson, Ph.D., (1981), *The History of Evolutionary Thought*, p. 112, Apologetics Press Inc. Note: #183 *Life and Letters of Charles Darwin*, Vol.II, p. 60, (1898), D. Appleton & Co. New York.
8. Ibid., p. 65.
9. Ibid., p. 66.
10. Ibid., p. 67.
11. Norman L. Geisler, (1999), *Baker Encyclopedia of Christian Apologetics*, p. 181, Baker Books, Grand Rapids, Michigan 49516.
12. Bert Thompson, Ph.D., (1981), *The History of Evolutionary Thought*, p. 181, Apologetics Press Inc.
13. Ibid., p. 108.
14. Ibid., pp. 107-108.
15. Ibid., p. 108.
16. Ibid., p. 124, Note: #212 & #117, Morris, Henry M., (1974), *The Troubled Waters of Evolution*, Creation-Life Publishers, San Diego, California. p. 61.
17. Ibid., p. 128, Note: #209 & #219, Huxley, Leonard, (1900) Life and Letters of Thomas Huxley. Appleton, New York. Vol. 1, p. 69. (letter to his sister Elizabeth, Nov. 21, 1850).
18. Ibid., p. 128. Note: Huxley, (1896) T.H. Darwiniana. D. Appleton & Co., New York. p. 467.
19. Ibid., p. 136
20. Norman L. Geisler, (1999), *Baker Encyclopedia of Christian Apologetics*, p. 198.

NOTES

21. Ibid., p. 198. Note: Dewey, John, (1934), *A Common Faith*, p. 31.
22. Ibid.
23. Ibid.
24. *The Columbia Encyclopedia*, 5th Edition, (1993), p. 1171 (on Ernst Haeckel).
25. Henry M. Morris, (1981) *Scientific Creationism*, 9th printing, p. 179.
26. Ibid., p. 179. Note: #1 Letter from Charles Darwin to W. Graham, July 3, 1881, Life and Letters, 1, p. 316, cited by G. Himmelfarb, Darwin and the Darwinian Revolution, (London: Chatto & Windus, (1959), p. 343.
27. Ibid., pp. 179-180, Note: Thomas Huxley, Lay Sermons and Reviews, (New York: Appleton, 1871), p. 20.
28. Edward McNall Burns, (1958) *Western Civilizations*, p. 773, 5th Edition, (on Friedrich Neitzsche).
29. Ibid.
30. Jacques Barzun, (2000), *From Dawn to Decadence*, p. 671, (on Nietzsche).
31. Edward McNall Burns, (1958), *Western Civilizations*, 5th Edition, p. 852, (on Adolf Hitler).
32. *The Columbia Encyclopedia*, 5th Edition, (1993), p. 1257, (on the Holocaust).
33. Carl J. Friedrich and Zbigniew K. Brzezinski, (1956), *Totalitarian Dictatorship and Autocracy*, p. 249, Frederick A. Praeger, Publisher, New York.
34. Ibid., pp. 250-251, Note: #163, Hermann Rauschning, (1940) Hitler Speaks, (1939).
35. James D. Bales, Two Worlds Christianity and Communism, (date unknown) p. 105. Lambert Book House, Box 4007, Shreveport, Louisiana 71104.
36. Carl J. Friedrich and Zbigniew K. Brzezinski, (1956), *Totalitarian Dictatorship and Autocracy*, p. 247, Frederick A. Praeger, Publisher, New York.
37. John Foxe, Rewritten and updated by Harold J. Chadwick, (1997), *The New Foxe's Book of Martyrs*, pp. 326-327, (on Christian Persecution).
38. William A. Dembski, (1999), *Intelligent Design*, p. 294, Notes: chapter 7, on Richard Dawkins quote: The Humanist, 57, January/February 1997) "Is Science a Religion?".
39. Kyle Butt, *Reason & Revelation*, July, 2008, Article: "The Bitter Fruits of Atheism," 28(7):49, (on William Provine, an atheist).
40. James D. Bales, (1976), *How Can Ye Believe?*, p. 17, Notes: #16, #17, Charles Darwin, *Life and Letters of Charles Darwin*, Vol. I, pp. 282, 285.
41. Dan Barker, (2008), *Godless*, p.219, (Evolution not blind chance?).
42. *Merriam Webster's Collegiate Dictionary, 10th edition*, p. 313.

NOTES

43. Ibid., pp. 313-314.
44. Kyle Butt, *Reason & Revelation*, July, 2008, "The Bitter Fruits of Atheism," 28(7);50, Note: Peter Singer, (1983) Pediatrics, 72[1]:128-129, "Sanctity of Life or Quality of Life."
45. Henry M. Morris, (1981) *Scientific Creationism*, p.197, (on Julian Huxley, "What is Humanism?).
46. Kyle Butt, *Reason & Revelation*, July, 2008, Article: "The Bitter Fruits of Atheism," 28(7):52, (on Abortion).
47. Kyle Butt, *Reason & Revelation*, August, 2008, Article:"The Bitter Fruits of Atheism (Part II)," 28(8):57. (Aldous Huxley: "Ends and Means," (1937) pp. 270, 273).
48. Ibid. 28(8):57, (Kyle Butts comments).
49. Kyle Butt, *Reason & Revelation*, Article: "The Bitter Fruits of Atheism," 28(7):50.
50. The Evidences of Christianity, A Debate between Robert Owens and Alexander Campbell, (April 1829). McQuiddy Printing Company, Nashville (1957).
51. Lee Strobel, *The Case for a Creator*, (2004), p. 99, Quote: Quentin Smith, atheist.

CHAPTER 3

1. William J. Federer, America's God and Country, (1994), p. 69, FAME Publishing Inc., Coppell, Texas, (Quote from Werner von Braun).
2. Henry M. Morris, (1997), *That Their Words May Be Used Against Them*, p. 22, Quote: from Stenger, Victor L., "Was the Universe Created?" Free Inquiry, (Summer 1987), p. 26.
3. Lee Strobel, (2004), The Case For a Creator, p. 31, Quote: from Ernst Mayr,1 Notes: 1, p. 309, Zondervan, Grand Rapids, Michigan 49530.
4. Ibid., p.17, Quote: from Richard Lewontin 1, Note: 1, P.307.
5. John C. Whitcomb, Jr., Th.D., and Henry M. Morris, Ph.D., (1967) *The Genesis Flood*, pp. 235-236, Quote: from Fred Hoyle, *Frontiers of Astronomy*, pp.317-318, (New York, Harper's, 1955).
6. Ibid., pp. 236-237, Quote: from George Gamow, "Modern Cosmology," The New Astronomy, Edited by Editors of The *Scientific American*, p. 23, (New York, Simon and Schuster, 1955).

NOTES

7. Lee Strobel, (2004), *The Case for a Creator*, p. 69, Quote: from John Polkinghorne 2, Notes: p. 312, Quarks, Chaos, and Christianity, (New York, Crossroad, 1994, xii).
8. Webster's New World Dictionary, (1962), pp. 234,769.
9. Henry M. Morris, (1966, 6th printing), *The Twilight of Evolution*, p. 33, (on Entropy), Baker Book House, Grand Rapids, Michigan.
10. Ibid., p.33, (on Thermodynamic Laws).
11. Ibid.
12. Henry M. Morris, (1981, 9th printing), *Scientific Creationism*, p. 25, (on Entropy), Creation Life Publishers, San Diego, California.
13. Norman L. Geisler, (1999), *Baker Encyclopedia of Christian Apologetics*, p. 725, (on Third Law of Thermodynamics), Baker Books, Grand Rapids, Michigan 49516.
14. Bert Thompson, (1999) The Scientific Case For Creation, pp. 20-21, Quote: Dr. Robert Jastrow, (1978) pp. 48-49, God and The Astronomers, (New York, W.W. Norton) Apologetics Press, Inc., 230 Landmark Drive, Montgomery, Alabama 36117-2752.
15. Henry M. Morris, (1997), *That Their Words May Be Used Against Them*, p. 69, Quote: Jesse L. Greenstein, "Dying Stars," *Scientific American*, vol. 200, (January 1959), p. 46, Institute for Creation Research, San Diego, CA.
16. *Merriam Webster's Collegiate Dictionary*, 10th Edition, (1996), p. 387.
17. Bert Thompson, (1999), The Scientific Case For Creationism, pp. 20-21, Quote: Dr. Robert Jastrow, (1977), *Until the Sun Dies*, p. 19, (New York, W.W. Norton), Apologetics Press, 230 Landmark Drive, Montgomery, Alabama 36117-2752.
18. Ibid., pp. 20-21, Quote: Robert Jastrow, (1978), p. 111, God and The Astronomers, (New York, W.W. Norton).
19. Webster's New World Dictionary, (1962), p. 769.
20. Ibid., p. 368.
21. Henry M. Morris, (1981), *Scientific Creationism*, 9th printing, p. 25, (on Thermodynamics), Creation Life Publishers, San Diego, California 92115.
22. Ibid., pp. 42-43.
23. Henry M. Morris, (1997), *That Their Words May Be Used Against Them*, p. 69, Quote: Jesse L. Greenstein, (1959), "Dying Stars," *Scientific American*, p. 46.
24. Bert Thompson, (2002), The Scientific Case For Creation, p. 23, Quote: Robert Jastrow, (1978), *God and the Astronomers*, (New York, W.W. Norton), Apologetics Press, Inc., 230 Landmark Drive, Montgomery, Alabama 36117-2752.

NOTES

25. Bert Thompson, (1999), The Scientific Case For Creation, p. 21, Quotes: from Robert Jastrow, who quotes Arthur Eddington, (1978) God and the Astronomers, pp. 48-49, (New York, W.W. Norton), Apologetics Press, Inc., 230 Landmark Drive, Montgomery, Alabama 36117-2752.
26. Henry M. Morris, (1997), *That Their Words May Be Used Against Them*, pp. 73-74, Quote: Jeremy Rifkin, (1980), *Entropy: A New World View*, p. 6, (New York: Viking Press).
27. Ibid., p. 74, Quote: John Ross, (July 7, 1984), "2nd Law of Thermodynamics," Letter-to-the-Editor, Chemical and Engineering News, vol.58, p. 40. Ross was at Harvard University.
28. Bert Thompson, Ph.D. and Brad Harrub, Ph.D., *Investigating Christian Evidences*, p. 7, Quote: Michael Lemonick, (June 25, 2001) Time magazine: "How the Universe Will End."
29. Ibid., p. 12.
30. Henry M. Morris, (1981), *Scientific Creationism*, 9th printing, p. 26.
31. Henry M. Morris, (1997), *That Their Words May Be Used Against Them*, p. 72, Quote: H.S. Lipson, (May 1980), "A Physicist Looks at Evolution," Physics Bulletin, p. 138, vol. 31.
32. Bert Thompson, Ph.D. and Brad Harrub, Ph.D., (2003), *Investigating Christian Evidences*, p. 146, Isaiah 40:22; "circle of the earth."
33. Ibid., pp. 148-149.
34. Ibid., p.152. (2 Sources mentioned: |1| H.L. Perutz, (1964), pp. 64-65; *Scientific American*, November; |2| Dean Havron, (1981), "Curious Cure-Alls," Science Digest, 89|8|:62, September.
35. Dan Barker, (2008), *Godless*, pp. 71-72, Ulysses Press, P.O. Box 3440, Berkely, CA 94703.
36. John D. Morris Ph.D., (April 2010), Acts & Facts, p. 18, Article: "A Barrier to Evolution."
37. Dennis Alexander, (2008), "Creation or Evolution," pp. 138-139.
38. John D. Morris Ph.D., (April 2010), Acts & Facts, p. 18, Article: "A Barrier to Evolution."
39. Norman L. Geisler, (1999), *Baker Encyclopedia of Christian Apologetics*, p. 724, (on Thermodynamics), Baker Books, a division of Baker Book House Company, P.O. Box 6287, Grand Rapids, MI 49516-6287.
40. John D. Morris Ph.D. (April 2010), Acts & Facts, p. 18, Article: "A Barrier to Evolution."

NOTES

CHAPTER 4

1. Norman L. Geisler, (1999), *Baker Encyclopedia of Christian Apologetics*, p. 120, (explanation of Causality), Baker Books, a division of Baker Book House Company, Grand Rapids, MI 49516-6287.
2. Ibid., p. 121.
3. Lee Strobel, (2004), *The Case for a Creator*, pp. 97-98, Quote: from William Lane Craig-Muslim Causality argument, Zondervan, Grand Rapids, Michigan 49530.
4. Henry M. Morris, (1997), *That Their Words May Be Used Against Them*, p. 10, Quote: Alan H. Guth, and Paul J. Steinhardt, (May 1984), "The Inflationary Universe," *Scientific American*, vol. 250, p. 128. Quote: from Alan H. Guth, (September 1997), p. 54, "Cooking Up a Cosmos," Astronomy, vol. 25, p. 54.
5. Ibid., p. 24, Quote: Edward P. Tyron, (March 8, 1984), "What Made the World?" *New Scientist*, vol. 101, pp. 14, 15, 16.
6. Ibid., p. 22, Quote: Victor L. Stenger, (Summer 1987), "Was the Universe Created?" Free Inquiry, pp. 26, 29, 30.
7. Bert Thompson, (2002), *The Scientific Case for Creation*ism, p. 65, (Causality indisputable) Apologetics Press, Inc., 230 Landmark Drive, Montgomery, Alabama 36117-2752.
8. *Merriam Webster's Collegiate Dictionary*, 10th Edition, Subject: "antecedent," p. 48.
9. Bert Thompson, (2002), *The Scientific Case for Creation*ism, pp. 37-38, (Comments on Stenger, Tyron and Guth), Apologetics Press, Inc. 230 Landmark Drive, Montgomery, Alabama 36117-2752.
10. Ibid., pp. 22-23, Quote: Robert Jastrow, (1977), Until The Sun Dies, p. 21, (New York: W.W. Norton).
11. Lee Strobel, (2004), *The Case for a Creator*, pp. 98-99, Quote: William Lane Craig, on matter existing without a cause is illogical. Zondervan, Grand Rapids, Michigan 49530.
12. Bert Thompson, (2002), *The Scientific Case for Creation*, p. 70, Quote: David Hume, Greig, J.Y.T., ed. (1932), Letters of David Hume (Oxford: Oxford University Press), 1:187.
13. Ibid., p. 13, Quote: Sir Fred Hoyle, (1981b), "Hoyle on Evolution," Nature, 294:105, 148, November 12.

NOTES

14. Ibid., p. 21, Quote: Robert Jastrow, (1977), Universe is totality of all matter, *Until the Sun Dies*, p. 31. (New York: W.W. Norton).
15. Henry M. Morris, (1997), *That Their Words May Be Used Against Them*, p. 25, Quote: Victor F. Weisskopf, (September/October 1983), "The Origin of the Universe," American Scientist, vol. 71, pp. 474, 480.
16. Bert Thompson, (2002), *The Scientific Case for Creation*, p. 46, ("matter or mind?") Quote: Fred Hoyle and Chandra Wickramasinghe, (1981), p. 139, *Evolution from Space*, (London: J.M. Dent & Sons).
17. Lee Strobel, (2004), *The Case for a Creator*, p. 248, Quote: Thomas Huxley, "Mr. Darwin's Critics," Contemporary Review, (November 1871). Quote: Edmund O. Wilson, Consilience, (New York: Vintage, 1998), 132.
18. W.E. Vine, Merrill F. Unger, & William White Jr., (1984), *An Expository Dictionary of Biblical Words*, p. 741, "Mind" (Greek-noun: "NOUS").
19. Ibid., p. 742, "Mind" (Greek-verb: "PHRONEO").
20. Dan Barker, (2008), *Godless*, p. 219, (on "spirit").
21. Lee Strobel, (2004), *The Case for a Creator*, p. 249, (reality of the "mind"-"soul").
22. Ibid., p. 249, Quote: Wilder Penfield, The Mystery of the Mind, (Princeton: Princeton Univ. Press, 1975), xiii.
23. Ibid., Quote: Wilder Penfield, The Mystery of the Mind, p.79.
24. Ibid., Quote: Lee Edward Travis, (on Wilder Penfield's demonstrations of the human Mind), "Response," in Arthur C. Custance, The Mysterious Matter of Mind, (Grand Rapids, Mich.: Zondervan and Richardson, Texas: Probe Ministries, 1980), 95-96.
25. Ibid., p. 250, Quote: Sir Charles Sherrington, by Karl L. Popper and John C. Eccles, The Self and Its Brain, New York: Springer-Verlag, 1977), 558.
26. Bert Thompson, and Brad Harrub, (2003), pp. 26-27, *Investigating Christian Evidences*, Quote: Norman L. Geisler, (1984), "The Collapse of Modern Atheism," The Intellectuals Speak Out About God, pp.140-141, ed. Roy A. Varghese (Chicago, IL: Regnery), pp. 129-152.
27. Ibid., p. 27, (about Dr. [Sir] John Eccles), Quote: Norman Cousins, (1985), "Commentary," in Nobel Prize Conversations, (Dallas, TX:Saybrook). [This book is a record of conversations that occurred in November, 1982 at the Isthmuis Institute in Dallas, Texas, among four Nobel laureates: Sir John Eccles, Ilya Prigogine, Roger Sperry, and Brian Josephson.].
28. Ibid., p. 29, Quote: John C. Eccles, (1984), "Modern Biology and the Turn to Belief in God," The Intellectuals Speak Out About God, ed. Roy A. Varghese

NOTES

(Chicago Il: Regnery Gateway), pp. 47-50.

29. The Evidences of Christianity, (1957), "A Debate Between Robert Owen, of Lanark, Scotland and Alexander Campbell, President of Bethany College, VA. Held in Cincinnati, Ohio, in April, 1829. (Nashville: McQuiddy Printing Company, 1957). Quote: Alexander Campbell: "What is man? Whence came he? Whither does he go?" p. 13.
30. Mesa Verde Country, 2010 Travel Planner, p. 8, (Mesa Verde Cliff Dwellings), Visitor Information Bureau, P.O. Box HH, Cortez, CO 81321-0930.
31. Ibid., p. 7.

CHAPTER 5

1. Henry M. Morris, (1997), *That Their Words May Be Used Against Them*, p. 109, Quote: Theodosius Dobzhansky, "Changing Man," Science, vol. 155, no. 3761 (January 27, 1967), p. 409.
2. Ibid., p. 111, Quote: Julian Huxley, Associated Press Dispatch, November 27, 1959, Address at Darwin Centennial Convocation. Chicago University, see *Issues in Evolution*, edited by Sol Tax (University of Chicago Press, 1960).
3. Wayne Jackson, Eric Lyons, Kyle Butt, (2008), Surveying The Evidence, pp. 65-66, Quote: Neil deGrasse Tyson, from Michael Brooks, (2006), "In Place of God," *New Scientist*, 192[2578]:8-11. (regarding recent poll—15% of scientists not atheists—why?).
4. Ibid., p. 66. (comments by authors, Jackson, Lyons, Butt on "poll").
5. Ibid., p. 69, Quote: Eugenie Scott, (preventing Creationists from public schools). Niles Eldridge, (2001), p. 178, The Triumph of Evolution and the Failure of Creationism, (New York: W.H. Freeman).
6. Ibid., p. 73, Quote: (2004, p. 119), Eugenie Scott, Evolution vs. Creationism: An Introduction, (Los Angeles CA: University of California Press).
7. Ibid., p. 73, Quote: from National Academy of Science's book, "creation science is not science," p. 2, (1999), *Science and Creationism*, (Washington D.C.: National Academy Press), second edition.
8. Henry M. Morris, (1997), *That Their Words May Be Used Against Them*, Quote: National Association of Biology Teachers, (Policy adopted by NABT Board, March 15, 1995), "Statement on Teaching Evolution," (to restrict teaching of Creation as science in public classrooms). pp. 1, 3.

NOTES

9. Ibid., p. 385, Quote: from Eugenie C. Scott, p. 25, ("avoid debates" with Christians), "Monkey Business," The Sciences, (January/February 1996), pp. 20-.25.
10. Charles L. Rulon, *Skeptical Inquirer*, (May/June 2007), Article: "Debating Creationists," pp. 63, 64, (reasons for science teachers not to debate "Creationists").
11. Bert Thompson, (1981), *The History of Evolutionary Thought*, pp. 142-143, (on Ernst Haeckel's, Biogenic Fraud), Footnotes: 254, Davidheiser, Bolton, see footnote #242, "History of Evolution II," IN: And God Created. Kelly L. Seagraves, Editor. Creation-Science Research Center. San Diego, California, 1973. p. 93.
12. Ibid., pp. 142-143, Quote: Prof. L. Rutimeyer's comments on Haeckel's Fraud. Footnote: #256. p. 143.
13. Lee Strobel, (2004), *The Case for a Creator*, p. 48, (Interview with Dr. Jonathen Wells, on Haeckel's fraud), Zondervan, Grand Rapids, Michigan 49530.
14. Ibid., (Wells, on Haeckel).
15. Ibid., p.49, (Wells, on Haeckel continued).
16. Ibid., p.50, (Wells, on why the deceit continues today).
17. Jerry A. Coyne, (2009), Why Evolution is True, p. 78, (defends Haeckel's fraud), Viking, Published by the Penguin Group, Penguin Group (USA) Inc. 375 Hudson Street, New York, New York 10014, U.S.A.
18. Burt Thompson, Wayne Jackson, (1992), *Christian Evidences*, p. 63, Quote: Sir Arthur Keith, (on embryo recapitulation hypothesis), The Human Body, Thornton, Butterworth, London, 1932, p. 94.
19. Ibid., p. 63, Quote: Dr. George W. Simpson, (ontology doesn't repeat phylogeny), Life, An Introduction to Biology, Harcourt-Brace, New York, 1957, p. 352).
20. Jerry A. Coyne, (2009), Why Evolution is True, pp. 39-40, (Archaeopteryx) Viking, Published by Penguin Group, Penguin Group (U.S.A.) Inc. 375 Hudson Street, New York, New York 10014, U.S.A.
21. Richard Dawkins, (2009), *The Greatest Show On Earth*, p. 159, (Archaeopteryx), Free Press, a Division of Simon & Schuster, Inc., 1230 Avenue of the Americas, New York, NY 10020.
22. Ibid., p. 160, (Birds come from "a single ancestor").
23. Kyle Butt and Eric Lyons, (2005), Truth Be Told, "Exposing the Myth of Evolution," pp. 78-79, Apologetics Press, Inc 230 Landmark Drive, Montgomery, Alabama 36117, U.S.A.

NOTES

24. Lee Strobel, (2004), *The Case for a Creator*, p. 57, (Jonathan Wells/archaeopteryx), Zondervan, Grand Rapids, Michigan 49530.
25. Henry M. Morris, (1997), *That Their Words May Be Used Against Them*, p. 191,Quote: Alan Feduccia, p. 792, ("Archaeopteryx....in the modern sense, a bird."), "Evidence from Claw Geometry Indicating Arboreal Habits of Archaeopteryx," Science, vol. 259 (February 5, 1993).
26. Jerry Fausz Ph.D., Article: "Morphing Flight: Beyond Irreducible Complexity," *Reason & Revelation*, 30(1):1; 30(1):2; 30(1):3; 30(1):4, January 2010, vol. 30, No. 1. Quote: Matthew Vanhorn, (2004), "Words of a Feather," Apologetics Press [On-line], URL:http://www.apologeticspress.org articles/2610. Quote: Caleb Colley (2004), "Bat Vision," Apologetics Press [On-line], URL:http://www.apologeticspress.org/articles2633. Quote: Jerry Fausz, (2008), "Designed to Fly," *Reason & Revelation*, 28[2]:9-15, February, [On-line], URL:http://www.apologeticspress.org/articles/3599.
27. Lee Strobel, (2004), *The Case for a Creator*, pp. 58-59, (Interview: Dr. Jonathan Wells, on fake dinosaur/bird, archaeoraptor). Quote: Alan Feduccia, Note-40, Kathy A. Svitil, "Plucking Apart the Dino-Birds," Discover, (February 2003). Quote: Alan Feduccia, Note-41, Ibid.
28. Edward McNall Burns, (1958 5th Edition), *Western Civilizations*, "Their History and Their Culture," p. 426, Quote: Erasmus, (on sacred relics of the Cross), W.W. Norton & Company, Inc., New York.
29. Henry M. Morris, (1981, 9th printing), *Scientific Creationism*, p. 178, (Explanation on Darwinist views on history, culture, and politics), Creation-Life Publishers, San Diego, California 92115.
30. Ibid., pp. 179-180, Note-1, Quote: Charles Darwin, Life and Letters, I, p. 316, "Letter from Charles Darwin to W. Graham, July 3, 1881, cited by G. Himmelfarb, Darwin and the Darwinian Revolution, (London: Chatto & Windus, 1959), p. 343. Quote: Thomas Huxley, Lay Sermons, Addresses and Reviews (New York: Appleton, 1871,), p. 20.
31. Henry M. Morris, (1997), *That Their Words May Be Used Against Them*, p. 442, Quote: George Gaylord Simpson, "The Biological Nature of Man," Science, vol. 152 (April 22, 1966), p. 474.
32. Ibid., p. 441, Quote: Henry Fairfield Osborn, "The Evolution of Human Races," Natural History, (January/February 1926), reprinted in Natural History, vol. 89, (April 1980), p. 129.
33. Marvin L. Lubenow, (1995, 5th printing), *Bones of Contention*, p. 86, "Java

NOTES

Man," Baker Books, a division of Baker Book House Company, P.O. Box 6287, Grand Rapids, MI 49516-6287.

34. Edward McNall Burns, (1958, 5th edition), *Western Civilizations*, p. 4, (Java Man), W.W. Norton & Company Inc., New York.
35. Lee Strobel, (2004), *The Case for a Creator*, p. 61, (Java Man), Zondervan, Grand Rapids, Michigan 49530.
36. Marvin L. Lubenow, (1995, 5th printing), *Bones of Contention*, pp. 86-87, (Java Man), Baker Books, a division of Baker Book House Company, P.O. Box 6287, Grand Rapids, MI 49516-6287.
37. Ibid., p. 87, (Lunenow's conclusions on Java Man).
38. Lee Strobel, (2004), *The Case for a Creator*, pp. 61-62, Note-50: "342 page scientific report," (No human evolution in Java Man), Hank Hanegraaff, The Face That Demonstrates the Farce of Evolution, 52.
39. Ibid., pp. 62-63, Quote: Jonathan Wells on Java Man and evolutionist's imagination.
40. *Merriam Webster's Collegiate Dictionary, 10th edition*, p. 911, ("postulate").
41. Brad Harrub, Ph.D., Bert Thompson, Ph.D., (2003), *The Truth About Human Origins*, pp. 89-90, (on Piltdown Man). Apologetics Press, Inc., 230 Landmark Drive, Montgomery, Alabama 36117-2752.
42. Ibid., pp. 88-89, (on Nebraska Man), Note: "see Gregory (1927), W.K. Gregory, (1927), "Hesperopithecus Apparently not an Ape nor a Man," Science, 66:579-581, December.
43. Marvin L. Lubenow, (1995, 5th printing), *Bones of Contention*, p. 66, (on Neanderthal Man), Baker Books, a division of Baker Book House Company, P.O. Box 6287, Grand Rapids, MI 49516-6287.
44. Ibid., p. 82, (Neanderthal/Neandertal continued).
45. Ibid., p. 62, (Neanderthal/Neandertal continued).
46. Ibid., pp. 68,70, (Neanderthal and mtDNA).
47. Ibid., p. 70, (mtDNA)
48. Ibid., pp. 70-71.
49. Brad Harrub, Ph.D., Bert Thompson, Ph.D., (2003), *The Truth About Human Origins*, pp. 128-129, (mtDNA and Neanderthal). Apologetics Press, Inc. 230 Landmark Drive, Montgomery, Alabama 36117-2752.
50. Ibid., pp. 129-130, Quote: Luigi Cavalli-Sforza, Luigi Luca, (2000), *Genes, People, and Languages*, p.35, (New York, North Point Press).
51. Ibid., p. 131, (mtDNA and Neanderthal) Quote: Marvin L. Lubenow, (1998),

NOTES

"Recovery of Neandertal mtDNA: An Evaluation," CEN Technical Journal, 12[1]:87-97.

52. Ibid., pp. 133-134, (mtDNA and Neanderthal) Quote: J.J. Hublin, F. Spoor, M. Braun, F. Zonneveld, and S. Condemi, (1996), "A Late Neanderthal Associated with Upper Palaeolithic Artifacts," Nature, 381:224-226, May 16. Quote: Randall White, in Tim Folger and Shanti Menon, (1997), "...Or much like us?," Discover, 18[1]:33, January. Quote: Marvin L. Lubenow, (1998), "Recovery of Neandertal mtDNA: An Evaluation," CEN Technical Journal, 12[1]:87-97.

53. Marvin L. Lubenow, (1995, 5th printing), *Bones of Contention*, p. 67, (Age dating and Neanderthal), Baker Books, a division of Baker Book House Company, P.O. Box 6287, Grand Rapids, MI 49516-6287.

54. Ibid., p. 73, (Neanderthal skull, dated, 5,710 years ago, Quote: Michael H. Day, Guide to Fossil Man, fourth edition (Chicago: University of Chicago Press, 1986), 128-29.

55. Brad Harrub, Ph.D., Bert Thompson, Ph.D., (2003), *The Truth About Human Origins*, pp. 41-42, (Johanson and "Lucy"), Apologetics Press, Inc., 230 Landmark Drive, Montgomery, Alabama 36117-2752, Quote: Donald C. Johanson, Tim D. White, and Yves Coppens, (1978), "A New Species of the Genus Australopithecus (Primates: Hominidae) from the Pliocene of Eastern Africa," Kirtlandia, 28:2-14.

56. Ibid., p. 42, Harrub and Thompson, (on "Lucy").

57. Marvin L. Lubenow, (1995, 5th printing), *Bones of Contention*, pp. 173-174, Quote: Mary Leakey, Note: 36, Mary D. Leakey, "Footprints in the Ashes of Time," *National Geographic*, April 1979, 446. Quote: Russell H. Tuttle, Note: 37, Tuttle, National History, 64. Note: 38, R.H. Tuttle and D.M. Webb, "The Pattern of Little Feet," (abstract), American Journal of Physical Anthropology, 78:2 (February 1989): 316. Note: 39, R.H. Tuttle and D.M. Webb, " Did Australopithicus afarensis make the Laetoli G Footprint Trails?" (abstract), American Journal of Physical Anthropology, 1991 Supplement: 175.

58. Ibid., p. 175, (Laetoli Footprints are Human—Not "Lucy's"!).

59. Ibid., pp. 52-53, (KP 271, Kanapoi Elbow Fossil), Note-15, Bryan Patterson, Anna K. Behrensmeyer, and William D. Sill, "Geology and Fauna of a New Pliocene Locality in North-western Kenya," Nature 226 (6 June 1970): 918-21. Note-16, Bryan Patterson and W.W. Howells, "Hominid Humeral Fragment from Early Pleistocene of Northwestern Kenya," Science 156 (7 April 1967):

NOTES

65. Bracketed material added for clarity. Originally the stratum was thought to be Pleistocene, but later it was determined to be of Pliocene Age. See endnote 15.
60. Ibid., p. 53, (KP 271 is like modern humans, not like "Lucy"), Note-18, Henry M. McHenry, "Fossils and the Mosaic Nature of Human Evolution," Science 190 (31 October 1975); 428.
61. Brad Harrub, Ph.D. Bert Thompson Ph.D., (2003), *The Truth About Human Origins*, p. 44, (on "Lucy's brain size about the same as the chimpanzee).
62. Ibid., p. 49, ("Lucy's" pelvis too small for birth), Quote: Martin Hausler and Peter Schmid (1995), "Comparison of the Pelvis of Sts 14 and AL288-1: Implications for Birth and Sexual Dimorphism in Australopithecines," Journal of Human Evolution, 29:363-383.
63. Ibid., pp. 50-51, ("Lucy's" locking Wrists made for knuckle-walking), Quote: Brian G. Richmond and David S. Strait (2000), "Evidence that Humans Evolved from a Knuckle-Walking Ancestor," Nature, 404:382-385, March 23. Quote: William Kimbel, Donald C. Johanson, and Yoel Rak (1994), "The First and Other New Discoveries of Australopithecus afarensis at Hadar, Ethiopia," Nature, 368;449-451, March 31.
64. Ibid., pp. 50, 51, 56, 57, ("Lucy" not missing link as supposed), Quote: Donald C. Johanson and Maitland Edey (1981), Lucy: The Beginnings of Humankind, pp. 257-258, 277.
65. Lee Strobel, (2004), *The Case for a Creator*, p. 19, (the Miller experiment).
66. Ibid., p. 37, (The Miller experiment interview with Jonathan Wells), Quotes: Note-12, See: Michael Florkin, "Ideas and Experiments in the Field of Prebiological Chemical Evolution," Comprehensive Biochemistry, 29B (1975), 231-60. Note-13, See: Sidney Fox and Klaus Dose, Molecular Evolution and the Origin of Life, (New York: Marcel Dekker, revised edition 1977), 43, 74-76. Note-14, John Cohen, "Novel Center Seeks to Add Spark to Origins of Life," Science 270 (1995), 1925-26.
67. Ibid., p. 38, (Wells, on Miller experiment).
68. Ibid., p. 39, (Wells comments on Human inability to make a living cell).
69. Henry M. Morris, (1997), *That Their Words May Be Used Against Them*, p. 43, Quote: Dr. Klaus Dose, p. 348, "The Origin of Life; More Questions Than Answers." *Interdisciplinary Science Reviews*, vol. 13, no. 4 (1988), pp. 348-356. Dose is Director, Institute for Biochemistry, Johannes Gutenberg University, West Germany.

NOTES

70. Ibid., p. 55, Quote: Sir Fred Hoyle, and Chandra Wickramasinghe, p. 148, *Evolution from Space* (New York: Simon & Schuster, 1984), 176 pp. Quote: Sir Fred Hoyle, and Chandra Wickramasinghe, p. 415, "Where Microbes Boldly Went." *New Scientist*, vol. 91 (August 13, 1991), pp. 412-415.
71. Bert Thompson, Ph.D., (2002), p. 73, The Scientific Case For Creation, (the Law of Biogenesis), Apologetics Press, Inc. 230 Landmark Drive, Montgomery, Alabama 36117-2752.
72. Ibid., p. 73, (Law of Biogenesis).
73. Ibid., p. 74, (Law of Biogenesis).
74. Bert Thompson, pp. 94, 99, *The History of Evolutionary Thought*, Quote: Louis Pasteur, footnote #164, Quoted in footnote #158 pp. 4-5. Sidney W. Fox and Klaus Dose, Molecular Evolution And The Origin Of Life. Marcel Dekker. New York. 1977. p. 2. (Louis Pasteur's statement that "spontaneous generation" has been proven false) Apologetics Press, Inc., 230 Landmark Drive, Montgomery, Alabama 36117-2752.

CHAPTER 6

1. Bert Thompson Ph.D., (2002), The Scientific Case For Creationism, pp. 129-130, (Law of Probability), Apologetics Press, Inc., 230 Landmark Drive, Montgomery, Alabama 36117-2752.
2. Michael J. Behe, (1996), *Darwin's Black Box*, p. 39, (Quote: Charles Darwin, (1872), *The Origin of Species*, 6th ed., (1988), New York, University Press, New York, p. 83, Note: #24) The Free Press, A Division of Simon & Schuster Inc., 1230 Avenue of the Americas, New York, NY 10020.
3. Ibid., p. 70, (Bactcrial Flagellum), Note: #8, "A good general introduction to flagella can be found in Voet and Voet, pp. 1259-1260. Greater detail about the flagellar motor can be found in the following: Schuster S.C., and Khan, S., (1994) "The Bacterial Flagellar Motor," Annual Review of Biophysics and Biomolecular Structure, 23, 509-538, Caplan, S.R., and Kara-Ivanov, M. (1993) "The Bacterial Flagellar Motor," International Review of Cytology, 147, 97-164.
4. William A. Dambski, (1999), *Intelligent Design*, p.177, ("Behe's irreducibly complex biochemical systems), Inter Varsity Press, P.O. Box 1400, Downers Grove IL 60515.

NOTES

5. Ibid., p. 178, (incomplete bacterial flagellum doesn't function).
6. Ibid., (complex specified information "CSI" of a flagellum is over "500 bits.").
7. Ibid., p. 166, (500 bits means no chance "probability bound").
8. Bert Thompson, Ph. D., (2002), The Scientific Case For Creation, p. 131, (Law of Probability), Apologetics Press, Inc., 230 Landmark Drive, Montgomery, Alabama 36117-2752.
9. Henry M. Morris, (1997), *That Their Words May Be Used Against Them*, p. 55, Quote: Sir Fred Hoyle and Chandra Wickramasinghe, p. 148, Evolution From Space, (New York: Simon & Schuster, 1984).
10. Bert Thompson Ph. D., (2002), p. 132, *The Scientific Case for Creation*, Quote: Dr. Morowitz, (1968, p. 99), (Estimate on life's probability by chance). Apologetics Press, Inc., 230 Landmark Drive, Montgomery Alabama 36117-2752.
11. Stephen C. Meyer, (2009), *Signature in the Cell*, p. 204, "Wistar Institute," (skeptical chance of evolutionary theories of life mathematically). Harper Collins Publishers, 10 East 53rd Street, New York, NY 10022.
12. Ibid., p. 208, (MIT biochemist, Robert Sauer's estimates, probability on 100 amino acid proteins at random).
13. Ibid., p. 210, (Molecular biologist, Douglas Axe's estimate on 150 amino acid sequences by chance).
14. Ibid., pp. 211-212, (Molecular biologist, Douglas Axe's estimate on 1-functional protein of length of 150 amino acids by chance.
15. William A. Dembski, (1999), *Intelligent Design*, p. 166, ("probability bound," no chance, estimate: "10-150."). Inter Varsity Press, P.O. Box 1400, Downers Grove, IL 60515.
16. Bert Thompson Ph.D. (2002), The Scientific Case For Creation, p. 132, (Carl Sagan's estimate on evolution of life on Earth in 1973, p. 46,) Communications With Extra-Terrestrial Intelligence, (Boston, MA: MIT Press). Apologetics Press, Inc., 230 Landmark Drive, Montgomery, Alabama 36117-2752.
17. Ibid., p. 138, (Spontaneous generation of life is "logically impossible.").
18. Ibid., p. 139, Quote: Murray Eden, (1967, p. 109), "Inadequacies of Neo-Darwinian Evolution as a Scientific Theory," Mathematical Challenges to the Neo-Darwinian Interpretation of Evolution, ed. Paul S. Moorhead and Martin M. Kaplan, Wistar Symposium No. 5 (Philadelphia, PA: Wistar Institute).
19. Henry M. Morris, (1997), *That Their Words May Be Used Against Them*, p. 55, Quote: Sir Fred Hoyle and Chandra Wickramasinghe, p. 148, Evolution From

NOTES

Space, (New York: Simon & Schuster, 1984).

20. Henry M. Morris, *Scientific Creationism*, p. 62, Quote: Frank B. Salisbury, "Doubts About the Modern Synthetic Theory of Evolution," American Biology Teacher, (September 1971), p. 336, Footnote #1.
21. William A. Dembski, (1999), *Intelligent Design*, "Foreword", p. 10, Quote: Michael J. Behe, ("Scrabble Letters" sequences point to intelligent design). Inter Varsity Press, P.O. Box 1400, Downers Grove, IL 60515.
22. Michael J. Behe, (1996), *Darwin's Black Box*, p. 5, (Behe doesn't reject natural selection "completely", but doesn't explain "molecular life."). The Free Press, A Division of Simon & Schuster Inc., 1230 Avenue of the Americas New York, NY 10020.

CHAPTER 7

1. W.E. VINE, Merrill F. Unger & William White Jr. (1984), *An Expository Dictionary of Biblical Words*, p. 593, (inspiration defined), Thomas Nelson, Inc., Publishers, Nashville, Tennessee.
2. Jean Sloat Morton, Science In The Bible, (1978), p. 10, (Introduction, the Bible), Moody Bible Institute of Chicago.
3. Bert Thompson, Ph.D. and Brad Harrub, Ph.D., (2003), *Investigating Christian Evidences*, p. 145, ("proofs" of Biblical inspiration), Apologetics Press, Inc., 230 Landmark Drive, Montgomery, Alabama 36117-2752.
4. Ibid., p. 149, ("springs" and "trenches" in the Oceans).
5. Ibid., p. 150.
6. Jean Sloat Morton, (1978), Science In The Bible, p. 121, ("paths of the sea"), The Moody Bible Institute of Chicago, IL.
7. Ibid., p. 49, ("hydrologic or water cycle").
8. Bert Thompson, Ph.D. and Brad Harrub, Ph.D., (2003), *Investigating Christian Evidences*, pp. 146, 152, ("life...in the blood."), References: H. F. Perutz, (1964), *Scientific American*, pp. 64-65, November. Dean Havron, (1981), "Curious Cure-Alls," Science Digest, 89[8]:62, September.
9. Neil R. Lightfoot, (2005, 4th printing), *How We Got the Bible*, p. 152, ("The Canon"), Published by Baker Books, a Division of Baker Book House Company, P.O. Box 6287, Grand Rapids, MI 49516-6287.
10. Norman L. Geisler, ((1999), *Baker Encyclopedia of Christian Apologetics*, p.

NOTES

80, (the Canon of the Bible), Published by Baker Books, a division of Baker Book House Company, P.O. Box 6287, Grand Rapids, MI 49516-6287.

11. Josh McDowell, (1979), Evidence That Demands a Verdict, p. 38, (Synod of Hippo), Quote: F.F. Bruce, 15/113, Here's Life Publishers, Inc. P.O. Box 1576, San Bernardino, CA 92402.
12. Neil R. Lightfoot, (2005, 4th printing), *How We Got the Bible*, pp. 154-155, (Old Testament Canon), Baker Books, a division of Baker Book House Company, P.O. Box 6287, Grand Rapids, MI 49516-6287.
13. Ibid., p. 155, (Old Testament Canon by 464-424 B.C.).
14. Ibid., Quote: Josephus, *Against Apion*, 1:8.
15. Neil R. Lightfoot, (2005, 4th printing) p. 153, (New Testament evidence that the Old Testament complete.), Baker Books, a division pf Baker Book Company, P.O. Box 6287, Grand Rapids, MI 49516-6287.
16. Josh McDowell, (1979), Evidence That Demands a Verdict, p. 31, (Jesus Confirms Old Testament complete.), Here's Life Publishers, Inc., P.O. Box 1576, San Bernardino, CA 92402.
17. Neil R. Lightfoot, (2005, 4th printing), *How We Got the Bible*, p. 154, Published by Baker Books, a division of Baker Book House Company, P.O. Box 6287, Grand Rapids, MI 49516-6287.
18. Ibid., p. 155.
19. Josh McDowell, (1979), Evidence That Demands a Verdict, p. 36, Here's Life Publishers, Inc., P.O. Box 1576, San Bernardino, CA 92402.
20. *Merriam Webster's Collegiate Dictionary*, (1996, 10th edition), p. 461.
21. *Nelson's New Illustrated Bible Dictionary*, General Editor, Ronald F. Youngblood, Consulting Editors, F.F. Bruce & R.K. Harrison, (1995), p. 304, Thomas Nelson Publishers, Nashville.
22. Everett Ferguson, (1971), *Early Christians Speak*, p. 24, (Irenaeus), Sweet Publishing Company, Austin, Texas.
23. Josh McDowell, (1979), Evidence That Demands a Verdict, p. 37, (Irenaeus), Here's Life Publishers, Inc., P.O. BOX 1576, San Bernardino, CA 92402.
24. Neil R. Lightfoot, (2005, 4th printing), *How We Got the Bible*, p. 157, (Muratorian Fragment), Published by Baker Books, a division of Baker Book House Company, P.O. Box 6287, Grand Rapids, MI 49516-6287.
25. Gary R. Habermas, (1997, 2nd printing), *The Historical Jesus*, pp. 111, 113, (Clement of Rome and Muratorian Fragment), College Press Publishing Company, Joplin, Missouri.

NOTES

26. Ibid., p. 111.
27. Ibid., (Ignatius).
28. Everett Ferguson, (1971), *Early Christians Speak*, p. 23, (Ignatius), Sweet Publishing Company, Austin, Texas.
29. Dan Barker, (2008), *Godless*, pp. 277-278, Ulysses Press, P.O. Box 3440, Berkeley, CA 94703.
30. Lee Strobel, (1998), *The Case for Christ*, p. 230, (Interview with Dr. Gary R. Habermas), Zondervan Publishing House, Grand Rapids, Michigan 49530.
31. Henry H. Halley, *Halley's Bible Handbook*, (1965, 24th edition), p. 743, (Ignatius), Zondervan Publishing House, Grand Rapids, Michigan 49506.
32. Neil R. Lightfoot, (2005, 4th printing), *How We Got the Bible*, p. 157, Published by Baker Books, a division of Baker Book House Company, P.O. Box 6287, Grand Rapids, MI 49516-6287.
33. Norman L. Geisler, (1999), *Baker Encyclopedia of Christian Apologetics*, p. 81, Published by Baker Books, a division of Baker Book House Company, P.O. Box 6287, Grand Rapids, MI 49516-6287.

CHAPTER 8

1. Kyle Butt, (2006), *Reason & Revelation*, Article, "The Predicted Messiah," 26(1):1, Apologetics Press, Inc., 230 Landmark Drive, Montgomery, AL 36117-2752.
2. Ibid., 26(1):2, Quote, David Baron, (2000 reprint), *Rays of Messiah's Glory*, p. 16, (Jerusalem, Israel: Kern Ahvah Meshihit).
3. Ibid., Quote, David Baron, (200 reprint), *Rays of Messiah's Glory*, p. 18, (Jerusalem, Israel: Kern Ahvah Meshihit).
4. Ibid., Quote, David Baron, (2000 reprint), *Rays of Messiah's Glory*, p. 20, (Jerusalem, Israel: Kern Ahvah Meshihit).
5. Ibid., Quote, Risto Santala, (1992), p. 22, The Messiah in the Old Testament: In the Light of Rabbinical Writings, trans. William Kinnaird (Jerusalem, Israel: Keren Ahvah Meshihit).
6. *Nelson's New Illustrated Bible Dictionary*, Ronald F. Youngblood, General Editor, F.F. Bruce & R.K. Harrison, Consulting Editors, (1995), pp. 1135-1136, Thomas Nelson Publishers, Nashville, Tennessee.
7. Kyle Butt, (2006), *Reason & Revelation*, Article, "The Predicted Messiah,"

NOTES

26(1):2, Quote, Aaron Kligerman, (1957), *Old Testament Messianic Prophecy*, pp. 19-20, (Grand Rapids, MI: Zondervan).

8. Gesenius, (1957), Hebrew-English Lexicon to the Old Testament, Translated by Samuel P. Tregelles, p. 818, "Shiloh," Wm. B. Eerdmans Publishing Company, Grand Rapids, Michigan.
9. W.E. Vine, Merrill F. Unger & William White Jr., (1984), *An Expository Dictionary of Biblical Words*, p. 182, "Christos" (Christ), Thomas Nelson, Inc., Publishers, Nashville, Tennessee.
10. Ibid., p. 9, "Mashiach," "anointed one."
11. *Holman Bible Dictionary*, Trent C. Butler, General Editor, Marsha A. Ellis Smith, Forrest W. Jackson, Phil Logan, Chris Church, Contributing Editors, (1991), p. 957, Holman Bible Publishers, Nashville, Tennessee.
12. Everett Ferguson, (1990 reprinted), *Backgrounds of Early Christianity*, pp. 329-330, Herod the Great, Wm. B. Eerdmans Publishing Co., 255 Jefferson Ave. S.E., Grand Rapids, Mich. 49503.
13. *Holman Bible Dictionary*, Trent C. Butler, General Editor, Marsha A. Ellis Smith, Forrest W. Jackson, Phil Logan, Chris Church, Contributing Editors, (1991), p. 910, Holman Bible Publishers, Nashville, Tennessee.
14. Merrill F. Unger, (1962), *Archaeology and the New Testament*, p. 64, the Census and tax enrollment, Zondervan Publishing House, Grand Rapids, Michigan.
15. Ibid., p. 65, Luke's Gospel and "Quirinius," Footnote 27: Bearing of Recent Discoveries on the Trustworthiness of the New Testament, (1915), pp. 223ff., Journal of Roman Studies VII, 1917, pp. 271ff. Footnote 28: Bearing of Recent Discovery, p. 300.
16. Gary R. Habermas, (1997, 2nd printing), *The Historical Jesus*, p. 173, (Luke 2:1-5), College Press Publishing Company, Joplin, Missouri.
17. W.E. Vine, Merrill F. Unger & William White, Jr., (1984), *An Expository Dictionary of Biblical Words*, p. 844, ("Pentecost,"), Thomas Nelson, Inc., Publishers, Nashville, Tennessee.

CHAPTER 9

1. Josh McDowell, (1979), Evidence That Demands a Verdict, Volume I, p. 166, (Messianic prophecies), Here's Life Publishers, Inc., P.O. Box 1576, San Bernardino, CA 92402.

NOTES

2. Ibid., p. 167, Quote, Peter Stoner, mathematical probabilities, Science Speaks, 27/100-107.
3. Ibid., Quote, Peter Stoner.
4. William A. Dembski, (1999), *Intelligent Design*, p. 166, (Probability Bound 10-150), InterVarsity Press, P.O. Box 1400, Downers Grove, IL 60515.
5. Josh McDowell, (1979), Evidence That Demands a Verdict, Volume I, p. 167, Quote H. Harold Hartzler, *American Scientific Affilliation*, Goshen College, (Stoner's Math Estimates Confirmed), Here's Life Publishers, P.O. Box 1576, San Bernardino, CA 92402.
6. Kyle Butt, (2006), *Reason & Revelation*, January, 2006, Article, "*The Predicted Messiah*," 26[1]:3, (Protevangelium), Apologetics Press, Inc. 230 Landmark Drive, Montgomery, AL 36117-2752.
7. *Merriam Webster's Collegiate Dictionary, 10th edition*, (1996), p. 938, ("Prot"), Merriam-Webster, Incorporated, Springfield, Massachusetts, U.S.A.
8. Ibid., p. 401, ("evangel").
9. Kyle Butt, (2006), *Reason & Revelation*, January, 2006, Article, "*The Predicted Messiah*," 26[1]:3, Quote, Aaron Kligerman, (1957), *Old Testament Messianic Prophecy*, p. 13, (Grand Rapids, MI:Zondervan). Quote, Charles A. Briggs, (1988), *Messianic Prophecy: The Prediction of the Fulfillment of Redemption through the Messiah*, p. 77, (1988 reprint), (Peabody, Massachusetts: Hendrickson).
10. W.E. Vine, Merrill F. Unger, William White, Jr., (1984), p. 246, (Hebrew "mashiach" "anointed one; Messiah."), Thomas Nelson, Inc., Publishers, Nashville, Tennessee.
11. Kenny Barfield, (1995), *The Prophet Motive*, pp. 123-124, Note #8, Alfred Edersheim, *The Life and Times of Jesus the Messiah*, (1883, rprt. Grand Rapids: Eerdmans, 1969), vol. II, pp. 710 741; Note #9, A. T. Pierson, God's Living Oracles (London: James Nesbit, 1908); Note #10, James E. Smith, *The Promised Messiah*, (Joplin, MO,: College Press, 1984). See especially, pp. 475-478. Note #11, J. Barton Payne, EBP (New York: Harper & Row, 1973), pp. 645-650.
12. Josh McDowell, (1979), Evidence That Demands a Verdict, Volume I, pp. 144-166, (61 prophecies), Here's Life Publishers, Inc., P.O. Box 1576, San Bernardino, CA 92402.
13. Homer Hailey, "Outline", Ed. C. Wharton, "Diagrams," (March 1960), *The Scheme of Redemption*, p. 14, ("The Two-Fold Promise to Abraham and its Fulfillment").

NOTES

14. Kyle Butt, (2006), *Reason & Revelation*, January, 2006, Article, "*The Predicted Messiah*," 26[1]:2, Quote, Risto Santala, (1992), *The Messiah in the Old Testament: In Light of Rabbinical Writings*, trans. William Kinnaird (Jerusalem, Israel: Keren Ahvah Meshihit).
15. Ibid., 26[1]4, Quote, Robert M. Cohen, "leprous one," (n.d.; also see Parsons,2003-2006). "Why I know Yeshua is the Jewish Messiah," [On-line], URL: http://www.imja.com/Atonem.htm]. Other reference in Notes, John Parsons, (2003-2006), "Hebrew Namesof God: The Mashiach as Revealed in the Tanakh," [On-line], URL:http//www.hebrew4christians.com/Names_of_G-d/Messiah/messiah.httm. 16. Ibid., 26[1]:4.

CHAPTER 10

1. Josh McDowell and Bill Wilson, (1993), *A Ready Defense*, p. 135, Biblical criticism, Thomas Nelson, Inc., Published in Nashville, Tennessee.
2. Norman L. Geisler, (1999), *Baker Encyclopedia of Christian Apologetics*, pp. 769-770, Julian Wellhausen background, Baker Books, a division of Baker Book House Company, P.O. Box 6287, Grand Rapids, MI 49516-6287.
3. Josh McDowell, (1975), *More Evidence That Demands a Verdict*, p. 29, Wellhausen and the Documentary Hypothesis, Campus Crusade for Christ International, Arrowhead Springs, San Bernardino, CA 92414.
4. Ibid., Documentary Hypothesis authors unknown.
5. Norman L. Geisler, (1999), Baker Encyclopedia of *Christian Evidences*, p. 770, Pentateuch authors hypothetically wrote from 9th century B.C. to 5th Century B.C., Baker Books, a division of Baker Book House Company, P.O. Box 6287, Grand Rapids, MI 49516-6287.
6. Edward McNall Burns, (1958, 5th edition), *Western Civilizations*, pp. 618-619, on George Wilhelm Hegel's philosophy, W.W. Horton & Company Inc., New York.
7. Norman L. Geisler, (1999), Baker Encyclopedia of *Christian Evidences*, p. 710, Spinoza doubted Moses authorship, Baker Books, a division of Baker Book House Company, P.O. Box 6287, Grand Rapids, MI 49516-6287.
8. Flavius Josephus, (AD 90-95), *The Life and Works of Flavius Josephus, Against Apion*, 1.8, the five books of Moses, Translated by William Whiston, A.M., John C. Winston Company, Philadelphia.

NOTES

9. Josh McDowell, (1975), *More Evidence That Demands a Verdict*, p. 94, Talmud, Philo, on Mosaic authorship, Campus Crusade For Christ International, Arrowhead Springs, San Bernardino, CA 92414.
10. Kenny Barfield, (1995), *The Prophet Motive*, p. 252-253, Isaiah's Date, Published in 1995, Gospel Advocate Company, P. O. Box 150, Nashville, Tennessee 37202.
11. Ibid.
12. *Dickson's New Analytical Bible*, (1973), p. 1454, Sennacherib's invasion of Judah failed, John A. Dickson Publishing Co., Chicago.
13. Edward McNall Burns, (1958), *Western Civilizations*, p. 66, (Assyrian Empire), W.W. Horton & Company Inc., 1958, 5th edition, New York.
14. Merrill F. Unger, (1956), *Archeology and the Old Testament*, p. 267, Sennacherib's invasion of Judah, Zondervan Publishing House, Third Edition 1956, Grand Rapids, Michigan.
15. Flavius Josephus, (AD 90-95), *The Life and Works of Flavius Josephus*, p. 321, 1:2, Isaiah's Prophecy and Cyrus, Translated by William Whiston, A.M., John C. Winston Company, Philadelphia.
16. Norman L. Geisler, (1999), Baker Encyclopedia of Christians Apologetics, p. 253, Josephus on Old Testament Canon, Baker Books, a division of Baker Book House Company, P.O. Box 6287, Grand Rapids, MI 49516-6287.
17. Flavius Josephus, (AD 90-95), *The Life and Works of Flavius Josephus, Against Apion*, 1:8, Hebrew Canon, John C. Winston Company, Philadelphia.
18. Kenny Barfield, (1995), *The Prophet Motive*, p. 256, similar backgrounds of Isaiah, Micah and Amos, Gospel Advocate Company, P.O. Box 150, Nashville, Tennessee 37202.
19. Ibid., p. 255, "anti-supernatural barrage."
20. James C. Vanderkam, (1994), *The Dead Sea Scrolls Today*, p. 16, "Paleography," William B. Eerdmans Publishing Company, 255 Jefferson Ave. S.E., Grand Rapids, Michigan 49503.
21. Ibid., p. 17, "Accelerator Mass Spectrometry."
22. Ibid., p. 19, "Internal Allusions."
23. Ibid., p. 18, "Table One."
24. Kenny Barfield, (1995), *The Prophet Motive*, p. 255, Isaiah Scroll at Qumran, Gospel Advocate Company, P.O. Box 150, Nashville, Tennessee 37202.
25. Norman L. Geisler, (1999), *Baker Encyclopedia of Christian Apologetics*, p. 367, Isaiah's writing styles, Baker Books, a division of Baker Book House Company, P.O. Box 6287, Grand Rapids, MI 49516-6287.

NOTES

26. Ibid., p. 367-368.
27. Kenny Barfield, (1995), *The Prophet Motive*, p. 253, style differences, Gospel Advocate Company, P.O. Box 150, Nashville, Tennessee 37202.
28. Randall Price, (1997), *The Stones Cry Out*, p. 162, historical King David, by World of Biblical Ministries, Inc., Published by Harvest House Publishers, Eugene, Oregon 97402.
29. Ibid., p. 163, David continued.
30. Ibid., p. 165, David continued.
31. Ibid., pp. 165, 167, "House of David" (stele).
32. Ibid., p. 169, Hazael and David stele.
33. Ibid., p. 170, historical King David verified.
34. Gary K. Brantley, (1995), *Digging for Answers*, pp. 121-122, "House of David" stele, Apologetics Press, Inc., 230 Landmark Drive, Montgomery, Alabama 36117.
35. Ibid., p. 123, historical King David verified.

CHAPTER 11

1. Kyle Butt & Eric Lyons, (2006), *Behold! The Lamb of God*, pp. 86-87, Jewish concept of two Messiahs, Apologetics Press, Inc., 230 Landmark Drive, Montgomery, Alabama 36117-2752.
2. Ibid., p. 87, Quote, Ankerburg, John, John Weldon and Walter Kaiser, (1989), The Case for Jesus the Messiah (Chattanooga, TN: John Ankerburg Evangelistic Association). Quote, Robert H. Cohen, (no date), "Why I know Yeshua is the Jewish Messiah," [On-line],URL: http://www.imja.com/Atonem.html. Quote, Parsons, John (2003-2006), "Hebrew Names of God: The Meshiach as Revealed in the Tanakh," [On-line], URL:http://www.hebrew4christians.com/Names_of_G-d/Messiah/messiah.html.
3. David S. Ariel, (1995), *What do Jews believe?*, p. 226, problem of Messiah's death, Schocken Books Inc. New York, U.S.A.
4. Kyle Butt & Eric Lyons, (2006), *Behold! The Lamb of God*, pp. 87-88, Rabbinical misunderstanding of the Messiah, Apologetics Press, Inc., 230 Landmark Drive, Montgomery, Alabama 36117-2752.
5. *Holman Bible Dictionary*, General Editor, Trent C. Butler, (1991), p. 1312, the Synagogue, Holman Bible Publishers, Nashville, Tennessee.

NOTES

6. Everett Ferguson, (1987), *Backgrounds of Early Christianity*, p. 449, office of high priest, William B. Eerdmans Publishing Co., 255 Jefferson Ave. S.E., Grand Rapids, Michigan 49503.
7. *Nelson's New Illustrated Bible Dictionary*, General Editor, Ronald F. Youngblood, Consulting Editors, F.F. Bruce & R.K. Harrison, (1995), high priest Annus, Thomas Nelson Publishers, Nashville, Tennessee.
8. Everett Ferguson, (1987), *Backgrounds of Early Christianity*, p. 331, high priest Joseph Caiaphas, William B. Eerdmans Publishing Co., 255 Jefferson Ave. S.E., Grand Rapids, Michigan 49503.
9. Ibid., p. 24, prefect Sejanus appointed Pontius Pilate.
10. Ibid., p. 331.
11. *Merriam Webster's Collegiate Dictionary*, 10th Edition, (1996), p. 637.
12. Everett Ferguson, (1987), *Backgrounds of Early Christianity*, p. 24, Tiberius/ Sejanus, William B. Eerdmans Publishing Co., 255 Jefferson Ave. S.E., Grand Rapids, Michigan 49503.
13. Ibid., p. 331.
14. Dan Barker, (2008), *Godless*, a historical Jesus?, Ulysses Press, P.O. Box 3440, Berkeley, CA 94703.
15. Gary R. Habermas, (2nd Printing, 1997), *The Historical Jesus*, pp. 187-188, Nero's Christian Persecution, mentions Christ, Foot Note 3, Tacitus, 15.44. College Press Publishing Company, Joplin, Missouri.
16. Ibid., p. 189.
17. Kyle Butt & Eric Lyns, (2006), *Behold! The Lamb of God*, pp. 10-11, Quote, Bruce, F.F. (1953), *The New Testament Documents—Are They Reliable?*, (Grand Rapids, MI: Eerdmans), fourth edition.
18. Gary R. Habermas, (2nd Printing, 1997), *The Historical Jesus*, p. 192, Josephus mentions Christ, College Press Publishing Company, Joplin, Missouri.
19. William Whiston, *The Life and Works of Flavius Josephus*, Antiquities 20:9, Brother of Jesus, John C. Winston Company, Philadelphia.
20. Gary R. Habermas, (2nd Printing), *The Historical Jesus*, p. 193, Arabic text of Josephus, College Press Publishing Company, Joplin, Missouri.
21. Kyle Butt & Eric Lyons, (2006), *Behold! The Lamb of God*, pp. 11-12, Josephus and Rome, Quote, Bruce, (1960), pp. 102-104.
22. *Holman Bible Dictionary*, General Editor, Trent C. Butler, (1991), p. 896, casting "lots," Holman Bible Publishers, Nashville, Tennessee.
23. *Nelson's New Illustrated Bible Dictionary*, General Editor, Ronald F.

NOTES

Youngblood, Consulting Editors, F.F. Bruce & R.K. Harrison, (1995), p. 1136, scourging by whip, Thomas Nelson Publishers, Nashville, Tennessee.

CHAPTER 12

1. Gary R. Habermas, "*The Historical Jesus*, p. 9, (2nd printing 1997), College Press, Joplin, MO.
2. Everett Ferguson, The Church of Christ, pp. 62-63, (1996), Wm. B. Eerdmans, 255 Jefferson Ave., S.E., Grand Rapids, Michigan, 49503.
3. Dan Barker, *Godless*, pp. 277-278, (2008), Ulysses Press, P.O. Box 3440, Berkeley, CA 94703. (Foreword Copyright, 2008 Richard Dawkins).
4. Norman L. Geisler and Frank Turek, *I Don't Have Enough Faith to be an Atheist*, p. 300, (2004), Crossway Books, a publishing ministry of Good News Publishers, 1300 Crescent Street, Wheaton, Illinois 60187.
5. Norman L. Geisler, *Baker Encyclopedia of Christian Apologetics*, p. 188, New Testament fragments, Jose O'Callahan, (1999), Baker Books, a division of Baker Book House Company, P.O. Box 6287, Grand Rapids, MI 49516-6287.
6. Ibid., p. 529.
7. Ibid.
8. Ibid.
9. a. Everett Ferguson, *Early Christians Speak*, p. 23, (1971), Sweet Publishing Company, Austin, Texas. b. Norman L. Geisler, and Frank Turek, *I Don't Have Enough Faith to be an Atheist*, p. 368, (2004), Crossway Books, a publishing ministry of Good News Publishers, 1300 Crescent Street, Wheaton, Illinois 60187.
10. Gary R. Habermas, *The Historical Jesus*, (2nd printing, 1997), College Press, Joplin, MO.
11. Lee Strobel, *The Case for Christ*, p. 230, (1998), Zondervan Publishing House, Grand Rapids, Michigan 49530.
12. Norman L. Geisler, *Baker Encyclopedia of Christian Apologetics*, pp. 188 and 529, (1999), Baker Books, a division of Baker Book House Company, P.O. Box 6287, Grand Rapids, MI, 49516-6287.
13. Norman L. Geisler and Frank Turek, *I Don't Have Enough Faith to be an Atheist*, Table 14:2, p. 369, (2004), Crossway Books, a publishing ministry of Good News Publishers, 1300 Crescent Street, Wheaton, Illinois 60187.

NOTES

14. Everett Ferguson, *Backgrounds of Early Christianity*, p. 38, (1987), Wm. B. Eerdmans Publishing Co., 255 Jefferson Ave. S.E. Grand Rapids, Mich. 49503.
15. Josh McDowell, compiled by Bill Wilson, *A Ready Defense*, p. 228, (1993), Wm. B. Eerdmans Publishing Co., 255 Jefferson Ave. S.E. Grand Rapids, Mich. 49503.
16. Ibid., p. 230.
17. Ibid.
18. Everett Ferguson, *Backgrounds of Early Christianity*, p. 58, (1987), Wm. B. Eerdmans Publishing Co., 255 Jefferson Ave., S.E. Grand Rapids, Mich. 49503.
19. Norman L. Geisler, and Frank Turek, *I Don't Have Enough Faith to be an Atheist*, p. 303, (2004), Crossway Books, a publishing ministry of Good News Publishers, 1300 Crescent Street, Wheaton, Illinois 60187.
20. Josh McDowell, Evidence That Demands a Verdict, Vol. 1, p. 224, (1972, 1979), Here's Life Publishers Inc., P.O. Box 1576, San Bernardino, CA 92402.
21. Gary R. Habermas, *The Historical Jesus*, (2nd printing, 1997), College Press, Joplin MO.
22. Ibid., pp. 230-231.
23. Everett Ferguson, *Early Christians Speak*, p. 23, (1971), Sweet Publishing Company, Austin, Texas.
24. Gary R. Habermas, *The Historical Jesus*, p. 231, (2nd printing, 1997), College Press, Joplin MO.
25. Ibid., p. 233.
26. Everett Ferguson, *Early Christians Speak*, p. 23, (1971), Sweet Publishing Company, Austin, Texas.
27. Ibid., p. 241.
28. Gary R. Habermas, *The Historical Jesus*, p. 235, (2nd printing, 1997), College Press, Joplin MO.
29. Josh McDowell, Evidence For Christianity, p. 267, (2006) Thomas Nelson Inc., Nashville, Tennessee.
30. Everett Ferguson, *Early Christians Speak*, p. 241, (1971), Sweet Publishing Company, Austin, Texas.
31. Ibid., p. 24.
32. Ibid., p. 25.
33. Ibid., p. 241.
34. Flavius Josephus, *Antiquities of the Jews*, p. 598, Book XX, Chapter 9, Translated by William Whiston, A.M., John C. Winston Company, Philadelphia.

NOTES

35. Ibid., p. 599.
36. Gary R. Habermas, *The Historical Jesus*, p. 192, (2nd printing, 1997), College Press, Joplin MO.
37. Flavuis Josephus, *Antiquities of the Jews*, p. 535, Book 18: Chapter 3, Translated by William Whiston, A.M., John C. Whiston Company, Philadelphia.
38. Lee Strobel, *The Case for Christ*, p. 75, (1998), Zondervan Publishing House, Grand Rapids, Michigan 49530.
39. Ibid., p. 78-79.
40. Ibid.
41. Ibid., p. 80.
42. Flavius Josephus, *Dissertation I*, p. 904, Translated by William Whiston, A.M., John C. Whiston Company, Philadelphia.
43. Ibid., p. 905.
44. Gary R. Habermas, *The Historical Jesus*, p. 193, (2nd printing, 1997), College Press, Joplin MO.
45. Ibid., pp. 193-194.
46. Ibid., p. 195.

www.ingramcontent.com/pod-product-compliance
Lightning Source LLC
Chambersburg PA
CBHW082105230426
43671CB00015B/2615